AF522226

Judicial Creativity in Constitutional Interpretation

Judicial Creativity in Constitutional Interpretation

V.R. JAYADEVAN
Reader in Law
Government Law College
Ernakulam (Kerala)

DEEP & DEEP PUBLICATIONS PVT. LTD.
F-159, Rajouri Garden, New Delhi - 110 027

JUDICIAL CREATIVITY IN
CONSTITUTIONAL INTERPRETATION

ISBN 978-81-8450-383-8

Printed in India at MAYUR ENTERPRISES
WZ Plot No. 3, Gujjar Market, Tihar Village, New Delhi - 110 018

Published by DEEP & DEEP PUBLICATIONS PVT. LTD.,
F-159, Rajouri Garden, New Delhi - 110 027 • Phone : 25435369, 25440916
E-mail : ddpubs@gmail.com • ddpbooks@yahoo.co.in
Showroom :
2/13, Ansari Road, Daryaganj, New Delhi - 110 002 • Telefax : 23245122

Contents

PART II

Preface

Interpretation of law as a discipline has a very brief history. Though one hears of the glossators from the days of the illustrious Roman Empire, interpretation did not have much relevance even during the Middle Ages. Even in the beginning days of the modern era, interpretation did not have much significance. This could be attributed to two reasons. Primarily law at that time was developed by the judges than by the legislature, who emphasized on concepts than on words for explaining rights and duties. Secondly, in that pre-Austinian era, relationship between law and language was not well established. But with the arrival of the era of legislation the entire scenario has changed. Judiciary was divested of the power to make law and a separate organ for enacting law—the legislature—came into existence. Such a change brought along with it the increased importance of language. All these changes were given a further boost by the then emerged school called Analytical Positivism which influenced every walk of social life. Consequent to these, there was a steady but gradual decline in the importance of the judiciary and judges as lawgivers. It was in such a situation in which it had to play the second fiddle to the legislature that judiciary appeared in a role of interpreting the laws enacted by the legislature. It is such a development of judicial process that paved in due course the way for the science of interpretation of law. It may not be wrong, in a way, to state that the discipline of interpretation of statutes is developed from the attempt of the judiciary to bring back the glory it enjoyed during the Middle Ages.

With the inauguration of the era of written constitution, judicial power began to be recognized as inclusive of the power to interpret the constitution and to nullify the enacted laws contrary to the constitution. The fact that constitution is a document expected to live longer without being amended, added more significance to the vibrant role of the judiciary in constitutional interpretation. Small wonder, inauguration of the era of written constitutions provided more scope for judicial play. In the succeeding age, the common law countries with written constitutions witnessed a flamboyant and imaginative judiciary, which formulated policies, brought in new principles and at times imported new ideas and norms in the process of interpreting constitutions. Undoubtedly the role played by the judiciary in interpreting constitutions to keep them vibrant and socially relevant has been conspicuous. All these are true of the judiciary in India.

The role played by the Indian judiciary in the constitutional development of the nation cannot be down rated. During the last six decades, its role as the interpreter of the Constitution has been kaleidoscopic. As the protector of the people, it has defended them from the legislative and executive onslaughts, guided and supported and at times frowned at those in power. Above all, by the innovative interpretation of its provisions, the judiciary kept the fragrance and freshness of the basic document. The greatest contribution to Indian constitutional jurisprudence came undoubtedly from the Indian Supreme Court. It has nurtured the Constitution in multifarious ways. It has interpreted the document in the light of the principles drawn from England and America, and at times it explained the difference of the Indian Constitution from that of the west. However, the Indian Supreme Court stands ahead of the judiciary of other countries in one respect. Unlike them, it in certain cases introduced concepts into the Constitution from outside and interpreted the constitutional provisions in the light of such judicially infused concepts, which may be the paradigm of innovative interpretation of the Constitution.

This book is a study about the scope and extent of creativity of and innovation by the Indian judiciary in interpretating the Constitution. Contribution of the Supreme Court in three prominent areas of the Indian Constitution is examined here. The provisions dealing with judiciary, the provision for amending the Constitution and the interrelation between fundamental rights and directive principles are the areas under examination.

Part I deals with the creativity of the Supreme Court in interpreting the constitutional provisions dealing with the judiciary. Part II deals with judicial innovation in dealing with the constituent power of Parliament in amending the Constitution. Part III deals with its creativity in interpreting fundamental rights in the light of the provisions contained in directive principles in accordance with the concept of social justice.

Chapter 1 is the general introduction. The Chapter 2 deals with the concept of judicial independence and how the Supreme Court developed it through various decisions. Chapter 3 deals with the innovations brought forth by the Supreme Court in construing the provisions dealing with appointment of judges to the higher judiciary and considers how the Court developed the concept of consultation between the President and the Chief Justice of India so as to suit the requirements of the concept of judicial independence. The Chapter 4 examines the various aspects of conditions of service of the judges of the higher judiciary including appointment of temporary judges, transfer of judges of the High Court and the procedure for removal of judges of both High Court and the Supreme Court and discusses the issues in these areas on the face of demands of independence of judiciary. Chapter 5 discusses how the Court dealt with appointment of judges of the lower judiciary and the conditions of their service with a view to achieving independence of judiciary. It also examines how far the Supreme Court was able to protect the lower judiciary from the threat to its independence from the High Court.

The second part comprises of the study of the doctrine of basic structure. Chapter 6 deals with the contribution of the Apex Court in construing and limiting the power of Parliament to amend the Constitution and in this attempt to introduce the doctrine of basic structure. Chapter 7 studies how the court developed the doctrine from constitutional provision and examines how the doctrine was made use of by the Court to assess the constitutionality of legislative and executive authorities and how it was developed as a tool for constitutional interpretation.

The third part deals with the innovation made by the Supreme Court in the interpretation of the fundamental rights. Understanding that there is no conflict between fundamental rights and directive principles, the Supreme Court, by 1970's entered the era of harmonious construction of the rights and the directives. But the 1980's witnessed a more innovative interpretation of the fundamental rights when the apex court began to explain them in the light of the non-justiciable directive principles. Chapter 8 glances through the extent of creative contribution of the Supreme Court in interpreting the fundamental rights in the light of social justice and by reading the directives contained in Part IV.

This book is thoroughly revised and updated version of the research work for which the Cochin University of Science and Technology, Cochin, awarded me Ph.D. This work would not have been possible but for the blessings and unstinting support I received from many persons. I remember the paternal affection of my teacher and the supervising guide Prof. (Dr.) N.S. Chandrasekharan whose blessings, I believe are there in my academic and professional life. But for his constant encouragement, I would not have succeeded in completing this work. I am deeply indebted to Prof. (Dr) P. Leelakrishnan, formerly Professor and Dean, Faculty of Law, Cochin University for his constant support and valuable pieces of advice. I will be failing in my duty if I do not remember at this moment, the debt I owe to my teacher the late Prof. G. Viswanatha Sharma. My mother, who has been a constant source of encouragement for me, sacrificed many of her personal interests and aspirations for my benefit, remained with prayers in times of tumult and trouble and found her rejoice in my happiness. I owe a lot to her inspiration, support and sacrifices for whatever little achievements I have had in this life. I respectfully dedicate this book to my mother and my teachers.

Moreover, I remember with gratitude all the members of the faculty, School of Legal Studies who encouraged me to complete the work. I take this opportunity to express my gratitude to the librarians of the School of Legal Studies and the General Library, Cochin University, the Govt. Law College, Ernakulam and the Delhi University. I owe a lot to the librarians of the American Library, Chennai, the High Court of Kerala, the Indian Law Institute, the Govt. Law College, Thrissur and to Adv. Jimmy John and Adv. Raju Abraham for giving me access to their libraries. I am also grateful to Mr. Peter Tense who helped me in preparing the final draft of both the thesis and the book and also to M/s. Deep & Deep Publications for publishing this book.

V.R. JAYADEVAN

PART I

1

Introduction

"We are under a Constitution, but the Constitution is what the judges say it is . . ."

—(Justice Hughes)

Common Law primarily consists of the judge-made law. In the common law system judiciary plays a creative role by formulating, developing, re-modelling[1] and at times breaking down[2] legal concepts from among the ideas and views prevailing in the community and by adapting legal concepts to the changing times. Thus we find the emergence, through judicial process, of different principles, concepts, rules and standards[3] (norms) in various branches of law.[4] Though the self-

1. "...common law is predominantly *judge-made law*. Under it the judge is the creator, interpreter, and modifier of laws. Even when he merely "interprets" law, he may well be creating it." Henry J. Abraham, *The Judicial Process* (1962), p. 13. (Emphasis supplied).
2. P.H. Levy, *Introduction to Legal Reasoning* (1948), p. 9.
3. "Modern juristic analysis shows that law operating through four distinct categories—principles, standards, concepts, and rules", G.W. Paton, *A Textbook of Jurisprudence* (1972), p. 236.
4. Morris, R. Cohen, "The Process of Judicial Legislation" in *Law and the Social Order, Essays in Legal Philosophy* (1967), p.112. He has rightly posed

imposed rule of *stare decisis*,[5] which came into existence at a later stage of development of common law,[6] imposed some restraint on judicial creativity, judicial decisions were considered a major source of law.[7] It is evident that there is high scope for play of judicial wisdom in the inductive process, which is the hallmark of common law.[8] In other words, judiciary had played a very significant role in the making of law.[9]

Nevertheless with the advent of the era of legislation, Parliament became the centre of law-making corresponding to which there was a change in the role of the judiciary. In the changed circumstance, judicial power was identified more with interpretation of statutes enacted by Parliament than with creation of legal concepts by heuristic judicial innovation. Judiciary had to function within the parameters of the words used in the statutes enacted by legislature, and the innovative role of the judiciary became considerably reduced.[10]

---

the question thus, "If judges never make law, how could the body of rules known as the common law ever have arisen or have undergone the changes which it has?".

5. "Adherence to precedent does not come naturally to every judge. Sometimes it is a discipline that he must impose upon *himself*." (Emphasis supplied) Patrick Devlin, *Samples of Law Making* (1962), p. 20.
6. R.M. Jackson, *The Machinery of Justice in England* (1972), pp. 12-13. He observes, "After printed reports became available during the sixteenth century there was more precision in citation; cases are cited by name and the court is expected to follow them. But the judge was not *bound* to follow earlier decisions: the older view was that 'that precedent is evidence, the best possible evidence, of rules of law, but *not more than that;* and that if the law which precedent purports to embody is erroneous, unreasonable, or even intolerably inconvenient, the precedent may be disregarded.' This attitude lasted until about the middle of the last century when a further hardening took place and our courts adopted a theory of 'absolutely binding' precedent." See also C.K. Allen, *op. cit.* at p. 232.
7. See, Fitzgerald (Ed.) *Salmond on Jurisprudence* (1966), p. 114.
8. Allen, C.K., *Law in the Making*, (1964) p. 161.
9. R.M. Jackson, *op. cit.* at p. 14. "Statutes were construed to be in conformity with the common law whenever possible. The older statutes had been so construed, and had become surrounded with such a mass of case-law that lawyers usually thought of the case-law and not of the statute." See also, Abraham, *op. cit.* at p. 20.
10. "In the interpretation of statutes the judge is still more closely tied to his material." Patrick Devlin, *op. cit.* at p. 3.

Be that as it may, the scope of the societal requirement of judicial law-making was such that the ushering in of the statutes could not totally abrogate the same. Nor, was it possible for statutes to meet all the demands of the legal system. For, statute law in contradistinction with the judge-made law was slow to react to the problems offered by the society. Even after the emergence of Parliament as the principal law-maker, there were areas in which either the absence of or lacunae in the existing law was there. In short, even in the wake of the enacted law, there was ample scope for judicial legislation. In such instances, judiciary continued to create law. Thus, even in an age of statutes new legal rights and liabilities began to emerge solely due to the handiwork of judges.[11]

Though statutes have got certain clear advantages in laying down the law, they may be replete with certain inherent defects. Legislature may not be able to pin point all the aspects and ramifications of a statute. And at times, words used in the statutes may be unclear in meaning either due to advancement of time or due to improper drafting. Moreover, there was no dearth of gray areas in the enacted laws which without interpretation could not be applied to novel issues.[12] In such contexts, it becomes the bounden duty of the judiciary to interpret the words and expressions in statutes in such a manner as to infuse sense into them. For such meaningful interpretation, statutes will be treated by judges as manifestation of certain ideals, attitudes, standards or evaluations.[13] Judges, in such cases, will be moved by certain operative conceptions, which direct towards a goal[14] rather than by the words in the statutes.

11. For instance, see *Ryland* v. *Fletcher,* (1868) L.R. 3 H.L. 330; *Donough* v. *Stevenson,* [1932] A.C. 562. For a discussion of the creative role of judges, see, Benjamin N. Cardozo, *The Nature of Judicial Process,* (1995).
12. "Judges should apply the law that other institutions have made; they should not make new law. That is the ideal, but for different reasons it cannot be realized fully in practice. Statutes, and common law rules are often vague and must be interpreted before they can be applied to novel cases. Some cases, moreover, raise issues so novel that they cannot be decided even by stretching or reinterpreting existing rules. So judges must sometimes make new law, either covertly or explicitly." Ronald Dworkin, *Taking Rights Seriously,* Universal Law Publishing, New Delhi, (1995) p. 82.
13. Alf Ross, *On Law and Justice,* (1958), p. 138.
14. *Id.* at p. 137.

In short, lacunae in statutory law provided room for continuance of the active and innovative role of judiciary in diverse ways. Emergence of the rules of statutory interpretation itself is an instance of judicial creativity. Over and above that, while interpreting statutes, courts used to construe words, usages and expressions in them in the light of the common law concepts.[15] The spirit and application of common law was thus retained by judiciary while interpreting statutes.[16] Such attempts to construe statutes in accordance with common law concepts[17] opened the scope for judicial creativity in statutory construction. In short, in interpreting statutes also judges stole opportunities for exhibiting some amount of creativity, which at times has been criticized as amounting to judicial supremacy. Even in England, where sovereignty of Parliament is accepted, judicial innovation has been justified on the ground that "the moral significance of the ideal of the rule of law provides judges to reject legislative supremacy."[18] For legislative supremacy bereft of any restraints is "inconsistent with the rule of law and is therefore politically undesirable."[19]

INTERPRETATION OF WRITTEN CONSTITUTION

It is in this background that interpretation of written constitution becomes significant. Constitution gives identity to the legal system and hence is considered as the basic law of the

---

15. "Then there are the older statutes which create new criminal or quasi criminal offences: but the judges make them submit to inquiries suggested by the common law; do they or do they not, for example, exclude the principle *actus non reus nisi mens sit rea*?" Devlin, *op. cit.* at p. 3. See also R.M. Jackson, *op. cit.* at p. 14. "Statutes were construed to be in conformity with the common law whenever possible. The older statutes had been so construed, and had become surrounded with such a mass of case-law that lawyers usually thought of the case-law and not of the statute." See also, Abraham, *op. cit.* at p. 20.
16. Abraham, *op. cit.* at p. 20.
17. The holding of Sir Edward Coke in the *Bonhams Case*, 8 Co. Rep. 113: LXXVII Eng. Rep. 638 is the best example of such a trend. He observed in that case that Acts of Parliament are controlled by common law and that Acts contrary to common law are void. (at p. 652) For this observation, see, *infra*, chapter VI, n. 84 and the accompanying text.
18. Richard Ekins, "Judicial Supremacy and the Rule of Law", 119 LQR 127.
19. *Id.* at p. 128.

land. Just like any other law, constitution also is enacted. But, it is different from the other laws in the sense that it contains the general norms of the legal system and it lays down the principles upon which the government is erected. It is the very framework of the body politic.[20] Even in the wake of such differences from ordinary laws, Constitution is all the more a statute.

However, a constitution has significant differences from ordinary statutes. It is the basic law from which other statutes in a legal system derive their validity. Apart from being a legal document, a constitution is a political and social document as well.[21] Unlike the ordinary statutes, constitutions come to stay for longer periods so as to provide stability to the legal system for which the process of their amendment is cumbrous. All these factors have to reflect in their interpretation also. Hence, as in the case of any other statute, while interpreting a constitution, though the judiciary has to identify the legislative intent of its makers, the interpretation has to be made in such a manner as to avoid 'ruling by the dead hands.'[22] The significance of constitutional interpretation is that it should enable the constitution to be a live document and to have its existence for long without being amended. All these imply that emergence of the era of written constitutions added a new perspective to statutory interpretation and to the very role of the judiciary in it. In other words, constitutional interpretation arranged the stage for a more creative and imaginative role for judges in statutory interpretation. Such creativity in constitutional interpretation has many dimensions. It may pertain to adoption of certain rules particular to the constitutional interpretation or in selecting the method of construing the words in the basic document. Courts are reluctant to construe provisions in constitutions in a narrow and pedantic manner. Words in the constitutions are given liberal content by courts[23] enabling them

20. K. Shanmukham, *N.S. Bindra's Interpretation of Statutes* (1997), p. 857.
21. Salmond, *op. cit.* at p. 84. He observes that a constitution has both *de jure* and *de facto* existence. It is pertinent to note that the Constitution of India has been characterized as a social document. See, Granville Austin, *The Constitution of India—The Cornerstone of a Nation.* (1966), p. 50. He says, "The Constitution of India is first and foremost a social document."
22. Alf Ross, *op. cit.* at p. 144.
23. Bindra, *op. cit.* at p. 857.

to contain the changes of time without formal amendments. Spirit and nature of the Constitution are considered as important in its interpretation.[24] As mentioned above, as the Constitution comes to stay for longer periods, it would be necessary that words and expressions in it are given a meaning in accordance with the advancement of time.[25] Otherwise, the basic document will have to face frequent amendments.

Judicial creativity in interpreting constitution has yet another dimension. There are occasions in which the court will have to interpret various provisions dealing with a common theme, where mere interpretation of the words and phrases used in those provisions may not be adequate for satisfying the object for which they are enacted. In such cases, the judiciary will have to identify, formulate and select certain concepts, norms or values relevant to all of those provisions and introduce them into the Constitution. All those provisions will then be interpreted with a view to upholding the concept or norm so introduced by the judiciary. In other words, the criteria for construction as well as the content of provisions will be the outcome of judicial labour. In some instances, such creativity to figure out the expressions in constitutions has been influenced by the common law concepts like public policy[26] or natural law.[27] Introduction of such concepts or norms was justified on the ground that interpretation of the Constitution without them would defeat the very purpose of enacting the Constitution. They are instances in which judiciary can be considered as at the zenith of its creativity in constitutional interpretation. An early instance of such innovation in constitutional interpretation in the United States is seen in the famous case of *Marbury* v. *Madison*.[28]

---

24. For a general discussion of interpretation of constitutions, see, Seervai, *Constitutional Law of India*, Vol. I (1993), p. 172 *et. seq*.
25. Interpretations of the expressions like 'due process of law', in the Constitution of the United States and of equality, life and freedom of speech and expression in the Indian and U.S. Constitutions are some examples of this trend.
26. "As a historic fact it cannot be denied that the vast body of constitutional law has been made by our courts in accordance with their sense of justice or public policy." Morris Cohen, *supra*, n. 4 at p. 138.
27. See, Roger Cotterrell, *The Sociology of Law An Introduction* (1992), p. 228.
28. 1 Cranch 137, (1803).

This multi-dimensional creativity in constitutional interpretation by the judiciary is discernible in India also. Though in the initial stages the Indian Supreme Court had been traditional and strict, one finds a progressive outlook on the part of the Court in diverse lines subsequently. The decision in the *Bengal Immunity Company* v. *State of Bihar*,[29] that the Supreme Court was not bound by its own earlier decisions could be considered as prognostic of the future judicial attitude. The Court accepted that the rules for interpretation of the Constitution were different from those of the ordinary statutes. By the latter half of the seventies, the Indian judiciary became very progressive in construing various constitutional provisions. One of the significant innovations of the judiciary is found in the interpretation of the fundamental rights enshrined in our Constitution. While interpreting constitutional provisions dealing with fundamental rights, the Court was influenced by various schools of law like imperative theory,[30] the natural law theory[31] and sociological jurisprudence.[32] Freedom from the shackles of emergency and the acceptance of the sociological approaches to the law by the 1980's paved the way for a more active and vibrant role for the judiciary particularly in the constitutional interpretation. Through progressive interpretation, the contents of the concepts of equality,[33] life,[34] personal liberty,[35] reasonableness,[36] minority rights,[37] inter-

---

29. A.I.R. 1951 S.C. 661.
30. See for example, *A.K. Gopalan* v. *State of Madras*, A.I.R. 1950 S.C. 27.
31. *Maneka Gandhi* v. *Union of India*, A.I.R. 1978 S.C. 597.
32. See, for instance, *Bandhua Mukthi Morcha* v. *Union of India*, (1984) 3 S.C.C. 161 where it was held that a person or class of persons to whom legal injury is caused by violation of fundamental rights is unable to approach the Court on account of poverty or disability, any member of the public acting bona fide can move the Court for relief under Article 32. See also *H.M. Hoskot* v. *State of Maharashtra*, (1978) 3 S.C.C 544, *M.C. Mehta* v. *Union of India*, A.I.R. 1987 S.C. 1086 and *Subshash Kumar* v. *State of Bihar*, A.I.R. 1991 S.C. 420.
33. *E.P. Royappa* v. *State of Tamilnadu*, (1974) 4 S.C.C. 3.
34. 34 *Francis Corellie* v. *Union Territory of Delhi*, A.I.R. 1981 S.C. 146; *Olga Tellis* v. *Bombay Municipal Corporation*, A.I.R. 1986 S.C. 180.
35. *Govind* v. *State of M.P.*, (1975) 2. S.C.C. 148 where it was held that right to personal liberty included in it right to privacy also.
36. *State of Bombay* v. *F.N. Balsara*, A.I.R. 1951 S.C. 318 where it was held that to determine reasonableness, directive principles can be a guideline.
37. *St. Stephens College* v. *Delhi University*, A.I.R. 1992 S.C. 1630.

relationship between various fundamental rights[38] and the scope of the right to approach the judiciary against the violation of fundamental rights[39] have been substantially widened. In short, one does not find dearth of instances of judicial innovation for constitutional innovation.

Over and above these, there have been instances in which the Indian judiciary evolved and introduced into the Constitution certain values and norms not specifically mentioned anywhere in the Constitution and applied them for the purpose of interpreting its provisions. Though the Constitution contains elaborate provisions on different aspects, there are certain silent postulates upon which it rests. Many provisions in the Constitution are incorporated on the basis of some such presumptions. For instance, unlike the Constitution of the United States,[40] the Constitution of India does not explicitly provide that legislative, executive and judicial powers are vested with Parliament, Executive and the Judiciary respectively. Nor does it provide whether the conventions of parliamentary form of government are applicable in India. These indicate that for properly interpreting certain provisions judiciary will have to imply some postulates in the Constitution and construe the words in accordance with them. All these leave much scope for creation and introduction of norms by the judiciary in the process of interpretation of the Constitution. Has the judiciary appropriately selected the values, concepts and norms for interpretation of the Constitution? Can the Indian judiciary be said to be successful in construing the provisions in accordance with such judicially created concepts or norms?

Unlike the innovation with reference to the specific provisions of the Constitution, or a particular aspect in it, with reference to which one finds vacillation in the approach of the judiciary, there are certain instances where the judiciary exhibited consistency in its creative attitudes. In the history of constitutional interpretation in India, one perceives three major areas where the judiciary has maintained consistency in its

38. *Maneka Gandhi* v. *Union of India*, A.I.R 1978 S.C. 597.
39. *S.P. Gupta* v. *Union of India*, 1981 Supp. S.C.C. 87.
40. Article I, section I, Article II section I, para 1 and Article III section I para 1.

innovative approach. While interpreting the provisions dealing with or involving judicial authority, while examining the scope of the power of Parliament to amend the Constitution and while explaining the meaning and content of individual rights in the background of social justice, one finds the Supreme Court at the zenith of its creativity.

The Constitution contains elaborate provisions dealing with judiciary. Provisions dealing with the judiciary are contextually provided in the Indian Constitution. It contains provisions for establishment and functioning of the Union Judiciary consisting of the Supreme Court and the State Judiciary consisting of High Court and subordinate judiciary. There are provisions establishing various courts regulating appointment and conditions of service of judges. A peripheral reading does not reveal anything in common among these provisions. Is there any principle the Court has to keep in mind while construing those provisions? Though no guidance is given by the Indian Constitution, as the decades passed by when the provisions dealing with the judiciary came for its consideration, the Supreme Court realized the necessity of tagging these provisions to the concept of independence of the judiciary lest the objectives of these provisions should be destroyed. Hence while interpreting those provisions, the Court could not ignore the concept of independence of the judiciary.[41] But, as the concept was absent in the document, the court had to import the same into it. How far has the Court kept the concept of independence of judiciary in mind while construing the provisions? What is the scope of the concept of independence of the judiciary so developed by the judiciary?[42] Could the Court figure out and maintain a meaningful concept by the interpretation of those provisions? These are some of the

41. For the concept of independence of the judiciary as developed by the Court, see *infra*, (Chapter, 2).
42. The concept of independence of judiciary is very wide. It includes many things like regulation of appointment, service conditions, removal, freedom of a judge from his colleagues and higher judiciary, appointment as members of various commissions and executive posts after retirement and so on. However, aspects, which do not directly affect any of the provisions of the Constitution do not fall within the purview of the study.

questions that arise in relation to the judicial creativity in the constitutional interpretation in this area.

Interpretation of the provision dealing with amendment of the Constitution is another aspect in which the Court was forced to look out for a norm outside the Constitution for construing scope of the constituent power. This has been the moot issue before the judiciary in all countries with written constitution. The issue was judicially attended to by the Supreme Court of the US within a few years of the arrival of the Constitution. The US Supreme Court took a consistent stand of upholding the constituent power as unlimited. Deviating, from the path laid down by the US Supreme Court, however, the Indian Supreme Court introduced certain limitations on the constituent power of Parliament. But, as the Indian Constitution does not stipulate any limitations on the constituent power save certain procedural ones, the court was constrained to introduce the same *dehors* the Constitution. By introducing into the Constitution, a norm judicially developed, namely, the basic structure the Court sought to construe the scope of the amending power. How far was the Court successful and justified in selecting and developing the norms and construing the provisions relating to amendment in the light of such judicial norms is an aspect which needs examination in relation to the judicial creativity in construing the scope of the constituent power.

Relationship between the ruler and the ruled is constitutionally explained in the form of fundamental rights. Wide understanding of fundamental rights is a threat to the power of the rulers while explaining them in a pedantic manner may cause their desuetude. Small wonder, interpretation of fundamental rights has ever been a moot issue in India as it has been elsewhere. An examination of judicial response right from 1950's will show that the Supreme Court was experimenting with different kinds of interpretation of those rights. During the early stages, the Court was inclined to construe them in a pedantic style. Of late, however the Court realized that a strict legal interpretation of fundamental rights might not satisfy the purpose for which they were enacted. On the other hand, for a proper enjoyment, they should be given a liberal outlook. By the 80's the court began to read the fundamental rights keeping a foot on social realities. This was explicit in the interpretation of the right to equality and right to life in Part III by which the court tried to make them socially relevant. In this venture, the Court began to read similar concepts contained in Directive Principles of State Policy into those fundamental rights. The feature that distinguishes the interpretation of these two fundamental rights is that the court was drawing energy and content from the provisions in Directive Principles of State Policy. In this exercise, the court reading the directives into those fundamental rights as a result of which the otherwise non-justiciable directives were made part of the judicially enforceable fundamental rights. The consequence of such an interpretation was the achievement of social justice through fundamental rights, which, in the previous decades were considered as hindrance to it. The extent of creativity involved in interpreting the fundamental rights with a view to achieving social justice is undoubtedly a question that requires scrutiny.

These areas are thus related to the civil liberties, the kingpin of modern democracy. Independence of judiciary is a *sine qua non* for the protection of civil liberties. Unbridled constituent power is likely to restrict the scope of those rights. And to make enjoyment of fundamental rights a reality, it is highly necessary that they should be explained in the light of social justice. The common thread running through these areas of examination is the judicial attempt to limit the exercise of power in an uncontrolled manner. Enforcement of fundamental rights is a limitation on the arbitrary legislative or executive power while regulation of the constituent power was necessitated by the attempt of Parliament to alter the basic document to enable unopposed governance of the nation. However, for checking arbitrariness of any kind, it is very essential that judiciary shall be absolutely insulated of other powers and remains independent. It is also worth mentioning that the above three areas were traditionally beyond judicial examination. Appointment of judges is considered as an executive function and their termination is by the legislature. The power to amend the constitution is vested on the supreme legislative body while implementation of directive principles is within the legislative and executive domain. The present work is an excursus into the contribution of the Indian Supreme Court in interpreting the Constitution in the above areas.

2

Independence of Judiciary : An Overview

Functions of the State are generally classified into three: legislative, executive and judicial.[1] Such a classification was in existence from very ancient times though the nomenclature used to denote these functions during those times was different.[2] In the ancient and medieval models of administration, monarchy was the only recognized form of administration. As the king was believed to be the representative of God on earth,[3] he was empowered to enact, execute and interpret the laws. In other words, though the three aspects of administration were identified as different, all of those powers were concentrated in one hand. Natural law

1. "It is submitted that the three basic and essential functions in the administration of any independent state are legislative, executive and judicial." Yardley, *Introduction to British Constitutional Law* (1964), p. 64.
2. See for instance, Earnest Barker (Ed.) *The Politics of Aristotle* (1958), Chapter XIV, pp. 188-200. He refers to those functions as deliberative (legislative), executive and judicial.
3. Rama Jois, *Legal and Constitutional History of India*, Vol. I (1990), pp. 666-67.

theory, which held the sway during those days, emphasized that laws owed their origin to God and hence law was considered infallible.[4] Due to such an axiomatic assertion of infallibility of law, justifiability of law was not a question. Judicial function—to interpret the laws—in that context was only of subordinate importance in comparison with the legislative and executive functions and it was carried out by the king himself or by his nominees.[5]

Elapse of time brought in along with it corresponding changes in legal philosophy also. The idea of laws having divine support was received reconsideration and the same was given footing on rational and pragmatic grounds.[6] Consequently, infallibility of law was questioned. Concomitant to these developments, the view that power had a tendency to corrupt became acceptable. Hence, it was realized that unification of powers—legislation, execution and interpretation—in one authority has a tendency to nurture and promote arbitrariness. In was in the wake of such an ideological shift from supra-mundane level to the terrestrial plane that the doctrine of separation of powers was given birth. The theory of separation of powers propounded that the three basic functions of the State viz. legislative, executive and judicial should be vested in different and independent persons or bodies.[7] These powers may bė held by authorities that are co-ordinate but independent in their respective fields. Nevertheless, even after the emergence of the doctrine of separation of powers the practice of holding the three powers by the same person or body used to exercise

---

4. God is infallible. Hence, natural law, which is his product, should also be infallible for, "The *Lex aeterna* is divine reason, known only to God and 'the blessed who see God in his essence.' It is god's plan for the universe, a deliberate act of God and everything, not only man, is subject to it." Lord Lloyd and M.D.A. Freeman, *Lloyd's Introduction to Jurisprudence* (1985), p. 109.
5. "The Monarch is the "fountain of justice", being technically present in all his courts of law, responsible for many judicial appointments, and exercising the prerogative of mercy in respect of persons convicted in the courts." Yardley, *op. cit.* at p. 66.
6. *Lloyds, op. cit.* at p. 123.
7. Legislation is to be done by the legislature, implementation by the executive and interpretation of such laws and judging by the judiciary and such bodies should be independent of one another.

the three kinds of powers. Evidently, the idea of separation of such functions reflected in the doctrine of separation of powers[8] was not put into practice till the eighteenth century. Constitutions framed subsequent to the emergence of the theory of separation of powers attempted to incorporate this concept into their Constitutions.[9] This in its turn led to a rational approach of questioning the validity of the enacted laws and their justifiability.

I. EMERGENCE OF JUDICIARY AS AN INSTITUTION

An important consequence of the adoption of the doctrine of separation of powers was the conferment of a prominent status to the judicial function. Judiciary had to be raised to a position of high significance on par with other organs of administration of the State.[10] Judicial function was to be discharged by an authority, which was independent of the legislative and executive wings. In other words, the doctrine helped the judiciary to stand upon its own legs.[11] Unlike the separation of powers in the case of legislative and executive functions,[12] there should be least interference with judicial function so as to maintain uncompromised independence of the judiciary.[13]

---

8. For the doctrine, see, Montesquieu, The *Spirit of Laws*, The Great Books of the World (Vol. 30) (1978).
9. See for instance, the Constitutions of the U.S.A, France, Australia, Canada and India.
10. "...of the three powers above mentioned, the judiciary in some measure next to nothing." Montesquieu, *op. cit.* at pp. 71-72.
11. See, for instance, Irving R. Kaufman, "The Essence of Judicial Independence," 80 Col. L. R. 671.
12. See, E.W. Thomas, *The Judicial Process: Realism, Pragmatism, Practical Reasoning and Principles*, Cambridge (2005) p. 77. He observes that though there is separation of powers, it is not possible to maintain total separation between them. The doctrine has been understood as the formula of 'core functionalism', which says that there should not be interference by one with the core functions of the other.
13. *Id.* at p. 78. He observes, "In respect of the judiciary, however, this perception is best removed from the context of the separation of powers doctrine altogether and advanced as a critical constitutional doctrine; the independence of the judiciary. For the legislative and executive branches of government to refrain from interfering with the judicial function, they must respect that independence itself and not just the core judicial

India also was no exception to the above-mentioned process. During the ancient[14] and medieval periods, the King, the executive head, was a three-in-one constitution, who exercised legislative,[15] executive and judicial functions. Though judicial function was recognized as a separate one, there was no separate organ for it.[16] The King during those times was considered as the fountainhead of justice. It was with the arrival of the British that the judiciary got an independent status of a separate institution. But, the concept of independence of judiciary began to flourish in our country only in the post independence era.

2. INDEPENDENCE OF THE JUDICIARY: THE CONCEPT

In common parlance, 'independence' means 'not depending on authority or control; not depending on another thing for validity or on another person for one's opinion or livelihood and unwilling to be under obligations to others'.[17] This is all the more true of judiciary also. The concept fundamentally means that judiciary as an institution has to be free from any control of supervision and that judges would not have to budge before others. "In the most basic and usually the least important sense, independence would mean that the judge had not been bribed or was not in some other way a dependent of one of the parties."[18] Independence of judiciary would certainly mean freedom of the institution from others. However,

---

function. *Another way of making the point would be to say that judicial independence is an integral part of the judiciary's core function. But, however the point is made, the level of legislative and executive restraint from interference in the judicial function must be necessarily high if judicial independence is not to be compromised.*" (Emphasis supplied).

14. There are reference to the fact that in the classical Vedic age, the ultimate court of justice was the King in Council. Though the code writers and commentators opine that king could not decide case personally, the king presided over the court and decrees given under his name. See, K.P. Jayaswal, *Hindu Polity*, (1955) p. 313.
15. However, the legislative power of the King was limited. See, Rama Jois, *op. cit.* at p. 627.
16. For details, see, *infra*, n 49.
17. See *The Concise Oxford Dictionary*.
18. Martin Shapiro, *Courts: A Comparative and Political Analysis* (1981), p. 19.

when the term 'independence' qualifies 'judiciary', it commands a wider connotation. It is wide enough to include independence not only from an outside authority but also from itself. In other words, the expression 'independence of the judiciary' encompasses freedom not only from its sister authorities like legislature and executive as well as from the public but also from the judicial hierarchy.

In English law, judicial independence consists of three motifs—rule of law, the functional specialization of the judiciary and the autonomy of the legal profession.[19] It also implies that even when hierarchically established, each court, how-low-so-ever it is, would be the final authority over matters falling within its jurisdiction. Appellate and higher courts with administrative jurisdiction would not have any control over their judicial functioning.[20] The ultimate safeguard of judicial independence is to be sought in the judge himself and not outside, for it is the inner strength of the judge which alone would save the judiciary.[21] In relation to the higher judiciary, it indicates freedom from other branches of administration while with reference to the lower courts it is concerned also with independence from the higher courts. In short, it is clear that the phrase independence of judiciary has different meanings in different contexts.[22]

(a) The Traditional Concept

A study of the origin and development of the concept tells

19. *Id.* at p. 69.
20. A hierarchical view of the institution of judiciary is in itself bad. In this sense, the expression, 'subordinate judiciary' is wrong as it smacks a sense of dependence on some other authority. See Upendra Baxi, *Courage, Craft and Contention, the Supreme Court in the 80's* (1985), p. 25.
21. "Timidity of mind ill goes together with the office of a judge. Weak characters cannot be good judges." H.R. Khanna, *Judiciary in India and Judicial Process* (1985), p. 25.
22. It is observed that to the senior members of the Press, independence of the judiciary means independence of the appellate judiciary only. The social meaning of independence of judiciary is that no change in so far as the system suits the upper echelon of the Bar and resourceful activators of the court system. *Id.* at pp. 25, 35. For politicians, independence of judiciary would sound quite a different tone like approval of government policies. See generally, Mohan Kumaramangalam, *Judicial Appointments* (1973).

us that till the advent of the second half of the twentieth century, 'independence of the judiciary' was a very narrow one. Its traditional view covered only formal matters like appointment, tenure, salary, transferability and removal of judges and their status after retirement. The concept meant only independence from the other institutions wielding power, namely, legislature and executive. Though independence of judges could be reverberated in the words of Chief Justice Edward Coke, fruitful attempts to free judiciary from the other organs can be traced only to the beginning of eighteenth century. The first move towards this direction in Britain can be seen in the Act of Settlement, 1700.[23] It tried to keep the British judiciary free from the executive. It was this statute which replaced the tenure of judges on Majesty's pleasure with the tenure of members of judiciary during their 'good behaviour' and provided for their removal upon address in both Houses of Parliament.[24] In other words, it was by the Act of Settlement that tenure of judges was freed from executive control and left under the control of judges themselves. The concept of independence of judiciary in this narrow sense was implemented in the U.S. also by its Constitution.[25] Such a concept is found in Constitutions of different countries including that of India.[26]

(b) The Modern Version

However, the scope of the traditional concept of independence of judiciary ended there. Notwithstanding the acceptance of the concept, one is able to find a number of instances in which administrators tried to subdue the spirit of independence exhibited by judiciary. It is in such a context that the concept of judicial independence began to grow so as to reach its modern form. The modern concept of independence of judiciary, unlike the traditional one, is more dynamic. It has many facets. Apart from the procedural and technical aspects of

23. 12 and 13 will c. 2. For the text, see *Chitty's Statutes of Practical Utility* Vol. III (1912), p. 661 *et.seq.*
24. *Id.* Sec. 3 (8). It was replaced by section 5 of Judicature Act, 1875, 38 & 39 Vict. C. 77.
25. See, the Constitution of the United States, Article III.
26. See, the Constitution of India, Articles 124(2), (4) and (5), 125, 217(1) 218 and 233 to 236.

the traditional concept, it contains some substantive elements of independence. The modern concept for instance, conceives internal and external independence of judges including their independence from colleagues and superiors as an essential ingredient of independence of judiciary.[27] The modern idea of judicial independence implies that judiciary should be free not only from the legislature, executive and the public, but also from the prejudices of the judiciary itself.[28] The concept thus includes internal, external, individual (personal), collective (institutional), functional and substantive forms of independence.[29] The expression therefore, implies avoidance of subjection of the will of a Judge to his colleagues or superiors in any way.[30] Inauguration of the era of judicial activism which brought judiciary as a centre power has amplified the significance of judicial independence.

3. NECESSITY OF JUDICIAL INDEPENDENCE

The need for judicial independence can never be over-emphasized. Judiciary is the institution where questions of law are analyzed threadbare and tested on the touchstone of axiomatic principles. Opinions and observations from such analysis bring about changes in the law, according to the requirements of the changing times. The role played by the judiciary, in other words, is that of a catalyst.

---

27. Simon Shetreet, "Judicial Independence: New Conceptual Dimensions and Contemporary Challenges," in Simon Shetreet and Jules Deschenes (Ed.), *Judicial Independence: A Contemporary Debate* (1985), p. 590.
28. "... it is necessary to remind ourselves that the concept of independence of the judiciary is not limited to independence from executive pressures or influence but is is a much wider concept which takes within its sweep independence from may other pressures and prejudices. It has many dimensions, namely, fearlessness of other power centres, economic or political and freedom from prejudices acquired and nourished by the class to which the judges belong." *Per* Justice Bhagwati in *S.P. Gupta v. Union of India*, 1981 Supp. S.C.C. 87 at p. 223.
29. Simon Shetreet, "Judicial Independence: New Conceptual Dimensions and Contemporary Challenges," in Martin Shapiro and Simon Shetreet, *op. cit.* at pp. 590-95. One cannot however, forget the fact that there are certain institutional factors within and outside the judges that are *likely* to affect their independence. See also E.W. Thomas, *op. cit.*, pp. 241-50.
30. Alfred Denning, *Road to Justice* (1955), p. 11.

The power conferred on judiciary is to interpret and explain the law, including the Constitution.[31] The primary aim of judiciary while interpreting law is to render justice. While thus interpreting the law, the judge would make law in a manner of what is called 'interstitial legislation'. His expressions and usage in the judicial dialect, at times, would be more valuable than the words used in statutes. This is particularly true of the common law system. The common law system owes much of its strength, credibility and above all uniformity and unity to the system of precedents. Unlike the civil law system followed in Europe, in common law countries judiciary was and continues to be the main law-maker. Even after the assumption of law-making function by the legislature, judiciary continued to play a vital role in the interpretation, application and in certain cases, creation of law.[32] Much of the English law and of the Indian law also is nothing but the views and opinions of judges well-versed in law. Many statutes are only legislative restatements of such judicial opinions. Such importance was given to the views of the judiciary and confidence was reposed on the opinions of judges by all only because of the independence of the institution. It is rightly said,

> "...much of the authority enjoyed by common law precedent has stemmed from the high status, *independence and substantial salaries* accorded to the judiciary in common law countries."[33]

In other words, there is an undeniable link between judicial independence and the authenticity of the law made by the judiciary. It is beyond comprehension as to what would happen if such an important organ were derided of its absolute independence and made dependent on another authority or person. The least that can be stated of such a predicament is that if the views of judges are based upon extraneous considerations they would lack authenticity and might enjoy scant respect.

---

31. See, for instance, *Marbury* v. *Madison*, Cranch 137 U.S. (1803).
32. See, *supra*, chapter I, n. 12.
33. Dennis Lloyd, *The Idea of Law* (1977), p. 276. (Emphasize supplied).

Independence of judiciary is important at least for four reasons. Firstly, it ensures that the judges to whom the duty of defining and regulating the governmental functions are entrusted carry out such duty impartially. Secondly, it guarantees the liberties of the subject as against other persons and bodies. Thirdly, it creates a law-abiding habit in the nation. And fourthly, it grounds the authority of the State upon the rule of law.[34] A judge can exercise his powers and discharge his duties effectively and honestly only if he is not susceptible to fear of any kind and pressures including those from other organs of the State.[35] Hence, independence of judges is, and must always be the best security for the stability of State. Liberty, democracy and rule of law can be said to be the holy trinity for a secured life in the modern world. Destruction of one of them would cause crumbling down of others also. And the holy trinity of liberty, democracy and rule of law depends upon the independence of the judiciary.[36] In the absence of judicial independence, there is a chance that fundamental rights enshrined in the Constitution could be easily abolished[37] leading to destruction of life and liberty of the people. In short, it is necessary that judges should be free from all sorts of influences and pressures adversely affecting their independence, so that judicial decisions are rendered without fear, favour or ill-will and dispensation of justice is not hampered. Impartiality in the decision-making process will be ensured only if such independence is secured.[38] Independence of the judiciary should be there for the benefit of the litigant and not for

---

34. Holdsworth, Sir William, *A History of English Law* Vol. X. (1966), p. 644. See also R.F.V. Heuston, *Essays in Constitutional Law* (1961), p. 49. He observes, "An independent judiciary is an indispensable requisite of a free society under the Rule of Law.
35. "It is axiomatic that the person who is to decide...disputes can discharge his functions effectively only if he be not susceptible to pressure of the citizen, and what is much more important, of the State." Khanna. H.R., *op. cit.* at p. 16.
36. *Id.* at p. 20.
37. As happened, for instance, during the emergency in 1975-77.
38. "(I)t is to be instilled in every mind that where fear is, justice cannot be; ... "Justice Khanna, H.R. "Need to Preserve Image of Judiciary", I J.B.C.I. pp. 241-42.

providing place for arbitrariness of judges. It is not a homily to the Judge but the right of every litigant.[39] Justice Frankfurter has rightly observed: "The most prized liberties themselves presuppose an independent judiciary through which these liberties may be, as they often have been vindicated."[40]

Independence of judiciary has an added significance in a federal state. In a state with federal Constitution, questions regarding the scope, extent and validity of the exercise of legislative power by various legislative authorities might arise. Similarly, there may be questions relating to constitutional validity of laws. The power to determine such issues is vested with the judiciary.[41] Judiciary may not be able to exercise these functions unless it is fully independent. As Lord Simmons observed, "in a federal system absolute independence of judiciary is the bulwark of the constitution against encroachment whether by legislature or by the executive."[42] Moreover, in a federal state, judiciary plays the role as an umpire in disputes between the federation and the states or in contentions between different units, which constitute the federation.[43] In the modern world, disputes between the State and individuals are very common. The State is the biggest litigant. In such a context, it is imperative that the body, which settles disputes, should be independent of influences likely to be exerted by the State. The importance of judiciary in such a situation, and the role it may have to play in dispensing justice to one and all even against executive excesses cannot be overemphasized.[44] In short, it may not be an exaggeration to state that the very existence of the federal Constitution depends upon the independent functioning of the judiciary. All these indicate

39. See, Article 10 of Universal Declaration of Human Rights.
40. *U.S.* v. *United Mine Workers,* 330 U.S. 258, 311: 91 L.Ed. 884, 922.
41. Seervai, *Constitutional Law of India,* Vol. I (1991), p. 260.
42. *R.* v. *Kirby exp. Boil-makers Society of Australia,* (1957) A.C. 288 at p. 315.
43. See, the Constitution of India, Article 131.
44. However, it is doubtful whether this aspect of judicial independence was properly perceived by Dr. Ambedkar, the President of the Constituent Assembly when he observed that there was nothing wrong in appointing retired Judges in different posts and that the restrictions constitutionally envisaged on the members of the Public Service Commission for such appointments were not to be applied to retired Judges. C.A.D., Vol. VIII, pp. 678-79.

the importance of judicial independence in India since its Constitution carries some federal features. Justice Bhagwati has rightly observed, "...the independence of the judiciary is a fighting faith of our Constitution. Fearless justice is a cardinal creed of our founding document."[45] Comments of several members of the Constituent Assembly also suggest that they were aware of the importance and need of judicial independence.[46] Perhaps, it is taking these factors into consideration that the apex court held that independence of judiciary formed one of the ingredients of basic structure of the Constitution.[47]

Judicial independence is so cardinal that when decisions by independent judges posed some threats, there were attempts on the part of the organs of the State and others to malign the benign independence of judiciary. Such instances are not lacking in England, America and India.[48] Such attempts were so grave that they threatened the very existence of judiciary. Hence, it became the bounden duty of the judiciary to check such inroads on its own existence. In such cases, the major medium in its attempts to salvage judicial independence was its power to interpret the Constitution and statutes. The Indian judiciary has played a very constructive role towards this direction. In the wake of legislative and executive inroads on the judiciary, it will be interesting to know the role played by the judiciary in India to uphold its own independence. How has the Supreme Court chiseled out the concept of independence of judiciary from the provisions of Indian Constitution, which do not specifically provide for it? Was the Supreme Court able to inculcate the modern, dynamic concept of independence of judiciary into the Indian legal system? By construing the provisions of the Constitution, was the Court able to hold out and sustain the

---

45. *Union of India* v. *Sankalchand Seth,* A.I.R. 1977 S.C. 2328 at p. 2355.
46. B. Shiva Rao, *The Framing of India's Constitution—A Study* (1968), p. 490.
47. *Shri Kumar Padma Prasad* v. *Union of India,* (1992) 2 S.C.C. 428. For a discussion of basic structure, see, *infra,* chapters VI and VII.
48. Dismissal of the Chief Justice Edward Coke in England by King James I, the court packing plan by Theodore Roosevelt in the United States of America and supersession of Hedge, Shelat and Grover, JJ for appointing A.N. Ray and appoointment of M.H. Beg overriding H.R. Khanna as the Chief Justice of India bear testimony to this trend.

judicially envisaged concept of judicial independence? For a satisfactory evaluation of the contribution of the Supreme Court in this respect the innovations made by it in nurturing the traditional concept of judicial independence are to be analyzed. It is to be examined how the Court treated and manured the concept of judicial independence and how far the Court was able to uphold the independence of an institution of which it is the head.

For examining the development of the concept of independence of judiciary through the contributions of the Supreme Court, it is very much necessary to have a look at the status accorded to judiciary in India from the ancient times.

4. STATUS OF JUDICIARY IN INDIA AND THE CONCEPT OF INDEPENDENCE OF THE JUDICIARY

(a) Judiciary in Ancient India

As said above, in India, during ancient times, there was no separation between the organs of administration though there was demarcation of the administrative functions. Judiciary was not given any separate status. The King himself was considered as the fountainhead of justice and there was no appeal against his decisions.[49] In short, in the ancient India, one may find references to the judicial function even though he may not be able to identify an institution called judiciary. However, as is evidenced from *Dharmasastras* utmost respect was given to laws and the administrators of those times tried to keep judiciary independent.[50] In other words, seeds of modern concept of judicial independence were there even in ancient India.

(b) Judiciary During the British Era

A study of the concept of judicial independence in India during the British regime calls for an understanding of the institution of judiciary during that period.

49. A.S. Altekar, *State and Government in Ancient India* (1949), p. 247.
50. Justice A.M. Bhattacharjee, *Hindu Law and the Constitution* (1994), pp. 5-6. He compares the ancient British jurisprudence with that of the ancient Indian legal thought and observes that while in Britain the King was above law in India the King could not deviate from the path chartered by law. See also, K.P. Jayaswal, *supra* note 14.

The era of British administration in India can be divided into four on the basis of formation and development of judiciary, namely (1) 1600-1726, during which period administration of justice in the three Presidency towns of Madras, Calcutta and Bombay was at a rudimentary stage and was totally dissimilar;[51] (2) 1726-1774 during which period the judiciary had been organized under the Charter Act 1726[52] in the three Presidency towns; (3) 1774-1861 when for the first time Crown offered to create the Supreme Court, which would be manned by persons who were not accountable to the Company, i.e. to the executive in any manner,[53] and (4) 1861-1950 during which period one finds rather well organized judicial establishments at the higher level.[54]

(i) Judiciary during the Regime of the East India Company

Administration by the East India Company (1600-1857) was marked by the establishment and management of judiciary by the Company itself. Courts other than the Supreme Court[55] were manned and financed by the Company through its nominees. Under this system certain functions like settlement of civil disputes and administration of criminal justice were assigned to nominees of the Company who were not even qualified to be appointed as Judges.[56]

---

51. See, M.P. Jain, *Outlines of Indian Legal History* (1981), p. 11. This stage can be further divided into three as follows: (a) the earliest stage marked by recognition of the rudimentary concepts of judiciary. (b) the second stage when the executive head viz., the Governor General in Council wielded the highest judicial function also, and (c) when more subordinate courts were created and manned by the executive. This division is more true of Madras Presidency where the British established their factory at the earliest. The other two Presidency towns of Bombay and Calcutta, which became under the British control later, exhibited the features of second and third period even during the first period. Again, the hierarchy of courts, the jurisdiction of the courts, the modes of administration of justice and the like were different in the three Presidency towns during these stages.
52. For a discussion of the Act, see, *id.* at pp. 38-44.
53. The Regulating Act, 1773, Stal. 13 Geo. 3 C.63.
54. The Indian High Courts Act 1861, 23 & 25 Vict. C. 104; The Indian high Courts Act, 1911, 1 & 2 Goe. V.C. 18; The Government of India Act 1915, 5 & 6 Geo. V, C. 61 and the Government of India Act, 1935.
55. Established by the Regulating Act, 1773.
56. E.g. The Charter Act, 1661. See, for a brief, but, nice description, H.P. Debey, *A Short History of the Judicial Systems of India and Some Foreign Countries* (1968), p. 10.

Since the judges were nominated by the Company, during this period, the administration of justice was fully under the control of the executive. Judges were appointed not on considerations of their legal qualifications or knowledge but of their pliability to the executive.[57] The conditions of judicial service were also not desirable. Instances like non-payment of salary, suspension from service for assertion of independence, treating it as insubordination were there.[58] In Madras, in 1678, it was resolved that the Governor in Council would be the High Court of Judicature.[59] In Calcutta, the judicial administration was in its rudimentary form with concentration of all of the powers in one and the same officer.[60] In short, "executive never relished the idea of judicial independence, it always wanted to keep the court under its thumb."[61]

The Charter Act, 1726 provided for the creation of the Mayor's Court in all the three Presidency towns. It was in the same lines of the Charter Act, 1687, which introduced the Mayor's Court in Madras.[62] Mayor was to be chosen from among the members of the Mayor's Court known as Aldermen. Aldermen were to hold the post for life. Vacancies were to be filled by selecting persons from the prominent inhabitants of the towns by Mayor and Aldermen and not by the Governor in Council. In other words, there was an attempt to bifurcate judiciary and executive.[63] The same led to an impasse between the executive and the judiciary.[64] There were two choices left for the Company: (a) to keep the judiciary as it was but to define the vague points by means of law and regulation or (b) to make the executive all the more predominant and weaken the judiciary. Lot fell for the latter option, it being easier, though at

57. It was "suggestive of the prerogative run mad." Keith, A.B. *Constitutional History of India* (1936), p. 39 as quoted in M.P. Jain, *op. cit.* at p. 26.
58. M.P. Jain, *op. cit.* at pp. 24-25. For instance, as the Company could not tolerate the independence exhibited by John St. John, a Judge of Recorder of the Mayor's Court, he was removed from the office.
59. *Id.* at p. 14.
60. *Id.* at p. 34.
61. *Id.* at p. 27.
62. Debey, *op. cit.*, pp. 26-28.
63. Due to the importance of the Charter in the spheres of law and justice, it was called the 'Judicial Charter'.
64. M.P. Jain, *op. cit.* at p. 22.

the cost of judicial independence.[65] The result was the Charter Act, 1753.[66] As a consequence, the judicial system tended to be a branch of the executive government.

However, some stray incidents of attempts to keep judiciary independent are discernible even when the Company was the administrator. Warren Hastings, the first Governor General, through his judicial plans introduced substantial changes into the judicial system in India. It was by the plan of 1772 that he laid down the foundation of the adalat system.[67] In 1780 there was another plan by him for mutually separating judicial and revenue functions (collection of revenue and deciding revenue disputes).[68] Thus, there existed adalats—the company courts—and the Supreme Court—the Crown Court—simultaneously with concurrent and conflicting jurisdictions.[69] The benign target of Hastings was to separate judiciary from the executive. For that purpose he appointed Elijah Impey the then Chief Justice of the Supreme Court of Calcutta as the Judge of the Sadr Diwani Adalat to avoid involvement of the Governor in judicial matters. It may seem paradoxical that Impey was later recalled by the Crown on the ground that he compromised his independence as a judge by accepting the post as judge of Adalat since that was an office at the sufferance the Company and the judge was removable by it.[70]

---

65. *Ibid.*
66. It re-introduced the system of appointment and dismissal of Mayor and Aldermen by Governor in Council. (*Id.* at p. 44.) It is criticized to be the creator of executive ridden judiciary. "Justice, therefore, was too much of a 'political force'." (at p. 51).
67. By the integrated administrative and judicial plain of 1772, a well established adalat system was created under the Company with the Sadr Diwani Adalat and Sadr Fouzdari Adalat at the apex of the civil and criminal courts respectively. The former consisted of the Governor and his council members while the latter consisted of the Judges appointed by Nawab on the advice of the Governor. M.P. Jain, *op. cit.* at pp. 61-62. See also Rama Jois, *op. cit.*, pp. 144-45.
68. M.P. Jain, *op. cit.* at p. 65. There was another administrative plan in 1774 which is not of relevance here. *Id.* at p. 118.
69. *Id.* at p. 118.
70. *Id.* at pp. 122-23. This gesture reveals that the Crown was well aware that the judicial officers under the Company never enjoyed the independence required for discharging judicial function properly.

Some changes in the status of judiciary as an independent institution were brought forth by the Regulation Act 1773.[71] It created a Supreme Court[72] with judges to be appointed and liable to be dismissed by the Crown.[73] Unlike the English East India Company, the Crown, who appointed the Judges, did not have any direct interest in matters relating to administration of India. Therefore, judges could take decisions against the Company personnel without fear or favour. Hence, that scheme of administration of justice under the Regulation Act, 1773 was in some way conducive to independence of the judiciary and it enabled Judges to take decisions without fear or favour in respect of the matters before them, whoever be the parties. Thus, for the first time in the history of India a judiciary not only free from the executive but which could control and supervise the executive came into existence.

However, after the term of Hastings, the merger of revenue and judicial functions was advocated to lessen the expenses of the administration and the same was effected in 1786. Needless to say, it resulted in destruction of independence of judiciary. It was during the term of Lord Cornwallis (1786-1796) that by Regulation II of 1793, India again experienced the much-desired bifurcation of judicial function from the revenue and executive functions. This Regulation provided for the judicial scrutiny of members of the executive also.[74] The reforms were however, limited to the lower levels of administration. Yet it could be stated that separation of judiciary from the executive, one of the pre-conditions for judicial independence, got materialized to some extent under the regime of Lord Cornwallis.

This trend got further impetus during the term of Lord Wellesly. It was decided during his term that the Governor General or his council members should not sit as Sadr Diwani Adalat. Thus it was provided by Regulation II of 1801[75] that separate judges should be appointed for Sadr Diwani and Sadr Nizamat Adalat. But, it appears that the reasons for such

71. 13 Geo. III C. 63.
72. It was to have civil, criminal, admiralty and ecclesiastical jurisdictions. See Regulation Act, 1773, sections 13, 15 and 16.
73. *Id.* Section 13,
74. M.P. Jain, *op.cit.* at pp. 139-40.
75. *Id.* at p. 164.

separation were other than the pious wish to secure independence of judiciary.[76] In short, the judicial system that existed in India during the 17th and 18th centuries was one vacillating between the separation and unification of the judiciary with the executive for some times.[77]

(ii) Changes during the Crown Administration

Taking over the administration of the colony by the Crown in 1857 brought substantial changes in the Indian judicial structure also. In 1861[78] the Crown enacted the High Courts Act.[79] It abolished the Sadr Courts and the Supreme Courts and thereby terminated the existing conflict of jurisdictions. It authorized the Crown to establish High Courts in their place. Further, it prescribed the qualifications for judges who were to be appointed by the Crown. In short, in matters of jurisdiction, status and position, High Courts under the 1861 Act can be considered as the forerunner of High Courts under the Constitution of India. However, security of tenure of judges which is an essential ingredient of independence of judiciary became a reality only with the enactment of the Government of India Act, 1935 which provided that judges could be removed only on the grounds of misbehaviour or infirmity of mind or

---

76. *Id.* at pp. 164-65. Therefore, the judges were continued to be appointed by the Governor General in council and council members as well as civil servants had a vital role in dispensing justice.
77. Till 1814, there were no qualifications prescribed for Judges of the Sadr Adalat. By Regulation XXV of 1814, it was stipulated that only persons who had previous experience in discharging judicial functions be appointed judges of Sadr Courts. This system was in vogue till the establishment of High Courts in 1892. In the criminal side also there was no separation of the judiciary from the executive. Therefore, there was no guarantee against the misuse of functions by the executive authorities. (*Id.* at p. 166)
78. An interesting feature of the stages up to 1861 was that the concept of judicial independence was limited to the Presidency towns of Bombay, Calcutta and Madras. They were ruled according to separate codes of regulations. Hence these were called Regulations Provinces. In the Non-Regulation Provinces, no mature and well-advanced judicial system was prevalent. Nor were there any attempts to improve the status of the judiciary. There, all the powers concentrated in the hands of the executive.
79. 24 & 25 Vict., c. 104.

body.[80] Till then, judges were removable at the will of the Crown. The Government of India Act 1935 was a major break through in this regard. The Act provides for excluding members of Indian Civil Service from being appointed as the Chief Justice of the Federal Court created by the Act.[81]

Analysis of the judicial institutions of the British Raj reveals that India passed through stages with the following characteristics successively namely, (i) the judiciary and the executive were in a state of merger, (ii) judiciary was manned by persons who were appointed and controlled by the executive, and (iii) judiciary was conferred with some independence due to the mode of appointment and conditions of service though not with the substantive independence.[82]

(c) Judiciary—The Post-independence Scenario

As against the above background one may find that the post-independent scenario offers some progress in this respect. A perusal of the debate in the Constituent Assembly reveals that the members of the Assembly were very much concerned with judicial independence.[83] The provisions relating to the judiciary were incorporated in the Constitution with a view to providing utmost freedom and sense of security to judges and independence to the institution of judiciary. The Constitution was to contain provisions relating to appointment of judges to the Supreme Court of India,[84] High Court of various States[85] and general guidelines relating to appointment of judges to the

80. S. 220(2). Though there were a few legislation dealing with judiciary, they do not have any direct nexus with its independence. The Government of India Act, 1915 is worth mentioning as it empowered His Majesty to establish High Courts under Letters Patent (section 113). The Act in fact, is only a copy of the Indian High Courts Act, 1861. See, Debey, *op. cit.*, pp. 274-75.
81. The Government of India Act, 1935, S. 200(3) Proviso (i). It reads, "a person shall not be qualified for appointment as Chief Justice of India unless he is, or when first appointed to judicial office was, a barrister, a member of the Faculty of Advocates or a pleader; ..."
82. For a treatment of judicial administration from 1781-1861, see Anil Chandra Banarjee, *The Constitutional History of India*, Vol. I (1977), p. 349 *et. seq.*
83. *Supra*, n. 46.
84. Article 124(2).
85. Article 217(1).

subordinate courts.[86] From the experience during the pre-independent stage, the members of the Constituent Assembly were eager to make the power to appoint judges outside the free will and control of the executive. Thus, the power to appoint judges to the Apex Court and the various High Courts was not vested solely with the executive head namely, the President. Unlike the Constitutions of other countries, our Constitution provides for a novel method of appointing judges to these courts by the head of the executive after consultation with the Chief Justice and other judges. Similarly, judges of the lower judiciary are to be appointed by the State Executive only after consulting the High Court concerned. In short, the Constitution of India has brought out the conditions of service of the judicial members of both the higher and lower judiciary outside the purview and control of the executive. It has substituted the concept of 'service during pleasure' of the executive with service during 'good behaviour' of the judge. Moreover, in every matter relating to the service of judges of the higher judiciary, the President has to take decision only after *consulting* the Chief Justice of India, the head of the judicial family. Similarly, in matters relating to service conditions of subordinate judiciary also the State executive has no full and final control. Over and above these, total separation of the judiciary from the executive has been made a constitutional desideratum.[87] In short, the Constitution brought with it the traditional concept of judicial independence. However, there is neither specific mention anywhere in the Constitution that independence of judiciary has to be maintained nor do we get any clue from the constitutional provisions as to how it is to be maintained. The Constitution of India was enacted during a period when the concept of judicial independence was the traditional one. That may be the reason that the provisions in the Constitution do not provide for judicial independence as understood in the modern sense. In such a context, it would be worthwhile to look into the views of the Apex Court as to the

86. Article 233(1) and Article 234.
87. See, the Constitution of India, Article 50. It reads, 'The State shall take steps to separate the judiciary from the executive in the public services of the State."

concept of independence of judiciary under the Constitution. It would be meaningful to enquire whether the Court was able to figure out a sensible concept of judicial independence fitting to the requirements of the modern era from the constitutional provisions.

5. INDEPENDENCE OF JUDICIARY: JUDICIAL VERSION

The earliest case in which the concept was seriously dealt with by the Supreme Court was *Union cf India* v. *Sankalchand Seth*.[88] The Court held that the concept of judicial independence was an integral part of our Constitution,[89] which meant that it was indestructible. The concept of judicial independence, not specifically mentioned in the Constitution, was thus given an important place. In the *Judges Case*[90] the Court developed the concept further. Characterizing the concept as an institutional one,[91] the Court raised it as a shield for protecting the interests of individual judges from the assaults of the executive. A careful perusal of the judgements in that case reveals that the Judges set judicial independence as a desideratum to be achieved by the Constitution.[92] The individual dimensions of the concept was given shape in *Subhash Sharma* v. *Union of India*.[93] While re-considering the validity of the *Judges Case*, the Supreme Court opined that the concept of judicial independence included the personal freedom of judges. The Court held, "For the availability of an appropriate atmosphere where a Judge would

88. A.I.R. 1977 S.C. 2328.
89. Chief Justice Chandrachud agreed with the holding of Justice Krishna Iyer in *Samsher Singh* that independence of judiciary was the fighting faith of our Constitution, and observed that the provisions dealing with judiciary in our Constitution to protect it. (*id.* at pp. 2338-39). Justice Bhagwati also agreed with it and added that fearless justice was a cardinal faith creed of our founding document, which was part of our tradition, (at p. 2355). Justice Krishna Iyer observed that the creed of judicial independence was our constitutional 'religion', (at p. 2369).
90. 1981 Supp. S.C.C. 87.
91. *Id. per* Bhagwati, J. (at p. 221); Gupta, J. (at p. 345); Fazal, Ali, J. (at pp. 411-12) and Pathak, J. (at p. 705).
92. Bhagwati, J. (at p. 221); Fazal Ali, J. (at p. 408) and Tulzapurkar, J. (at p. 527) observed that the importance of the concept is such that it was to be treated as an ingredient of the basic structure of the Constitution.
93. A.I.R. 1991 S.C. 612.

be free to act according to his conscience it is necessary, therefore, that he should not be overburdened with pressure of work which he finds it physically impossible to undertake."[94] In *Sree Kumar Padma Prasad* v. *State of Assam*[95] it was observed that the prime motive behind incorporation of the provisions dealing with judiciary in the Constitution was judicial independence. The Court therefore held that the concept formed a feature of the basic structure of the Constitution of India. It implied that the Constitution could not be amended in any manner detrimentally affecting independence of the judiciary. This was confirmed later in *S.C. Advocates* v. *Union of India*.[96] The concept got a further dimension when the Court developed it as a norm for interpreting the constitutional provisions dealing with appointment and conditions of service of judges.

The view that judicial independence means independence of the judiciary from the executive alone belongs to the past. The modern concept of independence of judiciary encompasses within it freedom from pressures from any quarters. Unlike the traditional concept, which gives importance to independence of the institution, the modern concept emphasises the individual aspect also. This aspect was stressed in *Ravichandra Iyyar* v. *Justice A.M. Bhattachrjee*[97] by the Supreme Court when it was held that the concept of judicial independence was not limited to independence from the executive. It is a wider concept including within its sweep independence from any other pressures and prejudices.[98] The Court noted that the heart of judicial independence was "judicial individualism."[99] Therefore, the Court observed that the only constitutionally envisaged procedure for removal of judges was the one contained in Article 124 and that no body other than Parliament could initiate the procedure for their removal.

---

94. *Id.* at p. 636.
95. (1992) 2 S.C.C. 428.
96. (1993) 4 S.C.C. 441.
97. (1995) 5 S.C.C. 457.
98. *Id.* at p. 469. The Court observed thus, "It has many dimensions, viz., fearlessness of other power centres, economic or political, and freedom from prejudice acquired and nourished by the class to which the judges belong.
99. *Ibid.*

The Apex Court had opportunity to give life to the idea that the concept of judicial independence encompassed within it the concept of freedom of a judge from his colleagues. In *State of Rajasthan* v. *Prakash Chand,*[100] while determining an unusual set of issues,[101] the Court held that aspersions and intemperate language on judges from his colleagues would cast a slur on judicial independence.[102] This view was reiterated by the Court in *Chetak Constructions Ltd.* v. *Om Prakash.*[103] The Court observed that judges should not be browbeaten or maligned by lawyers or clients as that may affect performance of their duties in a free and fair manner.

A look at the development of the concept of independence of judiciary by the Supreme Court, in the background of the pre-independent scenario, reveals that judicial independence according to the modern and international standards has been tailored into the Indian legal system. While dealing with various aspects of the Constitution affecting judiciary, the Supreme Court relied upon the concept thus judicially developed. By a penetrating analysis of the concept, the Court was able to give it dynamic contents so as to satisfy the requirements of the modern era. Earlier, the Court explained the concept as one

100. (1998) 1 S.C.C. 1.

101. A judge of the High Court of Rajasthan while deciding cases made some damaging statements on judges including the Chief Justice of the High Court and the then Chief Justice of India. He further issued a notice to the Chief Justice of the High Court to show cause why contempt action should not be taken as he allotted some cases partly heard by the judge to another judge. It is in such a context that the matter was taken in appeal before the Supreme Court.

102. *Id.* at p. 25. The Court observed, "Besides when made recklessly... it [intemperate language] amounts to interference with the judicial process. The foundation of our system which is based on the independence and impartiality of those who man it, will be shaken if disparaging and derogatory remarks are permitted to be made against Brother Judges with impunity. It is high time that we realize that the much cherished judicial independence has to be protected not only from outside forces but also from those who are in integral part of the system. Dangers from within have a much large and greater potential for harm than dangers from outside."

103. A.I.R. 1998 S.C. 1855. It arose out of a suit for injunction. It was alleged that there was some connection between the Judge of the High Court who heard the matter and one of the respondents. Hence the matter was referred to the Supreme Court.

bound within the parameters of constitutional provisions. However, later the Court began to interpret the provisions in the Constitution dealing with the judiciary in the light of and in accordance with the dynamic concept of judicial independence. The modern concept of judicial independence reflects a fundamental change in the approach of the courts. This approach of the Court in construing the constitutional provisions in the light of the concept of judicial independence, and of developing the concept in that process requires a closer look to assess the extent of judicial creativity.[104]

104. Such analysis is attempted in the following chapters of this Part.

3

Selection of Judges to the Higher Judiciary and the Process of Consultation

I. INTRODUCTION

Judicial independence and mode of appointment of judges, particularly, that of the higher judiciary are interlinked.[1] Hence, in a study about the independence of judiciary, examination of the mode of selection of judges is of high importance. The mode of selection and appointment of judges to the higher judiciary varies from nation to nation. In some countries people elect them.[2] In

1. See, Carlo Guarnieri & Patrizia Pederzoli, *The Power of Judges, A Comparative Study of Courts and Democracy*, OUP (2002), p. 18. See also Ajith Kumar, "Appointment of judges of the Supreme Court and High Courts" 7 Ac.L.R. p. 137 at p. 138 [1983]. He observes that judicial independence depends to a great extent on the composition of the Court.
2. Constitutions of some States in the U.S. provide for popular election of judges to the respective State Supreme Courts. See Emmettee S. Redford et. al., *Politics and Government in the United States* (1965), p. 530

others, legislature[3] or executive[4] selects them, and in some other countries the executive and legislative organs together select them.[5] In election by the people, obviously the popular will prevails. Hence the candidate would have to get popular support. Such elections may be contested on party basis with declared policies. This procedure therefore is fraught with the danger that it is likely to affect the free and independent thinking of the judges. In such a context while exercising the adjudicatory functions judges may be persuaded more by considerations of popularity or ideology than by principles and concept of justice. The same defect may be there to some extent even if selection is entirely with the legislative or executive body since in a democracy both are constituted by and therefore reflect the political will of the people. Hence, there also political will than judicial quality will count.[6]

It is in this context that a deep look into the significant role played by the Supreme Court of India towards securing independence of judiciary by a creative interpretation of the constitutional provisions dealing with selection of judges to the higher judiciary becomes highly relevant. Elaborate provisions

3. Judges of the erstwhile U.S.S.R. Supreme Court were so selected. See the Constitution of the U.S.S.R. Articles 105-06.
4. For instance in the U.K. judicial appointments to the Court of Appeal, House of Lords and to offices of the Lord Chief Justice and President of the Family Division are made by the Prime Minister after consultation with the Lord Chancellor who himself is an executive nominee. See S.A. de Smith, *Constitutional and Administrative Law* (1973), p. 365. See also J.A.G. Griffith, *The Politics of the Judiciary* (1978), p. 17.
5. Appointments to the U.S. Supreme Court for instance are done so. Constitution of the United States, Article II, Section 2, para 2 "He (the President) shall have the Power . . . and he shall nominate, and by and with the Advice and Consent of the Senate, shall appoint . . . Judges of the Supreme Court. . . ". There, on arisal of a vacancy to the post of judges to the Supreme Court, names would be proposed by the President and that would be scrutinized by the Senate, i.e. the legislature, see Rocco J. Tresolini and Martin Shapiro, *American Constitutional Law* (1970), p. 44.
6. Though nomination is a good method there also political eminence than judicial quality will be counted. See Harold, J. Laski, *A Grammar of Politics* (1979), p. 545. See also Norman Dorsen, "The Selection of US Supreme Court Justices", *International Journal of Constitutional Law*, 2006 4(4), 652-63.

relating to appointment of judges to the Supreme Court[7] and High Courts[8] are contained in the Constitution of India. The Constitution stipulates that before appointing judges to the Supreme Court and High Courts the Chief Justice of India, shall always be consulted.[9] For appointment of judges to High Courts, the Chief Justice of the respective High Court and the Governor are also being consulted. The significant feature of this system is the involvement of the Head of the Union Judiciary in the appointment of judges to the Supreme Court and Head of the State judiciary concerned in the matter of appointment of judges to High Courts. Thus, unlike the provisions in other constitutions, the unique feature of the Indian Constitution is that in it, the judiciary also plays a part in the process, which presumably is to rule out legislative or executive control over the judiciary so as to secure independence of the judiciary.

Appointment of judges of the higher judiciary under the Indian Constitution like under every other constitution is considered as an executive function.[10] As the Head of the Union Executive, the President acts on the aid and advice of the Council of Ministers.[11] Is there not a chance then, that judicial appointments may be influenced by political affinity? Is it not then a serious threat to judicial independence? Undoubtedly

---

7. The Constitution of India, Article 124 (2), "Every Judge of the Supreme Court shall be appointed by the President by warrant under his hand and seal after consultation with such of the judges of the Supreme Court and the High Courts in the State as the President may deem necessary for the purpose and shall hold office until he attains the age of sixty-five years:
   Provided that in the case of appointment of a judge other than the Chief Justice, the Chief Justice of India shall always be consulted:...."
8. *Id*. Article 217 (1), "Every Judge of a High Court shall be appointed by the President by warrant under his hand and seal after consultation with the Chief Justice of India, the Governor of the State, and, in the case of appointment of a Judge other than the Chief Justice, the Chief Justice of the High Court. . ."
9. The only exception to this rule is the appointment of the Chief Justice of India himself. See Constitution of India, proviso to article 124 (2).
10. *S.P. Gupta* v. *Union of India,* 1981 Supp. S.C.C 87. *Per* Bhagwati, J. (at p. 226); Fazl Ali J. (at p. 411); Desai J. (at p. 596) and Pathak J. (at p. 710).
11. Constitution of India Article 74 (1). See also *Samsher Singh* v. *State of Punjab,* A.I.R. 1974 S.C. 2192.

there has to be some control[12] on the executive in the matter of appointment of judges to ensure that the persons with right calibre, integrity and craftsmanship alone are appointed.[13] Obviously, the quality and quantity of the output is proportionate to the quality of the judge.[14] Such qualities could be assessed and extraneous considerations avoided only by a competent authority. The best authority, which can assess such judicial quality and competence, is now the judiciary. Though the Constitution provides clearly for a process of consultations in judicial appointments,[15] it is silent on the questions like the nature of consultation, whether the President is bound by the opinion tendered by the consultants and in case of conflict *inter se* whose opinion is so binding. It is in this backdrop that construction of the provisions dealing with the appointment of judges to the Supreme Court and High Courts by the apex court becomes significant. Has the Supreme Court explained the provisions in the light of the concept of independence of judiciary?

2. APPOINTMENT OF JUDGES TO HIGH COURTS

The procedure for appointing judges to High Courts is contained in Article 217(1). It stipulates that for appointing judges to the High Court, the President shall consult the Chief Justice of India, the Chief Justice of the High Court concerned and the Governor. Two important questions therefore arise in

---

12. The mode of appointment of judges to the U.S. Supreme Courts involves a process of control on the executive by the legislative body and hence prevents the possibility of executive arbitrariness in selection. See *supra,* n. 5, see also Lorry C. Berkson, "Judicial Selections in the U.S". 9 J.B.C.I. 424 (1982).
13. The qualities which a judge should possess were succinctly stated by Justice Bhagwati in the following words ". . . they should be of stern stuff and tough fibre, unbending before power, economic or political, and they must uphold the core principle of the rule of law which says, 'Be you ever so high, the law is above you'" *S.P. Gupta v. Union of India,* 1981 Supp. S.C.C. 87 at p. 224.
14. Law Commission of India, LXXX Report, p. 6. See also, *Subshash Sharma* v. *Union of India,* A.I.R. 1991 S.C. 631 in which the Court observed that "the quality of the judiciary cannot remain unaffected. . . by the process of selection of judges." (at. p. 640).
15. *Supra,* n. 7 & 8.

relation to the appointment of judges to High Courts, namely, the nature and scope of consultation and the question of primacy in case of conflict of opinions of the consultants. These questions came up for consideration before the Supreme Court on more occasions than one.

For answering the above questions, the meaning of the term consultation has to be examined. The common meaning of the term is to deliberate, or to seek information or advice from persons.[16] A meaningful consultation is not a formal process of eliciting of opinion of another with reference to a matter. Being a prelude to an action there must be a free transfer of ideas between the parties with full disclosure of all the relevant materials. Consultation can be of two types. In the first type the consulting person, being the sole beneficiary,[17] has the maximum discretion to accept or reject the opinion. In the second[18] where the consultant or a third person is the beneficiary, such discretion would be limited, especially when the consultant is an expert. Appointment of judges to the higher judiciary belongs to the second category.

The question relating to the nature of consultation (though not in the context of appointment of judges) arose in *Sankalchand Seth v. Union of India*[19] in the context of transfer of judges. It was decided by a bench of five judges.[20] The Court held that consultation in this context should be by obtaining the view of the Chief Justice of India for which full facts and circumstances should be supplied to him, and that deliberation is the quintessence of such consultation;[21] that the President should communicate to the Chief Justice of India the details and that

16. See *the Concise Oxford Dictionary.*
17. Consultation between the physician and the patient is an example of this kind of consultation. Though the patient is not always able to judge whether the opinion of the physician is correct or not, being the sole beneficiary of the opinion of the physician, he is free to decide whether the same is to be accepted. Similarly, the President seeking the advice of the Supreme Court under Article 143 also falls under this category
18. See Constitution of India Articles 124 and 217. Consultation under Article 103 also falls under this category.
19. A.I.R. 1977 S.C. 2329. For a discussion on the case see *infra*, "Transfer of Judges" in Chapter 4.
20. Chandrachud, C.J., Bhagwati, Krishna Iyyer, Fazal Ali and Untwalia JJ.
21. *Id* at p. 2347 (*per* Chandrachud J.).

the Chief Justice of India should provide in return with all the information available with him. They may discuss but may disagree and they may confer but may not concur. Consultation should, therefore, be real, substantial and effective based on full materials.[22] Consultation was a condition precedent for transfer in which ordinarily the views of the Chief Justice of India should prevail.[23] In short, the judges agreed as to the content of the term 'consultation'. But it is doubtful whether by such a holding the Court was able to evolve a meaningful concept of consultation as what has actually come out of the decision was only a formal concept of consultation rather than a substantive one. For, the decision left much scope for unilateral action by the President even after consultation. Hence, it resulted in reducing consultation to a mere formality.[24] The holding was reexamined in *S.P. Gupta* v. *Union of India,*[25] [popularly known as the *Judges Transfer Case*] and later the *Supreme Court Advocates-on-Record* v. *Union of India*[26] in the context of the appointment of judges to the higher judiciary.

The Court in the *Judges Case* unanimously held that though the power of appointment of judges resides in the President, it was not to be exercised arbitrarily,[27] for that was to be exercised only after consultation with the highest echelons of the judiciary

22. *Id* at pp. 2379 -2380, 2384 (*per* Krishna Iyer J., for himself and Fazal Ali J.).
23. *Id.* at p. 2387. (*per* Untwalia J.)
24. It appears that only Justice Untwalia understood the true significance of the expression as he insisted that the opinion of the Chief Justice of India was binding on the President (*Id.* at p. 2387).
25. 1981 Supp. S.C.C. 87 (Hereinafter the *Judges Case*)
26. (1993) 4 S.C.C. 441. (Hereinafter *S.C. Advocates*)
27. *Supra,* n. 25 *per* Bhagwati, J. (at pp. 224), 226; Gupta, J. (at pp. 346), 347; Fazl Ali, J. (at p. 322); D.A. Desai J. (at pp. 709), 715; Tulzaparkar, J. (at p. 524); Venkitaramaiah, J. (at p. 785) and R.S. Pathak J. (at p. 710) The Court thus approved the view that none wields absolute power in this matter. During the discussion in the Constituent Assembly, Ambedkar also held the view that none should hold such absolute power, not even the Chief Justice of India however independent he appears to be. He said ". . . the Chief Justice is a very eminent person. But after all the Chief Justice is a man with all the feelings, all the sentiments and all the prejudices which we as common people have; and I think, to allow the Chief Justice practically a veto upon the appointment of judges is really to transferred the authority to the Chief Justice *which we are not prepared to rest in the President or the Government of the day*", C.A.D., Vol. VIII, p. 258. (Emphasis supplied).

and that consultation was a mandatory one. The Judges said that the power of consultation with the judiciary in the matter of appointment of judges has to be real, and with "full and identical facts"[28] that the consultation has to be full and effective.[29] It was also held that all parties should provide all available details,[30] and that consultation should be "purposeful, result-oriented and of substance.[31]" Undoubtedly, these observations of the court are with a view to restraining the executive excesses in judicial appointments and hence are conducive to judicial independence. However, the holding of the court that the executive was free to take any decision whatever be the advice tendered by the Chief Justice of India[32] destroyed the salutary effects of the above observations.

The second question, namely, whose opinion is to be given weight for consideration by the President in case of a conflict was also examined by the Court in the *Judges Case*. Though Article 217(1) stipulates that before appointing a High Court judge, President has to consult the Chief Justice of India, Chief Justice of High Court and the Governor. The provision does not however, delineate the consultative process as to whether there has to be inter-consultants discussion. Nor does it throw light as what is to be done in case of conflict of opinions of the three consultants. The question therefore was whether the President was free to accept the advice of any of them or whether the opinion of the any of the three consultants deserves precedence. In the *Judges Case*, it was argued on behalf of the petitioners that as the Chief Justice of India was the head of the judiciary, his opinion deserved primacy over the other two consultants. Turning down the plea, the majority held that the opinion of the Chief Justice of India merited no primacy over the other two consultants in the matter of appointment of judges to High Courts.[33] Some of the judges went to the extent of holding that

28. *Supra*, n. 25 *per* Bhagwati, J. (at p. 227) and *per* Tulzaparkar, J. (at p. 557).
29. *Id. per* Bhagwati, J. (at p. 253).
30. *Id. per* Desai, J. (at p. 634).
31. *Ibid.*
32. *Id per* Bhagwati, J. (at p. 226); *per* Desai J. (at p. 598); *per* Pathak, J. (at p. 709). and Venkitaramaiah, J. (at p. 791).
33. *Id. per* Bhagwati, J. (at p. 228); Fazl Ali, J. (at p. 439); Desai, J. (at p. 608); Pathak J. (at p. 713) and Venkitaramiah, J. (at p. 785).

since the Chief Justice of the High Court concerned being the person in touch with the incumbents to the post, his opinion was entitled primacy.[34] Fortunately no judge opined that Governor's opinion had priority over that of the other two.

The decisions in the *Judges Case* produced two undesirable results in the issue of appointment of judges. It left the final decision in the selection of judges in the higher judiciary to the executive, as the phrase 'after consultation with' was held not to amount to have a binding effect on the consulting person.[35] Further, it gave no primacy to the opinion of the Chief Justice of India over that of the other two.

Though the Court held that consultation by the President with the judiciary was not an empty formality it could not make any useful substance of this discussion due to its ambivalent stand. Some of the judges were cementing the view that judicial appointment was an executive act by emphasizing that the President was bound by the advice of the Council of Ministers.[36] The insistence on consultation brought forth no substantial effect since the Court held that the presidential act of appointment of judges was to be done on the basis of the advice of the Council of Ministers as envisaged in Article 74(1). This in effect amounts to depriving consultation its content and its significance in Article 217 (1) for securing independence of judiciary. Though the Court innovatively brought out the importance of judicial independence from among the various constitutional provisions, it seems, it could not effectively implement the same as the Judges found nothing wrong in the executive brushing aside the opinions of the judicial heads without any objective criteria. Resultantly there may be

---

34. *Id. per* Bhagwati, J. (at p. 229); Fazl Ali, J. (at p. 439); Desai, J. (at p. 605) and Venkitaramaiah, J. (at p. 785).
35. "The Story of Judges Case is not a pleasant one to tell. It is here that the majority of the judges performed the so called solemn function of handing over the independence of judiciary to the Executive by acknowledging gracefully the authority of the Council of Ministers (Prime Minister) to appoint High Court judges even against the advice of the Chief Justice of the High Court and the Chief Justice of India. So the judiciary is on trail". See B.R. Sharma, *Judiciary on Trail—Appointment, Transfer and Accountability* (1989), and preface p. x.
36. *Supra,* n. 25 *per* Desai J. (at p. 598); *per* Pathak J. (at p. 707) and *per* Venkitaramaiah J. (at p. 791).

instances when the judiciary will be forced to function with persons unacceptable to it. The holding to that extent clearly forfeited independence of judiciary to the executive fiat.

It is submitted that the Court ought to have examined the question why consultation is provided for in the matter of appointment of Judges. For, judiciary knows its requirements better than the executive and also the required qualities and qualifications[37] of persons competing for judicial posts. Such qualities could be better assessed by the judiciary than the executive. Therefore consultation can be considered as of substance and not an empty formality only when the President is not able to ignore the views of consultants in the absence of valid and weighty reasons.[38] It implies that the executive should have the freedom to reject the views of the judiciary only if the person recommended by the judiciary is ineligible on other grounds like moral turpitude or involvement in criminal cases which may be known better to the executive.

The holding of the Court in relation to the second question also deserves closer examination. Is the view that in the matter of appointment of High Court judges the opinion of the Chief Justice of India has no primacy over the views of the Governor or the Chief Justice of High Court justified? When there is a conflict between the opinion of the Chief Justice of India and that of the Chief Justice of the High Court, it is unwise to leave

37. The qualities and qualifications required of a judge have been succinctly stated by a judge of the U.S. Supreme Court thus: "Judicial independence, of course has its corollary of judicial responsibility. The judge must be of the stuff that goes to make a good judiciary. What is the stuff of which I speak? Legal knowledge? Yes, and of sufficient quality to determine the applicable rule of law in a given case together with the wisdom to apply it with clarity and despatch. Ability to discover facts? Yes, and an ability to recognise truth and separate it from the chaff. A firm but understanding heart? Yes, and the courage to declare a just decision and enforce it. Integrity? Yes. . . A conscience? Yes, . . . it must be a conscience which at the close of each day's work may whisper softly, 'today you were truly worthy to wear the robe and enjoy the appellation of a judge. . .' " Tom, C. Clark, " Judicial Self-regulation—The Potential" 35 Law and Contemporary Problems, pp. 37-39(1970). This view was quoted with approval by the Law Commission of India, LXXX Report at p. 31. See also *supra*, n. 13.

38. *Cf*. Krishna Iyer J. In *Samsher Singh* v. *State of Punjab*, A.I.R. 1974 S.C. 2192.

the choice to the Government. There is a view that the opinion of the Chief Justice of the High Court has to be preferred on the ground that the Chief Justice of the High Court is in a better position to assess the fitness of the incumbent to the judicial post as he practices in his court.[39] But one has to keep in mind the possibility of the Chief Justice of High Court being an aspirant for the post of judge in the Supreme Court is not absolutely independent in forming his opinion as the Chief Justice of India in this regard.[40] The Chief Justice of the High Court may not be as free as the Chief Justice of India to take an objective decision on another ground also. The candidate being personally known to the Chief Justice of the High Court one cannot totally rule out the possibility of personal considerations or prejudices in forming the opinion. On the other hand, the Chief Justice of India can have the advantage of knowing all details before he makes his opinion by calling for necessary information from the Chief Justice of the High Court and the Governor and hence is more competent to take an objective decision on the basis of the known details than the Chief Justice of the High Court. Moreover, before forming his view he can have also the advantage of the views of other judges of the Supreme Court and the High Court so as to form a correct view about the candidate.[41] Above them all, rejecting the recommendations of the Chief Justice of India—the head of the judiciary—and accepting the opinion of the Chief Justice of the High Court is likely in the long-run to demoralize the hierarchical structure of the institution.

There is also a question as to whose opinion is to be preferred in case of a conflict between the Chief Justice of India and the Governor. When there is a conflict of opinions between the Chief Justice of India and Governor[42] of the State it is unwise to leave the choice to the President. The Chief Justice of India is the head of the judicial institution and is independent of

39. *Supra*, n. 34.
40. The absolute independence of the Chief Justice of India is attributable to the absence of a chance for further promotion. See Seervai, *Constitutional Law of India*, Vol. II (1984), p. 2444.
41. *Supra*, n. 25 *per* Pathak, J. at p. 714. See also Seevai, *op. cit.*, at p. 2446.
42. While discussing the incorporation of the provision, Krishna Chandra Sharma and S.L. Saksena observed in the Constituent Assembly that Governor need not be consulted. See, C.A.D., Vol. VIII, pp. 661-62.

the executive. The Governor on the other hand is a nominee of the Central Government and is terminable by it wherefore he is always likely to offer views palatable to the Central Government. In such a situation, it is doubtful whether he would express views unpalatable to the Central Government. The competence of Governor to express views is also to be examined. The post of Governor requires no special qualifications or knowledge. It is purely a political post. The post of the Chief Justice of India is therefore incomparable with that of the Governor of a State. It is not proper to equalize the views of the two authorities that are placed at different pedestals. Needless to say that in case of conflict of views of the Chief Justice of India and the Governor of the State weight has to be given to the opinion of the Chief Justice of India. It is unfortunate that the majority in the *Judges Case* while not giving primacy to the view of the Chief Justice of India, did not take these factors into account.

For upholding the executive power to appoint the judges, some of the judges[43] relied upon the practices prevailing in England and America which needs deep examination. For, the constitutional provisions and conventions prevailing in those countries in judicial appointments are different from those of India. In the U.S., judiciary does not participate in the appointment of judges.[44] While the Indian Constitution specifically provides for the participation of judiciary in the matter of appointment of judges to High Courts and the Supreme Court. As there is basic difference between the selection of judges in the U.S. and India it may not be proper to compare these two and seek assistance from the U.S.

---

43. Some of the Judges referred to the practices prevailing in England and America. Justice Bhagwati (*supra*, n. 25 at p. 230) and Justice Pathak (at p. 712) refer to the practice in England while Justice Desai makes a reference to the practice prevailing in the U.S. (at p. 593) in this regard.
44. See the Constitution of the U.S. Article II, Sec. 2, Para 2. There political affiliations, personal friendship with the President, religious and ethnic affiliations, geographical and sectional factors and above all "caprice of fortune" may play considerable role in judicial appointments since selection is made by the Executive. See also Martin Shapiro and Rocco Tresolini, *American Constitutional Law* (1975), pp. 42-49. But the Senate which is part of the Congress operates as check on the executive arbitrariness in this regard. See Constitution of U.S., Article II, Sec. 2, Para 2. *Supra* n. 5.

Likewise, there is basic difference between the English and the Indian Constitutions. The English Constitution is unwritten and unitary while ours is written and federal. As against the English Constitution, we have accepted separation of powers though not in a traditional sense.[45] Our Constitution has provided for judicial review even against parliamentary excesses whereas in England judicial review is not available against Parliament. In England the present system of appointment of judges to the higher judiciary has been in existence for quite a long time. Hence, appointment of judges by the executive may not be considered as stigmatic[46] as it is in India where judiciary also plays the role of arbiter in disputes in which state is a party and where the federation or its different constituents may be parties.[47] In England, out of convention Lord Chancellor also participates in the selection of judges to the higher judiciary. In short, in both America and England in the process of appointment of judges, no role is assigned to the judiciary while in India it is otherwise.[48] It is considering these differences that the makers of our Constitution made it clear that India would have a mode of selection of judges different

45. *Ram Jawaya Kapoor* v. *State of Punjab,* A.I.R. 1955 S. C.549.
46. See International Bar Association Code of Minimum Standards of Judicial Independence as adopted in the Plenary Session of the 19th Biennial Conference New Delhi in 1982. Article 2 (b), "appointments and promotions by a non-judicial body will not be considered inconsistent with judicial independence in countries where by long historic and democratic tradition, judicial appointments and promotions operate satisfactorily". Article 2.14(b) of the Universal Declaration of the Independence of Justice as adopted in Montreal proclaims that participation of the legislature or the executive in judicial appointments will be consistent with judicial independence if made after consultation with members of the judiciary. For the text of the declaration, see, Martin Shapiro and Jules Deschenes, *op. cit.* at p. 447 *et. seq.* See also Hilaire Barnet, *Constitutional and Administrative Law* (1996), p. 127.
47. "If this litigant can select judges suitable to itself that would be the end of judicial system which has till now served admirably as the citizen's palladium against unconstitutional laws and arbitrary executive action." Palkhaiwalla, "A Judiciary Made to Measure", in *Our Constitution Defaced and Defiled* (1974), p. 100.
48. The Indian Law Commission has observed that where the executive was appointing judges it should be assisted by judicial commission consisting of judges, lawyers, academicians, laymen, etc. See *Law Commission of India, LXXX Report,* p. 8.

from both England and America.[49] Examined in this background, it is doubtful whether the practices prevailing in UK and US would enlighten the interpretation of the provisions dealing with appointment of judges under the Indian Constitution.

Further, the practice of appointing judges exclusively by the executive is not suited to modern times. It is the relic of the executive ridden State of the ancient and medieval ages when the judges were considered as the servants of the executive[50] and independence of judiciary was not counted as a virtue. Moreover, the long practice followed hither to in India is that the opinion tendered by the Chief Justice of India is accepted. That crystallized constitutional convention also justifies the view that the opinion of the Chief Justice of India has to prevail. Thus, though the court innovatively explained the concept of judicial independence, and some of the observations were conducive to it, analyzed from different angles, the decision of the *Judges Case* on this count is not conducive to judicial

---

49. "In Great Britain, the appointments are made by the Crown without any kind of limitation whatsoever, which means by the executive of the day. There is the opposite system in the United States, where, for instance, appointments of the Supreme Court . . . shall be made only with the concurrence of the Senate of the United States. It seems to me, in the circumstances we live today, where the sense of responsibility has not grown to the same extent to which we find it in the United States, it would be dangerous to leave the appointments to be made by President without any kind of reservation or limitations, that is to say that the executive of the day. Similarly, it seems to me that . . . appointments which the executive wishes to make subject to the concurrence of the Legislature . . . involves the possibility of the appointments being influenced by the political pressures and political considerations. The draft articles, therefore, steers a middle course . . . The provision in the articles is that where should be consultation of persons who are *ex-hypothesi* well qualified to give proper advice in matters of the sort . . ." B.R. Ambedkar, C.A.D., Vol. VIII, p. 258. Such a mode of selection of judges was considered as of great import by Union Consultative Committee. See Alice Jacob and Rajeev Dhawan, "Appointment of Supreme Court Judges and Contemporary Politics in India", [1975] C.U.L.R. 15 at p. 18. See also Siva Rao, *Framing of India's Constitutions' Select Documents* Vol. IV, (1968), p. 173.
50. "The interpretation of law is the work of the Crown in its Courts, done through judges who have been and who are counsellors and representatives of the Crown." Anson, *The Law and Custom of the Constitution*, Vol. I (1907), p. 2.

independence. Viewed in this light, the words and phrases in the Constitution dealing with appointment of judges to the higher judiciary need a more progressive construction. In short, the decisions in the *Judges Case* were too technical and literal warranting reconsideration. Small wonder that the *Judges Case* was reconsidered by the Supreme Court after a decade. In *Subhash Sharma* v. *Union of India,*[51] (*Subhash Sharma,* for short) while dealing with certain issues though different from those in the *Judges Case,* the Supreme Court doubted the correctness of the *Judges Case* on the ground that the decision reduced the primacy of position of the Chief Justice of India in the consultative process and denuded 'consultation' its true meaning.[52] The Court criticized the holding of the *Judges Case* that the recommendation of the Chief Justice could be re-opened by the President as it might adversely affect the non-political nature of judiciary.[53] As the issue needed a detailed examination, the Court referred these questions of consultation to a larger bench. These questions thus arose in a series of writ petitions in the Supreme Court and was heard along with *Supreme Court Advocate on Record v. Union of India*[54] *(S.C. Advocates* for short).

In *S.C. Advocates,* the Court observed that the questions relating to the meaning of 'consultation' with the judiciary in

51. A.I.R. 1991 S.C. 631. This was a writ petition under Article 32 of the Constitution to issue directions to the Central Government to fill up the vacancies of judges of the Supreme Court and the High Courts.
52. The Court doubted the correctness of the *Judges Case* as to the non-binding nature of the opinion of the Chief Justice of India in the matter of judicial appointments and also the denial of primacy to the opinion of the Chief Justice of India. Observing that the view of exclusive executive privilege in the matter, after consultation with the judicial organ, is an over simplification of a sensitive and subtle constitutional sentience and that judicial independence was of crucial importance and that for it the Chief Justice of India should be given pride of case in the matter of selection of judges, the court referred the matter to a larger bench. The reference was made taking note of the need that, "Constitutional phraseology would required to be read and expounded in the context of Constitutional philosophy of separation of powers to the extent recognised and adumbrated and the cherished value of judicial independence." *Id.* at p. 641.
53. *Id.* at p. 640.
54. (1993) 4 S.C.C. 441.

matters of judicial appointments were to be considered in the light of 'independence of judiciary', a basic feature of our Constitution which was essential to secure Rule of Law and preservation of the democratic system.[55] The Court therefore held in clear terms that 'consultation' in the matter of appointment of judges[56] envisaged the decision of the President in accordance with the opinion of the consultants and that rejection of such opinions should only be for valid and weighty reasons.[57]

Justice J.S. Verma[58] opined that in the matter of judicial appointments the provisions for consultation found a place in the Constitution to avoid political considerations. He also observed that diversion from the Government of India Act, 1935[59] negates full discretion to the executive in the matter.[60] In such a context, he said that the process of appointment of judges to the higher judiciary was an "integrated consultative process" to select the best ones.[61] Justice Rangavel Pandian stated that judges alone could assess qualities like professional ability and legal knowledge of the incumbents for judicial posts.[62] He also observed that consultation amounted to a limitation on the power of the President to appoint judges.[63] So consultation is mandatory and should not be "easily brushed aside as an empty formality or futile exercise or a mere casual one attached with

---

55. *Id.* at p. 680.
56. Constitution of India, Articles 124 (2) & 217 (1). See *supra*, n. 7.
57. The decision was rendered by a majority of 8:1. The majority consisted of J.S.Verma, Dayal, Ray, Dr. Anand, Barucha, Rangavel Pandian, Kuldip Singh and Puncchi, JJ. Justice Ahmadi however dissented.
58. Justice Verma speaking for himself, Dayal, Ray, Dr. Anand and Barucha, JJ.
59. Section 200 of Government of India Act 1935 provides that appointments to the posts of judges of the Federal Court could be effected by the Crown under her warrant and seal without being advised by the judiciary. But Seervai observes that the judges of the High Court were to initiate proceeding to appoint judges under the Act. See Seervai, *Constitutional Law of India*, Vol. III, (1996), pp. 2956-57. However, that seems to be incorrect, as that was not a statutory mandate but only a constitutional convention under the Government of India Act.
60. *Supra*, n. 54 at pp. 691-92.
61. *Id.* at p. 709.
62. *Id.* at p. 558.
63. *Id.* at p. 564.

no sanctity."[64] Agreeing with the views expressed above, Justice Kuldip Singh held that the opinion of the judiciary was binding on the executive, as it knows the character, integrity and ability of the persons.[65] He further explained that the executive could have no knowledge of the fit person to the judicial post and hence consultation in the matter of appointment of judges amounted to one between a layman and a specialist. Therefore, the view of the specialist, namely, the judiciary should prevail.[66] Justice Puncchi disagreed with the view in the *Judges Case* in so far as it amounted in effect to recognition of arbitrary power in President in appointing judges. He pointed out that to prevent encroachment of the 'executive minded persons' to the judiciary, it was necessary that opinion of the judiciary should carry some weight.[67] In short, the decision in *Judges Case* in this respect was overruled.

The above decision in the *S.C. Advocates* is rendered after taking the perspective of the Constituent Assembly in relation to independence of judiciary into account. While enacting the provisions dealing with judiciary[68] the Constituent Assembly had taken utmost care to ensure independence of judiciary. The objective of the Constituent Assembly in enacting those provisions was primarily to secure judicial independence.[69] The Assembly was not ready to confer full and unconditional power on any of the organs of the Government—even in the

64. *Id.* at p. 564. He observed that the provision was *sine qua non* since the State was the biggest litigant (*Id.* at p. 569). Quoting Decimus Junius Juvenalis, a Roman satirist, he poses the question, *quis custodiet ipsos custodes* ? (But who is to guard the guards) (*Id.* at p. 559).
65. *Id.* at p. 663.
66. To reach his conclusion he drew support from the opinion of Justice Krisha Iyer in *Samsher Singh v. State of Punjab*, A.I.R. 1974. S.C. 2192 (*Id.* at p. 665) and also from the intention of the framers of the Constitution to confer only limited powers to the executive (at p. 667).
67. *Id* at pp. 721, 725 and 726.
68. Articles 124-39 relating to the Union Judiciary consisting of the Supreme Court, Articles 217-28 dealing with High Courts and Articles 230-37 dealing with the lower judiciary.
69. The Constituent Assembly had a unanimous view that India should have an independent judiciary. For instance, see the opinions of H.V. Kamat, K.M. Munshi and Naziruddin Ahmad in C.A.D., Vol VIII, pp. 218-27. See also *supra*, chapter II, n. 44.

President—in the matter of appointment of judges.[70] The *Judges Case* interpreted the provisions relating to appointment of judges keeping in mind the stand of the Constituent Assembly that consultation did not amount to concurrence but narrowly without fully keeping in mind the perspective of the Assembly in relation to judicial independence.[71] The *S.C. Advocates*, on the other hand, attempted to construe the provisions in a holistic manner with a view to securing judicial independence instead of embarking upon a piece meal analysis of various provisions as was done in the *Judges Case*. As a consequence, the Court held that the President was bound by the opinion tendered by the Chief Justice of India. The question of binding nature of the opinion of the Chief Justice of India indicates the weight it carried in the formation of the view of the President. By the term 'President,' the Indian Constitution denotes the President aided and advised by the Council of Ministers.[72] So in all executive matters the President has to act only in accordance with the advice tendered by the Council of Ministers. Appointment of judges being an executive function is not an exception to this rule. However, the provision for consultation with the judiciary raises a question as to the precedence of the advice tendered by the Council of Ministers under Article 74(1) and the opinion tendered by the judiciary under Article 124 (2) and 217(1). It is in such a context that the Court held that the advice tendered by the Council of Ministers should be in accordance with the opinion of the Chief Justice of India and the

70. See *supra*, n. 49. In determining the general objective of the legislature, the intention which appears to be in accordance with "convenience, reason, justice and legal principles" should be presumed to be the true one. See P. St. J. Lananglann (Ed), *Maxwell on Interpretation of Statutes* (1976), p. 199. It is accepted in judicial process that when the literal interpretation defeats the intention of the legislation and these likely to cause unreasonableness "some violence to the words" may be done to achieve a rational construction.

71. The issues of the mode of appointment of judges, the person with final say in the matter, the meaning of consultation with Chief Justice of India and other judges of Supreme Court and whether it means concurrence should be considered with emphasis on the independence of judiciary. See S. Sahai, "Role and Status of the Judiciary in Indian Government", 8, J.B.C.I. 442 at p. 444 (1981).

72. *Supra*, n. 54 at p. 701.

norms indicated there in.[73] In other words, the Court held that the requirements of Article 74(1) of the Constitution were circumscribed by the requirement of Articles 124 (2) and 217 (1). Such a construction was justified by the Court on the principle that when there are two provisions of law operating on the same set of facts one of which is special, that would prevail over the general one.[74] Absence of provisions for consultation with any authority for appointing Comptroller and Auditor General[75] and Chief Election Commission[76] also underlines the importance of consultation and the weight the opinion of the consultants carry in judicial appointments.[77] Thus for the maintenance of independence of judiciary the Court conferred importance to the opinion of the judiciary in the matter of appointment of judges. When with such an objective, precedence is given to the opinion of the judiciary it should be value-packed and should be distinguishable from that of others for the merit it contains.

It is with such a view that the Court held that the opinion of the judiciary was expressed through the Chief Justice of India with whom the President had to hold consultations before appointing judges to High Courts. However, the Chief Justice of India was not supposed to render a personal opinion in the matter. Before conveying his opinion to the President, he has to consult his senior colleagues in the Supreme Court who are

73. *Ibid.*
74. *Id.* at p. 696. Here the principle applied is *Generalia Specialibus Non Derogant* which means in case of a conflict, a special provision will prevail over a general one.
75. See the Constitution of India, Article 148 (1). It Reads, "There shall be a Comptroller and Auditor General of India who shall be appointed by the President by warrant under his hand and seal and shall only be removed from office in like manner and on the like grounds as a Judge of the Supreme Court."
76. See the Constitution of India, Article 324 (2). It runs thus, "The Election Commission shall consist of the Chief Election Commissioner and such other number of Election Commissioners, if any, as the President may from time to time fix and the appointment of the Chief Election Commissioner and other Election Commissioners shall, subject to the provisions of any law made in that behalf by Parliament, be made by the President."
77. This fact was taken note of by Justice Kuldip Singh (*supra, n.* 54 at p. 665).

likely to be conversant with the affairs of the High Court to which appointment was to be made. The Chief Justice of India has also to ascertain the views of one or more senior judges of the High Court concerned whose opinion according to him is significant in the matter. The opinion of the Chief Justice of the High Court deserves the greatest weight in this regard and it should also be formed after consulting two senior judges of the High Court.[78] That is why it was held that the opinion of the Chief Justice of India was to be formed after "participative consultative process"[79] which represented the view of the institution of the judiciary to select the best ones.

Once thus the Court provided a different colour and content to the nature of opinion of the Chief Justice of India that is liable to cause a change in the nature of 'consultation' under Article 217(1). Unlike in the past the President could not brush aside the opinion of the Chief Justice of India in the matter of appointment of High Court judges. Therefore, as a normal rule the final opinion of the Chief Justice of India was binding on the President.[80] But the President could counter his view in exceptional cases and that too only on sound materials.[81]

The dilemma of determining the primacy of opinion of consultants under Article 217(1) also arose in the *S.C. Advocates Case*. Dealing with this issue, the Court held[82] that in the matter of appointment of judges to High Courts, the Chief Justice of India should form his view only after consulting his colleagues who are conversant with the affairs of the High Court. He also has to consult one or more judges of the High Court whose views according to him would be significant in forming his view. The opinion of the Chief Justice of the High Court should be given the greatest weight in this regard. According to the court, the High Court Chief Justice has to form his view after consulting at least two Judges of the High Court.

It is clear from the holding that the Court deviated from the holding in the *Judges Case* and refused to recognize any

78. *Supra*, n. 54 at p. 702.
79. *Id.* at p. 693.
80. *Id.* at p. 700.
81. *Ibid.*
82. *Id.* per Verma, J. at pp. (701-02) and Pandian, J. (at pp. 571-72).

conflict between the views of the Chief Justice of India and the Chief Justice of High Court. The opinion of the Chief Justice of India to which primacy is given in *S.C. Advocates* encompasses within it the opinion of the High Court Chief Justice. By the requirement that before recommending, the Chief Justice of India has to necessarily consult the High Court Chief Justice, the Court was able to give due weightage to the opinion of the latter and avoid any conflict between them. Thus, neither the Chief Justice of India nor the Chief Justice of the High Court has to project his personal views. By insisting on the formation of the view of the Chief Justice of India after consulting judges of the Supreme Court and High Courts, the Court was able to give an institutional flavour to his opinion.[83]

The decision of *S.C. Advocates* has been thoroughly criticised by Seervai as one, which paid no attention to the rules of interpretation.[84] He opined that the decision was in violation of the "well settled principles of interpretations, namely, that the function of the Court is to ascertain the meaning of any provision of the constitution by referring to the language used, and if the language is unambiguous, to give the provision its plain ordinary meaning."[85] He also alleges that the decision was rendered in favour of the constitutional philosophy and values which are inimical to the interpretation of constitutional provisions.[86] He concludes that the decision was not actually warranted because the only question before the Court was whether consultation with the Chief Justice of India under Articles 124 (2) and 217 (1) amounted to concurrence.[87] He also viewed that it could not amount to concurrence as that may lead to a situation in which the term consultation would always be construed as concurrence.

On a peripheral reading, one may find the criticisms of Seervai as valid which, on a deep reflection can be understood to be otherwise. First of all, the decision does not convert the term consultation to concurrence. It just gave superiority to the

83. *Id. per* Verma, J. (at p. 699) and Kuldip Singh, J. (at p. 669).
84. Seervai, *Constitutional Law of India*, Vol, III (1996), pp. 2941-53.
85. *Id.* at p. 2942.
86. *Id.* at p. 2944.
87. *Id.* at p. 2952

opinion of the Chief Justice of India considering his absolute independence. The Court in the case was giving primacy and binding nature to the opinion of the Chief Justice of India not as the individual nor in his personal capacity but as the Head of the judiciary. It was held,[88]

> "At the same time, the phraseology used indicated that giving absolute discretion or the power of veto to the Chief Justice of India as an individual in the matter of appointments was not considered desirable, so that there should remain some power with the executive to be exercised as a check, whenever necessary. The indication is, that . . . the selection should be made as a result of participatory consultative process. . . It was for this reason that the word 'consultation' instead of 'concurrence' was used, but that was done merely to indicate that absolute discretion was not given to anyone, not even to the Chief Justice as an individual, much less to the executive, which earlier had absolute discretion under the Government of India Acts."

The criticism of Seervai that there cannot be constitutional philosophy or value to interpret the constitutional provisions also seems to be incorrect. It is axiomatic that the interpretation of the constitution is different from that of ordinary statutes as constitution stands on a higher pedestal. It is supposed to exist for a longer period. Therefore, interpretation of a Constitution should be to advance its philosophy. Further, when two constructions of the same provision are possible that which does not lead to absurdity should be accepted. For these reasons, avoidance of an interpretation to the term 'consultation' conferring unilateral power in the executive damaging independence of judiciary cannot be considered as unwarranted.

Thus, the Court has given a go-by to the strict literal interpretation of the constitutional provisions only with the object of maintaining independence of judiciary, taking the values and history of the Indian Constitution into account.

88. *Supra*, n. 54 at pp. 692-93.

While interpreting the term 'consultation' assistance of the mischief rule of interpretation can also be sought for.[89] In matters of judicial appointments other Constitutions as well as the predecessors of the Constitution of India like the Government of India Act, 1935 do not provide for consultation with members of judiciary. Deviating from them the Indian Constitution specifically provides for such consultation. It is indicative of the intention of the makers to restrict the powers of the executive and to emphasize consultation with the judiciary to appoint judges. Though the Court has not expressly mentioned the relevance of the rule, its impact is clear from the ruling of the majority,[90]

> "Thus, even under the Government of India Act, 1935, appointments of Judges of the Federal Court and the High Courts were in the absolute discretion of the Crown. . . when the Constitution was being drafted, there was a general agreement that the appointments of Judges in the superior judiciary should not be left to the absolute discretion of the executive, and this was the reason for the provision made in the Constitution imposing the obligation to consult the Chief Justice of India and the Chief Justice of High Court. . . . *This clear departure in the constitutional scheme from the earlier pattern in the Government of India Acts. . . . is a sure indication that. . . the constitutional provision cannot be construed to read therein the absolute discretion or primacy of the Government of India to make appointments of its choice, after completing formally the requirement of consultation, even if the opinion given by the consultants of the judiciary is to be contrary.*"

It appears therefore, that the Court interpreted the

89. The Mischief Rule was first applied in the *Heydon's Case*, 3 Co.Rep.7a. In *Re Mayfair Property Co.* (1898) 2 Ch. 28 Lindley M.R. stated the principle thus, "In order to properly interpret any statute *it is necessary now. . . to consider how the law stood when the statute to be construed was passed, what the mischief was for which the old law did not provide,* and the remedy provided by the statute to cure the mischief." (at p. 35) (Emphasis supplied). See also Maxwell, *op. cit.* at p. 40.
90. *Supra*, n. 54 at p. 691. (Emphasis supplied).

constitutional provisions dealing with judicial appointments without sacking the canons of constitutional interpretation. It is submitted that overruling of the *Judges Case* and the innovative interpretation of the provisions dealing with appointment of judges to High Court do not violative the basic principles of interpretation. It, on the other hand, furthers the objective for which these provisions are incorporated into the Constitution.

Will not conferment of an absolute discretion to the Chief Justice of India to recommend the names of judges lead to arbitrariness? To hold that the CJI had the full power to control judicial appointments would clearly be against the intention of the Constituent Assembly.[91] And it is also true that the Constitution does not confer any veto power on the CJI in relation to judicial appointments. Nor could the Court for the same reason go so as to hold that 'consultation' amounted to 'concurrence'. It is because of these factors that the Court held wisely that the President could disagree with the view of the Chief Justice of India and refuse to appoint as according to the opinion of the Chief Justice of India. But such non-appointment of the recommended person would be only for "good reasons,"[92] the same should be communicated to the Chief Justice of India for reconsidering his view and also to express the reconsidered view.[93] Similarly, if the other judges of the Supreme Court with whom the Chief Justice of India held consultation hold the view that the recommendation of the Chief Justice of India should be withdrawn, in public interest the President can refrain from appointing him.[94] Such a restraint on the power of the Chief Justice of India checks arbitrariness and caters independence of judiciary. The holding of the Supreme Court in this regard therefore is a creative one.

Even after the decision in *S.C. Advocates* certain doubts regarding the nature of the opinion of the Chief Justice of India in the matter of judicial appointments persisted. This came for consideration of the judiciary when the advisory opinion was

---

91. C.A.D., Vol. VIII, p. 258.
92. *Supra*, n. 54 at p. 706.
93. *Ibid.*
94. *Ibid.*

sought by the President in *Special Reference No. 1 of 1998*.[95] Agreeing with the decision in *S.C. Advocates*, the Court held that the Chief Justice of India had to form his opinion in the matter of appointment of Judges to High Courts after consultation with a collegium consisting of two senior-most judges of the Supreme Court. In making a decision, they would take into account the view of the Chief Justice of the High Court concerned and the views of other Judges of the High Court and views of the Judges in the Supreme Court 'who are conversant with the affairs of the High Court concerned' into account.[96] The Court opined that the best information regarding the appointee would come from the Chief Justice and Judges of the High Court and those of the Supreme Court.[97] The holding is highly creative and can be considered as an extension of *S.C. Advocates Case*. In *S.C. Advocates*, the Court emphasized the necessity of excluding the arbitrariness of the executive. In *Special Reference*, the Court tried to rule out all chances of arbitrariness of the Chief Justice of India in the selection of Judges by holding that he has to recommend a person only after taking into account the views of the collegium of Judges, and other judges of Supreme Court conversant with the affairs of the High Court and of the Chief Justice and other judges of the High Court concerned. The Court held that judicial review would be available if the recommendation is not that of the Chief Justice of India and his colleagues.[98] It is also available if in taking the decision, the views of the Chief Justice and senior judges of the High Court and of the judges of the Supreme Court who have knowledge about the High Courts have not been sought or considered by the Chief Justice of India and his colleagues. Similarly, judicial review would also be available when the appointee lacks

---

95. (1998) 7 S.C.C.739. Faced with an unprecedented impasse over the appointment of judges of the Supreme Court and transfer of judges of High Courts, the President sought the opinion of the Supreme Court on 27.7.1998. See, "President seeks SC's opinion on judges' postings," *The Times of India*, Mumbai, Tuesday, July 28, 1998, p. 1.
96. *Id.* at p. 767.
97. *Id.* at p. 768.
98. *Id.*, p. 768.

eligibility.[99] As a result of the decisions in *S.C. Advocates* and *Special Reference,* the Court has ruled out arbitrariness likely to impede judicial independence both on the part of the Executive and/or the Chief Justice of India in this respect. The creative element of the decision in *Special Reference* lies in further developing the expression 'consultation' in Article 217(1) from consultation between the President and Chief Justice of India to consultation between the Chief Justice of India and judges of the Supreme Court and High Court including the Chief Justice of that High Court making such consultation mandatory. Now the emerging position appears to be that consultation between the President on the one hand and the Governor and the Chief Justice of High Court on the other envisaged by Article 217(1) has relevance only in one situation namely, where the President considers whether the person recommended by the Chief Justice of India is suitable and whether the Chief Justice of India should reconsider his recommendation.

Undoubtedly, the thrust of the holdings in the *S.C. Advocates* and *Special Reference* was to check the arbitrariness of the executive, viz., the President. Are the propositions for consultation between the Chief Justice of India and his 'collegium' effective to prevent his arbitrariness? The functioning of the consultative process as envisaged by the *S.C. Advocates* and the *Special Reference* came to lime light in *Shanti Bhushan* v. *Union of India.*[100] It was a petition challenging the

---

99. Earlier, the scope of judicial review was extended to cases of violation of the requirements of Article 217. In *Shree Kumar Padma Prasad* v. *Union of India*, [(1992) 2 S.C.C. 428] the Court struck down an appointment of a judge to the High Court of Assam on the ground that he did not satisfy the required conditions for appointment in Article 217(2) (a). The Court held that the requirements in Article 217 were prescribed for protecting the independence of the judiciary, which according to the Court was a basic structure of the Constitution. In *Special Reference,* (*supra,* n. 95) the Court went to extent of widening the requirements for appointment by making consultation with the colleagues and other judges mandatory and extending the scope of judicial review so as to cover those aspects also. The Court held thus, "Similarly, if in connection with an appointment or a recommended appointment to a High Court, the views of the Chief Justice and senior Judges of the High Court have not been sought or considered by the Chief Justice of India and his two senior most puisne Judges, judicial review is available." (*Id.* at p. 768).

100. (2009) 1 S.C. 657. For a discussion of the case, see *infra*, Chapter 4, 66-72.

extension of the term of an Additional Judge, who was found to be ineligible to be appointed as a permanent judge. After giving the Additional Judge extension for two terms, the Chief Justice of India, accepting the recommendation of the Chief Justice of the High Court concerned, appointed him as a permanent judge without consulting the collegium.[101] The court in *Shanti Bhushan* dismissed the petition on technical reasons.[102] The facts of the case reveal that there is no effective consultative process between the Chief Justice of India and his senior colleagues as a result of which the possibility of arbitrariness of the Chief Justice of India cannot be ruled out. Needless to say, in such a context, the threat to judicial independence comes from within the juidiciary.

3. SELECTION AND APPOINTMENT OF JUDGES TO THE SUPREME COURT

The Constitution of India contains provisions for appointment of judges to the Supreme Court.[103] It is mandatory that for appointing judges to the Supreme Court, the President has to consult the Chief Justice of India. He may in addition, consult other judges of the Supreme Court and High Courts. There are a few issues, which are common to both the appointment of judges to the Supreme Court and High Courts. The nature of consultation with the Chief Justice of India, and the effect of the opinion of Chief Justice of India are common to both.

Referring incidentally to the appointment of judges to the Supreme Court, some of the judges[104] held in the *Judges Case* that consultation with the judicial authorities had been provided for in the Constitution to check executive arbitrariness in this respect. However, the holding of the Court that in appointing Judges to High Courts consultation should be meaningful and of substance and cannot be an empty formality has application

101. *Id.* at p. 677.
102. For a critique of the case, see, K.N. Chandrasekharan Pillai, "A Comment on *Shanti Bhushan* v. *Union of India*", (2009) 2 S.C.C. 46 (J).
103. *Supra*, n. 7.
104. *Supra*, n. 25 *per* Bhagwati, J. (at p. 232) and Desai, J. (at p. 638).

mutatis mutandis to appointment of Judges to the Supreme Court also. Specifically dealing with this issue in the *S.C. Advocates* Case, the Court held that the power of initiation of the name of the person to be appointed as the judge of the Supreme Court is fully vested with the Chief Justice of India.[105] This means that the proposal of the name of the person to be appointed as the judge of the Supreme Court is to come from the Chief Justice of India and the President is to consult the Chief Justice of India in case of the disagreement with the proposal. How then is the requirement of consultation with 'such judges of the Supreme Court' satisfied? The Court held that the Chief Justice of India is to form his opinion in consultation with two senior most colleagues and that before sending his final opinion, the Chief Justice of India has to consult two senior-most judges of the Supreme Court.[106] He has also to ascertain the opinion of the senior-most judge of the Supreme Court who has come from the High Court of the recommendee.[107] In the view of the Court, the requirement of consultation with 'other judges' under Article 124(2) stands satisfied by this procedure.[108] In other words, the Chief Justice of India is not supposed to project his personal view in this respect but an institutional view as the head of the judiciary.[109] Therefore, the Court held that his opinion has to carry the greatest weight. It deserved primacy normally and is binding on the President.[110]

In what circumstance then is the view of the Chief Justice of India not binding? The Court identified the exceptional circumstances in which the opinion of the Chief Justice of India was not binding on the President. When the President feels that the recommendee of the Chief Justice of India was not suitable to the post, he may return the recommendation with reasons for reconsideration. If on such a return, the Chief Justice of India does not agree, but the judges with whom the Chief Justice of

---

105. *Supra,* n. 54 at p. 705.
106. *Id.* at p. 702.
107. *Ibid.*
108. *Ibid.*, In the Constituent Assembly itself, a view was canvassed by Rohini Kumar Chowdhury that for appointing Judges to the Supreme Court, a panel of Judges be consulted. See, C.A.D., Vol. VII, p. 898.
109. *Supra,* n. 54 at p. 702.
110. *Id.* at p. 703.

India consulted earlier, agree with the President that the recommendee was unsuitable, the President need not appoint the recommendee of the Chief Justice of India.[111] But, if the judges unanimously agree that the recommended person should be appointed, the President has no option but to abide by the opinion of the Chief Justice of India.[112] It is not difficult to see that the consequences of the decision are revolutionary.

By the decision in the *S.C. Advocates*, the Court has formulated certain new principles. The Court denied the President the power to initiate the name of the person to be appointed as judge of the Supreme Court. He is also denied the power to appoint a person as the judge without the approval of the Chief Justice of India. The only power conferred on the President is to refrain from appointing a person when there is disagreement between the Chief Justice of India and his consultants. In other words, the Court erected judicial supremacy in the matter of appointment of judges to the Supreme Court. But it did not confer absolute and arbitrary power on the Chief Justice of India also. The Chief Justice of India could invoke his power of recommending the person only after consulting his senior colleagues and by taking their views into account. As a result of such a procedure of appointment, there is a possibility of non-appointment of suitable persons as judges. But the Court observed that in public interest such a predicament was preferable to the one in which wrong and unsuitable persons are appointed.[113]

In the wake of the holding two specific issues involved in the matter of appointment of judges to the Supreme Court become relevant. One is whether under Article 124(2) the President has the discretion to decide whether there has to be any consultation at all with other judges of the Supreme Court and High Courts. The other is whether the President has the discretion to decide the judges to be consulted. These questions arise in the context of the expression "after consultation with *such of the Judges of the Supreme Court and the High Courts* in the States *as the President may deem necessary for the purpose. . .*" in

111. *Id.* at p. 704.
112. *Ibid.*
113. *Ibid.*

Article 124(2). In other words, the question is whether the expression "as the President may deem necessary" qualifies the term 'consultation' or whether it qualifies the expression "such of the Judges."

The answer to the first question depends upon the definition, scope and extent of the discretion of the President to consult other judges under Article 124(2). Is the President duty-bound to consult them? Could he dispense with such consultation in cases he deems fit? These issues have not specifically attracted the attention of the Court since the matter did not come up for adjudication in any case before it.[114] However, there is a view that under Article 124(2) the President has the discretion to decide whether there has to be any consultation with other judges.[115] What could then be the parameters of the discretion of the President in the light of the decision of the Supreme Court in the *S.C. Advocates Case*?

The holding of the Court that the initiation of the name of the person should always come from the Chief Justice of India operates as a limitation on the President to initiate the same. When the President is denied the power to initiate the name of the appointee, there is circumspection of his discretion to consult other judges for such initiation. When a power is not vested with an authority, consultation for exercising that power is also meaningless and irrelevant. It is therefore clear from the holding of the *S.C. Advocates* that the President is bereft of the discretion to consult other judges to initiate the name of the person to be appointed to the Supreme Court.

---

114. However in the *S.C. Advocates*, Justice Puncchi dealt with the issue without much deliberation on the conflict between the opinion tendered by such judges and the opinion of the Chief Justice of India. *Supra*, n. 54 at p. 721.

115. See Seervai, *Constitutional Law of India*, Vol. II (1984), p. 2188. On a literal interpretation of the provision, he opines that as the first Proviso to Article 124(2) stipulates that the Chief Justice of India should always be consulted in the matter of appointment of judges to the Supreme Court other than the Chief Justice of India, there is an implication that the President had the freedom to decide whether consultation with other judges was necessary. But for a contrary opinion, see, Kashmir Singh, "Appointment of The Judges of the Supreme Court" in B.P. Singh Schgal (Ed.), *Law, Judiciary and Justice in India* (1993), p. 112 at 117.

Further, the holding of the Court that the opinion of the Chief Justice of India is binding on the President in normal circumstances significantly reduced his power to appoint judges. It means that the President can appoint only a recommendee of the Chief Justice of India and no one else. The discretion of the President to consult other judges under Article 124(2) is only a supplementary and ancillary one to streamline his power to appoint judges. Since the power of the President to appoint judges is restricted, it is meaningless to presume that the President enjoys absolute discretion to consult for exercising that power. If the other judges consulted by the President agree with the recommendation of the Chief Justice of India, consultation becomes redundant, as even without that the President could appoint the nominee of the Chief Justice of India. Even if they disagree with the suggestion of the Chief Justice of India, the President is bound by the opinion of the Chief Justice of India as it has precedence over that of other consultants of the President. That is, in either occasion, consultation between the President and other judges is without any consequences.

But, as mentioned above, the President is conferred with the power to refrain from appointing a person though recommended by the Chief Justice of India, if on reference by the President and on further consultation by the Chief Justice of India there is disagreement between the Chief Justice of India and his consultants as to the suitability.[116] Perhaps that is an occasion in which the President could effectively consult 'other judges' under Article 124(2). If on consultation, such other judges opined that the recommendee was unsuitable, on its basis the President may form an opinion that the person is unsuitable, and he can return the recommendation to the Chief Justice of India for reconsideration which, as mentioned above may lead to non-appointment of the person recommended by the Chief Justice of India. In other words, the power being limited to decide that the nominee of the Chief Justice of India is not to be appointed, the discretion to consult under Article 124(2) relates to matters of such non-appointments only. One of

116. *Supra*, n. 111.

the remarkable features of the decision in *S.C. Advocates* is that without expressly referring to the discretion of the President to consult, the Court has effectively restricted its scope by restricting his powers to appoint Judges.

The second question is whether this provision empowers the President to pick and choose the consultants he likes. If he is given such a freedom the chance that the President may select judges who may render views acceptable to him and avoid others cannot be ruled out. In such a context, the very concept of consultation in Article 124(2) as expounded by the Supreme Court in various decisions including the *Judges Case* and the *S.C. Advocates Case* may lose its content.[117] To be meaningful and of substance, it should not be optional for the President to pick and choose the persons with whom he would hold consultations. The category of persons with whom consultation is to be held should be predetermined. And it should be known to the consulting person, the consultants and the public. In such circumstances only it could be assured that the process of consultation is effected without personal prejudices of the consulting person. Therefore, to construe the discretion of the President to consult Judges of the Supreme Court and High Courts under Article 124(2) in accordance with the spirit of *S.C. Advocates* it should be given a restrictive interpretation. The discretion to hold consultation should be limited to consultation with senior Judges of the respective courts other than those consulted by the Chief Justice of India. Such a construction is necessary for upholding judicial independence.[118] The number of judges to be consulted may be decided by the President as that does not directly affect judicial independence.

It is clear from the above discussion that the scope of the discretion of the President to consult such other judges under

117. *Supra,* n. 25 & 54. See also the observation of Justice Subba Rao in *Chandra Mohan* v. *State of U.P.*, A.I.R. 1966 S.C. 1987 that in the matter of appointment of District Judges the constitutional mandate to consult in Article 233 would be vitiated by the Governor in two ways: either by not consulting persons who are necessarily to be consulted or by consulting persons who need not be consulted as per the Constitution.

118. There is a view that the President should consult the senior judges of both the Supreme Court and High Courts. See Kashmir Singh, *supra,* n. 115 at p. 118.

Article 124 (2) is effectively limited by the Supreme Court. The discretion of the President to consult other judges being executive in nature it would come under Article 74(1). If absolute discretion is given to the President in this respect a situation would ensue in which Article 74(1) controls the provisions of Article 124(2) which the Supreme Court wanted to avoid[119] for upholding independence of the judiciary.

The ruling of the *S.C. Advocates Case* is an improvement on yet another aspect also. Appointment of judges to the Supreme Court was being effected from the category of Judges of the High Courts having five years of experience[120] without giving due weight to *inter-se* seniority of judges of the same High Court and seniority on an all India basis.[121] The Court in the *S.C. Advocates Case* held that appointment of judges to the Supreme Court should be recommended by the Chief justice of India only after considering the seniority of the judges of the same High Court and seniority on an all India basis.[122] This rule can be digressed from only in exceptional cases where there are some 'strong cogent reasons to justify a departure'.[123] Such a ruling is sufficient to check arbitrariness of the Chief Justice of India. The decision in *S.C. Advocates* thus on the one hand puts restrictions on the power of the Chief Justice of India to recommend persons to the posts of Judges in the Supreme Court and on the other limits the discretion of the President to appoint the Judges as well as to make consultations with *other Judges* for the purpose. Obviously, this holding is capable of instilling confidence in the minds of judges and upholding independence of judiciary.

The nature of the opinion of the Chief Justice of India with reference to appointment of Judges to the Supreme Court also was considered by the Court in the *Special Reference*.[124] There were two major issues raised in this respect. (1) Whether the

---

119. *Supra*, n. 74.
120. The Constitution of India, Article 124(3)(a).
121. As a matter of rule seniority on an all India basis had not been considered as a criterion for being appointed as a judge of the Supreme Court.
122. *Supra*, n. 54 at pp. 702-03.
123. *Id.* at p. 702.
124. *Supra*, n. 95.

Chief Justice is bound to consult only two senior judges of the Supreme Court before making his recommendation, and (2) Whether the Chief Justice was entitled to act solely in his individual capacity when he is required to reconsider his recommendation. The Court affirmed that the opinion of the Chief Justice of India, which commanded primacy, was to be formed only in consultation with a collegium of Judges.[125] Reaffirming faith in the competence of the collegium of Judges to select the best person to the highest judicial forum, the Court held that the collegium should consist of the Chief Justice of India and four senior most Judges of the Supreme Court.[126] It was held that the Chief Justice of India was not to tender opinion in his individual capacity. To assure that the recommendation of the Chief Justice of India represented the views of the members of the collegium, the Court held that their views should be in writing.[127] The Court expected that the collegium would make its recommendations in consensus.[128] To check any arbitrariness on the part of the Chief Justice in this respect, the Court further held that if he was in the minority, he should not press for the appointment. Moreover, if the recommendation was returned by the President for reconsideration, decision is not to be taken by the Chief Justice individually. In such a case, it is for the collegium to withdraw or reiterate the recommendation.[129] The Court held that the opinion of the Chief Justice of India without consulting his colleagues was not binding on the President.[130] This decision exhibits very high innovation of the judiciary on many counts in construing the consultative procedure for appointment of

125. *Id.* at p. 763.
126. *Id.* at p. 764.
127. *Ibid.*
128. *Id.* at p. 765.
129. *Id.* at p. 766. The Court visualized a situation in which some of the members of the collegium have retired between the initial recommendation and its return for reconsideration by the President, The Court held that in such a context, the collegium should be reconstituted by filling up the vacancies with the senior-most Judge to deal with the matter. The Court was particular that the number of Judges who reconsider non-appointment should be as large as those who recommended the appointment.
130. *Id.* at p. 762.

Judges to the Supreme Court. It is creative in the sense that the Court has transformed the content of consultation in Article 124(2) from one between the President and the Chief Justice of India into one between the Chief justice of India and his colleagues in every aspect of recommendation and reconsideration in the processes of appointment of Judges to the Supreme Court. The peculiarity of the consultative process as envisaged by the decision is that by it the Court was able to rule out the possibility of arbitrariness of the Chief Justice of India in two ways. He was denied the power to recommend a person if the majority of the Judges in the collegium was against such appointment. Similarly, if the President returned the recommendation for reconsideration of the Chief Justice, he can recommend the appointment again only if the original recommendation is unanimously reiterated by the collegium. Thus in every sense, the Court tried to see that the view of the Chief Justice of India represented the view of the judiciary. Incorporation of the condition that the views of the collegium should be in writing helps an objective evaluation whether the recommendation of the Chief Justice was made in accordance with their view. Such an extended construction of the expression 'after consultation with the Chief Justice of India' excludes even a distant possibility of arbitrariness either of the executive or that of the Chief Justice of India and is therefore conducive to judicial independence. While the drive behind the decision in the *S.C. Advocates* was subjugation of executive prejudice, the thrust of the *Special Reference* lies in curbing the arbitrariness of the Chief Justice of India. From the point of view of judicial independence, *Special Reference* undoubtedly is a step forward from *S.C.Advocates.*

4. SELECTION AND APPOINTMENT OF THE CHIEF JUSTICE OF INDIA

The importance of the office of the Chief Justice of India need not be over emphasised. The office of the Chief justice of India has been specifically mentioned in the Constitution.[131]

131. Article 124(1).

Being the head of the Apex Court,[132] though *primus inter pares,*[133] he is *pater familias* of the judiciary and is highly influential in framing the judicial policies.[134] Apart from judicial functions and powers, he holds administrative powers like the power to constitute the benches of the Supreme Court.[135] He has functions of advising the President in certain important matters.[136] He also wields legislative powers like the power to frame rules to regulate the conditions of service of servants of the Supreme Court.[137]

Article 124(2) stipulates that judges to the Supreme Court should be appointed by the President after consultation with such of the Judges of the Supreme Court and High Courts he deems fit. The first proviso makes compulsory the requirement of consultation with the Chief Justice of India only in the matter of appointment of Judges other than the Chief Justice of India. In such appointments consultation by the President with other Judges of the Supreme Court is discretionary. The Constitution does not specifically envisage the pre-requisite of consultation with any body in the matter of appointment of the Chief Justice of India. Since the Constitution does not contain any guideline as to a mandatory procedure, appointments of the Chief Justice of India were being effected by the conventional procedure of selecting and appointing the senior-most Judge of the Supreme

---

132. *Ibid.*
133. *Supra,* n. 54 *per* Puncchi, J. at p. 714. See also Baxi, *The Indian Supreme Court and Politics* (1980), p. 41.
134. "On him rests the tone and tradition of the highest Court of the land, the law laid down by which, is the law of the country. . . as the Head of the judiciary, he would lay down the principles and practices to be followed in the administrations of justice all over the country". See, The Law Commission of India, XIV Report at pp. 38-39. See also Baxi, *op. cit.* where he opines at pp. 41-42 : "In a sense, the focal points of these relations is the Chief Justice of India, who though *primus inter pares* has a considerable role in maintaining a cohesive functioning of the Court in normal times. In abnormal times, the responsibilities are ever heavier: the Chief Justice of India has to be anxiously vigilant in defense of the Court and the values of the Constitution."
135. See, the Supreme Court Rules, 1966, Order VII.
136. Articles 124(2), 217(1) and 217(3).
137. Article 146(2).

Court though there were some incidents of breaking of the convention.[138]

In 1958, in its attempt to improve the judiciary, the Law Commission of India in its XIV report suggested certain changes in the mode of selection of the Chief Justice of India. It opined that the office of the Chief Justice of India was of high importance. He has a key role to play in upholding independence of the Judiciary. For effecting changes favourable to the judiciary it is highly necessary that the person holding the post of Chief Justice of India should remain there for a reasonably long time.[139] It therefore suggested that the Chief Justice of India should be selected on the basis of merit and competence rather than on the basis of seniority.[140] But if the required qualifications and qualities are found in the senior most Judge of the Supreme Court, undoubtedly he has to be appointed.[141]

The above criterion for the selection of the Chief Justice of India was proposed by the Law Commission for upholding judicial independence. Though the Commission referred to the

---

138. Four times the convention was broken. The first was in 1952 when Justice Patanjali Shatri was tried to be superseded. The Government could not implement it as all the bench Judges of the Supreme Court expressed their willingness to tender resignation. For a discussion, see Kuldip Nayar, "The Thirteenth Chief Justice" in Kuldip Nayar, *Supersession of Judges* (1973), p. 9 at 12. For the second time the seniority was over looked when Justice Imam was super seeded as the Chief Justice of India by Justice Gajendragadkar in 1968. But that was due to the persistent illness of Justice Imam disabling him to continue as a Judge. See Amiya K. Chaudhuri, "Appointment of a Chief Justice : a Study of a Controversy in a New Perspective" in Verinder Grover (Ed.), *Courts and Political Process in India* (1989), p. 152 at 174. The convention was again broken in 1973 when Justice A.N. Ray was appointed the Chief Justice of India superseding Justices Hegde, Grover and Shelat who were senior to him. As a result all the three Judges resigned. For a detailed discussion of every aspect of the incident, see Kuldip Nayar, *The Supersession of Judges* (1973). The fourth incident of such a break was in 1976 when Justice M.H. Beg was appointed the Chief Justice of India superseding Justice H.R. Khanna who was the senior-most judge.
139. *Law Commission of India, XIV Report*, p. 39.
140. "Considering the importance of the office, appointment by seniority may not always be advisable". *Ibid.*
141. *Ibid.*

qualities required of the Chief Justice of India,[142] it did not make clear as to who should determine the merit and competence of the persons to fill the highest office of the judiciary. As per the constitutional provision, the only person necessarily involved in the process of selection and appointment of the Chief Justice of India is the President. If the choice of the Chief Justice of India is unilaterally left with the President, the purpose of the Law Commission to effect a shift over to the merit criterion from the seniority rule would stand defeated as the matter may fall solely within the purview of the executive. Even in the matter of the appointment of Judges of the Supreme Court or High Courts, selection is effected by the President only after consultation with certain constitutional authorities. The case of appointment of Judges to the lower judiciary also is not different. In such a context, it cannot be inferred that a unilateral power is conferred on the President in the matter of appointment of Chief Justice of India. Conferment of such a power on the President has not been envisaged by the makers of the Constitution.[143]

However, the proposal of the Commission was not carried out by constitutional or statutory amendments. Later developments proved that the recommendation to appoint Chief Justice of India on merit gave rise to serious consequences. In 1973, when three senior-most Judges of the Supreme Court were superseded and a junior Judge Justice A.N. Ray was appointed the Chief Justice of India, to meet the criticisms against that appointment, justification was sought from the Report of the XIV Law Commission, which prepared the criteria of merit and competence over seniority.[144]

Further, initial appointments to the higher judiciary are effected on the basis of merit, integrity and competence of the incumbents. Such merit is determined only after consultation

---

142. *Ibid.* It observed, "To perform the duties of the Chief Justice of India, there requires a judge of ability and experience, but also a competent administrator capable of handling complex matters that may arise from time to time, a shrewd judge of men and personalities and above all, a person of sturdy independence, and covering personality who would on the occasion arising be a watch-down of the independence of the Judiciary".
143. *Supra*, n. 49.
144. See, Mohan Kumaramangalam, *Judicial Appointments* (1973), pp. 12-13.

with authorities that could extend impartial opinions to the President. The most important among them is the Chief Justice of India.[145] As a result of judicial decisions, in certain cases his opinion now carries considerable weight[146] and in others it is binding on the President.[147] If the Chief Justice of India could be chosen by the President in a unilateral manner, it is likely that one who would agree with the views of the Executive in matters of appointment of judges may be appointed the Chief Justice of India. Consultation in Article 124(2) becomes then a mere meaningless exercise, since the executive can appoint one who would always agree with its views as the consultant. Such a procedure is also hidden with the danger that the merit of a judge to be the Chief Justice of India is likely to be determined by the Executive on the basis of the nature of the decisions rendered by him in the judicial side. Persons who render important judgements in deciding cases against the executive may not be considered for the highest judicial post by the executive. That exactly is what happened in 1973[148] and in 1976.[149] Such a process of selection of the Chief Justice of India poses therefore a serious threat to judicial independence, as it is likely that judges may try to be in the good books of the

---

145. In matters of judicial appointments, the President is advised by the Chief Justice of India, the Chief Justice of High Courts, and the Governor of the State. But, among them the only absolutely independent person is the Chief Justice of India.
146. See, for instance, *Ravichandra Iyyar* v. *Justice A.M. Bhattacharjea*, (1994) 5 S.C.C. 457 in which it was held that allegations of misconduct of judges of the High Courts should be looked into by the Chief Justice of India and *Veeraswamy* v. *Union of India*, (1991) 3 S.C.C. 655 in which it was held that no criminal action could be registered without consulting the Chief Justice of India.
147. *S.C. Advocates*, *supra*, n. 54.
148. See Palkhiwala, *op. cit.* at p. 93 where he observes, "But on 25 April 1973, the three senior most judges of thte Supreme Court—J.M. Shelat, K.S. Hegde and A.N. Grover who had decided the monumnetal case against the Government (Kesavananda Bharathi)—were superseded..."
149. Justice H.R. Khanna has reproduced in his autobiography the following conversation which he had with his wife on the evening of the day in which he wrote the judgement in *A.D.M. Jabalpur* v. *S. Sivakant Sukla*, (A.I.R. 1976 S.C. 1276) which he decided against the government: "... I have prepared a judgement which is going to cost me the Chief Justiceship of India." H.R. Khanna, *Neither Roses Nor Thorns*, p. 80.

government by exercising their administrative and judicial powers in a manner palatable to the executive, with a view to reserving a berth to the post of the Chief Justice of India. Since judges to the higher judiciary—High Courts and the Supreme Court—are appointed after a thorough scanning process after consultation, among other things, as to their integrity, character knowledge of law and ability to decide cases, one cannot say that merit would stand totally excluded even if the seniority rule is followed in appointing the Chief Justice of India.

It is in this context that one has to examine the holding in the *S.C. Advocates Case*.[150] The Court recognized that there was a convention of appointing the senior-most Judge of the Supreme Court as the Chief Justice of India and that the outgoing Chief Justice of India could make the proposal well in advance.[151] Only if there is any doubt as to the fitness of the senior-most judge of the Court, the convention could be breached. So the Court held that there was no reason to depart from the convention and to evolve any new norm for the appointment of the Chief Justice of India. The Court therefore concluded that there was no need for any other consultative process or norm in the matter of appointment of Chief Justice of India.[152] The creative element of the decision lies in making

150. (1993) 4 S.C.C. 441.
151. *Id.* at p. 706.
152. *Ibid.*, The Court held, "Apart from the two well-known departures, appointments to the office of Chief Justice of India have, by convention, been of the senior most Judge of the Supreme Court considered fit to hold the office, and the proposal is initiated in advance by the outgoing Chief Justice of India. The provision in Article 124(2) enabling consultation with any other Judge is to provide such consultation, if there be any doubt about the fitness of the senior-most Judge to hold the office, which alone may permit and justify a departure from the longstanding convention. For this reason, no other substantive consultative process is involved. There is no reason to depart from the existing convention and, therefore, any further norm for the working of Article 124(2) in the appointment of Chief Justice of India is unnecessary."
Justice Pandian, also observed that the expression 'Judge' in Article 124(2) included Chief Justice of India also and hence the consultative process in appointing Judges in which the opinion of the Chief Justice of India has primacy was applicable in the appointment of the Chief Justice of India also.

independence of the judiciary the norm for placing controls on exercise of executive powers in recognizing the convention of appointing the senior-most judge of the Supreme Court as the Chief Justice of India and in making the opinion of the outgoing Chief Justice of India binding on the President in the normal circumstances. By its holding that when the President entertains any doubt as to the fitness of the recommendee, he has to consult other judges under Article 124(2) before he takes a decision,[153] the Court placed fetters on the arbitrary exercise of power by the Executive in the matter of appointment of the Chief Justice of India. The decision thus places the judiciary in a prominent position in the matters of appointment of the Chief Justice of India also. Undoubtedly, such decision is taken by the Court for the purpose of upholding independence of judiciary.

A reading of *S.C. Advocates* makes it clear that the Court interpreted the provisions for appointment of judges to the higher judiciary in a deductive style drawing the conclusions in relation to them by applying the major premise of independence of judiciary.[154] The major premise applied by the Court is that all constitutional provisions dealing with judiciary should be interpreted in a manner conducive to judicial independence.[155] The minor premise is that provisions relating to appointment of judges are provisions dealing with the judiciary. The conclusion

153. *Id.* at p. 706.

154. For a discussion on the deductive style of reasoning see I.M. Copie, *Introduction to Logic* (1996), p. 205 *et. seq.*

155. *Supra*, n. 54 *per* Verma, J., "These questions have to be considered in the context of independence of judiciary, as a part of the basic structure of the Constitution; . . ." (at p. 680).
Per Pandian J., " . . . the constitutional assurances, relating to the basic service conditions are . . . not the be all and end all . . . More than the above, one other and inseparable vital condition is absolutely necessary for timely securing the independence of the judiciary . . . that concerns the methodology followed in the matter of sponsoring, selecting an appointing a proper and fit candidate to the . . . higher judiciary". (*Id.* at p. 521).
Justice Kuldip Singh also spoke in the same tone. He said that independence of judiciary was a basic feature of the Indian Constitution and for its maintenance judicial appointments should not be left to the executive will. The Chief Justice of India and Chief justices of High Courts are better equipped to identify suitable persons to the posts of judges of higher judiciary. (*Id.* at pp. 649, 663).

is that provisions relating to appointment of judges should be interpreted with a tilt in favour of judicial independence. The purpose of incorporating the provisions dealing with the judiciary in the Constitution was to uphold and maintain independence of judiciary. That was not lost sight of by the makers of the Constitution also.[156] The interpretation of the provisions dealing with appointment to higher judiciary rendered in the *S.C. Advocaes Case* is in line with this constitutional objective. Therefore, undoubtedly it can be said that the Supreme Court has rightly construed the words in the provisions relating to judicial appointment in the context of judicial independence, instead of interpreting them in a formal manner divorced from its conceptual context[157] which folly it committed in the *Judges Case.*

Thus a journey from the *Judges Case* through *S.C. Advocates* to the *Special Reference 1998* reveals that the Court has been highly creative in interpreting the concept 'consultation' in the matter of appointing Judges to the higher judiciary. The problem involved in the term 'consultation' was identified in the *Judges Case* in which the concept was considered by the Court as a device for checking arbitrariness of the President. It was given a serious consideration in *Subhash Sharma. S.C. Advocates* rendered the term a true content. In *S.C. Advocates,* and *Special Reference* the Court developed consultation as a tool for checking despotism of the judicial authorities also. That is clear from the holding that the President is not bound to appoint if the recommendee is not a fit person. Further, in *Special Reference,* the Court fully developed consultation from as one between the President and the Chief Justice of India to one between the Chief Justice of India and the collegium of judges. Such a holding helps avoid arbitrariness of both the executive and the judiciary in the matter of appointment of Judges. In short, the Supreme Court by innovative workmanship in the *S.C. Advocates* and *Special Reference* was able to edify the concept of judicial independence to its modern dynamic functional style as against the traditional cabined one.

156. *Supra,* n. 69.
157. "... the words are images of matter; and except they have a life of reason and invention, to fall in love with them is all one as to fall in love with a picture". Francis Bacon, *Advancement of Learning Book 1,* p. 25.

Conditions of Service of Judges of the Higher Judiciary

I. INTRODUCTION

Security of tenure constitutes another important aspect of independence of the judiciary, since it involves the problem of independence of judges during the long span of their tenure. Security of tenure is of high significance as its presence is necessary for exercising truly judicial mind by judges.[1] Without such security one may find it difficult to keep up one's character, individuality, honesty, and courage as a Judge.[2] Among the conditions of service, those relating to appointment for short periods, transfer and removal of judges deserve special attention. These matters are so intertwined with independence

---

1. Judicial officers have to perform the duties of office "without fear or favour affection or ill-will". See the Constitution of India, the oath of affirmation, Schedule III.
2. For the concept of independence of judiciary, see, *Supra*, Chapter 2.

of judiciary, that exercise of power by the executive in relation to any one of them is likely to affect the security of tenure of Judges thereby causing adverse impact on the independence of the Judges.[3] In modern times the concept of security of tenure is wide enough to include due promotion also.[4]

The concept of security of tenure of judges, which forms such an important aspect of the concept of independence of judiciary is, but, of recent origin. It has two aspects. Smooth life when one adorns the judicial office and protection against indecorous exit out of the office. The former is the negative and the latter, the positive aspect of the concept of security of tenure. However, the view that independence of judiciary and security of tenure of judges are indelibly linked did not gain recognition in the early days when judiciary was established as a separate organ of the State.[5] In Grate Britain, the concept emerged only in the eighteenth century.[6] Till then, judicial service was at the pleasure of the Crown which meant that judges were to serve only during the pleasure of the Crown. They were known as the King's Judges.[7] It just meant that continuance in and conditions

3. "Among the traditional safeguards of judicial independence, the most notable is that of tenure. It means that a judge has a guaranteed right to reach the mandatory age of retirement or until the expiry of his term of office and may not be removed except for incapacity or proved misbehaviour. It also means that the term of office, emoluments and other conditions of service or judges (such as e.g. age of retirement) shall not be altered to their detriment. When this elementary safeguard is destroyed and the judges are put on the sufferings of the executive or military governments, the independence of the judiciary is the first victim." L.M. Singvi, *Freedom on Trial* (1991), p. 166.
4. By due promotion is meant promotion as Chief Justice of High Court from among puisne Judges or elevation to the Supreme Court and also the appointment of the Chief Justice of India. Though each such instance is a fresh appointment, by convention, the senior most judges are so appointed. This practice leads to a legitimate expectation for such elevation. The Court in the *Judges Case*, while dealing with the question of regularizing Additional Judges of High Court, held that such conventions paved the way for legitimate expectations for judges in the matter of promotion those higher posts.
5. See *supra*, "Independence of the Judiciary: The Concept" in Chapter 2.
6. The Act of Settlement, 1702. 12 and 13 Will. 3 c 2. For the text see, *Harlsbury's Laws of England*, Vol. 51.
7. See, Anson, *Law and Custom of the Constitution*, Vol. I, p. 2.

of service of a judge was unilaterally determined by the Crown. Change came with the Act of Settlement of 1701. It specified that judges could continue in service during "good behaviour" instead of that the pleasure of the Crown.[8] It further stipulates that salaries and other privileges of Judge of the Supreme Court and High Courts should not be varied to their disadvantage after retirement. Security of judicial tenure was thus assured for the first time by the Act of Settlement.[9]

Across the Atlantic, in the United States, the Constitution itself protects these two aspects of security of judicial tenure.[10] Many modern states have incorporated the concept of security of judicial tenure in their Constitutions. The Constitution of India also guarantees security of tenure of Judges of the Supreme Court and High Courts[11] in the sense that the conditions of service cannot be varied to their disadvantage after their appointment.[12] Further by providing for a detailed procedure for removal of Judges, the Constitution extends protection against chances of arbitrary removal.[13]

The Supreme Court had occasion to pay its attention on the aspects of service conditions of judges of the higher judiciary, mainly on the appointment of judges for temporary periods, transfer of Judges of High Courts and the procedure for removal of Judges of the higher judiciary. How far the Court has been

---

8. Section 3 of the Act stipulates that thereafter judges should hold office *qualdive se bene gerbit* instead of *durate bene placito masto.*
9. "But equally important in the history of constitutional freedom is the independence of the judiciary from the executive; secured in Britain after a traumatic struggle by the Act of Settlement." Lord Hailsham, "The Independence of the Judicial Process", 7 J.B.C.I. 21 at p. 23 (1978).
10. The Constitution of the United States, Article 3, Section 1, Paragraph 1. "...the Judges both of the Supreme and inferior Courts shall hold their offices during good behaviour, and shall receive for their services a compensation, which shall not be diminished during their continuance in office."
11. The Constitution of India, Articles 125 and 221.
12. *Id.*, Article 125(2) Proviso. It reads, "Provided that neither the privileges nor the allowances of a Judge nor his rights in respect of leave of absence of pensions hall be varied to his disadvantage after his appointment." Article 221(2) Proviso. "Provided that neither the allowances of a Judge nor his rights in respect of leave of absence or pension shall be varied to his disadvantage after his appointment."
13. *Id.*, Articles 124(4) and (5) and Article 218.

successful in examining those aspects of the Constitution in the light of the concept of judicial independence? Could the Court give a strong footing for independence of judiciary by the construction of those concepts? An examination of questions would be fruitful in the wake of the recent decisions in these areas.

2. APPOINTMENT OF JUDGES TO HIGH COURTS FOR TEMPORARY OR SHORT PERIODS

The Constitution of India provides that a judge of the Supreme Court may continue in office till he attains 65 years of age[14] and a judge of High Court till he attains the age of 62[15] unless he resigns or is removed from office. In other words, once appointed, the judge of the Supreme Court or High Court should be able to hold office till retirement or removal. Undoubtedly, these provisions are designed to instill confidence and courage in the mind of judges to discharge their functions independently.

The implication of the above discussion is that appointment of judges for undetermined period is anathematic to security of tenure. Similarly, appointment of Judges for short terms with likelihood of extension or non-extension is also against the principle of the security of tenure[16] and therefore against independence of judiciary.[17] It is significant to note that at the time of enactment, there was no provision in the

14. Articles 124(2) The relevant portion of Article 124(2) reads, " Every Judge of the Supreme Court...shall hold office until he attains the age of sixty five years:..."
15. Article 217(1) Article 217(1): "Every Judge of a High Court...shall hold office,...until he attains the age of sixty two years:"
    But Additional Judges of High Courts are to continue in the office only for a period of two years from the date of appointment. See Article 224(1).
16. For such a view, see, Chandrapal, "Independence of Judiciary—Some Aspects of the Indian Experience", J.I.L.I. 282, 285290 (1982).
17. Joseph Story in his famous *Commentaries on the Constitution Law of the United States*, Vol. II has opined that appointment of Judges for short intervals would adversely affect independence of judiciary as Judges will have to depend heavily upon the appointing authorities. (Ss. 1613-1614) as cited in, *Id.* at p. 285.

Constitution dealing with appointment of temporary judges with a limited term of office. Incorporation of such provision in the Constitution of India was the subject matter of long deliberation in the Constituent Assembly. Finally, it was ruled out on the ground that it was against independence of judiciary.[18] Non-incorporation of such a provision was thus a deliberate one. It is also significant that while many sections in the Government of India Act 1935 were adopted as such in our Constitution,[19] the provision for temporary Judges[20] was not included. However, the Constitution in its original form had provided that if due to non-availability of persons, there was a lack of quorum of Judges in the Supreme Court, the Chief Justice of India, with the previous consent of the President and after consultation with the Chief Justice of the High Court concerned could request a Judge of the High Court to be an *ad hoc* Judge of the Supreme Court for a specified period.[21] Similarly, the Chief Justice of the High Court with the previous consent of the President may request a retired Judge of any High Court to sit and act as the judge of the High Court for a specific period.[22] Undoubtedly, these provisions were meant not for regular operations but only to tide over certain exigencies.

Finding that the provision dealing with appointment of retired judges to High Court was not sufficient to meet the requirements of disposal of cases, in 1956 Parliament amended Article 224[23] by the Constitution (Seventh Amendment) Act.

---

18. The view was expressed in the Constituent Assembly that appointment of temporary Judges would not be conducive to the independence of the judiciary. See, for instance, speeches of K.M. Munshi, and M.V. Kamath in the Assembly were against the appointment of temporary Judges. C.A.D., Vol. VII, pp. 670, 693.
19. For instance, section 200 of the Government of India Act provided for transfer of Judges of High Courts. The Constitution of India has adopted it as Article 222.
20. The Government of India Act, 1935, Section 101(2) Proviso.
21. The Constitution of India, Article 127. This Article was scarcely invoked.
22. *Id.*, Article 224. Presently, Article 224A.
23. It reads, "If by reasons any temporary increase in the business of a High Court or by reason of arrears of work therein, it appears to the President that the number of the judges of that court should be for the time being increased, the President may appoint duly qualified persons to be additional judges of the Court such period not exceeding two years as he may specify."

Thus a new provision was introduced into the Constitution which provided for appointment of Additional Judges who were to serve only for a maximum period of two years. The intent of the amendment is clear. If by the reason of temporary increase in the business of the High Court, or by reason of the arrears of cases a High Court is in requirement of an increased number of judges for a short period,[24] the President may appoint additional judges for a period not exceeding two years. The provision is meant to tide over certain emergencies. Such Judges are to be appointed only when two conditions are satisfied. The first and foremost one is the sitting permanent Judges are not able to dispose of arrears of or increase in the pending cases. At the same time such pending should not warrant appointment of more permanent Judges. It is therefore clear that there was a correlation between appointment of Additional Judges with the workload pending in a High Court. The number and term of Additional Judges appointed should be such that by the end of the term of Judges so appointed, the pendency should be eliminated. Therefore, it need not be specifically mentioned that the provision should not be invoked when the increase in workload is not of a temporary nature. In other words, Article 224(1) is only a provision that enables the President to appoint judges for meeting short-term requirements. In such a context, if the provision enables the President to appoint Judges with tenure of short-term duration with a chance of further such appointment is contrary to the original intention of the makers of the Constitution.[25] For, like a permanent Judge, an Additional Judge is also to be appointed either from the Bar or lower judiciary. So, when the exigency for

---

24. There may be instances of temporary increase in the pending works of the High Courts for one reason or the other. For instance, litigation in connection with an election or claims filed in connection with winding up of a company may cause such arrears. But there is no yardstick to determine what is meant by the term arrears. But the Law Commission in its XIV Report has laid down a criterion to determine the same at p. 91.
25. *Supra*, n. 18. This practice of appointing temporary Judges for short periods is peculiar to India.

his appointment ends, he has to return to his erstwhile office which creates embarrassment for both the Bench and Bar.[26]

What is the extent of damage appointment of temporary judges could cause on independence of judiciary? Such an issue came for the Consideration of the court while dealing with a matter relating to election in *Krishna Gopal* v. *Prakashchandra*.[27] Though no distinction based on constitutional provisions was drawn between permanent and temporary judges, Justice H.R. Khanna speaking for a five-member constitution bench held that 'in the interests of justice' election petitions should be heard by permanent judges.[28] This holding indicates that temporary judges do not enjoy the same amount of independence as permanent judges and therefore they may not be able to decide cases in which Government has an interest as impartially as permanent judges.

Tenure of judges acquires added importance when the issue is one of fundamental rights. Fundamental rights are guaranteed against the government and judiciary is considered

26. The restriction to practise as an Advocate in the High Court in which one was a permanent Judge is incorporated in Article 220 to protect independence of the judiciary as such persons should not have an opportunity to influence the Bench as a retired judge. This provision was incorporated to the Constitution after a long deliberation. However, this restriction is not applicable to an Additional Judge. Thus, if a person served as an Additional judge in a High Court for two years, after the term, he can resume practice in the same court. But if he is appointed as a puisne judge, in that court, he cannot resume practice even if he held the office only for a day or two. This is a matter of violation of equality also.
27. AIR 1974 SC 209. That was a petition filed against the decision of the High Court of Madhya Pradesh. The petition was filed before the High Court under Article 80A of the Representation of the Peoples Act. The court posted the matter before a judge appointed under Article 224A of the Constitution. The decision is challenged on the ground that an election petition could not be decided by a judge appointed under Article 224A.
28. *Id*. at p. 216. "It seems indeed desirable that election petition should ordinarily, if possible, be entrusted for trial to a permanent judge of the High Court even though we find that additional or acting judges or those requested under Article 224A of the Constitution to sit and act as judges of the High Court, if assigned for the purpose by the Chief Justice, are legally competent to hear those matters... The election petition filed by the appellant shall now be heard by a permanent judge who may be assigned for the purpose by the learned Chief Justice."

as the guardian of those rights. So absence of the security of tenure leads to violation of fundamental rights. In other words, there is a reasonable nexus between protection of fundamental rights and security of tenure of the judges, which is an essential ingredient of independence of judiciary. In *Re Special Courts Bill, 1978,*[29] the court found a reasonable nexus between the tenure of judges who decided cases and the fundamental right under Article 21 of the Constitution. It was held that clause 7 of the Bill, which provided that Additional Judges could decide cases that arose in connection with the national emergency was struck down as violative of Article 21 as they did not enjoy security of tenure.[30]

These two holdings indicate that tenure of judges has an undeniable correlation with their independence. What role the Supreme Court can and has played in its determining the scope and parameters of the provision empowering the President to appoint temporary judges? This enquiry is highly relevant and important in evaluating the creative contribution of the Supreme Court in securing independence of the judiciary. In the *Judges Case*[31] much of the arguments was over this provision and its unscrupulous invocation by the government.

Dealing with this aspect the Court held[32] that appointment of Additional Judges to High Courts should also be in accordance with the procedure envisaged by Article 217(1).[33] It means that irrespective of whether one is appointed a permanent or temporary judge, the President should consult the Chief Justice of India, the Chief Justice of the High Court concerned and the Governor to satisfy the requirement of Article 217(1) and also in compliance of the procedure in it. The Court held that though the period for which an Additional Judge is to be appointed is to be determined by the executive,

---

29. AIR 1979 SC 478. That was a petition challenging the provisions of the Special Courts Bill, 1978 as violative of the Constitution. Clause 7 of the Bill, provides that judges of the special courts can be either from sitting or retired judges of the High Courts.
30. *Id.* at pp. 517-18.
31. 1981 Supp. S.C.C. 87.
32. *Id. per* Bhagwati, J. (at p. 241); Gupta, J. (at pp. 346-47); Desai, J. at p. 610; Pathak, J. (at p. 716) and Venkitaramaiah, J. (at p. 874).
33. For the text of the Article, see, *supra*, Chapter 3, n. 8.

subject to a maximum period of two years fixed by the Constitution, such appointments could not be for short periods like three months or six months.[34] The Court further held that on expiry of the initial term of appointment of a person as an Additional Judge, for his reappointment, the procedure contained in Article 217(1) had again to be followed.[35] It means that there also consultative procedure with the Chief Justice of India, Chief Justice of the High Court concerned and the Governor of the State has to be repeated.

However, the Judges added that there was a right for such Additional Judges to be reconsidered for further appointment as Additional or permanent Judges.[36] In other words, in such appointments effected subsequent to their term as Additional Judges, they have a clear precedence over others who were not judges. The Court held so on the ground that there was a long standing practice that most of the persons who were initially appointed as Additional Judges were later confirmed as permanent judges on arisal of vacancies though there were a few exceptions. Such a long-standing practice therefore led Additional Judges to believe that they would be confirmed later. Such a long-standing practice, according to the Court has crystallized into a convention.[37] Similarly, such Additional Judges were given extended terms in the wake of continuance of the contingencies mentioned in Article 224(1). That is, there was a legitimate expectation on the part of the Additional Judges to continue as Judges. Some of the Judges observed that there were certain other factors which weighed in favour of Additional Judges for their continuance or re-appointment like their experience as Judges[38] and also the fact that it was not feasible

34. *Supra*, n. 31 *per* Bhagwati, J. (at p. 247); Gupta, J. (at p. 347); Tulzapurkar, J. (at pp. 527-28); Desai, J. (at p. 629) and Pathak, J. (contra) (at p. 716).
35. *Id. per* Bhagwati, J. (at p. 243); Fazl Ali J. (at pp. 471, 474); Desai, J. (at p. 613); Pathak, J. (at pp. 719-20) and Venkitaramaiah, J. (at p. 874).
36. *Id. per* Bhagwati, J. (at p. 241); Gupta, J. (at p. 348); Tulzapurkar, J. at p. 511; Desai, J. (at p. 626), Pathak, J. (at p. 718) and Venkiratamaiah, J. (at p. 815). However, Fazal, Ali J. held that the temporary Judges had neither such legitimate expectation nor any right to be appointed. (at p. 472).
37. *Id. per* Bhagwati, J. (at p. 244); Gupta J. (at pp. 241, 348); Tulzapurkar, J. at p. 511; Desai, J. (at p. 472); Pathak, J. (at p. 718) and Venkitaramiah, J. (at p. 815).
38. *Id. per* Fazal, Ali J., at p. 472.

to send them back to the Bar or the lower judiciary.[39] As a corollary of the legitimate expectation to be re-appointed, Additional Judges have got a right to approach the judiciary for not appointing them if such non-appointment or non-extension as the case may be was on extraneous grounds.[40] Such exclusion can be made only if they do not satisfy the qualifications and requirements mentioned in Article 217(1) and not for anything else. The Court further held that appointment of Judges to High Courts was not on probation[41] and therefore their performance as Additional Judges should not be a criterion for determining extension of their term as Additional Judges or appointment as permanent judges.[42]

While rendering the judgement on this issue, the Court was faced with certain hard realities. The government, ever since the incorporation of Article 224(1) in the Constitution, was invoking it in an indiscriminate fashion. Since its enactment, this was one of the most misused provisions of our Constitution. From 1956, the year of its enactment, till the date of the decision of the *Judges Case,* about one fifth of the total vacancies of judges of

39. *Id. Per* Bhagwati, J., (at p. 244) and Venkitaramiah, J., (at p. 804).
40. *Id. Per* Bhagwati, J. (at p. 245); Gupta, J. at p. 348; Tulzapurkar, J. at (p. 518); Desai, J. (at p. 640) and Venkiraramiah, J. (at pp. 817-18). Justice Bhagwati, Justice Desai and Justice Venkitaramiah held so on the ground that Additional Judges have a a right to be considered and a right not to be excluded on extraneous grounds. So they could approach the Court against such a decision. Justice Tulzapurkar reached such a conclusion on a different ground. He held that there was a valid classification between Additional Judges and a fresh appointee. Non-extension of the term of the former or not appointing him as a permanent judge is not 'appointment' in the real sense of the term. While that of the latter is actually appointment. So the former has a right to move the Court against a decision to exclude him. Justice Gupta held that non-extension of the term of an Additional Judge or not appointing him as a permanent judge of the High Court amounts to his termination. (*Id* at p. 348). However, he did not deal with the right of such Additional Judges to move the Court against such a decision for not appointing him.
41. *Id. Per* Bhagwati, J. (at p. 321); Gupta, J. (at p. 347); Tulzapurkar, J. (at p. 518); Desai, J. (at p. 618) and Pathak, J. (at p. 719).
42. *Id. Per* Bhagwati, J. (at p. 321); Gupta J. (at p. 347); Tulzapurkar, J. (at p. 519) and Pathak, J. (at p. 720).

various High Courts was filled up as Additional Judges.[43] That is, the majority of Judges appointed to various High Courts from the date of the incorporation of the provision was initially appointed as temporary, irrespective of whether there were the contingencies mentioned in Article 224(1).[44] Such Judges normally were later confirmed as permanent Judges. In other words, Article 224(1) was the "gateway" for the post of puisne judges to High Courts.[45] Additional Judges were dropped or given extension or were regularized exclusively at the whim and caprice of the executive.[46] In other words, appointment of Judges for temporary periods runs counter to independent decision making process of such judges and therefore it is against the very independence of the judiciary. The decision of the Court has to be analysed in the light of these facts.

A perusal of the decision proves that while rendering it, the Court has taken the rights of the Additional Judges into consideration as an integral part of the concept of independence of the judiciary. The decision of the Court that in every case of appointment of Judges to High Courts whether permanent or Additional—the procedure in Article 217(1) should be complied with is a welcome one. That demands that the President has to hold consultation with the Chief Justice of India, the Chief Justice of High Court concerned and the Governor even in the appointment of Additional Judges. The Constitution does not

---

43. *Id. Per* Venkitaramiah, J. (at p. 815). See also Satinder Mohan Mehta, "Appointment of Additional Judges in the High Courts: A Threat to the Independence of the Judiciary" in B.P. Singh Seghal, (Ed.) *Law, Judiciary and Justice in India,* (1993) p. 59 (at p. 64).
44. *Id. per* Desai, J., (at p. 619).
45. *Id. per* Bhagwati, J. (at p. 240) and Venkitaramiah, J. (at p. 801).
46. Instances of non-extension and dropping of Additional Judges even when vacancies of permanent Judges exist are not lacking in the history of Indian judiciary. Such dropping and non-extensions were effected at the whim and caprice of the Prime Minister. In the *Judges Case* itself, there were petitions against the dropping of Justices S.N. Kumar and O.M. Vohra Judges of the High Court of Delhi. Seervai has reminded us of the non-extension of Justice Aggarwal of Delhi High Court and Justice Lalith of the High Court of Bombay at the pleasure of the then Prime Mininister. Such incidents have led him to think that there was a similarity between that incident and the dismissal of Sir Edward Coke 360 years back as he was not acceptable to the then King. See, Seervai, *Constitutional Law of India,* Vol. II (1984) pp. 2295-97.

specifically stipulate that to appoint Additional Judges Article 217(1) should be complied with. Such a restriction on the power of the President is solely the creation of the Court. It is a fine incident of judicial innovation to protect independence of the judiciary in the matter of appointment of Judges for short duration. As a result of the decision, now the President cannot appoint Additional Judges without following consultative process under Article 217(1) and to that extent executive arbitrariness is curbed. For, it rules out the chances of selection of persons acceptable to the Executive and excluding of persons who are disliked by it. It also avoids the possibility of executive arbitrariness in selection and appointment of a person as Additional Judge when he is not qualified to be appointed as a puisne Judge of the High Court. Such a holding implies that all the formalities conceived by Article 217(1) are made applicable to appointments of Additional Judges also under Article 224(1). As a result of the holding, appointment of Additional Judges also has been subjected to the restrictions and safeguards to which the process of appointment of puisne Judges is dependent.

(a) Term of Appointment of Additional Judges

An important issue to which the court paid its attention was the discretion of the executive to determine the duration of the term for which Additional Judges may be appointed. The Constitution provides only the maximum period of two years for which Additional Judges could be appointed and it does not stipulate a specific minimum period for such appointments. The implication is that the President may appoint Additional Judges for any period not exceeding two years, as he ay consider necessary.[47] Does the provision empower the President to appoint Additional Judges even for short periods like three months or six months?[48] The court held that such short-term appointments or extensions were bad since it affected judicial

47. That was an argument raised by the Union of India. See, *supra* note 31 (at p. 224).
48. Terms of Justices O.N. Vohra, S.N. Kumar and S.B. Wad, Additional Judges of the High Court of Delhi were to expire on 6.3.1981. They were given extension for three more months. See *supra*, n. 34 (at p. 197).

independence and that it was not the intendment of Article 224(1).[49] Justice Bhagawati[50] observed that such appointments would be bad unless they have correlation with the cases pending in the court while Justice Gupta, Tulzapurkar and Desai held that such short appointments *per se* were unconstitutional.[51]

The holding of the court on this count is an instance of excellent creativity. By the decision, the freedom of the President to unilaterally determine the minimum duration of appointment of Additional Judges stands restrained. Actually, the President is not a competent authority to determine the period of service of such temporary requirement as that depends upon the number, disposability and nature of cases pending and the capacity of the judge. It is likely that the conclusions of the executive in this regard are based on extraneous considerations. Hence the decision of the court to deny the President the power to decide the term of appointment is certainly conducive to independence of the judiciary. Thus, while the Constitution limits the maximum period for which Additional Judges are to be appointed, the decision of the *Judges Case* has provided the criteria for the fixation of the minimum duration for such appointments.

(b) Extension or Regularization of Additional Judges

Yet another important issue in relation to appointment of Additional Judges is extension of the term of Additional Judges or their regularization as permanent Judges. In this respect the Court exhibited a very creative outlook in interpreting the constitutional provisions. While deciding this issue, the Court countenanced with a conflict between the power of the President to extend the term of Additional Judges or their regularization as the case may be on the one hand and the expectation of such temporary judges and the independence of the judiciary on the other. The Court rightly analyzed the issue on the basis of the long-standing practice of extending or

49. *Supra,* n. 34.
50. *Supra,* n. 31 (at p. 247).
51. *Supra,* n 34.

regularizing the term of Additional Judges, which has crystallized as a convention. It was held so on the basis of the convention that Additional Judges expected that on expiration of their initial term they would be regularized or given a further term as an Additional Judge. To give effect to the holding, the Court based its decision for conferring such a right to reappointment on three concepts namely, (a) consultative process under Article 217(1), (b) Legitimate expectation of Additional Judges and (c) their right to judicial review against wrongful dropping.

By the end of the term of an Additional Judge, there may be a question of appointing an Additional or permanent Judge. In such circumstances, the Additional Judge whose term has expired is also eligible to be re-appointed. If the executive has got a freedom to decide whether the sitting Additional Judge is to be appointed or not, its decision is likely to be influenced by the performance of the Judge during the initial term as the Additional Judge.[52] Referring to Article 217(1) that "*Every Judge of a High Court* shall be appointed by the President after consultation with...,"[53] the Court held that in instances where the sitting Additional Judges are also eligible to be re-appointed, the procedure envisaged by Article 217(1) should be complied with. The holding of the Court is to be understood and appreciated in the background of its observation that consultation under Article 217(1) was to check executive arbitrariness.[54] As a result of such a holding, the President is restrained from unilaterally deciding whether the Judge whose term has expired is to be dropped or not. In other words, the discretion of the President to decide whether the term of an additional Judge is to be extended or be regularized is effectively circumscribed by the creative reading of the consultative procedure under Article 217(1) to those instances also. The desirable impact of such a creative interpretation on judicial independence cannot be over emphasized.

52. That is, the executive may decide whether he is to be given extension on the basis of whether he, as an Additional Judge used to cater the interests of the government. If he did not, the government may unilaterally decide not to given an extension to him.
53. *Supra*, Chapter 3 n. 8.
54. *Supra*, Chapter 3 n. 27.

The second limb of the decision, namely the doctrine of legitimate expectation was incorporated to protect the interests of Additional Judges who took up the office in the background of the convention according to which in the majority of instances they were either re-appointed or regularized. In the absence of such a doctrine, the executive could altogether exclude the names of the persons who have served a term as Additional Judges for further appointment and thereby circumvent the requirement of consultation. For, consultation under Article 217(1) is only with reference to who is to be appointed from an already prepared list of persons. It does not include the concept of consultation as to who are to be included in the list to be considered for appointment. In other words, the executive can validly comply with the requirement of consultation even after excluding the names of such Additional Judges. It is likely that such a decision of the executive not to consider the name of a Judge for appointment may be influenced by the decisions rendered by him during his tenure as Additional Judge. Therefore, it is clear that to make 'consultation' under Article 217(1) as a check on the executive arbitrariness meaningful in instances of extension of Additional Judges, the concept of legitimate expectation becomes highly necessary. It therefore is unavoidable from the point of view of independence of judiciary.

The third limb of the holding of the Court is the right of Additional Judges to approach the judiciary against the breach of their legitimate expectation to be considered for further appointment. Conferment of the right to legitimate expectation without a right to enforce it would not be effective. Therefore, the Court held that if an Additional Judge was not considered for further extension or for regularization, or if he was dropped on extraneous considerations he has got a right to approach the Court to get his legitimate expectation established.[55] In short, the right of Additional Judges to legitimate expectation and his right to approach the judiciary go hand in hand and one without the other is barren.

Incorporation of the requirement of consultation is to restrain the power of the President to appoint judges. But the

55. *Supra*, n. 40.

concepts of legitimate expectation and the right of Additional Judges to judicial review operate as delimitation on the very process of consultation by the President. Unlike 'consultation' with the judiciary, the concept of legitimate expectation and the right of Additional Judges for judicial review are not found in the provisions of the Constitution. They are contributions of the judiciary to give life to consultation and thereby to effectively check the executive arbitrariness in the matter of appointment of judges where there are qualified persons who served a term as judges. These concepts therefore have an undeniable share in maintaining the security of tenure of temporary judges and also independence of the judiciary.

Can we say that the holding in the *Judges Case* in the matter of temporary Judges upholds judicial independence to its fullest extent? Were there other leeways left to the Court to uphold it? It is true that the doctrine of legitimate expectation and the right to approach the Court were the outcome of the creative interpretation of the constitutional provisions by the Court. It is also true that they were introduced by the Court to protect independence of judges. Certainly, they were thus meant for the purpose of securing judicial independence. However, it requires a thorough examination whether the concept helped to reach the desideratum of judicial independence.

An analysis of the doctrine of legitimate expectation reveals that it has two limbs. The first limb insists that Additional Judges have a right to be included in the panel of persons to be considered for appointment. The second limb on the other hand proscribes the President to deny reappointment to Additional Judges on extraneous grounds. These two limbs of the doctrine are linked by the Court with the requirement that even in a case where Additional Judges are available for reappointment, there should be consultation under Article 217(1) on the ground that consultation alone may be insufficient to protect judicial independence. Consultation for appointment of judges was considered by the Court as a check against executive arbitrariness. Such consultation alone may be insufficient to protect judicial independence, since the names of Additional Judges may not be included in the panel by the executive. Hence, the doctrine of legitimate expectation was incorporated by the Court to limit the freedom of the Executive of arbitrarily excluding Additional Judges from being re-appointed. Such a construction undoubtedly was for securing judicial independence.

It is true that the first limb of the doctrine restricts the discretion of the President to select the persons regarding whom consultation should be held. But such a restriction on the President did not mean that an Additional Judge would necessarily be re-appointed. Even in the wake of such a limitation on the discretion of the President, his power to decide whether an Additional Judge is to be re-appointed or not remains unaffected. It means that the first limb of the doctrine is insufficient to deter the President from deciding not to extend the term of Additional Judges on irrelevant grounds. Such grounds may include the independence the judge exhibited to render decisions unpalatable to the executive. It is in such a context that the second limb of the doctrine, which stipulates that the President cannot deny appointment to Additional Judges on extraneous considerations becomes relevant. It thus regulates the powers of the President to determine the eligibility of judges to be re-appointed. But the pit fall of the decision lies in the inability of the Court in not identifying and demarcating those extraneous grounds. It was just mentioned by the Court that performance of an Additional Judge could not be determinant of his eligibility to be re-appointed. The doctrine, in other words, leaves very wide discretion to the President to decide whether an Additional Judge is to be re-appointed or not. Further, the doctrine does not deal with the question whether the behaviour and integrity of an Additional Judge during his judicial tenure is a valid criterion in determining his re-appointment. Non-extension of the term of an Additional Judge on such grounds would detrimentally affect their independence. In other words, even in the wake of the protections judicially incorporated, chances for arbitrary non-extension of judges cannot be totally ruled out. The stigma of such a situation is that such a power of the executive not to effect re-appointment of judges amounts to their removal for which there are provisions in the Constitution.[56] Those

56. Article 124(4) and (5) and Article 218.

provisions are incorporated into the Constitution to assure security against any encroachment on judicial tenure from any quarters.[57] For a meaningful tenure for Additional Judges, such a protection should be extended to them also. Non-extension on the basis of behaviour or integrity of Additional Judges during the initial judicial tenure by the executive means that they are denied the protection offered to other judges appointed under Article 217(1) for removal by the procedure under Article 124(4) and (5). Such a predicament has undesirable effects on judicial independence. Additional Judges, just like puisne Judges, are entitled to enjoy the "tenure on good behaviour" and the procedure for removal under Article 124 should be applicable for them also.[58] Hence the question whether an Additional Judge has misbehaved or not should be determined according to the procedure under Article 124 read with Article 218. The executive shall on no account have the discussion to decide whether the term of Additional Judges be extended. As the doctrine of legitimate expectation does not rule out an arbitrary exclusion of Additional Judges, it cannot be said to be an effective sword for maintaining security of judicial tenure. The doctrine in other words cannot be said to protect judicial independence to the fullest extent.

Further, the doctrine does not prohibit reconsideration of the matters under Article 217(1), which had been considered at the time of initial appointment as Additional Judges. Such reconsideration is not specifically prohibited by the Constitution. However, reconsideration of such matters is not constitutionally contemplated either. For, one is appointed judge under Article 217(1) only if he satisfies the requirements thereunder. Such a test envisaged by the provision is to be undergone by the judge only once, as otherwise, it would reduce the initial appointment as one on probation.[59] The doctrine suffers from the defect that it facilitates such reconsideration. Moreover, the doctrine does not explain how there can be a comparison of the qualifications of Additional

57. For a discussion of the issue, see *infra*, "Removal of Judges" generally and nn. 263-65 particularly.
58. Seervai, *op. cit.* at p. 2308.
59. *Ibid.*

Judge who is available for reappointment with that of the outsiders in the panel for consideration for appointment who do not have judicial experience. Nor does the doctrine prohibit the President from appointing outsiders overriding Additional Judges on the ground of better qualifications. In other words, the doctrine does not object selection of outsiders even when Additional Judges with experience are available for appointment. But as one of the Judges in the *Judges Case* opined, dropping of Additional Judges may lead to their return to the bar or lower judiciary as the case may be, causing adverse results to independence of the judiciary.[60] In the interests of judicial independence, when there is a question of selection of Judges from among the Additional judges and outsiders, the former should be given a preference over the latter in view of their earlier experience at the Bench. Hence dropping of an Additional Judge without cogent reasons and appointing somebody else would be "unreasonable and perverse act."[61] In short, the doctrine leaves independence of the higher judiciary at bay. It implies that legitimate expectation of Additional Judges to be re-appointed for appointment is necessary for the maintenance of the concept of judicial independence.

The right to approach the judiciary is conferred on Additional Judges against the possible violation of their legitimate expectation. The right is therefore available only if the name of an Additional Judge is not included in the panel of persons to be considered for appointment or if an Additional Judge is denied reappointment on extraneous grounds. Hence non-extension of the term of an Additional Judge *ipso facto* would not enable him to invoke the right. In short, the scope of the right to enforce the expectation commensurate with the scope of the doctrine of legitimate expectation, which is limited. Apart from that judicial review as a remedy suffers from the systemic lacunae like huge expenditure and time lag,[62] which may render it an inadequate mechanism for protecting so important a feature as independence of the judiciary. Insurmountable expenditure and undue delay in getting justice

60. *Supra*, n. 39.
61. *Supra*, n. 31 at p. 816.
62. Seervai, *op. cit.* at pp. 2273-74.

may deter at least some of the judges from approaching the Court for establishing their legitimate expectation in cases where it is denied. So even if judicial review is effective in protecting the legitimate expectation of judges who may approach the Court, it is doubtful whether it is an efficient armoury to protect judicial independence as such. Hence, leaning heavily on judicial review alone for protecting an important postulate of our legal system like judicial independence may not be a wise step. The above discussion makes it clear that the doctrine of legitimate expectation coupled with the right to judicial review does not uphold judicial independence in the desired manner. It is therefore necessary to develop the doctrine further. It should be developed to confer a full-fledged right on Additional Judges to be re-appointed.[63] Such a development of the doctrine enables the eligible Additional Judges to be automatically re-appointed and does away with the requirements of further consultation under Article 217(1). Besides, it nurtures a circumstance in which Additional Judges would be able to discharge their judicial functions fearlessly. It creates a climate in which they can act without any fear of non-extension of tenure. Such a step would undoubtedly be one in the line of securing judicial independence.[64]

---

63. *Cf*. Upendra Baxi, *Courage, Craft and Contention* (1985), pp. 42-48.
64. Even in the case of re-appointment or regularization of an Additional Judge, the process of consultation contemplated by Article 217(1) could have been followed without affecting independence of the judiciary. In the reappointment of Additional Judge, the scope of consultation could be limited to the question whether the emergencies mentioned in Article 224(1) prevail in the High Court warranting appointment of an Additional Judge to the High Court. Similarly, in the regularization the only question over which consultation is to be carried out is whether there exists a vacancy of permanent Judge in the High Court. In both the cases the scope of consultation could be limited to the question of requirement of a Judge in the High Court and it does not extend to the question whether the sitting judge satisfies the requirement of an Additional Judge as contemplated by the constitutional provisions. The advantage of such a scheme is that the requirement of consultation under Article 217(1) stands satisfied without adversely affecting the interests of the judges and therefore that of the independence of the judiciary.

Hence, incorporation of the doctrine of legitimate expectation is certainly a signal to the opening up of a new era. It establishes that the judiciary was not willing to leave the issue of reappointment of Additional Judges to the province of executive discretion. The doctrine equated the issue of reappointment of Additional Judges with judicial independence. However, an appraisal of the doctrine as evolved by the Court reveals that it requires further elaboration for ensuring independence of the judiciary. The deficiencies in the doctrine discussed above are alive even after the decision in the *S.C. Advocates*,[65] as the issue was not dealt with in that case.

Questions relating to the procedure and practice of appointment of Additional Judges and extension of their terms as well as regularization as permanent judges came up for consideration of the Supreme Court in *Shanti Bhushan* v. *Union of India*.[66] The challenge of the petitioners in this case was that the two short term extension of the of the 2nd respondent as Additional Judge and the subsequent appointment as the puisne judge of the High Court was without complying with the process of consultation between the Chief Justice of India, his collegium and the Chief Justice of the High Court concerned[67] envisaged in S.C. Advocates and Special Reference 1 of 1998, was invalid.[68] Dealing with the petition, the Court held in tune with the guidelines of the Judges Case (as the issue of appointment of Additional Judges was not dealt with in S.C. Advocates and Special Reference 1 of 1998) that the rigour of the

65. (1993) 4 S.C.C. 441.
66. (2009)1 S.C.C. 657.
67. Before appointing judges to the High Court, the Chief Justice of India has to consult the collegium consisting of his senior colleagues and the opinion of the Chief Justice of the High Court concerned shall be given greatest weight. For a discussion on the issue, see, *supra*, Chapter 3 nn. 78-99 and the text attached thereto.
68. It was a petition under Article 32 of the Constitution filed in public interest seeking issuance of the writ of *quo warranto* for quashing the appointment of the 2nd respondent as a Judge of the High Court of Madras. He was appointed as an Additional Judge of the Madras High Court in 2003. Finding that he was unsuitable to be appointed as a permanent judge his term as Additional Judge was extended twice for short periods. Thereafter, in 2007 he was appointed as a permanent judge and was transferred in public interest to another High Court.

consultative procedure for appointing permanent judges to the High Court need not be followed in the case of regularization of an Additional Judge.[69] The court further held that though there was no right to extension of the term of Additional Judge, as the initial appointment was not on probation,[70] "unless the circumstances or events arise subsequent to the appointment as an Additional Judge, which bear adversely on the mental and physical capacity, character and integrity or other matters the appointment as a permanent Judges has to be considered" in accordance with the *Judges Case* and that due weightage should be given to him.[71] The view of the court that due weightage should be given to the Additional Judge impliedly give effect to the concept of legitimate expectation. But, the holdings that one should not be permitted to continue as an Additional Judge if he was not suitable to be appointed as a permanent judge and that the circumstances subsequent to his initial appointment would be considered for his extension or regularization[72] are potential threats to the independence of the judge. For, non-extension of the term of the judge on the basis of his performance or character after his initial appointment poses a serious threat to his independence as a judge.

If such a proposition is accepted, a question arises. What is to be done if there is an allegation that during his initial tenure, an Additional Judge had misbehaved? Is he entitled to be re-appointed? The power to deny extension by the executive on the ground of alleged misbehaviour may lead to the removal of a judge who has not really misbehaved. Such a situation affects independence of the judiciary. Compliance with the constitutionally contemplated procedure for removal of judges on the other hand upholds independence of the judges and it enables removal of a judge who is found to have misbehaved. Avoidance of an incompetent judge, no doubt, is in the public interest. But independence of the judiciary is the highest public interest.[73] Hence removal of Additional Judges should also only

69. *Supra*, n. 66 at p. 674
70. *Id.* at p. 674. See also *supra*, n. 41.
71. *Id.* at p. 675.
72. *Ibid.*
73. Justice Tulzapurkar observed, "Not to have a corrupt Judge or a Judge who has misbehaved is unquestionably in public interest but at the same time preserving judicial independence is of the highest public interest." *Id.* at p. 520. See also Seervai, *op. cit.*, at p. 2274.

be in accordance with the procedure contemplated by Article 124(4) and (5). There may be a circumstance in which there may not be enough time to initiate or complete proceedings under Article 124 against an Additional Judge within his tenure. Even in such a case he should not be denied reappointment by the procedure of consultation since it runs counter to judicial independence. In such a situation, the Additional Judge should be re-appointed and be removed only after a finding that he had misbehaved. Though such a course may appear to be roundabout, protracted or absurd, it is inevitable to protect judicial independence.[74]

(c) Appointment of Additional Judges vis-à-vis Requirement of Permanent Judges

The concepts as incorporated or identified by the Court on the power of the President to appoint Additional Judges viz. consultation with the Chief Justice of India, legitimate expectation and the right to judicial review are procedural in nature. Apart from them, the Constitution also contains some substantive limitations on the power of the executive to appoint Additional Judges. The Constitution stipulates that Additional Judges are to be appointed for disposing "temporary increase in business of High Court" or "the pending arrears" of cases.[75] In other words, Additional Judges could be appointed for meeting

74. Justice Gupta and Justice Tulzapurkar in their minority judgement opined that such a procedure was necessary to uphold judicial independence. Justice Gupta observed, "... the only reasonable course open, which dies not undermine independence of the judiciary, was to appoint the Judge for another term having a rational nexus with the volume of arrears pending in the High Court and then proceed with an inquiry into the allegations and remove the Judge if the allegations were found true, in accordance with the procedure laid down in clauses (4) and (5) of Article 124 read with Article 218." *Supra*, n. 31 at p. 348. Justice Tulzapurkar was more emphatic, "The other alternative, namely, to continue hi as an Additional Judge for another term or to make him permanent if a vacancy; is available an then take action for his removal under the regular process indicated in Article 124(4) and (5) read with Article 218 . . . may sound absurd but must be held to be inevitable if judicial independence, a cardinal faith of our Constitution, is to be preserved and safeguarded." *Id.* at p. 520.

75. Article 224(1), *supra*, n. 23.

out certain exigencies and not as a rule.[76] Such contingencies operate as limitations on the power of the President to appoint temporary judges.

A basic question arises here. What is meant by temporary increase in the business of the High Court and pending arrears of cases? Ascertainment of their meaning is very crucial for determining the constitutionality of exercise of the power by the President. The question whether the increase in or arrears of cases in a court can be considered as one under Article 224(1) depends upon two criteria. Has the number of cases filed or pending in the files of the court increased in such a proportion disabling the existing permanent judges to dispose them of? Secondly, is it likely that by appointing Additional Judges, the increase in the business or arrears could be disposed of? If answers to both the questions are in the affirmative, the situation could be treated as one falling within Article 224(1) warranting appointment of Additional Judges. If, on the other hand, answer to either or both the questions is in the negative, appointment of Additional Judges would not be justified. For, if the answer to the first question is in the negative, appointment of Additional Judges would be redundant. If the answer to the latter is in the negative, it implies that the increase in the cases is so unwieldy that it could not be disposed of by appointing Additional Judges and the circumstance calls for appointment of more permanent judges. However, the Court has not dealt with these issues. A proper construction of these expressions certainly would have been more effective as restraints on the executive in appointing Additional Judges than the procedural limitations.

It is clear from the above discussion that the President would be justified in appointing Additional Judges only if the existing number (and not the existing permanent judges) in a High Court is not sufficient to dispose of the pending cases. In other words, the President should be satisfied that the High Court is not in requirement of more permanent judges before appointing Additional Judges. It means two things. Before appointing Additional Judges, existing vacancies of permanent

76. Anand Prakash, "Appointment of High Court Judges under the Constitution of India—Issues and Perspectives", 9 JBCI 397 at p. 403, (1982).

judges should be filled up by the President. It also means that before appointing Additional Judges, the President should be satisfied that the prevailing circumstances in the High Court do not warrant appointment of permanent judges under Article 216.[77] That provision imposes a duty on the President to periodically review the strength of the number of judges in High Courts and if found necessary to increase the same. The Court held that it would be improper for the President to appoint Additional Judges while the posts of permanent judges remain vacant.[78] For, vacancy in the post of permanent judges implies that the existing judges are sufficient for disposing the cases pending in the files of the Court. The decision certainly is one rendered in view of the damaging consequences that may follow if the President is left with the power to exercise the power to appoint Additional Judges irrespective of the presence of permanent vacancies. However, the Court has not dealt with the question whether the President could appoint Additional Judges instead of increasing the number of permanent judges after reviewing their strength under Article 216. It is beyond doubt that invocation of Article 224 instead of Article 216 would also be violative of the concept of judicial independence.

That leads to a further question as to what is to be done if the President wrongly invokes his power to appoint Additional Judges? Can the Court pass an order quashing appointment of Additional Judges as unconstitutional on the ground that such appointments are made while the posts of permanent judges are left unfilled? The Court has not dealt with such an issue. The court however held that Additional Judges cannot be treated as permanent ones.[79] The *Judges Case*, to the extent to which it denied effective remedy in this respect has not been creative in upholding the independence of the judiciary.

The second question is whether even after filling up of the vacancies of permanent judges, or when there is no vacancy of

77. Article 216 reads, "Every High Court shall consist of a Chief Justice and such other Judges as the President may from time to time deem it necessary to appoint.
78. *Supra*, n. 31 *per* Bhagwati, J., (at p. 238); Tulzapurkar, J., (at p. 530); Desai, J., (at pp. 626-27) and Venkitaramaiah, J., (at pp. 805-06).
79. *Id.*, *per* Tulzapurkar, J., (at p. 530); Desai, J., (at p. 629); Pathak, J., (at p. 718) and Venkitaramaiah, J., (at p. 810).

judges, can the President appoint Additional Judges when due to the increase in the filing the sitting judges may not be able to dispose of the cases pending in the Court. In such a context, what the President has to do is to review the strength of judges in the High Court and increase the same.[80] Instead of increasing the strength of judges, can he appoint Additional Judges? Can there be a writ against the Union directing it to discharge the constitutionally mandated function? Can appointment of Additional Judges in such a context be quashed being violative of the Constitution?

The Court in the *Judges Case* held that in such a case, a writ of mandamus could not be issued against the Union of India directing it to exercise its powers under Article 216.[81] The Judges supplied different reasons for not issuing the writ of *mandamus*. Justice Bhagwati held that fixation of judge strength was purely an executive function and that there were no judicially manageable standards for guiding the discretion of the President in this respect. He further reasoned that there might be many constraints deterring the government from increasing the number of Judges.[82] Justice Tulzapurkar opined that appointment of Judges was an executive function and it might not be proper for the judiciary to usurp that function.[83] Justice Desai observed that non-appointment of judges makes the President answerable to the Parliament and not to the courts[84] while Justice Pathak reasoned that it was for the President to determine the number of Judges and not for the courts.[85] However, Justice Venkitaramiah in his dissenting view was willing to issue a writ of mandamus to the Union for the purpose on the ground that it was a power coupled with a duty and not merely a political function.[86] The result of the holding

80. *Id., per* Bhagwati, J., (at p. 246); Tulzapurkar, J., (at p. 530); Pathak, J., at (pp. 714-15) and Venkitaramiah, J., (at p. 804).
81. *Id., per* Bhagwati, J. (at p. 225); Tulzapurkar, J. (at p. 530); Desai, J. (at p. 617) and Pathak, J. (at p. 707). Justice Venkitaramiah, J. *contra* (at p. 916).
82. *Id.* at pp. 225-26.
83. *Id.* at p. 530.
84. *Id.* at p. 617.
85. *Id.* at p. 718.
86. *Id.* at pp. 915-16. He held that the power under Article 216 "is a power coupled with a duty and is not merely a political function... it appears to be inevitable that the Union Government should be directed to

of the Court is that if the President appoints Additional Judges even when from the prevailing circumstances he could have inferred the requirement of increased number of permanent judges nothing could be done through judicial proceedings. It is tantamount to a situation wherein the President is left with an uncontrolled discretion to appoint permanent or Additional Judge, as he likes. Appointment of Additional Judges in the place of permanent judges runs counter to the concept of independence of the judiciary and such a freedom on the part of the President is bad. Though the judges supplied different reasons for not issuing the writ of mandamus,[87] it is unfortunate that they did not consider the undesirable impact of the holding on independence of judiciary. In view of the independence of the judiciary, the question whether the judiciary has the power to direct the Union of India to review the strength of the judges is to be answered in the affirmative. So, the holding of the court that mandamus could not be issued against the Union of India to review the number of judges is wrong.

The holding of the Court is open to objections on other grounds also. In a democratic state, courts enjoy the ultimate authority to restrain the exercise of absolute and arbitrary powers by the administrative authorities.[88] Such authorities are not supposed to exercise their power in an arbitrary or absolute manner nor can they fail to discharge their public duties. Public authorities cannot exercise their discretion in an unreasonable manner. Without such judicial supervision, it is likely that there may be excesses by such administrative authorities.[89] That is why the judiciary enjoys ultimate authority to restrain exercise of administrative authorities. It encompasses both the power to check abuse of power[90] and non-performance of public duties

determine within reasonable time the strength of permanent Judges required for the disposal of cases... I am of the view that the Union Government which has the responsibility of appointing sufficient number of Judges in every High Court should be directed to review the strength of permanent Judges in every High Court, to fix the number of permanent Judges that should be appointed in that High Court on the basis of work-load. A writ in the above terms shall be issued to the Union Government."

87. *Supra*, nn. 81-86.
88. M.P. Jain and S.N. Jain, *Principles of Administrative Law* (1986), p. 425
89. *Padfield* v. *Minister of Agriculture, Fisheries and Food*, 1968 AC 997.
90. O. Hood Philips, *Constitutional and Administrative Law* (1975), p. 517.

by public authorities.[91] It is keeping this in mind that in India jurisdiction to issue writs has been conferred on the Supreme Court and High Courts.[92] The writ jurisdiction of the Supreme Court and High Courts empowers them to exercise judicial supervision over administrative authorities including the executive. The nature of the function under Article 216 to review the strength of permanent judges of High Court and change their number is a duty cast on the President.[93] If the strength of the permanent judges is not periodically reviewed and required changes effected, that is a failure of the government to exercise a constitutional duty. Hence, compliance with such a constitutional or statutory duty, may be required by issuing a writ of mandamus.[94] Though the court cannot direct the specific manner in which the duty is to be discharged,[95] it can direct the government to exercise its powers under 216 to review the strength of judges. Such a direction is in no way beyond the judicially manageable standards. Small wonder that after a decade the holding was subjected to judicial reconsideration.

In the *S.C. Advocates*,[96] the Court re-considered its holding in the *Judges Case* that the powers of the President to review the strength of judges of High Courts was not amenable to the review by the judiciary. The question that was posed before the Court was whether the power of the President to increase the strength of judges was amenable to judicial review. The court held that the function of the President to re-fix the strength of judges of High Courts under Article 216 was amenable to

91. *Id*. at p. 529.
92. See, the Constitution of India, Articles 32, 226 and 227.
93. See, *supra*, n. 31 at p. 915 (per Venkitaramiah, J.).
94. "If it is the constitutional or statutory duty of a Governor to exercise his discretion with respect to a certain matter, he may be required to do so, but, of course, the writ does not lie to direct the manner in which his discretion shall be exercised." *American Jurisprudence*, 2d Vol. 52 paragraph 141 quoted with approval by Venkitaramiah, J (*Id* at p. 912)
95. Such a restriction means that the court could not determine the number of judges to be increased. However, there was a view in the Constituent Assembly that the President should determine the number of judges on the advice of the Chief Justice of India or the Supreme Court. See, *CAD*., Vol. VIII, p. 657.
96. *Supreme Court Advocates-on-Record* v. *Union of India*, (1993) 4 S.C.C. 441.

judicial review.[97] The question was whether the President could appoint Additional Judges where he should have increased the number of permanent judges. The power of the President to review the strength of permanent judges has direct relation with his power to appoint Additional Judges. Therefore naturally ruling on the scope of the scope of the President to review the strength of permanent judges will have its impact on the scope of his power to appoint Additional Judges. Some of the Judges held so on the ground that review and re-fixation of the strength of judges was necessary to ensure speedy disposal of cases to 'secure that the operation of the legal system promotes justice' which is a directive principle, fundamental in the governance of our country. Further, non-increase in the number of judges may also affect the right of the people to have speedy trial, which is a requirement under Article 21. Therefore failure on the part of the President to discharge the function under Article 216 for re-fixing the same would call for issuance of writ of mandamus.[98] Justice Pandian held that the duty cast on the President under Article 216 was a mandatory obligation failure to perform which will result in negation of rule of law.[99] Accordingly, such non-discharge of such duty will call for issuance of writ.[100] While Justice Ahmadi held that if there was a willful and deliberate failure on the part of the executive to perform its duty under Article 216, a writ to direct the executive to perform its part could be issued.[101] The consequence of such a holding is

97. *Id. per* Justice Verma (for Dayal, Ray, Anand Barucha, JJ. and for himself) at p. 709; Pandian, J. at pp. 584; Kuldip Singh, J. at p. 675 and Ahmadi, J. at p. 639.

98. *Id. per* Verma, J. *et. al.* at pp. 708-09. The Court held thus, This is essential to ensure speedy disposal of cases, to 'secure that the operation of the legal system promotes justice'—a directive principle 'fundamental in the governance of the country' which, it is the duty of State to observe in all its actions; and to make meaningful the guarantee of the fundamental rights in Part III of the Constitution... Accordingly, it must be held that fixation of judge-strength in a High Court is justiciable; and if it is shown that the existing strength is inadequate to provide speedy justice to the people—speedy trial being a requirement of Article 21—in spite of optimum efficiency of the existing strength, a direction can be issued to assess the felt need and fix the strength of judges commensurate with the need..."

99. *Id.* at p. 584.

100. *Ibid.*

101. *Id.* at pp. 638-39.

that if the President decides not to review the strength of permanent judges in a High Court or not to increase their strength, mandamus could be issued. As a result of the decision, he may not be able to appoint Additional Judges without reviewing the strength of the permanent judges and increasing the same in necessary cases. Though the judges did not gear their decision to judicial independence, such a holding is certain to have favourable results on independence of the judiciary as the executive would not enjoy uncontrolled discretion to appoint Additional Judges. To that extent, the decision upholds judicial independence. The court further held that in taking a decision as to whether the number of judges should be increased, the opinion of the Chief Justice of India should carry greatest weight.[102] There also the discretion of the President to take the decision was taken away. Now, he has to take a decision in accordance with the opinion of the Chief Justice of India. By such a holding, the power of the President to appoint Additional Judges has been streamlined as he can venture to invoke Article 224 only if the Chief Justice of India opines that the existing conditions do not warrant appointment of permanent judges. In short, the power of the President to appoint Additional Judges under Article 224 was conditioned by the exercise of his power under Article 216. By such a holding, the power of the President to appoint Additional Judges has been streamlined as he can now venture to invoke Article 224 only if the Chief Justice of India opines that the existing conditions do not warrant appointment of permanent judges.

Will such a constitutional position lead to autocracy of the Chief Justice of India in matters of judicial appointments? The possibility of wielding autocratic power by the Chief Justice of India is very distant. While tendering opinion for appointing judges under Article 217(1), the Chief Justice of India is not expected project his personal view. He has to consult his

102. *Id.* at p. 709. They observed, "In making the review of the Judge-strength in a High Court, the President must attach great weight to the opinion of the Chief Justice of that High Court and the Chief Justice of India and if the Chief Justice of India so recommends, the exercise must be performed without due despatch."

colleagues. If the recommendation of the Chief Justice of India is not acceptable to the President, he can require the former to reconsider the suggestion. All these restraints are applicable in the matter of appointment of Additional Judges also in view of the holding that appointment of Additional Judges should also be in compliance with the procedure for appointing puisne judges.

As a result of the holdings of the Court in the *Judges Case* and the *S.C. Advocates*, the issue of appointment of Additional Judges is more or less settled. Now the President cannot act arbitrarily in the matter. He cannot appoint such temporary judges without filling up the existing vacancies of permanent judges. Nor can he appoint Additional Judges when the existing circumstances warrant increase in the number of permanent judges. In short, his power in this respect has been effectively circumscribed by the creative interpretation of the provisions in view of the concept of judicial independence.

3. TRANSFER OF JUDGES

The Constitution of India contains provision for transferring judges from one High Court to another High Court.[103] It stipulates that the President may transfer High Court Judges after consultation with the Chief Justice of India. The provision does not elaborate the mode and conditions of exercising that power. Though *prima facie* it may appear that this provision is innocuous and has no impact on judicial independence, it is yet another area that is bound to have a repercussion on independence of the judiciary. The makers of the Constitution might have presumed that the power being conferred on high constitutional authority, the President, it would be exercised with prudence and on rare occasions. But history tells us that this may not always be the case. Transfer of judges during the period of emergency is an instance where the presumption appears to be incorrect. There were allegations that

103. Article 222(1). It reads: "The President may, after consultation with the Chief Justice of India, transfer a judge from one High Court to any other High Court."

certain transfers were influenced by political considerations and therefore threatened the very independence of the judges.[104] Such incidents proved that Article 222(1) has the potential in the hands of the executive even to shake so cardinal a pillar of our Constitution like judicial independence.

Transfer being generally a condition of service of government servants, there cannot normally be a right not to be transferred in their case. But service of High Court judges is different from that of others. there is no master-servant relation between the government and the judges of the higher judiciary. They on the other hand, are on par with the executive and legislature.[105] Hence, questions relating to transfer of High Court judges cannot be considered in the lines of other government servants. Their service enabling them to decide cases without fear or favour also calls for independence. Hence, conditions of their service including change of the place of the service should only be of such a nature as not to pose any threat to their power to take independent decisions. Transfer should never be allowed to be used as a weapon to cow down the spirit of independent and impartial judges. Insistence on such a condition is important as otherwise the executive, with whom lies the power to transfer judges will be able to exercise it indiscriminately. And as in the case of non-extension of the term of Additional Judges, the possibility of exercising the power to transfer on political grounds and political considerations will be a live threat to independent judges. The fact that the executive is the biggest litigant makes the issue more complex. Is it not then necessary to define and delimit the power of the President to transfer High Court judges to protect judicial independence? Though the answer to this question should be in the affirmative the safeguards for preventing indiscriminate transfers are not explicitly stated in the constitutional provision. Hence, such delimitation of the executive powers has to be read into the

---

104. During emergency, a list of 56 judges to be transferred was prepared by the Union Government. See, Seervai, *op. cit.* at p. 2264.
105. *All India Judges Association* v. *Union of India*, (1993) 4 SCC 288. The court held, "The parity is between the political executive, the Legislators and the Judges and not between the judges and the administrative executive." (at p. 295).

provision of the Constitution. The Supreme Court was faced with this question in certain cases in which transfer of High Court judge was challenged before it.

Union of India v. *Sankalchand Seth*,[106] (*Seth*, for short) was the first case where transfer of High Court judges was challenged before the Supreme Court. The court by majority held that the power to transfer High Court judges was vested with the President and was executive in nature.[107] If it is an executive power of the President, is it not to be exercised solely in accordance with the advice of the Council of Ministers?[108] The view of the court is that it is not. The court was of the unanimous opinion that the President should not be left free to exercise the power in an indiscriminate manner. The power should not be used arbitrarily to toe the judges to the line of the executive.[109] Nor should it be used as a penal measure.[110] The court clarified that judges should be transferred only if it serves public interest[111] and that too only after consulting the Chief Justice of India.[112] However, the court held that consent of the

---

106. AIR 1977 SC 2328. It was an appeal against the decision of the High Court of Gujarat. There, the respondent, the then Chief Justice of Gujarat High Court who had just nine months to retire was transferred to the High Court of Andhra Pradesh. He challenged it before the Gujarat High Court on grounds *inter alia* that the transfer was without his consent which according to him was a condition precedent for transferring a High Court Judge under Article 222(1), that it was contrary to public interest and that it was without effective consultation with the Chief Justice of India. The petition filed by him before the High Court was allowed. The Union of India came in appeal to the Supreme Court.
107. *Id., per* Chandrachud J. (at pp. 2339-40); Bhagwati J., 2360 and Untwalia J., (at p. 2387).
108. Article 73(1). It reads, " There shall be a Council of Ministers with the Prime Minister at the head to aid and advice the President who shall, in the exercise of his functions, act in accordance with such advice : . . ." See also *Samsher Singh* v. *Union of India*, AIR 1974 SC 2192.
109. *Supra*, n. 106, *per* Chandrachud J., (at pp. 2339-40).
110. *Id., per* Chandrachud J., (at p. 2329); Bhagwati J., (at p. 2352) and Krishna Iyer J. (for Fazal Ali J. and for himself) (at p. 2383).
111. *Id., per* Chandrachud J., (at p. 2339); Bhagwati J., (at p. 2352); Krishna Iyer J. (for Fazal Ali J. and for himself) (at p. 2383) and Untwalia J., (at p. 2388).
112. *Id., per* Chandrachud J., (at p. 2346); Bhagwati J., (at p. 2366); Krishna Iyer J. (for Fazal Ali J. and for himself) (at p. 2370) and Untwalia J., (at p. 2387).

judge concerned was not a precondition for transfer.[113] The decision of the *Seth's Case* was reiterated in the *Judges Case*.[114] It was held that judges should not be transferred as punitive measure,[115] or to toe them to the executive line.[116] The court unanimously agreed that the power to transfer judges should be exercised by the President only in public interest[117] and that transfers should be effected only after consultation with the Chief Justice of India.[118]

It is submitted that the holding of the court to import restrictions on the executive power to transfer judges is to be analyzed in the background of the need to preserve judicial independence. Restriction on transfer of judges undoubtedly protects independence of the judiciary. By such a holding the President is checked from transferring judges for passing judgments unpalatable to the executive. In such circumstances, judges are relieved from the feeling that they are under a threat of transfer if they displease the executive by their decisions. The decision thus avoids a situation enabling the executive to encroach upon the independence of the judges to decide cases.

A penal transfer is one effected as punishment. The only constitutionally contemplated punishment for judges of the higher judiciary is their removal according to the procedure under Article 124(4) and (5).[119] Therefore, there cannot be a transfer in lieu of such removal. The holding that penal transfers are outside the scope of Article 222(1) is justified on many grounds. If a judge is one who deserves punishment, his retention in another High Court is as adverse to the image of the

113. *Id., per* Chandrachud J., (at p. 2341) and Krishna Iyer J. (for Fazal Ali J. and for himself) at p. 2381. However, Bhagwati J., (at p. 2362) and Untwalia J., (at p. 2393) who constituted the minority expressed the view that consent of the judge was a precondition for transfer.

114. 1981 Supp. SCC 87.

115. *Id., per* Bhagwati J., (at p. 334); Gupta J., (at p. 358); Tulzapurkar J., (at p. 535); Pathak J., (at p. 736) and Venkitaramaiah J., (at p. 840).

116. *Id., per* Bhagwati J., at p. 334

117. *Id., per* Bhagwati J., (at p. 337); Gupta J., (at p. 358); Fazal Ali J., (at p. 369); Tulzapurkar J., (at p. 535); Desai J., (at p. 670) and Pathak J., (at p. 735)]

118. *Id., per* Bhagwati J., (at p. 334); Fazal Ali J., (at p. 483); Tulzapurkar J., (at p. 533); Desai J., (at p. 659) and Pathak J., (at p. 733).

119. *Infra*, nn. 183-184.

judiciary as his retention in the same High Court. Transfer is not therefore a remedy to diseases like corruption or misbehaviour, which calls for penal actions. Transfers of such judges in such instances would only diminish the confidence of the public in the institution. Conferment of power on the executive to transfer judges as a penal measure may lead to other consequences also. It may encourage the executive to act discriminatively. It may for instance transfer only one judge who misbehaved while it may take steps to remove another from office. Acceptance of such penal transfers may nurture an atmosphere enabling the executive to find fault with judges whom it dislikes and transfer them.

Further, when penal transfers exist, people will be inclined to look at every transferred judge with suspicion. Viewed from these angles, it is clear that the power of the President to transfer judges as penal measure is detrimental to judicial independence. Hence, the holding of the court that such transfers are constitutionally anathematic emerges from the need to protect judicial independence.

(a) Public Interest

The activist role of the court in this respect extended further to the introduction of the concept of public interest as a further restriction on the power to transfer judges. This would mean that even if transfer is not penal, and even if it is not made due to unpalatable decisions, a transfer is not justified unless it is in the public interest. The President has to be satisfied that a transfer is in accordance with the demands of public interest. In other words, he is prohibited from transferring judges if public interest is indifferent to such a transfer. Incorporation of public interest as a restriction on transfer is a further control on arbitrary or penal transfers.

What is the concept of 'public interest' in relation to transfer of judges? Does the requirement of 'public interest' effectively check the arbitrary exercise of the power? Does it help maintain judicial independence? The judges in the *Seth's Case* and the *Judges Case* have tried to explain the concept of public interest not through a descriptive definition but through certain illustrations. Transfers can be said to be in public interest, they held, if made to serve national integration,[120] or to withdraw a judge from the circle of his favourites,[121] or on requirement of a better talent or expert in specific branch of law in a High Court,[122] or on demand of a person who is free from local politics.[123] The concept thus has got varying connotations[124] and may enable the executive to propose transfer of judges on extraneous grounds, which may be characterized as apparently in public interest on these and other grounds.

From the above observations of the judges, it is very clear that they did not have a concrete and well-defined idea of public interest. They have only a very vague idea of the concept. The concept of public interest as envisaged by them consisted of fragmentary ideas like national integration, requirement of a judge who is free from local politics and so forth. However, such a concept may not be able to operate as a shield of judicial independence against executive arbitrariness in different cases of transfers. In other words, even when a transfer is effected in accordance with the concept of public interest as contemplated by the judges, it may be quite against the spirit of judicial independence. The result of the holding is that a transfer would be constitutionally valid even when it poses a threat to independent judges. To curb this arbitrariness of *malafides* of the executive, the court should have developed a concept of public interest in which independence of the judiciary forms an essential element. In other words, the other elements constituting public interest should be given heed to only in so far as they do not contradict independence of the judiciary. For, as far as judiciary is concerned, its own independence is the highest public interest.[125]

---

120. *Supra* note at 99 *per* Chandrachud J., at p. 2344 and Untwalia J., at p. 2388.
121. *Id.*, at p. 2344 (*per* Chandrachud J.).
122. *Id.*, at p. 2388 (*per* Untwalia J.).
123. This view projected by Ambedkar in the Constituent Assembly was quoted by Tulzapurkar J., with approval in *supra* n. at p. 537.
124. Justice Desai observes, "The public interest like Public Policy it is an unruly horse." *Supra* n. 31 at p. 670. Seervai observes that there is no yard stick by which public interest can be measured. Seervai, *op. cit.*, at pp. 2389, 2362.
125. Seervai, *op. cit.*, at p. 2393.

(b) Consultation

In such a context a question arises here. How can it be determined that a transfer will be effected only in tune with the requirement of independence of the judiciary? Elucidation of the requirement of consultation with the Chief Justice of India as a restraint on the President gains relevance here. In the *Seth's Case,*[126] the court held that consultation with the Chief Justice of India should not be a formal one. The Chief Justice of India should ascertain whether the judge has any personal difficulty in being transferred or whether there is any humanitarian ground preventing the transfer.[127] The President should supply all relevant data to the Chief Justice of India and the Chief Justice should collect all necessary information from the President.[128] The opinion of the Chief Justice of India should be formulated on the basis of the information so made available.[129] In other words, the court held that consultation should be real, substantial and effective based on full and proper materials.[130] The holding in *Seth's Case* was reaffirmed in the *Judges Case*[131] These cases elevated the whole process of transfer of judges to a plane where transfer without meaningful consultation with the Chief Justice of India would be invalid and unconstitutional. The President would no more be able to exercise his power arbitrarily after a mere formal consultation. Such a holding is definitely conducive to judicial independence since the Chief Justice of India would alone be able to assess the impact of transfer on the independence of the judges in particular and on the judiciary in general. But the holding of the court that consultation with the Chief Justice of India does not mean his concurrence creates a situation that the opinion of the Chief Justice of India was not binding on the President.[132] It means

126. *Supra* n. 106.
127. *Id., per* Krishna Iyer, at p. 2384.
128. *Ibid.*
129. *Id.,* at pp. 2347 and 2377-80.
130. *Id., per* Krishna Iyer, at p. 2384.
131. *Supra* n. 115.
132. Justice Chandrachud observed, "After, consultation with the Chief Justice of India, it is open to the President to arrive at a proper decision of the question whether a judge should be transferred to another High Court because, what the Constitution requires is consultation with the Chief Justice, not his concurrence with the proposed transfer. (*Supra* note

that even after consulting the Chief Justice of India the President would be able to take a decision, which goes against the opinion of the Chief Justice of India. Such a holding paves a way for the exercise of the power of the President in his own way and he would be able to select the person to be transferred and the High Court to which he is to be so transferred. Conferment of such a power on the executive, enabling it to ignore the opinion of the Chief Justice of India will not promote judicial independence. The need for transfer, the person to be transferred and the place to which the judges to be transferred are matters known to the head of the judiciary than to the executive.[133] The question whether a transfer is in the interest of judicial independence can be assessed by judiciary and not by the executive. Therefore, it was inappropriate for the court to confer the President with the power to brush aside the opinion of the Chief Justice of India.[134]

The view of the *Seth's Case* and its confirmation in the *Judges Case*, conferring discretion on the executive to ignore the opinion of the Chief Justice of India in transferring High Court judges was modified and altered later in *S.C. Advocates*[135] which created the new law in this respect.[136] The court held that as in the matter of appointment of judges, transfer also should be

---

at 2348). Justice Krishna Iyer expressed the view thus, "...consultation is different from consentaneity. They may discuss but disagree, they may confer but may not concur." (*Id.* at p. 2368). Justice Untwalia held, "The Government, however ... is not bound to accept and act upon the advice of the Chief Justice. It may different from him and for cogent reasons may take a contrary view." (*Id.* at p. 2387).

133. Earlier, in *State of Assam* v. *Ranga Mohammed*, AIR 1967 SC 903, where the issue was the transfer of the judge of the lower judiciary, the Supreme Court had held that the view of the High Court would be binding on the Governor. For a detailed discussion of the case, see *infra*, Chapter 5 nn. 76-78.
134. International norms require that the ultimate power to transfer judges should reside in the judiciary itself. See, the Code of Minimum Standards of the Independence of the Judiciary adopted by the plenary session of the International Bar Association. Article 12 reads, "The power to transfer a judge from one court to another shall be vested in a judicial authority..."
135. (1993) 4 SCC 441.
136. The court reaffirmed that transfer of judges could only be on the ground of public interest. (*Id.* at pp. 585, 632, 675 & 700), and that the consent of the judge was not a condition for transfer (id. pp. 585, 675 & 700) but totally changed the concept of consultation under Article 222(1).

done only with the concurrence of the Chief Justice of India.[137] The proposal for transfer, the court held, was to be initiated by the Chief Justice of India. It therefore makes a substantial change from the holding in the *Judges Case* where it was held that the proposal for transferring a judge could be initiated either by the President or the Chief Justice of India. The court thus shifted the emphasis of consultation from the President to the Chief Justice of India. In effect, the procedure was changed from one of "President consulting the Chief Justice of India", into one of the "Chief Justice of India consulting the President". The process of consultation was reduced to an opportunity to the President to bring matters to the notice of the Chief Justice of India for a consideration as to whether his view need be altered, the final word being always with the Chief Justice of India and not the President. The whole process of transfer therefore revolves around the Chief Justice of India. The meaning rendered to 'consultation' in the *S.C. Advocates* checked fully the possibility of arbitrary transfer of judges by the President in two ways. The President cannot transfer judges contrary to the opinion of the Chief Justice of India. Nor can he refuse to transfer a judge contrary to the view of the Chief Justice of India. While in the *Seth's Case* and the *Judges Case* the emphasis was on the concept of public interest and the process of consultation was only a procedure for ensuring that transfers should be effected only in public interest, in the *S.C. Advocates*, the emphasis has been shifted to the very process of consultation in the interest of preserving independence of judiciary.[138]

---

137. "The provision requiring exercise of this power by the President only after consultation with the Chief Justice of India, and the absence of the requirement of consultation with any other functionary, is clearly indicative of the determinative nature, not mere primacy, of the Chief Justice of India opinion in this matter." (*Id.* at pp. 699-700).

138. Justice J.S. Verma observed, "Apart from the constitutional requirement of a transfer being made only on the recommendation of the Chief Justice of India, the issue of transfer is not justiciable on any other ground including, the reasons for the transfer or their sufficiency. The opinion of the Chief Justice of India formed in the manner indicated is sufficient safeguard and protection against any arbitrariness or bias, *as well as any erosion of independence of judiciary*" (at p. 708) (Emphasis supplied)

The holding of the court in the *S.C. Advocates* undoubtedly is an instance of judiciary creation through progressive interpretation of the law. The declaration of law that initiation of the proposals for and the decision of transfer rest with the Chief Justice of India has thus developed the dimensions of transfer jurisprudence and has furthered the cause of judicial independence.

A question may be raised in this context. Is it proper to confer such absolute powers on the Chief Justice of India? Is the Chief Justice of India infallible? Will he also not have, as a human being, his prides and prejudices?[139] So will not conferment of such a power on the Chief Justice of India lead to arbitrary transfer of judges? Such a possibility cannot be totally ruled out if an absolute power is conferred without some safeguard. Conferment of an absolute power on the Chief Justice of India does not seem to be a solution for executive arbitrariness. However the court in the *S.C. Advocates* has taken care to avoid substitution of judicial arbitrariness for the executive ones by laying down safeguards in the following lines,[140]

> "In the formation of his opinion, the Chief Justice of India, in the case of transfer of a Judge other than the Chief Justice of India, is expected to take into account the views of the Chief Justice of the High Court from which the Judge is to be transferred, any Judge of the Supreme Court whose opinion may be significant in that case, as well as the views of at least one other senior Chief Justice of a High Court, or any other person whose views are considered relevant by the Chief Justice of India."

Questions regarding formation of opinion by the Chief Justice of India for transferring Judges again came up before the court in *Special Reference, 1998*.[141] It was held that before forming

139. He is also a man with human failings. That was the chief reason for the framers of the Constitution to deny the Chief Justice of India the power to veto the proposal for appointment of judges. See, *C.A.D.*, Vol. VIII (at p. 258).

140. *Supra*, n. 135 at p. 706 (*per* J.S. Verma J., speaking for the court).

141. (1998) 7 SCC 739.

an opinion, the Chief Justice of India should obtain the views of the Chief Justice of the High Court from which the judge was to be transferred and the Chief Justice of the High Court to which he is sought to be transferred. He should also get the views of one or two judges of the Supreme Court who are able to provide materials to decide whether the proposed transfer should take place. These views should be considered by the Chief Justice of India and the four senior-most judges of the Supreme Court. These views and the views of each of the four judges should be communicated to the Government of India along with the proposal for transfer. The government is not bound by the opinion unless the opinion is formed in the above said manner. These decisions give a new dimension to the concept of consultation and they try to check arbitrariness of both the President and the Chief Justice of India in transferring judges. As a result of these decisions, consultation under Article 222 is not limited to one between the President and the Chief Justice of India alone. It has been developed as one between the Chief Justice of India and judges of the Supreme Court and High Courts. Just as consultation with the Chief Justice of India is the safeguard to check the arbitrariness on the part of the President, consultation between the Chief Justice of India and other judges operates as a safeguard to check arbitrariness on the part of the Chief Justice of India in effecting transfer of judges. In short, the Supreme Court while dealing with the issue of transfer of High Court judges *in S.C. Advocates* and *Special Reference, 1998* has developed 'consultation' as a device for protecting independence of judges both from the executive and the judiciary. Time alone can prove how far these restraints will check arbitrariness of the President and the Chief Justice of India in this respect.

(c) Judicial Review

Though in these cases, the Court interpreted the powers of the President to transfer judges under Article 222(1) very restrictively and as conditional there is no assurance that judges would be transferred only in compliance with those conditions. The President, for instance, may transfer judges without satisfying himself that it subserved public interest or without consulting the Chief Justice of India. Transfers may also be effected on certain extraneous conditions. In other words, incorporation of public interest and consultation *ipso facto* does not guarantee exclusion of arbitrary power of the President. In such a context, examination of transfers by the judiciary acquires high relevance. Though Article 222 does not explicitly mention judicial review of transfers, in the *Seth's Case*, the Court recognized such a right of the transferred judge to challenge the validity of transfer.[142] In the *Judges Case* also the Court has taken the judicial review of transfer for granted.[143] Such an interpretation of the provision by which judicial review was read into the constitutional scheme with a view to securing judicial independence is another instance of creativity in the transfer issue.

However, in the *S.C. Advocates* the Court took a quite different view of the matter. The Court held that transfers would be judicially reviewed only if they were effected without consulting the Chief Justice of India and in accordance with his recommendations.[144] It means that the judiciary would not examine the validity of transfers only on the ground that they were bereft of public interest or that they were effected on certain extraneous considerations. In other words, a transfer effected after consultation with the Chief Justice of India will not be reviewed by the judiciary even if it violated the constitutional norms. It implies that the recommendations of the Chief Justice of India were identified as an alternative to judicial review. The Court seems to have believed that the Chief Justice of India would recommend transfer of judges only in public interest. Such a holding is based on two grounds. (1) The Chief Justice of India recommends transfers only after consulting other Judges[145] and also that in recommending transfers, he

142. In the *Seth's Case*, the Court had no occasion to hold specifically that Judges had the right to approach the Court. But such a right was implicitly recognized by the Court as it allowed the petition.

143. In the *Judges Case* also the Court did not doubt the right of judges to challenge this transfer under Article 222(1). But, Justice Bhagwati (at p. 336), Desai J. (at p. 670), Pathak J. (at p. 738) and Venkitaramiah J. (at p. 836) have particularly mentioned that the power of the President to transfer judges under Article 222(1) is subject to judicial review.

144. *Supra*, n. 135 at p. 708 (*per* Verma J.).

145. *Id.* at p. 707.

would not be influenced by extraneous considerations, and (2) that such a recommendation carried with it a judicial element.[146] As a result of the decision, all cases of transfers effected in accordance with the recommendation of the Chief Justice of India would be outside the purview of judicial review. This holding was reconsidered by the Court in *K. Ashok Reddy* v. *Union of India*.[147] After analyzing the earlier decisions, the Court concluded that the power to transfer judges of High Court was vested with the highest constitutional functionaries of the state and it could be exercised by them only in accordance with the guidelines laid down in *S.C. Advocates*. These factors according to the Court operated as sufficient safeguards for ruling out arbitrariness in transferring judges. The Court therefore held that transfers of judges was a matter in which judicial review had a very exceptional role to play and that too on limited grounds.[148] The court further restricted the scope of judicial review by holding that when cases regarding transfer of judges were filed in any other court, the Supreme Court would be called upon to decide the same and that the same could be agitated by the transferred judge.[149] In short, the Court not only affirmed the holding in the *S.C.Advocates* that judicial review be restricted but also limited the jurisdiction to decide the matter to the Supreme Court.

Questions regarding formation of opinion by the Chief Justice of India for transferring judges and whether transfers of judges were amenable to judicial review again came up before the Court in *Special Reference, 1998*.[150] In that case the court held that judicial review in such cases was limited to transfers recommended or effected without following the procedure of consultation between the Chief Justice of India and other judges.

146. *Id.* at p. 708.
147. (1994) 2 S.C.C. 303. This was an appeal by special leave against the dismissal of a writ petition by the High Court of Andhra Pradesh. The petition was filed for declaration that judges were not liable to be transferred from one High Court to another, that transfers were likely to be on extraneous considerations leading to arbitrariness resulting in erosion of independence of the judiciary, and that the *Supreme Court Advocates Case* was in conflict with the decision of *Kesavananda Bharathi*.
148. *Id.* at p. 316.
149. *Ibid.*
150. *Supra*, n. 135.

The reason assigned by the Court was that such wide-based decision-making helps eliminate the possibility of bias or arbitrariness.[151] As a result of the decisions in *S.C. Advocates, Ashok Reddy* and *Special Reference*, the scope and extent of judicial review in transfers of judges has been substantially restricted. Such a holding is open to objections on many counts.

These decisions amount to exclusion of judicial review in cases where judges were transferred in accordance with recommendations of the Chief Justice of India. Exclusion of judicial review is open to objection as it now forms part of the basic structure of the Constitution, which cannot be taken away by any authority.[152] Moreover, such an exclusion of judicial review implies that the Court has taken the impartiality and infallibility of the Chief Justice of India for granted as if he would never act arbitrarily in transferring judges. But it may not always be correct. It is true that before recommending transfers the Chief Justice of India has to consult some of the judges. But impact of such consultation in the transfer process is yet to be known. Even if such consultation is carried out, the possibility of undue influence by such consultants upon the Chief Justice of India and omission on their part to take note of necessary factors for reaching correct decisions by the Chief Justice of India cannot be totally ruled out. Therefore, recommendations of the Chief Justice of India cannot always be treated as one containing all checks against arbitrary transfers. To add to all these, the Court has not explained as to what was to be done if the Chief Justice of India acted arbitrarily in transferring judges.

Further, the opinion of the Court that the recommendation of the Chief Justice of India for transferring judges contained judicial element is not correct. It, in fact, is a power in his administrative jurisdiction, which is subject to review by the judiciary.[153] Unfortunately, while ruling out judicial review, all

151. *Id.* at p. 771.
152. *Minerva Mills* v. *Union of India*, A.I.R 1980 S.C. 1789. For a discussion of the case and issue see, *infra*, Part II Chapter 7 n. 68.
153. There were a lot of occasions in which decisions of the Chief Justice of various High Courts in the administrative capacity have been challenged before the High Courts and Supreme Court. See, for example, *Dixitulu* v. *Chief Justice of the High Court of Andhra Pradesh*, A.I.R. 1979 S.C.

these considerations somehow escaped the attention of the Court. Hence the opinion of the Chief Justice of India cannot be considered as a substitute for judicial review.

A study of these cases reveals that in the *Seth's Case* and the *Judges Case* the Court gave predominance to the concept of public interest and judicial review as check on the power of the President to transfer judges. That is clear from the holding of the Court in these cases that to be valid, transfers should have been effected on public interest and to assure that consultation should be effected and that in violation of either of those conditions, judicial review would be available. In the *S.C. Advocates* and *Ashok Reddy* on the other hand, the Court placed pride of place to the process of consultation with the Chief Justice of India. Such a shift is clear from the holding in the *S.C. Advocates* that public interest is subsumed in the opinion of the Chief Justice of India,[154] that a transfer without consulting the Chief Justice of India alone would be invalid and that judicial review would be available only in cases of transfers without consultation with the Chief Justice of India.[155]

Apart from the interests of the judge so transferred, the question of transfer involves the larger issue of independence of the judiciary, which is a matter of public interest. It therefore indicates that the issue cannot always be left to be agitated by the judge concerned. There may be instances where the judge aggrieved by the arbitrary transfer is not interested in raising the issue before the Court. In such cases also it is necessary that the issue be brought before and settled by the judiciary. It thus indicates the necessity of liberalization of *locus standi* enabling persons other than the judge to challenge the constitutionality of transfers.

Though the issue was not raised in the *Judges Case*, some of the petitions in the case against transfers were filed by persons other than the judges transferred.[156] Thus, the Court took a very liberal and sensible stand holding that the issue of transfer of judges was one directly linked with independence of judiciary.

154. *Supra*, n. 135 at p. 707.
155. *Supra*, n. 138.
156. In that case, four petitions and one special leave petition were filed by Advocates of various High Courts challenging the constitutional validity of transfer of Chief Justices M.M. Ismail and K.B.N. Singh.

Such a stand of the Court permitting members of the public to agitate the issue was certainly an innovative interpretation of the constitutional provision conducive to judicial independence. However, in this respect also, in *S.C. Advocates* and *Ashok Reddy*, the Court took a very regressive step as it was held that the judges concerned alone could challenge transfers. Such a holding restrains the members of the public from bringing arbitrary transfers to the attention of the judiciary, leaving judicial independence and its credence at bay.

(d) Consent—A Valid Norm for Transfer?

Can consent of the judge to be transferred be taken as a reliable and effective criterion for transfer? Will it safeguard independence of the judiciary? Will it affect the power of the President to transfer judges in necessary cases? Incorporation of consent of the judge in cases of transfer was a moot issue from the *Seth's Case*[157] itself. The majority of judges considered its relevance[158] and impact and rejected the same. The Court did so mainly on two grounds. The first ground was that the requirement of consent was absent in Article 222(1) and the Court could not read something into a provision which was absent in it.[159] The Court further reasoned that what Article 222 conferred on the President was a power to transfer judges and if 'consent' of the judge was read into it, power would lose its teeth.[160] These views have been approved and accepted by the Court in the *Judges Case*[161] and *S.C. Advocates*.[162] Was the Court justified in dismissing 'consent' of the judge as anathematic?

157. AIR 1977 SC 2328.
158. The majority consisted of Chandrachud C.J., Krishna Iyer and Fazal Ali JJ., Bhagwati J., (at p. 2362) and Untwalia J., (at p. 2387) held that for transferring judges of High Courts, their consent was a condition precedent.
159. *Id. per* Krishna Iyer J., for Fazal Ali J., and for himself (at p. 2380).
160. *Id., per* Chandrachud C.J., (at p. 2341) and Krishna Iyer J., (at p. 2380). Justice Chandrachud further reasoned that since the power of the President to transfer was not an unlimited one but one subject to limitations like public interest and consultation, there was no requirement of 'consent' as a restraint on the power. (*Id.* at p. 2339).
161. *Supra*, n. 114 *per* Fazal Ali J. at p. 487; Tulzapurkar J. at p. 540; per Desai J. (at p. 663) and Venkitaramiah J. (at pp. 821-22).
162. *Supra*, n. 135 *per* Verma *et. al.* at p. 700; per Pandian J. (at p. 585) and Kuldip Singh J. (at p. 675).

The reasoning of the court that absence of the word 'consent' in the constitutional provision prevented it from incorporating it as a condition precedent for transfer is faulty. In its attempt to limit the power of the President to transfer judges, the court incorporated public interest and judicial review into Article 222(1) as restraints which were verbally absent in the provision. If the court considered their incorporation as not offensive to rules of constitutional interpretation, the same is no less true of the term 'consent' also. Moreover, securing consent of the judge is not novel, as such a practice has "become part of the procedure in the effective consultative process under Article 222.[163] Besides, as the State is the biggest litigant, it would only be fare that its powers to transfer judges are subject to his consent.

Further, it is true that what Article 222 confers on the President is a power. But that does not mean that the power should be unlimited. It is only a permissive power[164] to be sparingly used.[165] Restrictions imposed on this power through judicial interpretation[166] suffer from certain patent defects. There is a view that they were incorporated to obviate the necessity of consent.[167] The court could have incorporated consent as a valid condition precedent for transferring judges. Such a holding would have been more creative in securing judicial independence also. However, it is yet to be seen that the judge does not withhold his consent without any valid reasons.

(e) Policy Transfers—Are they Constitutional?

A related issue that has sprung up in the *Judges Case* was whether policy transfers were outside the scope of Article 222(1). Policy transfers are transfers arising out of a policy framed by the government. In other words, it can be considered as transfers on the basis of guidelines for selecting judges and places to be transferred. Policy transfers enjoy certain advantages over those without a policy. Transfers on policy

---

163. Upendra Baxi, *The Indian Supreme Court and Politics* (1980) p. 207.
164. Seervai, *Constitutional Law of India*, Vol. II (1984) p. 2389.
165. *Supra*, n. 114 *per* Pathak J. (at p. 798).
166. Such as public interest and judicial review.
167. Seervai, *op. cit.*, (at p. 2400).

assure that all transfers are on certain pre-determined criteria. It then forms part of conditions of service. Such a situation eliminates the possibility of executive arbitrariness, as the executive may not be able to unilaterally determine individual transfers. Moreover, when such a policy is laid down all judges enter the service with the prior knowledge that they would be transferred in accordance with the published criteria.

However, establishment of a policy *ipso facto* does not rule out the possibility of executive arbitrariness and the consequential threat to judicial independence. The President may frame arbitrary or vague policies and improperly implement them. Criteria for selecting judges for transfers, the places to which they are to be transferred may also be open to objection. Hence it would be dangerous to leave the formulation of the policy for transfer or its implementation solely to the executive fiat.

The Court in the *Judges Case* did not find policy transfers as outside the purview of Article 222 and dealt with it as constitutionally valid.[168] It was held that even such transfers were to be effected only in compliance with Article 222(1).[169] It was also held that in formulating such a policy of transfers, Chief Justice of India was to be consulted.[170] Thus, on the whole, the court was not willing to leave framing of policy for transfers as well as its implementation exclusively to the executive decision, presumably because of the fear that they may adversely affect judicial independence. Though the question was given reconsideration by the court in the *S.C. Advocates Case*, it did not gain much relevance in view of the holding that the transfer to be valid should be in accordance with the recommendation of the Chief Justice of India irrespective of whether it is in furtherance of a policy.[171] Recognition of policy transfers as not contrary to Article 222 and as constitutional is

---

168. *Supra* n. 114 *per* Fazal Ali J., (at p. 418), 425-26. Tulzapurkar J., (at p. 541), Pathak J., (at p. 739) and Venkitaramiah J. (at pp. 843, 846-47).
169. *Id., per* Fazal Ali J., (at p. 434); Tulzapurkar J., (at p. 541); Pathak J., (at p. 738) and Venkitaramiah J., (at p. 849).
170. *Id.*, per Fazal Ali J., (at p. 433); Tulzapurkar J., (at p. 541); Pathak J., (at p. 739) and Venkitaramiah J., (at p. 849).
171. *Supra*, n. 135 *per* Verma J. *et. al.* (at pp. 700-01).

an instance of judicial creativity. Evidently, the court was not willing to leave transfers to the discretion of the executive even under the garb of policy. Unwillingness of the court to leave formulation of policy for transfers fully to the executive and the insistence that even such policy transfers should be effected only after a further consultation with the Chief Justice of India also strengthens judicial independence through creative interpretation.

It is clear from the above discussion that the purpose of transfer policy should be smooth administration of justice[172] and independence of the judiciary. However, it is doubtful whether the transfer policy impugned in the *Judges Case* satisfied the above mentioned conditions. That policy was "to further national integration and to combat parochial tendencies bread by caste, kinship and other local affiliations."[173] Though impressive, emotive and high sounding national integration appears to be, it is an amorphous and irrelevant concept as far as transfer of judges is concerned. For, what judges are supposed to have is a "judicial approach" by holding the scales of justice between and among citizens, the States and the Centre. Concepts like national integration are matters to be achieved at political and administrative levels than through transfers of judges. Therefore, though the holding of the court that policy transfers were constitutionally valid is correct, the holding that the impugned letter as not unconstitutional is clearly wrong.

Thus, the travel from the *Seth's Case* through *Judges Case* to the *S.C. Advocates, Ashok Reddy* and *Presidential Reference* reveals that the issue relating to transfer of judges is settled without giving any room for doubt. The Court was experimenting with different combinations of restrictions on the power of the President to transfer judges. A comprehensive examination of all these cases reveals that the Court was successful in effectively checking the possibility of arbitrariness of the

172. *Cf.* the observation of Pathak J., "... any policy framed and adopted in this behalf must be tested on the criterion of public interest, and it must be clearly understood that "public interest" means here the interest of the administration of justice." (*Supra* n. 114 at p. 739).

173. See, the letter sent by the then Law Minister to the Chief Ministers quoted in the *Judges Case* by Justice Bhagwati. See, *supra*, n. 114 at pp. 194-95.

President. The court commands much appreciation for its holdings, but the effect of the holdings is yet to be seen.

4. REMOVAL OF JUDGES

The concept of security of tenure of judges is inextricably interwoven with the procedure for their removal. That is essentially so, because absence of a proper procedure for removal of judges proclaims lack of security of tenure. It is as important as, if not more important than, the conditions of service while continuing in service. For, absence of a proper procedure for removal of judges undoubtedly paves the way for lack of security of tenure and violates the principles of judicial independence.

The issue of removal has two aspects. The grounds for removal constitute the former and its procedure the latter. Both are so seminal as to claim a place in different Constitutions. Earlier in England, judges were removable at the pleasure of the Crown. This means that the grounds and mode of removal of judges were at the pure will of the Crown. Judges were removed for reasons known only to the Crown, which might even include declaration of judicial decisions objectionable or unpalatable to the Crown. There were instances of removal of judges for their independence.[174] At that time tenure of judges was determined by the terms of prerogative appointments.[175] Such appointments adversely affected judicial independence as "judges had to be good King's men, prepared to act as his confidential advisers."[176] By 1688, the situation changed and judges began to

174. Chief Justice Sir Edward Coke was a victim of such a scheme. He was dismissed by the then King James I for his independence as a Judge. "Bacon drew up a list of decisions of Coke which were objectionable. The King used them as ground for dismissing Coke. He did it by the writ of supersede as;" See Lord Denning, *What Next in Law,* (1982) at p. 10. Pemberton, a Judge during the last quarter of the seventeenth century also was subjected to similar treatment. See De Smith, *Constitutional and Administrative Law* (1973), p. 373.

175. S.A. De Smith, *op. cit.* at pp. 372-73.

176. *Id.* at p. 373. See also Alfred F. Havinghurst, "the Judiciary and Politics in the Reign of Charles II" (1950) 66 L.Q.R. (at p. 64). "Judicial office in Common Law courts, since their origin in the twelfth century had been the gift of the King."

be appointed 'for good beahaviour'. They were not removable at the pleasure of the Executive. The matter was statutorily settled by the Act of Settlement 1700.[177] The Act provided that judges would serve for good beahaviour[178] and not at the pleasure of the Crown. It was further stipulated that they should be removed only by an address by both the Houses of Parliament and an order of the Crown.[179] Thus for the first time in the history of judiciary, the grounds as well as the procedure for removal of judges were brought outside the purview of the subjective satisfaction of the Executive. Following the suit, the Constitution of the United States declared that judges shall enjoy a tenure during good behaviour.[180] It means that judges are removable only on misbehaviour. Judges are liable to be removed by impeachment[181] through a procedure by the legislature, namely the Congress.[182]

In India judges of the higher judiciary are removable only "by an order of the President passed after an address by each House of Parliament supported by a majority of total membership of that House and by a majority of not less than two-thirds of the members of that House present and voting has been presented to the President in the same session for such removal on the ground of proved misbehaviour or incapacity.[183] But unlike in the other nations our Constitution provides that Parliament has the power to pass a law regulating the procedure and removal of judges.[184] Thus in India also removal of judges is possible only through a procedure which simulates impeachment. It is clear that introduction of the concepts of

177. 12 & 13 Will.
178. *Id*. s. 3.
179. *Ibid*.
180. Article III, S. 1. The relevant portion of the provision reads, "... The judges, both the Supreme Court and inferior courts, shall hold their office during good behaviour, ..."
181. See, Raol Berger, *Impeachment, the Constitutional Problems* (1973), p. 122.
182. It is for the House of Representatives at the first instance and for the Senate finally to Judge whether there was the alleged misconduct. See, Edward S. Corwin, *The Constitution and What It Means Today* (1958), p. 11.
183. The Constitution of India, Article 124(4) and Article 217(1).
184. *Id*. Article 124(5). It reads, "Parliament may by law regulate the procedure for the presentation of an address and for the investigation and proof of the misbehaviour or incapacity of a Judge under clause 4."

'misbehaviour' and 'incapacity' as grounds of removal and the procedure for removal known as impeachment modified the tenure of judges as that on good behaviour. Unlike judges of the past, those in the modern era enjoy to some extent protection against executive onslaughts. Does such a scheme of removal offer absolute solution to the issue of political attack on judicial independence? Does it provide a scheme for removal of judges without damaging judicial independence? In fact impeachment was not a weapon fashioned to dismiss corrupt judges from their office. It originally was a device to make high officials of the Crown who are political offenders responsible to Parliament.[185] But somehow impeachment happened to be applied to judges also.[186]

Impeachment is defined as a "criminal proceeding against a public officer, before a quasi-political court..."[187] It is condemned that ever since its inception in 1386 in England; impeachment was "essentially a political (factional) weapon."[188] In America also it is considered as a political remedy.[189] The framers of the Constitution of the U.S. were conscious of this fact. Hamilton, an ace architect of the U.S. Constitution, observed that impeachment "will seldom fail to agitate the passions of the whole community.... In many cases it will connect itself with the pre-existing factions... and in such cases there will always be the comparative strength of the parties, than by the real demonstrations of innocence or guilty."[190] Mecaulay at the time of impeachment of Warren Hastings, made the following comment, [191]

> " ... it is certain that no man has the least confidence in this impartiality, when a great public functionary, charged with

185. Raol Berger, *op. cit.* (at p. 1).
186. *Id.* at pp. 3-4.
187. See *Black's Law Dictionary* (1990).
188. M.V. Clarke, "The Origin of Impeachment" in *Oxford Essays in Medieval History* (1964), pp. 164, 185 quoted in Berger, *op. cit.* at p. 59.
189. Wrisley Brown, "The Impeachment of the Federal Judiciary", 26 H.L.R. 68 at p. 705 (1912-13).
190. *The Federalist Papers* 65.
191. Quoted in J.C. Dougherty, "Inherent Limitations upon Impeachment." (1913) 23 Yale Law Journal 60 at p. 69.

a great state crime, is brought to their bar. They are all politicians. There is hardly one among them whose vote on an impeachment may not be confidently predicted before a witness has been examined."

Evidently, the question whether the person against whom impeachment motion is moved has committed any act liable to impeachment is determined on the basis of policies of political parties, which participate in the move. If the opinion of the members if formed on the basis of the view of the political parties to which they subscribe"... what then, is an impeachable offence? The only answer is that an impeachable offence is whatever a majority of the House of Representatives considers it to be at a given moment in history.... There are few fixed principles among the handful of precedents."[192] Initiation of charges against a person, his trial and the finding that the person is guilty are fully at the control of the legislature, which is a political body. Notwithstanding such a shortcoming even now it remains the sole method of removal of judges. It means that in many nations, judges are liable to be removed through a procedure at the control of legislatures.[193] In other words, impeachment only shifts the procedure for removal of judges from the executive to the legislature. Is it not then equal to transfer of a disease from organ of the body to any other rather than curing it? It seems that impeachment as a mode of removal of judges may continue to adversely affect the freedom of judges to decide cases fearlessly. For, determination of misbehaviour of judges depends upon the will of the majority party in the legislature. Therefore, it is doubtful whether even after the adoption of the mechanism of impeachment, independence of the judiciary is out of danger.

(a) Proof of Misbehaviour under Article 124

In such a context, it will be interesting to examine the

192. 116 Cong. Rec. H. 143113-3114 as cited in Berger, *op. cit.*, at p. 53, n. 1.
193. See for instance, the Constitution of the United States, Article I, Sec. 2; the Constitution of Australia, Section 72(ii) and the Constitution of India, Article 124(4).

construction of the provisions of the Constitution of India relating to removal of judges to assess how far the Supreme Court succeeded in insulating the judiciary from political caprice. The issues of removal of a judge of the higher judiciary came up before the Supreme Court for the first time in the history of Indian judiciary in 1991. In *Sub-Committee for Judicial Accountability v. Union of India,*[194] the question of removal of Justice Ramaswamy, one of the judges of the Supreme Court itself was examined by the Court.[195] In that case, the Court considered the nature of the procedure for removal of judges as envisaged by the Constitution. It examined the question whether removal is within the exclusive domain of Parliament and how misbehaviour or incapacity of a judge is to be proved.

The Court held[196] that in India, the procedure for removal of judges of the higher judiciary consists of two stages. The first one is as contained in Article 124(5) from the initiation of investigation and proof of misbehaviour or incapacity through a judicial processes and the second is as contained in Article 124(4) which is political in nature.[197] The latter commences only when the guilt of the judge is proved in accordance with clause (5).[198] The Court held that "there was a judicious blend of both judicial and political processes"[199] in the matter of removal of judges. The court further held that the judicial procedure should

194. (1991) 4 S.C.C. 699. (*Sub-Committee,* for short).
195. It was alleged that Justice Ramaswamy while he was the Chief Justice of the High Court of Punjab and Haryana committed financial improprieties and irregularities. Inquiries were ordered against him. He refused to co-operate with the same. Later a motion for his removal was presented in the House for his removal. But before the completion of the proceedings, the then Lok Sabha came to a premature closing. Writ petitions were filed before the Supreme Court pleading that the motion lapsed with the dissolution of the House and so the action for removal of a Judge therefore be dropped.
196. The case was decided by a majority of four to one. The majority consisted of Judges B.C. Ray, Venkitachalia, Justice, J.S. Verma. Justice S.C. Agarwal. Justice B.C. Ray delivered the judgement for the majority. Justice L.M. Sharma dissented.
197. *Supra,* n. 194 at pp. 747-48.
198. *Ibid.*
199. *Id.* at p. 731.

governed by the law enacted under Article 124(5) and hence the procedure was statutory in nature.[200] The court clarified that Parliament had no option but to pass the law for regulating the procedure for removal of judges.[201] The court further observed that the scope and ambit of the law enacted under Article 124(5) was wide enough to cover the entire process from the initiation of the motion till the final act of delivery of address as it ensured uniformity and reduced chances for arbitrariness.[202] Such a holding, it was observed, was justified on the ground that it upheld independence of the judiciary.[203] Being statutory in nature, the procedure is subject to judicial review[204] and hence non-compliance with the provisions of the law in the matter is liable to be struck down.

The Court declared that the second part of the process was parliamentary in nature.[205] However, the Court expressed the view that the procedure was not of the ordinary nature governed by the provisions in Articles 118, 119 and 122(1)[206] but was of a special nature governed exclusively by Article 125(4) and the law thereunder. Consequently, the Court declared that

---

200. *Id.* at p. 744. In accordance with Article 124(5), Parliament enacted the Judges Inquiry Act, 1968. It stipulated that if a motion for removal of Judges of the Supreme Court or of the High Court is presented in either House of Parliament, the Speaker or the Chairman as the case may be, shall constitute a Committee for inquiring into the misbehaviour or incapacity of the Judge. [s. 3(2)]. It shall consist of the Chief Justice of India or such other Judges of the Supreme Court, Chief Justice of a High Court or such other Judges of a High Court and a distinguished jurist. [s. 3(2)] After examining evidence, the Committee should then forward to the Speaker or Deputy Chairman as the case may be, its finding as to whether the Judge committed misbehaviour or suffered from incapacity. [s. 4(2)]. If the Committee found the Judge guilty, Parliament would be able to take up the matter and discuss the motion for removal of the Judge. [s. 6(2)]. If, on the other hand, the Committee found the Judge as not guilty, Parliament has no power to take up the motion. [s. 6(1)].
201. *Id.* at pp. 749-50.
202. *Id.* at p. 751.
203. *Id.* at pp. 748-49
204. *Id.* at pp. 744, 46. The Court held, "... the validity of law enacted by the Parliament under clause (5) of Article 124 and the stage upto conclusion of the inquiry in accordance with that law be governed entirely by statute would be open to judicial review..." (at p. 746).
205. *Id.* at p. 744.
206. *Id.* at p. 751.

unlike the ordinary parliamentary procedure which cannot be called in question on the ground of irregularity the procedure for removal of judges was judicially reviewable.[207]

Examining the second question, the Court observed that the prohibition imposed by Article 121 on Parliament to discuss the conduct of judges except on a motion of removal indicated that investigation and proof of misbehaviour of a judge should necessarily be outside Parliament and not within it.[208] The prohibition in Article 121 stands lifted and Parliament empowered to discuss and pass a motion for removal of a judge only when his misbehaviour is proved.[209] Further, in our legal system "proof means one through the judicial process,[210] and not through parliamentary one. The Court therefore concluded that Article 124(4), which stipulates for procedure within Parliament was not a complete code in itself for removal of the judges. Such a construction, of Article 124(4), reducing Article 124(5), which contains the judicial process to self-abnegation, cannot be given.[211] The Court further pointed out that as the motion for presenting an address for removal of judges as envisaged by Article 124(4) was on 'proved misbehaviour or incapacity 'the same should be proved elsewhere.[212] In short the Court held that misbehaviour or incapacity of judges should be proved by judicial process and not by a political process.[213] Consequently, the Court held that the judicial procedure contained in Article 124(5) was not an enabling one but mandatory.[214] Such being the position the Court held that Parliament was not free to strip the judicial process off from the procedure for removal of judges. By

207. The Court held, "Article 124(5) has no comparison with Article 119. Articles 118 and 119 operate in the same field viz... the normal business of the House.... Since Articles 118 and 124(5) operate in different files, ... a law made under Article 124(5) will override the rules made under Article 118 and shall be binding on both the Houses of Parliament. A violation of such a law would constitute illegality and could be immune from judicial scrutiny under Article 122(1).

208. *Id.* at p. 745.

209. *Id.* at p. 743.

210. *Id.* at p. 745.

211. *Id.* at pp. 744-45.

212. *Id.* at p. 743.

213. *Id.* at p. 745.

214. *Id.* at pp. 744-45.

such an interpretation, the Court was able to insulate investigation and proof of misbehaviour or a judge from the influence of political considerations.

Such a decision is justified on yet another ground also. The determination of misbehaviour is not an easy task. Misbehaviour means, conduct inappropriate to the particular role of actor.[215] Judicial misbehaviour is explained by Justice Ramaswamy[216] thus,

> "Wilful abuse of judicial office, wilful misconduct in the office, corruption, lack of integrity, or any other offence involving moral turpitude would be misbehaviour. Misconduct implies actuation of some degree of *mens rea* by the doer. Judicial finding of guilt of grave crime is misconduct. Persistent failure to perform the judicial duties of the Judge or wilful abuse of the office *dolus malus* would be misbehaviour. Misbehaviour would extend to the conduct of the Judge in or beyond the execution of the judicial office."

However, it was also held that "[E]very act or conduct or even error of judgement or negligent acts by higher judiciary *per se* does not amount to misbehaviour."[217]

It is clear that the process of evaluating evidence and proving of misbehaviour demands sound knowledge of the principles of law and requires judicial skill rather political awareness. Members of the legislature may not necessarily be blessed with such essential qualities. If removal for misbehaviour is left fully to the legislature, chances for removal of a judge who has not misbehaved is considerably high as its decision may not be based on proper evaluation of evidence. Such a situation is likely to instill fear in the minds of judges. It is clear that determination of misbehaviour of a judge by judicial process is very cardinal for eliminating political consideration from the procedure for removal. That may be the reason that in England traditionally though impeachment, the

---

215. See, *Black's Law Dictionary* (1990).
216. *Krishnaswamy* v. *Union of India* (1993) 4 S.C.C. 605.
217. *Id.* at p. 651.

punishment for misdemeanour and high treason is by Parliament, misbehaviour is determined by "civil forfeiture proceeding" before a Court.[218] In the U.S also every instance of misconduct is not considered as misbehaviour of the judge. Finding that the constitutionally envisaged procedure for impeaching judges was not an unmixed blessing, there have been demands for improving the same.[219] Thus, conduct of circuit, district and bankruptcy judges would be examined by the Judicial Conference and would be sent for impeachment only if found necessary.[220] Under the Government of India Act, 1935 also the executive could remove judges of the Federal Court only if the Judicial Committee of the Privy Council reported that the judge ought to be removed on grounds of misbehaviour or infirmity of mind or body.[221] These instances indicate that for maintaining judicial independence, the procedure for removal of judges should be under judicial control.

In short, the decision in *Sub-Committee,* that removal of a judge should be proved through a judicial process and that the removal procedure under Article 124 was amenable to judicial review are instances of judicial creativity with a view to protecting judiciary from the onslaughts of the legislature. By such an interpretation, the court was able to avoid the possibility of political consideration in the process of removal of judges of the Supreme Court and High Court and thereby to uphold independence of the judiciary.

Is proof of misbehaviour through the judicial procedure envisaged by the Constitution sufficient to remove a judge? The court had occasion to dwell upon the issue in *Sarojini Ramaswamy* v. *Union of India.*[222] The questions that arose for

---

218. Berger, *op. cit.* at p. 127.
219. See, F.S. Nariman, "The Ramaswamy Case," in Verinder Grover (Ed.) *Political Process and the Role of Courts,* (1997), p. 313 at 316.
220. The Judicial Councils Reform and Judicial Conduct and Disability Act 1980. For the text of the statute, see U.S. Statutes at Large (1980), Vol. 94, Part II, 2035 *et. seq.* in the *Sub-Committee,* the court had discussed the US position also. (See, *supra* n. 194 at p. 726).
221. See, the Government of India Act, 1935, S. 200(2)(a).
222. (1992) 4 SCC 506. In furtherance of the inquiry into the allegations of financial improprieties and irregularities made against Justice Ramaswamy, a report was filed by the Committee constituted under the

consideration in that case were whether the accused judge was entitled to subject the finding of the Committee which found him guilty, to judicial review, and if he was so entitled, at what stage of the proceeding—before or after the adoption of the motion for removal by Parliament—that he could resort to such judicial review.

If removal for misbehaviour is left fully to the political process, chances for removal of a judge who has not misbehaved is considerably high as the decision would normally be triggered by political considerations. Thus it is clear that determination of misbehaviour of a judge by judicial process is very cardinal for eliminating political consideration from the procedure for removal.

Decisions on these issues depended upon the question as to when misbehaviour under Article 124(4) is 'deemed to be proved.' If it is deemed to be proved by the finding of the Judicial Committee that the judge was guilty, judicial review should be available against such a finding. If, on the other hand, it is deemed to be proved only after adoption of the motion to that effect in the Parliament judicial review would not be available against such a finding immediately after the finding of the Committee. A reading of the Judges Inquiry Act, 1968 and the Rules thereunder proves that a finding of guilt by the Committee would not determine misbehaviour of the accused judge. It provides that if the Committee finds him not guilty, the proceedings have to be stopped then and there and Parliament cannot proceed with the matter.[223] Even if the Committee finds him guilty, removal takes place only if Parliament adopts a motion to that effect and the President orders his removal and not before it.[224] But before adopting such a motion, Parliament

Judges Inquiry Act, 1968. The accused judge requested for a copy of the report, so as to enable him to seek redress in the court of law if necessary. The present petition was filed by the wife of Justice Ramaswamy to direct the Committee to provide the accused, i.e. her husband with a copy of the report.

223. The Judges Inquiry Act, 1968. Sec. 6(1).

224. *Id.* S. 6(3). It reads, "If the motion is adopted by each House of Parliament in accordance with the provisions of clause (4) of Article 124 or, as the case may be, in accordance with that clause read with Article 218 of the Constitution, then, the misbehaviour or incapacity of the Judge shall be deemed to have been proved and an address praying for the removal of the Judge shall be presented in the prescribed manner to the

has to scrutinize the opinions of the majority of the members of the Committee, holding that the judge was guilty; the opinion of the dissenting member, if any, holding that the judge was not guilty[225] and the comment of the Judge against whom the motion is proposed is to be adopted.[226] The finding of the Committee therefore is only a recommendation, which may or may not be acted upon by Parliament.[227] Such a scheme and constitutional set-up make it clear, the Court held, that misbehaviour was not 'deemed to be proved' by the finding of the Committee that the Judge was guilty and that it is proved only when a motion to that effect is adopted by Parliament.[228] Therefore, the court held that misbehaviour of a judge is 'deemed to be proved' only after completion of the judicial and parliamentary procedures under Article 124.[229] Consequently, the Court came to the conclusion that the petitioner was entitled for review of the action for his removal only after and not before the completion of the parliamentary procedure.[230]

Does judicial examination of the validity of removal amount to judicial review of parliamentary action? Legislature being the final authority to determine matters within the House, no external authority should be competent to interfere with.[231] Procedure being a matter within the House, the House has to be its own judge and no review by the judiciary is permissible.[232] The Constitution of India also prohibits judicial incursion into parliamentary procedure.[233] If removal of judges under Article

President by each House of Parliament in the same session in which the motion has been adopted."

225. Supra, n. 222 at pp. 546-47.
226. *Id.* at p. 548.
227. *Ibid.*
228. *Id.* at p. 547.
229. *Id.* at p. 557. See also *Sub-Committee, supra* n. 194 at p. 748.
230. *Id.* at p. 573.
231. See, for instance, S.A. de Smith, *Constitutional and Administrative Law,* (1973) at pp. 321-22.
232. *Bradlaugh v. Gossett,* 12 Q.B. D. 271 (1884). Such a view taken beacause, most of the transactions in the House are political in nature and are beyond judicially manaageable standards. See also, *Coleman v. Miller,* 307 U.S. 433.
233. Article 122. It reads, "The validity of any proceedings in Parliament shall not be called in question on the ground of any alleged irregularity or procedure."

124 is treated as merely a procedure falling exclusively within the parliamentary procedure judiciary cannot review it.[234] In *Sarojini Ramaswamy*[235] the Court held that though removal of a judge under Article 124 was finalized only after the adoption of the motion in the House, determination of misbehaviour of the Judge by the Committee of Inquiry constituted under the Judges Inquiry Act, 1968 is a condition precedent for commencement of the parliamentary process culminating in the Presidential order of removal.[236] For, without such a finding, there is no foundation for adopting the motion for presenting an address to the President for removal of a judge.[237] This indicates that adoption of the motion is only parliamentary approval of a finding by a committee outside the Parliament. Such a parliamentary approval *ipso facto* cannot have the effect of excluding judicial review of a procedure on permissible grounds.[238] Therefore, intervention of the parliamentary part of the process in the matter does not totally exclude judicial review. The court drew justification for such a view from the decisions of *Re Keshav Singh*[239] and *Sub-Committee*[240] also. The Court further held that there was no meaning in excluding judicial review at the end of the process of removal of a judge where it is a composite process

234. A U.S. Court in *Halstead L. Ritter* v. *U.S.* 84 Court of Claims 293, (as cited in *supra*, n. 216 at p. 663) refused to interfere with a decision of the legislature to remove a judge on the ground that it was solely a parliamentary procedure.
235. *Supra*, n. 222.
236. *Id.* at p. 561.
237. *Id.* at p. 559.
238. *Id.* at p. 561. The Court held, "The clear indication, therefore, is that mere parliamentary approval of an action or even a report by an outside authority when without such approval the action or report is ineffective by itself, does not have the effecting of excluding judicial review on the permissible grounds."
239. A.I.R. 1965 S.C. 745.
240. (1991) 4 S.C.C. 699.
241. *Supra*, n. 222 at p. 569. It is clear from the holding of the Court that it used the expressions parliamentary proceedings and political process interchangeably. They are different through interconnected. But, in substance they denote the same thing, viz. The procedure that takes place inside the legislative house. However, the Court, at a later stage (at p. 569) used the more comprehensive expression "political question doctrine" which covers both the above expressions. A political question is one "which Courts will refuse to take cognizance, or to decide, on

of which parliamentary process forms a part.[241] For such a conclusion, the Court drew justification from the view of U.S. Supreme Court in *Kilburn v. Thomson*[242] and *Powell v. Mc Cormack*[243] that judiciary could not keep away from deciding issues on the ground that they were political in nature. The Court extended the scope of judicial review over such questions[244] observing that judicial review was the exercise of the inherent power of the Court to determine legality of an action and to award suitable reliefs.[245] The Court therefore came to a conclusion that its jurisdiction was wide enough to encompass determination of the questions of removal of judges.[246] The court also observed that since misbehaviour of a judge is 'deemed to be proved' only after completion of the whole process contemplated by Article 124 interdiction of judicial review in the process before its completion will help only to protract the procedure for removal of judges.[247] The Court concluded that only such a view would ensure preservation of the right, interest and dignity of the learned

---

account of their purely political character , or *because their determination would involve an encroachment upon the executive or legislative power." Black's Law Dictionary*. (Emphasis added)

242. 103 US 168 (1880). The House of Representatives passed a resolution for taking steps to realize the amount due to the US from a debtor and the plaintiff was directed to appear as witness. He refused to answer to some of the questions. The House of Representatives ordered his arrest for contempt of the House. He approached the court against trespass and false imprisonment. The defense was that being a question of contempt of the House, courts had no jurisdiction over the issue. The Court held, "Especially it is competent and proper for this Court to consider whether its [the legislature's] proceedings are in conformity with the Constitution and the law...." (at p. 390).
243. 395 U.S. 486 (1969). That was a petition by a member challenging the decision of the House of Representatives to exclude him from the House and denial of his seniority in the House on certain allegations against him. Accepting *Kilbourn* and *Baker* v. *Carr*, 369 US 186, (1962) it was held that the issue did not bar judicial examination of the issue as conferment of such a power on the Congress would be against the intent of the framers of the Constitution.
244. *Supra*, n. 222 at pp. 563-64.
245. *Id*. at p. 561.
246. *Ibid*.
247. *Id*. at p. 553.

Judge and commensurate with the dignity of all the institutions and functionaries involved in the process.[248]

By the decision in *Sub-Committee* the court made it clear that removal of judges was statutory in nature, that it was fully dependent upon judicial procedure involved in it and that Parliament could not take up the motion for removal in the absence of a finding of misbehaviour by a judicial process. Further, Parliament could not strip that judicial procedure contained in Article 124 to wield ultimate control. The court made it clear that such an interpretation which gave pride of place to the judicial process alone promoted independence of the judiciary.[249] In *Sarojini Ramaswamy*, the court went further and held that judicial review extended to parliamentary and political processes also. In other words, the court brought the entire process for removal of judges within the scope of judicial review.[250] In this sense, *Sarojini Ramaswamy* extends the logic of *Sub-Committee* and therefore undoubtedly is its befitting successor. As a result of these decisions, chances for arbitrary removal of judges by Parliament thus stands considerably reduced. Even the critics of these decisions agree on the creativity of these decisions.[251] In short, by a creative interpretation of the provisions in *Sub-Committee* and *Sarojini Ramaswamy*, the court was able to take removal of judges out of

248. *Id.* at p. 559.
249. *Supra*, n. 194 at pp. 740-41.
250. *Supra*, n. 222 at p. 559. The Court held, "In the event of an order of removal being made by the President under Article 124(4), the right of the Judge concerned to seek judicial review on permissible grounds would be for quashing the order of removal made against him on the basis that the finding of 'guilty' made by the Inquiry Committee in its report which matured into 'proved misbehaviour' on adoption of the motion by Parliament suffers from an illegality rendering it void resulting in the extinction of the condition precedent for commencement of the parliamentary process for removal in the absence of which there is no foundation for considering or adopting the motion for presenting an address to the President for removal of the judge and, therefore, no authority in the President to make the order of removal."
251. See for instance, Seervai, *Constitutional Law of India, Vol. III* (1996), pp. 2909-27. He observes, (at p. 2923) "I may add that in the *Judicial Accountability Case* and *Sarojini Ramaswamy's Case*, the Judges showed great solicitude that no injury was done to the Judges "dignity, position and reputation."

the control of the legislature and bring it under the control of judicial review and thereby to uphold independence of the judiciary.

(b) Impeachment—the Only Mode of Removal?

A question that was mooted abroad was whether impeachment by the legislature was the only mode of removal of judges who have misbehaved. The general view is that it is.[252] In the US, impeachment applies not only to high crimes and misdemeanours but also to acts which affect public welfare.[253] Hence, there is a strong view that the only constitutionally permissible method of removal of judges is impeachment.[254] However, in England, it is opined not to be the sole method for removal. There, impeachment was considered as a criminal procedure against misdemeanour and high treason while other instances of misconduct of judges could be dealt with in accordance with judicial proceeding, which is civil in nature.[255] One thing is clear from this. Judges cannot be removed except through a well-defined procedure on settled principles. Such a scheme is very much necessary for maintaining judicial independence. Members of judiciary should not be open tothreats of removal from unexpected quarters as such threats may adversely affect judicial independence. Hence, a meaningful concept of judicial independence should be wide enough to include within it safeguard against threats from any quarters—even from the public. Since the procedure for removal of judges of the higher judiciary in India simulate that of the other countries, these issues are live in India also. In *Ravichandra Iyyar* v. *Justice A.M. Bhattacharjea*,[256] the court had to deal with such an issue. In that case, the court held that our Constitution

252. Berger, *op. cit.* at p. 123.
253. W. Willoughby, *The Constitutional Law of the United States*, Vol. III, (1929), p. 1449.
254. Berger, *op. cit.* at pp. 123, 135-53.
255. *Id.* at p. 127 *et. seq.*
256. (1995) 5 SCC 457. That was a petition filed by a lawyer of the High Court of Bombay alleging that the Chief Justice of the High Court received huge royalty from a publisher abroad for his two books. The petition was to order the Central Bureau of Investigation to enquire into it and if found correct, to direct the Speaker to initiate action against the Judge under Article 124(4).

permitted removal of judges only when a motion was carried out with the requisite majority in both the Houses of Parliament recommending such removal by the President. It means that the Constitution of India does not permit any action by any agency other than the initiation of the action under Article 124(4).[257] The Constitution does not permit any forum other than the one contemplated to investigate or inquire into or discuss the conduct of a judge or the performance of his duties and on/off court behaviour except as per the procedure provided under Article 124(4) and (5) of the Constitution.

The court has reached such a conclusion on the ground that while there was an express provision regarding the subject in the Constitution, others not so mentioned are impliedly excluded.[258] By the holding the court has effectively curtailed scope of potential threats to judges from various quarters like scandalizing of judges by litigants, advocates or other members of the public.

Will such a restraint amount to curtailment of freedom of speech and expression guaranteed under Article 19(1)(a)? The court observed that advocates have the freedom of opinion under Article 19(1)(a) to criticize and condemn a judge and exercise of such an invaluable right in public interest should not be gagged.[259] However, the court held that exercise of such a right to criticize judicial conduct "must be measured, strictly rational, sober and proceed from the highest motives without being coloured by partisan spirit or pressure tactics or intimidatory attitude."[260] The court further held that exercise of

---

257. *Id.* at p. 482. The court held, "Our Constitution permits removal of the Judge only when the motion was carried with requisite majority of both Houses of Parliament recommending to the President for removal. In other words, the Constitution does not permit any other action by any agency other than the initiation of the action under Article 124(4) by Parliament....discussion of the conduct of a Judge or any evaluation or inference as to its merit is not permissible elsewhere except during investigation before the Inquiry Committee constituted under the [Judges Enquiry] Act for this purpose".
258. *Expressio unius exclusio alterius* is a principle accepted in constitutional interpretation. It means that express mention of one person or thing is exclusion of another. See Berger, *op. cit.*, pp. 137-41.
259. *Supra*, n. 256 at p. 478.
260. *Ibid.*

the right in violation of the above rule would call for punishment.[261] By the holding the court has harmoniously construed the freedom of speech and expression on the one hand and independence of the judiciary on the other and gave pride of place to judicial independence over the right to the freedom of expression. Such a view is justified, as judicial independence is more important than the fundamental rights. A contrary interpretation is likely to lead to a situation in which even an honest and sincere judge may at times be embarrassed due to scandalizing and demoralizing discussion about his conduct.[262]

While holding that removal procedure envisaged by Article 124(4) is the sole procedure for terminating the judges of the higher judiciary, the court held that the same can be invoked only against impeachable behaviour and not against "minor offences and abrasive conduct" of judges.[263] It is clear that the court identified a wide gap between mere misconduct on the one hand and impeachable misbehaviour on the other. The court observed,[264]

> "Yet every action or omission by the judicial officer in performance of his duties...may not be misbehaviour indictable by impeachment. But...may produce deleterious effect on the integrity and impartiality of the Judge. Every misbehaviour in juxtaposition to good behaviour, as a conditional tautology, will not support impeachment but a misbehaviour which is not a good behaviour may be improper conduct not befitting to the standard expected of a Judge."

In other words, there is a "yawning gap between proved misbehaviour and bad conduct inconsistent with the high office" of a Judge.[265] The court held that in such instances where the conduct does not warrant removal, the judge was to be kept

261. *Ibid.*
262. See also observations of Justice A.S. Anand in *Chetak Consttructions Ltd.*, v. *Om Prakash*, AIR 1998 SC 1855 that such scandalizing of judges affects judicial independence.
263. *Supra* n. 256 at p. 471.
264. *Id.* at p 479.
265. *Id.* at p. 482.

under supervision and control in a manner without affecting judicial independence. Analyzing the issue at the theoretical level, the court held that where misconduct does not amount to misbehaviour, the remedy lay in self-regulation by the judiciary. The court agreed with the juristic view[266] that control of the fate of judges by bureaucrats was unwise and therefore it would be prudent to have self-regulation.[267] It was held that if complaints relating to the conduct of a judge of a High Court are made by the Bar Association, the Chief Justice of the High Court should verify its truth from independent sources by an enquiry. He should consult the Chief Justice of India wherever necessary and once the matter has gained the attention of the Chief Justice of India, the Bar Association should suspend all actions to enable disposal of the matter. The Chief Justice of India may "tender such advice either directly or may initiate such action, as is deemed necessary or warrant under given facts and circumstance."[268] If the complaint relates to the Chief Justice of the High Court, the matter should be directly sent to the Chief Justice of India.[269] Such course, according to the court, facilitated nipping in the bud the conduct of the judge leading to loss of public confidence in the courts and to sustain public respect for the judiciary. Independence of the judiciary and the stream of public justice, the court held, would thus remain pure and unsullied.[270]

The court highlighted the role of the Chief Justice of India for regulating the conduct of judges in such cases where their conduct does not amount misbehaviour on specific grounds. The Chief Justice of India is known as the head of the judiciary. in matters of appointment and transfer of judges of the higher judiciary, the executive can act only according to his recommendations.[271] Likewise, for registering a criminal case against a judge prior consent and approval of the Chief Justice

266. *Id.* at p. 480. See also Irving R. Kaufman, "Chilling Judicial Independence", 88 Yale L.J. 681 (1978-79).
267. *Id.* at pp. 480-81. See also Harry T. Edwards, "Regulating Judicial Misconduct and Divining 'Good Behaviour' for Federal Judges," 87 Mich. L.R. 765 (at pp. 778-85).
268. *Supra,* n. 256 at p. 481.
269. *Ibid.*
270. *Ibid.*
271. *S.C. Advocates* v. *Union of India,* (1993) 4 SCC 441. For a detailed discussion of the case, see *supra,* Chapter 3.

of India should be obtained.[272] All these indicate that though first among equals, the Chief Justice of India has been conferred with a special status. Therefore, the court concluded that cases of judicial misconduct not amounting to 'misbehaviour' could be dealt with by the Chief Justice of India. The court held, "the yawning gap between proved misbehaviour and bad conduct inconsistent with the high office on the part of a non-cooperating Judge/Chief Justice of a High Court could disciplined by self-regulation through in-house procedure. This in-house procedure would fill in the constitutional gap and would yield salutary effect."[273]

The decision in *Ravichandra Iyyer* is remarkable for two reasons from the point of independence of judiciary. Firstly, it categorizes judicial misconduct as impeachable and non-impeachable and limits removal to the former. By such a holding, the court avoids chances of threats of removal for minor misconduct, which warrants merely a reproof, warning or a minor punishment as removal in such cases would be unfair and contrary to the principles of independence of the judiciary. Secondly, the decision brings such minor misconduct of judges under the control of the Chief Justice of India. By bringing such instances of misconduct fully under the control of the judiciary, likelihood of other authorities being a storehouse of threat to the freethinking of judges was avoided and judicial independence upheld. However, it is yet to be seen how far the Chief Justice of India could effectively regulate the conduct of judges and what punishment could be imposed upon them.

However, it is doubtful whether the provision dealing with removal of judges of the higher judiciary is without any lacunae. One of the patently visible defects of the provision is the inability of the judiciary to exclude a judge, who, according to it, is not to continue as a judge. Though an independent judge cannot be removed by the decision of Parliament, in the wake of the provisions, removal of a judge whose misbehaviour or incapacity is proved remains in the decision of the Parliament. This lacuna came to light when the misbehaviour of one of the judges of the High Court of Calcutta was proved by the inquiry conducted by the committee constituted by the Supreme Court.

---

272. *K. Veeraswamy* v. *Union of India*, (1991) 3 SCC 665.
273. *Supra*, n. 256 at p. 482.

The Chief Justice of India could do nothing but recommend to the government that the erring judge may be removed according to Article 124. It has to be accepted that the predicament is a discredit to the judicial system.[274]

Be that as it may, the decision in *Sub-Committee, Sarojini Ramaswamy* and *Ravichandra Iyyer* constitute a tribune in the matter of removal of judges of the higher judiciary. They can be considered as supplementary and complementary to each other. Each decision is fitted into the others in such a manner as to lay down an objective and just procedure for punishing the erring judges. *Sub-Committee* and *Sarojini Ramaswamy* lay down the law for cases of serious misbehaviour warranting removal of judges while *Ravichandra Iyyer* deals with instances of misconduct which do not call their removal. These cases bear testimony to the observation of the court in *Sub-Committee* that the provisions for removal of judges should be interpreted with a view to achieve judicial independence.[275] They also reveal as to what extent judiciary can be creative in interpreting the provisions dealing with the removal of judges with a view to securing independence of the judiciary.

---

274. The case of Justice Soumitra Sen that arose in 2008 reveals the defect of the present law. There were some allegations that while he was practicing as Advocate, he misappropriated money he received as the Court Receiver. An in-house committee appointed by the Chief Justice of India constituted to inquire into the allegations observed that he misappropriated money he received as the Court Receiver and reported on 1.2.2008 that he should be removed from office. On the basis of the report, the Chief Justice of India wrote to the Prime Minister "recommending the initiating of the proceedings for removal" contemplated by Article 217(1) read with Article 124(4). See, V. Venkatesan and Suhrid Sankar Chattopadhyay, "The Judiciary, Judges in the Dock," *Frontline*, Vol. 25, Issue 20, Sept. 27-Oct. 10, 2008 available at www. Hindu.net.nic accessed on 1.5.2009. However, the Rajya Sabha appointed a panel to "investigate the grounds on which the removal of Justice Soumitra Sen of the Calcutta High Court is prayed for." See, *The Hindu*, 31 May, 2009, Kochi, p. 10. In other words, the process has not started even after the elapse of more than a year of the letter written by the Chief Justice of India recommending his removal.
275. *Supra*, n. 194 (at p. 719). It was observed, "In interpreting the constitutional provisions in this are the Court should adopt a construction which strengthens the foundational features and the basic structure of the Constitution. Rule of law is a basic feature of the Constitution which permeates the whole of the constitutional fabric and is an integral part of the constitutional structure. Independence of the judiciary is an essential attribute of rule of law."

5

Independence of the Lower Judiciary

The Constitution of India envisages a system of judiciary with a three-tier arrangement. The union judiciary consists of the Supreme Court[1] and the State judiciary consists of the High Courts[2] and the subordinate courts.[3] By the expression 'subordinate courts', the Constitution means the judiciary consisting of courts below the High Court.[4] It includes District Courts and other civil and criminal courts. The provisions in the Constitution relating to subordinate courts deal with appointment, promotion and posting of judges of those courts and also with control of such courts by the High Court. The

1. See, the Constitution of India, Articles 124 to 147.
2. *Id.* Articles 217 to 232.
3. *Id.* Part VI Chapter VI.
4. The expression 'subordinate' in relation to courts is criticized as being one contrary to the notion of independence. "Indeed, the expression subordinate judiciary, all too often used by the appellate justices and embodied in the Constitution, violates the very notion of independent judiciary." Baxi, *Courage, Craft and Contention* (1985), p. 25. It may be recalled that neither the Supreme Court nor High Court is under the administrative control of any other authority.

distinguishing mark of the provisions in contradistinction with those dealing with the higher judiciary is that subordinate judiciary is brought fully and directly under the administrative control of High Court.[5]

Appointment, posting and promotion of district judges are to be effected by the Governor in consultation with the High Court.[6] Appointment of persons other than district judges is made by the Governor in accordance with the rules framed by him after consulting the State Public Service Commission and the High Court.[7] The High Court is vested with the power of control over district and other subordinate courts.[8] Though the Governor is the authority to appoint judges of the subordinate judiciary, it is evident that he does not enjoy a free hand in the matter. The consultative process envisaged in the matter checks the possibility of executive arbitrariness.

Just like every provision dealing with the higher judiciary, those dealing with the subordinate judiciary were enacted for securing independence of the institution.[9] On many occasions

5. Article 235, see, *infra*, n. 8. The Supreme Court being the highest court, is not under the control of any other authority. High Courts also are not under the supervisory control of the Supreme Court. See, *Chief Justice, High Court, Madhya Pradesh* v. *Mohan Kumar*, 1994 Supp. (2) S.C.C. 602.
6. Article 233. It reads, "Appointment of persons to be, and the posting and promotion of, district judges in any State shall be made by the Governor of the State in consultation with the High Court exercising jurisdiction in relation to such State."
7. Article 234. It reads, "Appointment of persons other than district judges to the judicial service of State shall be made by the Governor of the State in accordance with rules made by him in that behalf after consultation with the State Public Service Commission and the High Court exercising jurisdiction in relation to such State."
8. Article 235. "The control over district courts and courts subordinate thereto including the posting and promotion of, and the grant of leave to, persons belonging to the judicial service of a State and holding any post inferior to the post of district judge shall be vested in the High Court but nothing in this Article shall be construed as taking away from any such person any right of appeal which he may have under the law regulating the conditions of his service or as authorizing the High Court to deal with him otherwise than in accordance with the conditions of his service prescribed under such law."
9. See the view of Dr. B.R. Ambedkar in the Constituent Assembly. He said: "...the object of these provisions [the provisions dealing with the subordinate judiciary] is two-fold: first of all, to make provision for the appointment of district judges and subordinate judges and their

the Supreme Court had to deal with these provisions. What has been the attitude of the Supreme Court in construing these provisions? How far has the court successful in this task? It will be of interest to examine these aspects.

I. APPOINTMENT OF DISTRICT JUDGES

(a) 'Consultation' under Article 233

Appointment of judges is an executive function.[10] The Governor, when he effects appointments, can be assumed to act on the aid and advice of the Council of Ministers.[11] Unless bridled, such executive power is likely to run riot due to political consideration. Therefore, is it not necessary to render a construction to the provision whereby the power of the Governor to appoint District Judges is effectively restrained? The question was given a serious consideration by the Supreme Court in *Chandra Mohan* v. *State of U.P.*[12] The Court observed that under Article 233 the Governor[13] had to exercise his power after consultation with High Court and held that the requirement of such a consultation would be breached if it was effected with a different body or if no consultation was effected at all. Consultation with a committee consisting of a few judges

qualifications. The second object is to place the whole of the civil judiciary under the control of the High Court." *C.A.D.*, Vol. IX, pp. 1570-71.

10. *S.P. Gupta* v. *Union of India*, 1981 (Supp.) S.C.C. 87. See *supra*, Chapter, 3, n. 10.
11. Article 163 (1). It runs thus, "There shall be a Council of Ministers with the Chief Minister at the head to aid and advice the Governor in the exercise of his function except in so far as he is by or under the Constitution required to exercise his functions or any of them in his discretion. See also *infra*, n. 13.
12. A.I.R. 1966 S.C. 1987. Under the provisions of the U.P. Higher Judicial Services Rules framed under Article 309 certain persons were selected district judges by a committee consisting of two Judges of the High Court. The Court approved the selection. The petition and later the appeal were filed on the grounds *inter alia*, that the selection was not in consultation with the High Court as envisaged by Article 233 and hence was bad.
13. The Court said, "We are assuming for the purpose of these appeals that the "Governor" under Article 233 shall act on the advice of the Ministers. So, the "Governor" used in the judgement means Governor acting on the advice of the Ministers." *Id.* at p. 1990. (*per* Subba Rao J.)

of the High Court was not a valid one. The Court therefore insisted that the body to be consulted under Article 233 could be none other than the High Court. The reason was very well explained by the Court in the following words:[14]

> "The object of consultation is apparent. The High Court is expected to know better than the Governor in regard to the suitability or otherwise of a person, belonging either to the "judicial service" or to the Bar, to be appointed as a district judge. Therefore, a duty is enjoined on the Governor to make the appointment in consultation with a body which is the appropriate authority to give advice to him."

The Court thus clarified that the power of the Governor to appoint district judges was conditional upon consultation with High Court and violation of the condition would make the appointment unconstitutional. *Chandra Mohan* restricted the scope of the power of the executive by holding that the Governor could not appoint judges solely in accordance with the aid and advice of the Council of Ministers or in consultation with some judges of the High Court. In other words, by a creative interpretation of the provision, the Court had read down the mandate of Article 163(1) to the provision for consultation under Article 233.

What is the impact and influence of the view of the High Court, when consulted, on the Governor in appointing district judges? Is Governor bound by the view of the High Court? Or has he got an option after considering the views of the High Court to take a different view? In *Chandra Mouleswar* v. *Patna High Court*,[15] it was held that though consultation with the High Court as mandatory, the view of the High Court was not binding on the Governor notwithstanding the fact that High Court was better posited to know the relative merits of the candidates.[16] In other words, it is not unconstitutional for the

14. *Ibid*.
15. A.I.R. 1970 S.C. 370. The petitioner was officiating as Additional District Judge. The High Court issued an order declaring some of the respondents senior to him. He challenges the order under Article 32.
16. Referring to the scope of consultation in Article 233, the Court said, "The underlying idea of the Article is that the Governor should make up his mind after there has been a deliberation with the High Court... . The

Governor to take a decision contrary to the opinion expressed by the High Court. The view that the ultimate authority to appoint district judges was the Governor was accepted later in *Panduranga Rao* v. *State of A.P.*[17] and *Mani Subrat Jain* v. *State of Haryana*.[18] However, in *Panduranga Rao* the Court observed that though it was not obligatory for the government to appoint persons as according to the recommendations of the High Court, the government could convey the reasons for not appointing the persons so recommended.[19] The implication of the holding is that though the recommendations of High Court were not binding on the government, the court restricted the liberty of the executive to reject the recommendation without communicating the reasons to the High Court. The Court, however, struck a different note in this respect in *Hari Dutt* v. *State of H.P.*[20] and stressed on the importance of the opinion of High Court in selection of district judges. It was observed that High Court was the proper authority to determine as to the person to be so promoted. The Court observed,[21]

High Court alone knows their merits as also demerits. This does not mean that the Governor must accept what advice is given by the High Court but the Article does require that the Governor should obtain from the High Court its views on the merits and demerits of persons among whom the choice of promotion is to be limited." (*Id.* at pp. 374-75).

17. A.I.R. 1975 S.C. 1922. That was an appeal by Special Leave against the decision of the High Court of Andhra Pradesh. The government appointed six district judges of which only two were the recommendees of the High Court. Appointment of the persons who were not recommended and non-appointment of the appellant were challenged in this appeal.
18. A.I.R. 1977 S.C. 276. The appellants who were direct recruits asked for *mandamus* directing the respondents to appoint them as Additional District and Sessions Judge. The State government was not interested in posting them. The High Courts dismissed the petitions on the ground that the initial appointments were to be effected by the State government. They came in appeal by special leave.
19. *Supra*, n. 17 at p. 1924.
20. A.I.R. 1980 S.C. 1426. Appointments of certain persons as district judges by promotion on the basis of seniority were effected. The challenge of the petitioner was that as in the case of initial appointment of persons, appointment by promotion to the posts of district judges should also be on the basis of merit. The Court held that such appointments could either be on seniority or merit as decided by High Court.
21. *Id.* at p. 1430.

> Article 233 confers power on the Governor of the State to appoint persons either by direct recruitment or by promotion from amongst those in the judicial service as District Judges but this power is hedged in with the condition that it can be exercised by the Governor in consultation with the High Court. In order to make this consultation meaningful and purposive the Governor has to consult High Court in respect of appointment of each person as District Judge which includes an Additional District Judge and the opinions expressed by the High Court must be given full weight. Article 235 invests control over subordinate courts including the officers manning subordinate courts as well as the ministerial staff attached to such courts in the High Court. Therefore, when promotion is to be given to the post of District Judge from amongst those belonging to subordinate judicial service, the High Court unquestionably will be competent to decide whether a person is fit for promotion and consistent with its decision to recommend or not to recommend such person. The Governor who would be acting on the advice of the Minister would hardly be in a position to have intimate knowledge about the quality and qualification of such person for promotion.

Evidently, the Court in this case was reading the provision for consultation for appointing district judges in the light of the power conferred on High Courts to control the subordinate judiciary. The Court extended considerable emphasis and force to the opinion of the High Court in view of the opportunity it has to supervise, watch and control the members of the subordinate judiciary under Article 235 and therefore to assess the quality of the persons in the judicial service, which opportunity is not available to the Governor. The Court thus read the power of the Governor under Article 233 to appoint district judges in the light of the controlling power of the High Court under Article 235. Obviously, such a creative interpretation of Article 233 was made to rescue the subordinate judiciary from the controls and onslaughts of the executive. Such a construction of the provision is undoubtedly an instance of innovative interpretation of the Constitution. It can be considered as a significant step of the judiciary to materialise the ideal of separation of powers as envisaged by the makers of the Constitution.[22] Thus in each successive decision the Court was giving meaningful content to consultation with High Court with a view to securing independence of judiciary.

Clarifying and further explaining the position, the Court in *M.M. Gupta* v. *State of Jammu and Kashmir*,[23] held that as a matter of rule, for appointing judges, the Governor should accept the recommendations of the High Court. If the Governor finds "good and weighty reasons" for rejecting them, the same should be communicated to the High Court.[24] The Court feared that ignoring the recommendations of the High Court might lead to erosion of judicial independence. The Court held,

> "....persons who are interested in being appointed District Judge whether directly or by promotion, will try to lobby with the executive and curry favour with the Government for getting these appointments and there is every possibility of the independence of such persons so appointed being undermined with the consequence that the course of justice will suffer."[25]

What is the remedy if the Governor did not communicate the reasons for not accepting the recommendations of the High Court? The answer to this question is found in *State of Kerala* v. *A. Lakshmikutty*.[26] The question raised in that case was whether

22. See the Constitution of India, Article 50. It reads, "The State shall take steps to separate the judiciary from the executive in the public services of the State."
23. A.I.R. 1982 S.C. 1579. That was a writ petition filed against the decision of the State government to appoint certain persons as district judges in accordance with the recommendations of the sub-committee of the cabinet ignoring the recommendations of the High Court under the provisions of Constitution of Jammu and Kashmir which corresponds to Article 233 of the Constitution of India.
24. *Id.* at p. 1593.
25. *Ibid.*
26. A.I.R. 1987 S.C. 331. This case arose against the decision of the government of Kerala not to implement the recommendations of the High Court for appointing district judges on the ground that if appointments were effected on its basis, reservation could not be implemented.

High Court could issue a writ of mandamus for appointing district judges. The Court held that the government could reject the recommendations of the High Court only after communicating its difficulties in accepting them. It was further held that on receiving such intimation from the government, the High Court had an obligation to express its views after considering such facts and circumstances. The Court went a step ahead and held that if the government was not communicating its views to the High Court, a writ of *mandamus* could be issued to the government to place before the Court its difficulties in implementing the recommendations of the High Court.[27] The Court was of the view that it was the High Court and not the government which should adjudge the suitability of the candidate and therefore also the cycle of rotation for the purpose of reservation.[28]

As a result of the above decisions, the scope and extent of the concept of 'consultation' under Article 233(1) has become very clear. Now, Governor cannot appoint district judges without consulting High Court.[29] The recommendations of the High Court are not binding on the Governor.[30] Nevertheless, he cannot brush aside the opinion of High Court, as it knows the merits and qualifications of the candidates better than the executive does.[31] In other words, consultation under Article 233 with the High Court cannot be reduced to an empty formality.[32] It is clear that in these cases the Court rightly construed the significance of consultation with High Court. The reasons for the decision in *Hari Dutt* was the fact that the High Court was more competent than the executive to select the fit person as district judge. In *M.M. Gupta,* the decision was based on the need to prevent a situation of the power of the executive leading to nepotism, favouritism and shaking the very foundations of judicial independence. The decision in *Lakshmikutty,* could be seen as the first step towards judicial review of the decision of the government in the matter of appointment of district judges

27. *Id.* at p. 346.
28. *Id.* at p. 348.
29. *Chandra Mohan, supra,* n. 12.
30. *Chandra Mouleswar, supra,* n. 15.
31. *M.M. Gupta, supra,* n. 23.
32. *Chanda Mouleswar, supra,* n. 15.

in so far as the Court declared that government was under an obligation to state the reason why the recommendations of the High Court regarding appointment of district judges could not be implemented. All these decisions could be considered as indices to the view of the Court that in the matter of appointing district judges influence of the executive should be reduced to a minimum so as to protect judicial independence. The Court was exhibiting high creativity in emphasizing the importance of the recommendations of the High Court and construing the constitutional provisions accordingly.

Still later the Supreme Court went ahead of what it said in the previous cases and held that the power of legislature in the matter of appointment of judges to subordinate judiciary is very limited in view of independence of judiciary. In *State of Bihar* v. *Bal Mukund Sah*,[33] the question was whether the State legislature was competent to enact the Bihar Reservation of Vacancies in Posts and Services (for Scheduled Castes, Scheduled Tribes and Other Backward Classes) Act, 1991 as section 4 of the Act provided for reservation in direct recruitment to the posts of District Judges and other subordinate judges. The High Court struck down the advertisement in accordance with the Act on the ground that the same was *ultra vires* Article 233. Observing that the Constitution "underscores the felt need of separation of the Judiciary from the Executive" and that the Constitution has made separate provisions for subordinate judiciary[34] and that for preserving the independence of judiciary as envisaged by the Constitution, judiciary should be insulated from the interference of the legislature, for which consultation with the High Court is laid down under Articles 233 and 234.[35] Hence, no appointments could be made by the Governor to the subordinate judiciary without the rules framed in consultation with the High Court.[36] The court therefore, concluded that the state legislature has no role to play in the matter of appointment of District Judges and other subordinate judges[37] and the

33. (2000) 4 SCC 640
34. *Id*. at p. 681.
35. *Id*. at p. 686.
36. *Id*. at p. 688.
37. *Id*. at p. 689.

legislative power under Article 245 and the power to make rules under 309 should be read subject to Articles 233 and 234.[38]

(b) Scope of the Executive Power

What is the scope of the executive power under Article 233? Does it include the power to effect removal of district judges? The provision specifically mentions that the same extends to 'appointments, posting and promotion' of district judges.[39] In *State of Assam* v. *Kuseswar*,[40] the Court held that the power of the Governor under Article 233 encompassed both direct appointment of as well as promotion to be district judges.[41] That is, in the case of appointment of district judges either from the Bar or from the lower judiciary, appointment could be effected by the Governor. Such a view was taken by the Court on a literal construction of the provision which provides for "appointment of persons to be and posting and promotion of district judges" and on reading it in the light of Article 235, which vests High Courts with complete control over the judges subordinate to district judges. In *High Court* v. *State of Haryana*[42] the question whether the power of the Governor under Article 233 extends to confirmation of district judges arose for consideration of the Supreme Court. The Court rendered a restrictive interpretation to the power of the Governor to appoint district judges and held that appointment was complete with the actual placement of a person and that there remained

38. *Id.*, 683. The opinion was rendered by Justice Majmudar with which Justice Pattanaik (at p. 719) and Justice Banerjee (at p. 767) agreed while Sethi J., (who wrote judgement for Khare, J.) dissented.
39. *Supra*, n. 6.
40. A.I.R. 1970 S.C. 1616. That was an appeal against the quo warranto issued by the High Court declaring a district judge as not entitled to hold that office. The original petition was filed by the respondents who were convicted by the district judge whose appointment was held void.
41. *Id.* at p. 1618.
42. A.I.R. 1975 S.C. 613. A district judge was serving on probation. An inquiry was ordered against him in which he was exonerated. But the government wanted to extend the probation to which High Court dissented. The High Court ordered his confirmation. The government denied confirmation and reverted him. The judge challenged the decision of the government before the High Court. High Court held that confirmation was part of the act of appointment and hence with the Governor. That is challenged in this appeal by special leave.

nothing to be done thereafter. Confirmation on completion of probation is neither fresh appointment nor its completion and hence not under the control of the executive. By denying the executive the power to confirm district judges, the Court closed any possibility of leaving their tenure at the pleasure of the government. Therefore, the holding can be considered as an instance in which the Court has been creative in interpreting the scope of the executive power in Article 233 with a view to securing independence of judiciary.[43] Likewise, it was held that the provision did not confer power on the Governor to transfer district judges and that the power was exclusively with the High Court of the State.[44] In *State of Orissa* v. *Sudhansu*,[45] the Court held that though persons to be appointed as law officers or legal remembrancers are to be determined by the government, sparing of services of district judges for such posts could only be with the consent of the High Court and High Court could fix the term of such appointments to executive posts. The High Court was also competent to recall them from the executive posts at anytime it thinks fit and proper[46] and post them as district judges. In short, in view of independence of the judiciary, the extent of the restriction on the power of the executive under Article 233 has been gradually widened by the Supreme Court.

2. APPOINTMENT OF OTHER JUDGES OF SUBORDINATE COURTS

Appointment of judges other than district judges is regulated by Article 234.[47] In this matter also the Governor does

43. *Id.* at p. 623. See, *State of Assam* v. *S.N. Sen*, A.I.R. 1972 S.C. 1028. *infra*, nn. 95 and 96.
44. *State of Assam* v. *Ranga Mohammed*, A.I.R. 1967 S.C. 903. For a detailed discussion of the case, see, *infra*, nn. 76-78.
45. A.I.R. 1968 S.C. 647. That case arose out of the conflict between the High Court and the State Government. Some district judges were appointed law secretaries, legal remembrancers and members of tax tribunal. The High Court took a policy decision to recall such persons to judicial work. The Government did not agree with it. Hence some districts remained without district judges. A lawyer filed a petition to direct the Government to allow them to join as district judges. This is an appeal against it.
46. *Id.* at p. 652.
47. *Supra*, n. 7.

not wield an exclusive power. Such appointments are to be effected by the Governor only in accordance with the Rules framed by him after consultation with the High Court and the State Public Service Commission. In such a context, certain questions may arise. What is the scope of such consultation for framing Rules? Is the Governor bound by the views of the two consultants? If he is, by whose views is he bound in case of a conflict of views between the two consultants?[48] Usually, a judge of the High Court would be a member in the committee for selection of judges under Article 234. When selection of judges is by a committee in which a High Court judge is a member, has his opinion got weightage over that of other members? Such an issue was discussed by the Court in *Ashok Kumar* v. *State of Haryana*.[49] The Court held that in the matter of selecting judges to the subordinate judiciary, the opinion given by the judge of the High Court who is a member of the selection committee should normally be accepted, for he knows the character and quality of the candidates. His opinion should be rejected only for strong and cogent reasons recorded by the Chairman and members of the Public Service Commission. The Court further observed that a sitting judge and not a retired judge of the High Court should be the expert member of the Committee.[50] Later in *Durgacharan Mishra* v. *State of Orissa*,[51] the Court held that the Judge of the High Court who is a member of the selection committee was the competent person to advice

48. Such a question of primacy of conflicting opinions of consultants with reference to appointment of Judges to the higher judiciary was posed before the Court in both the *Judges Case* and *S.C. Advocates*. For a discussion, see *supra*, chapter III.
49. (1985) 4 S.C.C. 417. Appeal by special leave from the decision of High Court of Punjab and Haryana which quashed and set aside selection of persons to the Haryana Civil Services (Executive) and Allied Services by the Haryana Public Service Commission.
50. *Id.* at pp. 456-57. Such a view has been appreciated by jurists. See for example, Shariffil Hassan, "Supreme Court and Appointments to Judicial Service: A Need for Judicial Rethinking," 34 J.I.L.I. 125 (1992).
51. (1987) 4 S.C.C. 646. It was a petition under Article 32 challenging the validity of the list of Munsiffs prepared by the Public Service Commission. The name of the petitioner was excluded on the ground that he did not secure minimum marks for the viva voce as determined by the Commission for which there were no provisions in the Rules.

as to the special qualities required for judicial appointments. It may be in regard of the range of subjects of viva voce, standard of questions to be put to the candidates and the acceptance of the answers given thereof.[52] By these decisions, the Court emphasized that in the matter of selection of judges subordinate to district judges also the power of the executive was not unchecked. The creative element of these decisions is that the Court brought the process of selection under the control of the High Court by reading in the restrictions other than those found in the provision in Article 234 in relation to selection of judges other than district judges. In short, the role of High Courts was not limited to one of a consultant in the rule making process. It extended to actual selection process also. Conferment of primacy to the opinion of the judicial member over that of members of the Public Service Commission in the selection of judges highlights the vital role of High Court in this respect. The holding that rejection of the opinion of the judicial member of the committee should be only for recorded reasons carries with it the idea that unreasonable or prejudiced executive decisions are likely to be struck down.

In *A.C. Thalwal* v. *High Court of H.P*[53] the Supreme Court reiterated the above view and held that securing independence of judiciary is a bulwark of democracy. In view of *S.C. Advocates -on-Record,* and the constitutional scheme which assigned primacy of place to High Court, consultation under Article 234 was not a matter of mere formality. It has to be 'meaningful and effective' and the opinion of the High Court should enjoy primacy over that of the Public Service Commission.[54] In *Sanjay Singh* v. *U.P. P.S.C.,*[55] the Supreme Court reiterated the view that in the wake of Article 234, the Judicial Rules framed after

52. *Id.* at p. 653.
53. 2000 (7) SCC 1. Taking his previous military service into consideration, the appellant was given seniority over his seniors in the judicial service by about 11 years. Later, the High Court struck down the same. Hence the appeal.
54. *Id.* at p. 9.
55. (2007) 3 SCC 720. In this case, the petitioners were the unsuccessful candidates in the recruitment to the posts of Civil Judges (Junior Division). They challenged the selection under Article 32 of the Constitution on the ground that the evaluation of candidates 'by statistical scaling' led to lower ranking of meritorious candidates.

consultation with the High Court should prevail over the Rules framed for selection for non-judicial posts.[56]

A comparative study of the provisions dealing with appointment of judges to the higher judiciary on the one hand and the lower judiciary on the other and the response of the Supreme Court to the issues in them reveal some similarities and much contrasts. Appointment of judges to the higher judiciary is effected by the President while that of the subordinate courts is by the State executive namely the Governor. While appointing judges of the Supreme Court, the President has to consult the Chief Justice of India, and other judges as he deems fit. Judges of the High Courts are to be appointed by President after consulting the Chief Justice of India, the Chief Justice of the High Court concerned and the Governor. But judges of the subordinate judiciary are to be appointed by the Governor only after consulting the High Court concerned. A comparative study of the approach of the Supreme Court to the issues involved in relation to appointment of judges reveals that in dealing with the issues relating to the subordinate judiciary, the Court expressed mature views at an early stage itself while in construing the provisions relating to the appointment of judges to the higher judiciary, the Court expressed very conservative views. The Court had provided content to the concept of consultation in appointing judges to the subordinate judiciary in a manner fitting to the context as early as 1966 in *Chandra Mohan* as explained in *Hari Dutt* in 1980 in which it was opined that as a rule the view of the High Court should be accepted in appointing judges of the subordinate courts since the High Court is more qualified to determine whether a person is fit to be appointed as a judge of the subordinate court. The view that the judiciary is more competent than the executive to determine as to who is fit to be a judge should have effective application in relation to appointment of judges to the higher judiciary. But in the *Judges Case*, the Court had extended a very literal meaning to the provisions relating to appointment of judges of the Supreme Court and High Courts leading to conferment of arbitrary powers to the executive. In short, the Court showed enviable

56. *Id*. at p. 736.

creativity in construing the provisions relating to appointment of judges to the subordinate judiciary at a very early stage.

3. CONDITIONS OF SERVICE OF JUDGES OF THE LOWER JUDICIARY

Conditions of service of judges of the subordinate judiciary form another important aspect that has correlation with judicial independence. The Constitution does not contain any specific provision for them. The conditions of service are prescribed by the subordinate service rules made by the respective States. However, the Constitution provides that judges of the subordinate judiciary are under the control of the High Court.[57] What is the scope and extent of the powers so conferred on High Court? The Supreme Court had occasion to examine the scope and extent of this power on many occasions. Could the Supreme Court deal with the issue in a manner conducive to independence of judiciary?

In *State of West Bengal* v. *Nripendra Bagchi*,[58] the Court held that what is vested with the High Court under Article 235 was control over the subordinate judiciary and that "control is useless if it is not accompanied by disciplinary powers."[59] The Court concluded that the power therefore included disciplinary jurisdiction also. Further, it would not be possible for the High Court to run to the government for every instance of disciplinary action. In other words, the term 'control' in Article 235 denotes not only the day-to-day working of the subordinate judiciary but also the disciplinary jurisdiction over the presiding judge.[60] The Court made such a decision consciously to protect independence of the subordinate judiciary as it was observed that Article 235 was enacted with a view to securing independence of the judiciary.[61] Leaving of disciplinary power

57. See the Constitution of India, Article 235, *supra*, n. 8.
58. A.I.R. 1966 S.C. 447. The Government conducted a disciplinary inquiry against the respondent who was a district and session judge and dismissed him from the service without consulting the High Court. The High Court quashed the inquiry as well as the order of dismissal. The State filed an appeal against the order of the High Court.
59. *Id.* at p. 454.
60. *Id.* at p. 453.
61. *Id.* at p. 454.

to the Executive may destroy the very judicial independence.[62] Hence it was not agreeable for the Court to construe the provision in a narrow manner excluding the disciplinary jurisdiction. It is clear from the decision that the Court gave a wide perspective to the concept of 'control' keeping in view the need to protect judicial independence.

In *State of Haryana* v. *Inderprakash*,[63] relating to termination of service of a District Judge, the Court held that though the executive was the authority to dismiss judges, such termination should be done only on the advice of the High Court. In other words, though as appointing authority, the power of termination is vested in the Governor, that power can be exercised under Article 233 only subject to the recommendations of the High Court, since the power of control vested on the High Court includes disciplinary jurisdiction. The scope of Article 233 was thus construed in the light of Article 235 of the Constitution.[64] The Court reiterated its view that the power of the High Court under Article 235 would be meaningless unless it encompassed disciplinary powers. The

62. "Nothing is more likely to sap the independence of the magistrate than the knowledge that his career depends upon the favour of a minister." Islington Committee Report, para 337 at p. 701 as quoted by the Supreme Court in *id*. at p. 452.
63. A.I.R. 1976 S.C. 1841. The High Court opined that the respondent was incompetent to continue as a District Judge and recommended his reversion as a Chief Judicial Magistrate. Disregarding this recommendation, the Government ordered his retirement. The High Court struck down the order of the government. The State came in appeal.
64. The Court held, "The control vested in the High Court is that if the High Court is of the opinion that a particular Judicial Officer is not fit to be retained in service the High Court will communicate that to the Governor because, the Governor is the authority to dismiss. . . . In such cases, it is the contemplation in the Constitution that the Governor as the head of the State will act in harmony with the recommendation of the High Court. If the recommendation of the High Court is not held to be binding on the State, consequences will be unfortunate. It is in public interest that the State will accept the recommendations of the High Court. The vesting of complete control over the Subordinate Judiciary in the High Court leads to this that the decision of the High Court in matters within its jurisdiction will bind the State. 'The Government will act on the recommendation of the High Court. That is the broad basis of Article 235.' *Id*. at p. 1845. See also *Baldev Raj, infra*, n. 66 at pp. 2496-97.

Court explained the scope of disciplinary jurisdiction in a very wide perspective. It was observed that disciplinary jurisdiction did not mean merely the jurisdiction to award punishment for misconduct. It embraced the power to determine whether the record of the servant was satisfactory or not, so as to entitle him to continue in service till he attains the age of superannuating.[65]

In conformity with these decisions, the Court in *Baldev Raj* v. *Punjab and Haryana High Court*,[66] relating to a case of a subordinate judge held that the control of the High Court under Article 235 was exclusive and so in a disciplinary matter of the subordinate judiciary the Governor could not ignore the recommendations of the High Court and take a contrary stand in consultation with the Public Service Commission. As a result of these decisions, in the matter of termination of service, the executive power of the Governor under Articles 233 and 234 have been read down and made subject to the administrative control of the High Court under Article 235. In *Chief Justice, Andhra Pradesh* v. *Dixitulu*,[67] a constitutional bench of the Supreme Court had occasion to examine the scope of the power of the High Court under Article 235. Observing that the power was all comprehensive, the Court held,[68]

> "Article 235 is the pivot round which the entire scheme of the chapter revolves... The position crystallized . . . is that

65. *Id.* at p. 1844.
66. A.I.R. 1976 S.C. 2490. The appellant was servicing as a Subordinate Judge. The High Court recommended after due enquiry that his service should be terminated. But the Governor sought the view of the Public Service Commission which opined otherwise. So the judge was exonerated and retained in service. Though the High Court required the Governor to review the decision, he did no do it. The High Court therefore refused to pass posting order for the appellant. The petition filed by the judge before the High Court for posting and payment of salary was dismissed. The judge moved the Supreme Court in appeal.
67. A.I.R. 1979 S.C. 193. The respondents in the appeal were compulsorily retired by the High Court in two different cases. They approached the Administrative Tribunal which has got jurisdiction by virtue of Article 371-D. The Tribunal quashed the respective orders of the High Court. The High Court approached the Supreme Court against the order on the ground *inter alia* that in the context of the basic and fundamental scheme of the Constitution, servants of High Court and subordinate judiciary were outside its scope.
68. *Id.* at p. 201.

> the control over the subordinate judiciary vested in the High Court under Article 235 is exclusive in nature, comprehensive in extent and effective in operation."

The question in that case was whether judicial officers of the subordinate judiciary could be considered as in civil service and governed by the Administrative Tribunals under Article 371-D of the Constitution. Looking into the legislative history of Article 371-D, the Court observed that it was enacted with a view to catering certain objects having no nexus with independence of judiciary, which is vouchsafed by Article 235. Judicial independence was not a criterion for enacting Article 371-D. In such a context, if subordinate judiciary was brought under Article 371-D, the control vested in the High Court over it would be eroded.[69] The Court held that in view of the special provision in Article 235 for judges of the lower judiciary, they would not be considered as in "civil service" under Article 371-D and therefore their service matters could not be determined by Administrative Tribunals which settle disputes of civil servants.[70] Such an interpretation of the provisions with a view to achieving judicial independence is an instance where the Supreme Court has been highly innovative. Such an interpretation is justified on yet another reason also. Article 371-D is a general provision dealing with conditions of service of civil servants while Article 235 is a special one for controlling judges of the subordinate judiciary. Though judges could be generally called as those in civil service, since there is a special provision regulating their service in Article 235, a general provision in Article 371-D will not be applicable to them. For, it is accepted that in case of conflict between general and special provisions, the general one should give way to the special one.[71] By such an interpretation, judges of the subordinate judiciary were taken out from the jurisdiction of the Administrative Tribunals.

69. *Id.* at p. 207.
70. *Id.* at p. 208.
71. *Generalia specialbus non derogant* which means that the general provision should not derogate from the special ones. The Court however, did not specifically apply the maxim in this case. See Broom's Legal Maxims (2000), p. 443 *et. seq.*

Later, in *All India Judges Association* v. *Union of India*,[72] while extending the age of superannuation of judges of the subordinate judiciary from 55 to 60, the Court held that all such judges were not entitled for such an extension. It was held that at the age of 58, the High Court should assess and evaluate the performance of judges and they would be entitled for superannuation at the age of 60 only if so recommended by the High Court. By the decision, the Court extended the scope of Article 235 to the assessment of the performance of judges to determine their age of retirement.

Does the concept 'control' under Article 235 include the power to promote a judge of the subordinate judiciary? The Constitution vests the Governor with the power to promote a judge to be a district judge.[73] However, it does not specifically mention anything about the promotion of other judges. In *State of Assam* v. *Kuseswar*,[74] the question of promotion of a subordinate judge was dealt with by the Court. The Court held that the power to promote a judge subordinate to the district judge was vested with the High Court and that it was to be exercised in accordance with Article 235. It was held that the State government could not amend the regulating statute whereby High Court is divested of its power to control under Article 235 and the government is conferred with the power under Article 233 since such a course impairs independence of judiciary.[75]

Who has got the power to transfer a judge of the subordinate judiciary, the High Court or the Governor? That question came up before the Supreme Court in *State of Assam* v.

72. (1992) 1 S.C.C. 119. Petition under Article 32 for reliefs through directions for setting up of All India Judicial Service and for bringing about uniform conditions of service for members of the subordinate judiciary throughout the country.
73. Article 233, *supra*, n. 6.
74. A.I.R. 1970 S.C. 1616. The Civil Courts Act, 1967 was amended by the State to change the nomenclature of subordinate judge as Assistant District Judge. It was alleged that the amendment was for divesting the High Court with the power to promote sub-judges and to vest it with the Governor.
75. *Id.* at p. 1619. See also *High Court, Calcutta* v. *A.K. Roy*, A.I.R. 1962 S.C. 1704.

Rangu Mohammad.[76] The answer to that question depends upon determination of the issue under which Article the instance of transfer comes. Is the power to transfer included in the control exercised by the High Court under Article 235? Or does it fall within the power relating to 'appointment' of persons to be, and the posting and promotion of district judges under Article 233, by the Governor? The Court held that under Article 233 the word 'posting' read in the light of accompanying words, 'appointment' and 'promotion', meant only position or job to which one is appointed and 'not to station one at a place'. Therefore it did not carry with it the meaning of the word 'transfer'.[77] The Court further reasoned that transfer operates at a stage later to appointment and promotion. Moreover, the High Court knows the capacity for work of individuals and the requirements of a particular station. The Court observed that "however, well meaning a Minister may be he can never possess the same intimate knowledge of the working of the judiciary as a whole and of the individual Judges, as the High Court.... The Chief Justice and his colleagues know these matters and deal with them personally. There is less chance of being influenced by secretaries who may withhold some vital information if they are interested themselves."[78] Therefore the Court held that the High Court is better suited to make transfers and hence the power resides in the High Court.

Here also, the Court made a comparative analysis of Articles 233 and 235 for determining the scope and extent of the powers of the High Court. Article 233 was restrictively interpreted and the scope of Article 235 was widened so as to confer High Courts the power to transfer the District Judges. The Court arrived at such a conclusion because the High Court would be in a position to take an impartial decision in the

---

76. A.I.R. 1967 S.C. 903. The State Government issued a notification appointing some District Judges by promotion and some other by transfers. The notification is challenged in this case by the respondent as unconstitutional on the ground that transfers were to be effected by the High Court. The High Court held that transfers could be effected by High Court. The State came in appeal under Article 132 on the ground that the power to transfer district judges lies with it.
77. *Id.* at p. 906.
78. *Id.* at 907.

matter and such impartiality is the minimum requirement to ensure judicial independence. If the place of work of judges is likely to change according to the whim and fancies of the executive, or depending on whether the judges toe the line of the executive, independence of the judicial officers will undoubtedly be affected adversely.[79] The holding of the Court certainly reflects the judicial policy to uphold judicial independence.

In *State of U.P.* v *Batuk Deopathi Tripathi*[80] a different question came up for consideration. Does the power of the High Court to control the subordinate judiciary include the power to make Rules so as to exercise its control under Article 235 effectively? A constitutional bench of the Supreme Court held that though the power to frame Rules is conferred on the High Court under Article 225, that was not the sole repository of rule-making power. Article 235 vests power to control on the entire body of judges of the High Court,[81] but the High Court could prescribe the manner in which the power under Article 235 was to be exercised. For, a power to do a thing carries with it the power to regulate the manner in which it may be done. Moreover, the power under Article 235 comprises of numerous matters demanding considerations of minutest details.[82] If the

79. A comparison of this decision with that of *S.P. Gupta* v. *Union of India*, 1981 (Supp.) S.C.C. 87 makes it clear that the Court in that case held a very regressive view as it held that the power to transfer Judges of High Courts ultimately resided in the Executive. See *supra*, Chapter 4, n. 109.
80. (1978) 2 S.C.C. 102. The respondent joined the service as Munsiff and later promoted as a district judge. On request from the government, the High Court proposed his compulsory retirement. The decision was taken by an Administrative Committee constituted in accordance with the rules framed by the High Court recommended the retirement of the appellant. The decision was challenged by him in the High Court on the ground that the decision should have been taken by the High Court and not by an Administrative Committee constituted by the court.
81. *Id.* at p. 110. Article 229, which provides for appointment of officers and servants of the High Court, in contradiction to Article 235, confers power on the Chief Justice of India. Article 235 confers power on the High Court presumably for protecting the independence of the judiciary. See, *High Court of Judicature for Rajasthan*, v. *Ramesh Chand Paliwal*, (1998) 3 SCC 72, 87.
82. For an in-exhaustive list of those incidence, see, *Chief Justice, Andhra Pradesh* v. *Dixitulu*, A.I.R. 1979 S.C. 193.

whole High Court is required to consider every one of them, exercise of the control becomes delayed and confused. So, it will be effective only if a committee was conferred with an authority under Article 235.[83] Therefore, the Court held that the "seeds of the jurisdiction to frame rules regulating the manner in which the control over subordinate Courts is to be exercised are to be found in the very nature of the power. The High Court has therefore the power under Article 235 itself to frame rules for regulating the manner in which the thing may be done."[84] If the High Court is not having the power to decide the mode of exercising its control under Article 235, the very power conferred by the provision would be made nugatory. A power to do something envisages the power to do it effectively. Therefore, the Court cautioned that such rule making should not be exercised in derogation of or to dilute the powers constitutionally conferred on the High Court.[85] In short, the holding of the Court establishes the supremacy of the High Court.

In *B.S. Yadav* v. *State of Haryana*[86] a slightly different question arose for consideration. The question was whether under Article 235, High Court had the power to frame rules for regulating the conditions of service of the subordinate Courts.[87] Analysing the provision the Court held that the plane reading of Articles 235[88] and 309[89] reveals that the power to make rules for

83. *Supra*, n. 80 at p. 113.
84. *Id.* at p. 110.
85. *Id.* at pp. 110-11.
86. A.I.R 1981 S.C. 561. That was a writ petition filed under Article 32 questioning the fixation of seniority of judges by direct recruitment and promotion *inter-se* in the Punjab and Haryana superior judicial service under the rules framed by the Governor under Article 309. The Rules thus framed were amended time and again without consulting the High Court.
87. In *Batuk Tripathi*, the question was whether High Court had the power to frame rules for the purpose of exercising the power vested on it under Article 235. The question, here, on the other hand, is whether Article 235 confers on High Court the power to frame rules for regulating the conditions of service of judges of the subordinate courts.
88. *Supra*, n. 8.
89. Article 309 reads: "Subject to the provisions this Constitution, Acts of the appropriate Legislature may regulate the recruitment, and conditions of service of persons appointed, to public services and posts in connection with the affairs of the Union or of any State:

the subordinate judiciary is vested in the Governor and not in the High Court. The second part of Article 235 provides that the power of the High Court to control the subordinate Courts would be subject to the law in that behalf. Such a power cannot be subject to the law laid down by the High Court itself.[90] If the Constitution makers intended to confer High Court with a rule-making power, (which is legislative in nature) they could have specifically conferred the same on the High Court. Further, Article 309 clarifies that it is the Governor who has the power to make rules, and such an executive power is not violative of the controlling jurisdiction of the High Court under Article 235.[91] However, the power conferred on the Governor by Article 309 is not absolute. It provides that the power under Article 309 can be exercised 'subject to the provisions of the Constitution'. Therefore, the Court made the point clear that the legislative or rule-making power could not be exercised by the Governor in such a manner as to impair the power of the High Court under Article 235. Therefore, the Court held that application of the rules so made to each individual case should reside in the High Court and not in the Governor or the legislature.[92] It means

---

Provided that it shall be competent for the President or such other person as he may direct in the case of services and posts in connection with the affairs of the Union, and for the Governor of a State or such other person as he may direct in the case of services and posts in connection with the affairs of a State, to make rules regulating the recruitment, and the conditions of service of persons appointed to such posts until provision in that behalf is made by or under an Act of the appropriate Legislature under this Article, and any rules so made shall have effect subject to the provisions of any such Act."

90. *Supra*, n. 86 at p. 576.
91. *Id*. at p. 577.
92. *Id*. at pp. 578-79. The Court held, "The opening words of Article 309 'Subject to the provisions of this Constitution' do not exclude the provision contained in the first part of Article 235. It follows that though the legislature or the Governor has the power to regulate seniority of judicial officers by laying down rules of general application, that power cannot be exercised in a manner which will lead to interference with the control vested in the High Court by the first part of Article 235. In a word, the application of law governing seniority must be left to the High Court. ...though rules of recruitment can provide for a period of probation, the question whether a particular judicial officer has satisfactorily completed his probation or not is a matter which is exclusively in the domain of the High Court to decide."

determination of seniority of judges *inter-se* and decisions as to whether judges have successfully completed probation in accordance with Rules so framed are matters to be decided by the High Court.[93] The holding indicates that the rule making power cannot be exercised by the Governor in such a way as to destroy the control of the High Court under Article 235. Therefore the Court wished that in future the Governor might amend the Rules relating to the service of judges of the subordinate courts only in consultation with the High Court. The Court observed:[94]

> "Nothing will be lost thereby and there is so much to gain: Goodwill, expert advice and the benefit of the experience of a body which has to administer the Rules since the control over the Subordinate Courts is vested in it by Article 235."

In *B.S. Yadav* the Court was trying to effect a nice balance between powers of the High Court under Article 235 relating to control of subordinate courts and the rule-making power of the Executive under Article 309. The Court recognised the legislative power in such a manner as not to adversely affect the control of the High Court. In rendering such a construction, the Court has taken into account the damage that would happen to judicial independence by such impairment of control of the High Court. In other words, the power to frame rules and to implement them were not left free to the Executive. Instead they were made subject to judicial approval by insisting on the process of consultation before the promulgation of the rules and by vesting the complete power of application of the rules in the High Court itself by a creative interpretation of the constitutional provisions. Thus the possibility of executive

93. *Id.* at pp. 578-79.
94. *Id.* at p. 587. However, in *State of Jammu & Kashmir* v. *A.R. Zakkir*, 1993 Supp. (1) S.C.C.548, where the legislature failed to comply with the suggestion of the High Court to amend the J.K. Civil Service (Judicial) Rules to avail the reservation for its employees in the judicial service, the Court held that that writ of mandamus could not be issued against the legislature to enact law. (at p. 554).

arbitrariness is excluded and independence of the subordinate judiciary protected.

Similarly in *State of Assam* v. *S.N. Sen*[95] the Court held that under Article 235, High Court alone had the power to promote judges of the subordinate judiciary other than District Judges. It implies that the power to confirm such promotions also resides in the High Court.[96] In this case, the Court gave content to Article 235 in such a way as to exclude intervention of the Executive in the service affairs of the subordinate judiciary.

The Court examined the scope and extent of the power of the High Court to control subordinate judiciary under Article 235 in *Chief Justice, Andhra Pradesh* v. *Dixitulu*.[97] The Court enumerated the instances of the power of High Court to control the subordinate courts. The Court identified disciplinary jurisdiction and complete control over subordinate courts, power to suspend a member with view to disciplinary enquiry, transfer, promote and confirm persons subordinate to District Judges, transfer of District Judges, recall of District Judges posted on ex-cadre posts or on deputation, award of selection grade to members of the judicial service including District Judges, confirmation of District Judges, and premature and compulsory retirement of District and other Judges as part and parcel of the power of the High Court to control subordinate judiciary under Article 235.[98]

Is the control of the High Court limited to the power over the judicial officers or does it extent to control over ministerial staff of subordinate judiciary? The Court in *Lakshmikant Dhal* v.

95. A.I.R. 1972 S.C.1028.
96. *Id.* at p. 1030. In that the respondent was appointed Munsiff and later promoted as Additional Sub-Judge in a temporary post. He was subsequently confirmed in the post by the High Court. The Accountant General however objected it as the post was temporary. He filed the petition for getting him confirmed. The High Court allowed the petition. Hence the appeal.
97. A.I.R. 1979 S.C. 193. See, *supra*, n. 67.
98. *Id.* at pp. 201-02. In *High Court of Punjab and Haryana* v. *Iswar Chand Jain*, A.I.R. 1999 S.C. 1677, the Supreme Court held that inspection of subordinate courts also formed part of the power of the High Court to control subordinate courts under Article 235.

State of Orissa[99] held that in view of the decision in *S.P. Sampath Kumar* v. *Union of India,*[100] Article 235 extends over the ministerial staff of the subordinate judiciary also. It was therefore held that the Administrative Tribunal could not have jurisdiction over the ministerial staff of the District Courts as it would affect the power of the High Court under Article 235 to control subordinate judiciary.[101]

In *T. Lakshmi Narasimhachari* v. *High Court, Andhra Pradesh,*[102] an interesting question arose for consideration of the Supreme Court. In its attempt to harmonise the power of High Court under Article 235 with A.P. Civil Services (Classification, Control & Appeal) Rules 1963 which provided that appeal against the recommendation for dismissing a judge of the lower judiciary by the High Court would lie to the Governor. The Court held that in such a case, if an appeal was made by the dismissed judge to the Governor, he had to forward the appeal to the High Court for its reconsideration. However, the Court further held that the Governor was bound by the decision of the High Court in such a case also.[103] The Court held that only such a course would help avoiding erosion of control vested in the High Court under Article 235. Such a procedure would also satisfy the requirement of appeal and reconsideration as contained in Article 235.[104]

99. 88 (Supp.) S.C.C. 504. The appellants were selected for appointment of ministerial posts in the courts of district judges. The selection was vacated. It was challenged before the Administrative Tribunal, which dismissed the petitions on merit. The order of the Tribunal is challenged in appeal.
100. (1987) 1 S.C.C. 124. The Government agreed that the Administrative Tribunal constituted under the Administrative Tribunal Act 1985 would not have jurisdiction over the members and employees of the subordinate judiciary
101. *Supra* , n. 99 at pp. 504-05.
102. (1996) 5 S.C.C. 90. The appellant was a judge in the subordinate judiciary. There was an allegation that he forced a litigant to have illicit relationship with him. Charges were framed and after an inquiry by the district judge his removal from the service was ordered. Removal was effected by the High Court without referring the matter to the Governor. He appealed to the Governor who set the order aside. That was overruled by the High Court. Hence he came in appeal.
103. *Id.* at p. 98.
104. *Id.* at pp. 98-99.

Can High Court delegate the power under Article 235 to another authority? Every power envisages within its ambit the power to delegate it. An analysis of cases dealing with this aspect brings out that the Supreme Court recognized such a power with the High Court only to the extent of not damaging independence of the judiciary. The issue was discussed for the first time in *Samsher Singh* v. *State of Punjab*.[105] The Court held that the power conferred on the High Court under Article 235 was so important in upholding the dignity and independence of the subordinate judiciary, that the High Court cannot abdicate that power to an executive authority. While quashing the termination of the appellant on the basis of an inquiry conducted by the executive, the Court held that the subordinate judiciary was not only under the control of the High Court but also under its care and custody. Hence inquiry should have been conducted by the High Court through a district judge. And transfer of that power to an authority under the executive was in disregard of Article 235.[106] However, the Court recognized delegation of the power to control without marring independence of subordinate judiciary in *State of U.P.* v. *Batuk Deo Tripathi*[107] and *High Court of Judicature, Bombay* v. *Shirish Kumar Ranga Rao Patil*.[108] Such a construction of the power under Article 235 bears testimony to the resourceful interpretation of the Supreme Court for achieving judicial independence.

A survey of the landmark cases dealing with the subordinate judiciary highlights certain important features. Every decision, right from the earliest ones, stands testimony to

---

105. A.I.R. 1974 S.C. 2192. The appellants were terminated as members of the Punjab Civil Service (Judicial Branch) during probation. The termination was challenged by them on the ground *inter alia* that there was no proper inquiry. In the case of one of the appellants, the High Court required the Government to get the inquiry conducted by the Director of Vigilance.
106. *Id.* at p. 2207.
107. *Supra*, n. 80.
108. (1997) 6 S.C.C. 339. That was an appeal by special leave against the quashing of the removal of the respondent as the Civil Judge on proof of corruption on the ground that his dismissal was recommended by a Committee of Judges and not by the High Court. Allowing the appeal, the Supreme Court held that High Courts could delegate the powers conferred by Article 235.

the anxious effort of the Supreme Court to keep the subordinate judiciary free from the influence of the executive. The Supreme Court opposed every attempt of the respective State Governments to bring the subordinate judiciary under its wings. As freedom from executive control is its cardinal feature, it is evident from these cases that the apex court was championing the cause of judicial independence. Restrictive interpretation of the scope of the executive power under Article 233 in cases like *Chandra Mohan* and *Chandra Mouleswar* and cases exploring the extent of control of High Court under Article 235 bear testimony to this fact. The consistent holdings to reduce the power of the executive to appoint and dismiss judges of the subordinate judiciary and the residue of the powers including the disciplinary jurisdiction on the High Court is indicative of this attitude.[109] Conferment of such a wide and undefined power to High Court was justified by the Supreme Court in the following words,[110]

> "For the first time, in the country's history, appeared in the Constitution of India the concept of control over subordinate courts to vest in the High Courts. The quality of exclusive control of the High Court does not appear to be whittled by the constitutional device of all orders being issued in the name of the Governor as the head of State administration. When, therefore, the High Court exercising disciplinary control over the subordinate judiciary finds, after a proper enquiry, that a certain officer is guilty... and, therefore, recommends to the Governor his removal or dismissal, it is difficult to conceive how and under what circumstances such a recommendation should be rejected by the Governor acting with the aid and advice of the council of ministers.... It is in this context that this court has more than once observed that the recommendations of the

---

109. The only exception to this trend, perhaps, could be found in *Baradakanta Misra* v. *Orissa High Court*, A.I.R. 1976 S.C. 1899, where the Court agreed that the power to reduce the rank of a Judge was with the Executive. However, the Court held that the same could be effected by the executive only on the recommendation of the High Court.

110. *Beldev Raj* v. *Punjab and Haryana High Court*, A.I.R. 1976 S.C. 2490 at pp. 2496-97.

High Court in respect of judicial officers should always be accepted by the Governor. This is the inner significance of the constitutional provisions relating to the subordinate judiciary. Whenever in an extra ordinary case, rare in itself, the Governor fails, for certain reasons, that he is unable to accept the High Court's recommendations, these reasons will be communicated to the High Court to enable it to reconsider the matter. It is, however inconceivable that, without reference to the High Court, the Governor would pass an order which had not been earlier recommended by the High Court. That will be contrary to the contemplation in the Constitution and should not take place."

Such a view was given further impetus when Article 235 has been considered by the Supreme Court as a measure for self-introspection by the judiciary against corruption in it.[111]

4. CONTROL OF HIGH COURTS *VIS-A-VIS* INDEPENDENCE OF JUDICIARY

The above discussion reveals that very wide jurisdiction was conferred on High Courts over the subordinate courts for securing their independence. However, independence of judiciary requires check on curtailment of judicial freedom even from the colleagues of judges as well as from the higher judiciary.[112] So *a carte blanche* to the High Court in the guise of power to control the subordinate judiciary would violate the spirit of judicial independence. It is true that such a power is vested with the High Court to divest the executive of any control over the subordinate judiciary. Conferment of wide

111. *High Court of Judicature at Bombay* v. *Shrish Kumar Ranga Rao Patil*, (1997) 6 S.C.C. 339. Justice K. Ramaswamy for the Court held in an inimitable style thus, "The lymph nodes (cancer cells) of corruption constantly keep creeping into the vital veins of the judiciary and the need to stem it out by judicial surgery lies on the judiciary itself by its self-imposed or corrective measures or disciplinary action under the doctrine of control enshrined in Articles 235, 124(6) of the Constitution. It would therefore, be necessary that there should be constant vigil by the High Court concerned on its subordinate judiciary and self-introspection." (at p. 358).

112. For the concept, see, *supra*, chapter II.

powers in the higher judiciary may have the effect of avoiding control of executive over judiciary; but the question still remains whether such a measure protects to the fullest extent independence of judiciary. For, construction of the provision in such a way as to confer unrestrained power to the High Court is likely to mar the very concept of judicial independence. There are at least a few instances where the highest judicial forum of the State went wrong while exercising its power under Article 235. What remedy has the Supreme Court to offer against such aspersions on the judicial independence by the High Court? Is there any way out from such attacks on judicial independence from within the judiciary?

High Court, Calcutta v. *Amal Kumar*[113] is an interesting instance in which this issue has been discussed. The Supreme Court held that the power of the High Court to control under Article 235 was a complete one which contains in it the discretion to pass over a judge by others to the higher cadre even without initiating any disciplinary action against him. The holding amounted to acquiescence of the power with the High Court that without initiating a disciplinary action against a judge, his due promotion could be indefinitely withheld. The result of such a holding is that even when there is no disciplinary action pending against a servant, he would not be entitled to take up action against the High Court before any other authority for denial of promotion. The decision is open to objection as nowadays due promotion of judges forms part of legitimate expectation and breach of that expectation without due process is certainly violative of their independence. Therefore, the holding that control of High Court under Article 235 includes both disciplinary and non-disciplinary (administrative) jurisdiction is directed against the interest of judicial independence.

---

113. A.I.R. 1962 S.C. 1704. In this case, the High Court without promoting the respondent, a Munsiff promoted his juniors as Subordinate Judges. He made representation to the Governor. The High Court took the stand that no disciplinary proceedings were pending against the respondent and that his promotion was under its consideration. The petitioner contented that promotion of his juniors superseding his claim was violative of his rights, he filed a suit in the civil court for his promotion and salary which was allowed. The matter was taken in appeal by the High Court.

In *Tejpal* v. *State of U.P.*[114] the Court rendered a very constructive interpretation to the power to control vested in High Courts by Article 235 and checked exercise of the power in a perfunctory manner. The question that came up for consideration was whether the decision of the government to compulsorily retire a judge could be subsequently ratified by the High Court. It was held that it was for the High Court on the basis of assessment of performance and other aspects germane, to reach the conclusion whether a judicial officer is to be terminated as the power is vested in it. The Court agreed that in view of *Batuk Deo Tripathi,*[115] the decision could be taken by the Administrative Committee of the Court. But, High Court's ratifying the decision of the government to terminate a judge is wrong, as the initiative for removal should always come from the High Court.[116] Such a decision insists that the decision to remove a judge should always be taken by the High Court and what remains with the executive is only complying with its recommendation. Such a view is protective of the independence of judicial officers of the subordinate courts. In *Beena Tiwari v. State of M.P.*[117] services of the appellants who were officiating civil judges were found not satisfactory by the High Court and hence it was recommended that they were not to be confirmed. The Apex Court in appeal held that from the facts and records of the case, non-confirmation of the appellants as civil judges by the High Court was not justified.[118] The Supreme Court held that the High Court exceeded the limits of its jurisdiction in a

114. A.I.R. 1986 S.C. 1814. The appellant was serving as the district and session judge. The government decided that the appellant be prematurely retired. The Administrative Judge of the High Court agreed with the proposal and the Governor passed an order accordingly. Later the Administrative Committee of the High Court gave its approval to the recommendation of the Administrative Judge. A writ petition was filed in the High Court challenging the order of premature retirement *inter alia* on the grounds that the order was without the recommendation of the High Court and hence violated Article 235 and that it was violative Articles 14, 16 and 311(2) of the Constitution. That was dismissed. He came in appeal.
115. *Supra,* n. 80.
116. *Supra,* n. 114. at pp. 1820-21.
117. 1988 (Supp.) S.C.C. 213.
118. *Id.* at p. 218.

manner adversely affecting judicial independence. Hence the Court reversed the order and directed the government to reinstate them.

Iswar Chand Jain v. *High Court of Punjab and Haryana*[119] is another instance in which the exercise of control of the subordinate courts by the High Court under Article 235 was found by the Court as contrary to the spirit of independence of the judiciary. Trying to streamline the power of the High Court, the Supreme Court held that the power of the High Court under Article 235 to control subordinate judiciary was administrative in nature which was open to judicial review. The Court discouraged the exercise of the power by the High Court in an indiscriminate style, and observed.[120]

> "While exercising that control it is under a constitutional obligation to guide and protect judicial officers. If complaints are entertained on trifling matters relating to judicial orders . . . it would be difficult for him to discharge his duties in an honest and independent manner.... *If High Court encourages anonymous complaints to hold the field the subordinate judiciary will not be able to administer justice in an independent and honest manner. It is therefore imperative that the High Court should also take steps to protect its honest officers...*"

It is clear from the decisions discussed above that the intention of the Court was to check arbitrariness of the High Courts in controlling the subordinate courts. The Court made this point clear in *R.C. Sood* v. *High Court of Rajasthan*.[121] In this case, the Supreme Court had an opportunity to deal with an instance in which the High Court invoked its power to control

---

119. (1988) 3 S.C.C. 370. Here the appellant was an Additional District Judge. On allegations from the Bar Associations and some litigant there was a vigilance enquiry against him. On its basis, completion of probation was left undeclared leading to his termination. Earlier the High Court had given him an entry of satisfaction, which was later altered by it. But no material was placed before the Supreme Court for such alteration.
120. *Id.* at pp. 381-382. (Emphasis supplied).
121. 1994 (Supp.) S.C.C. 711.

under Article 235 in an arbitrary manner.[122] The Court observed that fairness and absence of arbitrariness was all the more important in any administrative act of the judiciary and that the power to control the subordinate courts under Article 235 should be exercised in a manner conducive to its independence from the executive.[123]

Does the supervisory jurisdiction of the High Court extend to criticizing judges of the subordinate judiciary and to punishing them for their mistakes and errors though intolerable? In *Kashi Nath Roy* v. *State of Bihar*[124] the Court expressed the view that it does not. The Court quashed an order of the High Court that the petitioner, a judicial officer should not, for certain mistakes committed by him in rendering a judicial decision, be allowed to deal with criminal matters. According to the Court correction of intolerable errors of subordinate judiciary by the superior courts should be "in a manner befitting, maintaining the dignity of the court and independence of the judiciary, convey its message in its judgement to the officer concerned through a process of reasoning, essentially persuasive, reasonable, mallow but clear, and result-orienting, but rarely as a rebuke".[125] The directive force of the principle behind the decision is very clear. It operates as a warning to the High Court that the power under Article 235 should not be exercised so as to damage independence of the judiciary. By such an interpretation of Article 235, the Supreme Court has excluded exercise of judicial

---

122. The petitioner was a district judge. Before that he was the Registrar of the High Court. He was placed under suspension on the ground that as Registrar, he was responsible for some patent mistakes crept into the notification inviting application to certain posts in the Rajasthan Higher Judicial Service. The Supreme Court observed that even after careful scrutiny there was no evidence to prove that the mistake committed was intentional to benefit any one in whom he had some interest.
123. *Supra*, n. 121 at p. 716.
124. (1996) 4 S.C.C. 539. In this case the petitioner was a judicial officer in the Superior Judicial Service. Application for bail was allowed by him which on appeal was rejected by the High Court. While deciding the appeal the judge of the High Court ordered that the petitioner should not thereafter sit on the criminal side. Hence, he file the petition under Article 32 of the Constitution. While deciding the case the Supreme Court referred to Article 235.
125. *Id.* at p. 541.

powers of the judges of the subordinate judiciary from the purview of control under Article 235.[126] The decision therefore undoubtedly is one which upholds independence of the subordinate judiciary. In *High Court of Judicature at Allahabad* v. *Sarnam Singh*,[127] the interest of the subordinate judiciary has been well taken care of by the Supreme Court. The apex court upheld the decision of the High Court that quashed the order for compulsory retirement of the respondent on the ground of allegations of corruption recorded by the inspecting judge without giving an opportunity to him to reply to the allegations. The court quoted[128] the observations in *M.S. Bindra* v. *Union of India*,[129]

> "To dunk an officer into the puddle of 'doubtful integrity', it is not enough that the doubt fringes on a mere hunch. That doubt should be of such a nature as would reasonably and consciously be entertainable by a reasonable man on the given material. Mere possibility is hardly sufficient to assume that it would have happened."

An instance of more intrusion into the independence of the lower judiciary came for examination of the Supreme Court in *Re 'K' A Judicial Officer*.[130] Reminding the High Court that its control over the lower judiciary is three dimensional, viz., administrative, judicial and disciplinary, the court cautioned the High Court in exercising its supervisory power against the

126. The cause of independence of judiciary was given further stimulus by the Supreme Court in *Madan Mohan Choudhuri* v. *State of Bihar*, A.I.R 1999 S.C. 1018 in which it was held that judge of the subordinate judiciary should not be compulsorily retired by the High Court on the ground of wrong judicial order, *bonafide* made by him.
127. (2000) 2 SCC 339.
128. *Id*. at p. 355.
129. (1998) 7 SCC 310, 317.
130. (2001) 3 SCC 54. The appellant was a Metropolitan Magistrate. She took cognizance of offences against certain PWD officials who furnished the courtroom in an improper manner under sections 380, 201 and 120-B IPC. In a petition under section 482 Cr. P.C. read with Article 227 of the Constitution, the High Court quashed the proceedings and passed some strictures against the appellant. The appeal under Article 136 is filed to remove the adverse remarks, which by the time were entered in the service records of the appellant.

judicial decision taken by a member of the lower judiciary. For, a :

> "Judge entrusted with the task of administering justice should be bold and feel fearless while acting judicially and giving expression to his views and constructing his judgment and order.... The availability of such fearlessness is essential for the maintenance of judicial independence."[131]
>
> And that,
>
> "The power to control is not to be exercised solely by wielding a teacher's cane; the members of subordinate judiciary look up to the High Court for the power to control to be exercised with parent-like care and affection."[132]

Reiterating the stand, *In the Matter of 'RV' a Judicial Officer*,[133] the Supreme Court required the "High Courts by stressing upon the need for restraint, care and circumspection while exercising its power of superintendence lest those who dispense justice to other should themselves suffer injustice."[134] The court therefore expunged the remarks adverse to the appellant made by the High Court while disposing of an appeal against the judgment given by the appellant.[135] These two recent

---

131. *Id.* at p. 63.
132. *Id.* at p. 65. However, the Supreme Court warned the High Court against the exercise of jurisdiction under Article 226 over the decision taken by the disciplinary committee authorized by the High Court under Article 235. The court opined that the court in its judicial side should not overstep the jurisdiction condoning or compromising with dishonest deeds of the subordinate judiciary. See, *High Court of Judicature* v. *Shashikant S. Patil*, (2000) 1 SCC 416.
133. (2004) 7 SCC 729. The appellant was a judge in the higher judicial service. An accused in a case pending before the appellant challenged the trial on the ground of delay. He furnished the reason for the delay before the High Court only after repeated demands by it. Hence, while disposing of the appeal, the High Court directed disciplinary proceedings against him against which this appeal is preferred.
134. *Id.* at p. 733.
135. The court however, gave liberty to the High Court to initiate action against him under Article 235.

decisions reveal how the Supreme Court became conscious of the fact that the judiciary itself poses a threat to judicial independence and suggested a remedy for the same by demanding the High Court not to exercise its power to superintendence over the subordinate judiciary along with its judicial power in an arbitrary manner. Hence, the court held that though the decision of the appellant was 'ill-advised' or 'misadventure,' it was not a misconduct or an act out of malice and hence, the observations adverse to the appellant made by the High Court were to be expunged.[136] The decision amounts to a declaration that the judicial power of the High Court should not be mixed up with its administrative power under Article 235, as the same is detrimental to judicial independence.

Though, the Supreme Court characterized the power of the High Court under Article 235 to control the lower judiciary as "comprehensive, exclusive and efficacious as it is to subserve the basic feature of the Constitution, i.e. independence of judiciary,"[137] the High Court was forewarned against exercising the administrative power to cow down the independence of the subordinate judges. This point was further vivified and summed up in *Ramesh Chander Singh* v. *High Court of Allahabad*,[138] where the High Court initiated disciplinary proceedings against the appellant on the basis of the allegation that he accepted illegal gratification for granting bail to an

136. For reaching the conclusion, and for protecting the independence of the lower judiciary, the Supreme Court has given a catena of reasons. It said that such observations against the judge of original jurisdiction is condemned unheard and so violative of natural justice, that the harm caused by such observations might be incapable of being undone and that it leads to a situation in which the judicial officer himself becomes a litigant as he has to file an appeal for expunging the observations which was not happy from the point of view of functioning of the judiciary system. (*Supra*, n. 130 at p. 65).

137. *Prakash Singh Badal* v. *State of Punjab*, (2007) 1 SCC 1, 43. It was an appeal challenging the decision of the High Court of Punjab not to quash a case registered against the appellant under the provisions of the Prevention of Corruption Act, 1988. One of the challenges of the petitioner was that the judge to whom his case was allocated for trial was so appointed by the government and hence the same was tainted with political ill-will.

138. (2007) 4 SCC 247.

accused person.[139] Castigating the order of the High Court to punish the appellant for the judicial order given by him, the apex court observed that there should be strong grounds for taking action, lest judicial independence should be affected. The court observed,[140]

> "If the High Court were to initiate disciplinary proceedings based on a judicial order, there should have been strong grounds to suspect officer's *bonafides* and the order itself should have been actuated by malice, bias or illegality. This court on several occasions has disapproved the practice of initiation of disciplinary proceedings against officers of the subordinate judiciary merely because the judgments/orders passed by them are wrong. The appellate and revisional courts have been established and given powers to set aside such orders. . . . While taking disciplinary action based on judicial orders, the High Court must take extra care and caution."

The Supreme Court further warned the High Court that though the supervisory power under Article 235 included the power to take action against a judicial officer if he acted 'in a manner as would reflect on his reputation or integrity or good faith or there is a *prima facie* material to show recklessness or misconduct in discharge of his duties or he acted in a manner to unduly favour a party or had passed an order actuated by corrupt motive', the High Court should keep in mind that 'Judges at all levels have to administer justice without fear or favour.' It was also observed that '[F]earlessness and maintenance of judicial independence are very essential for an

139. There was an inquiry conducted by the High Court in which it was not proved that the appellant judge accepted bribes as alleged in the complaint. The inquiring judge however, opined that bail was granted in disregard of judicial norms. Based on the report, the High Court initially decided to withhold two increments of the appellant, which he challenged in the High Court. By the judgement, the High Court issued notice to show cause why he should not be removed from service against which he filed appeal. In the appeal, the High Court held that he be reduced in rank. Hence this appeal.

140. *Supra*, n. *138*. at pp. 254-55.

efficacious judicial system. Making adverse comments against subordinate judicial officers and subjecting them to severe disciplinary proceedings would ultimately harm the judicial system at the grassroot level.'[141] Thus, the court called for great amount of care on the part of High Court before exercising its administrative power over the judicial power exercised by subordinate judges as the same might adversely affect the independence of the subordinate judiciary. Thus, even while the Supreme Court was conscious of keeping lower judiciary from the jaws of the executive and the legislature, it was all the more cautious that in the guise of protecting the subordinate judiciary, the High Court should not exercise its supervisory jurisdiction in manner detrimental to the independence of the subordinate judiciary.

The above discussion reveals that the status of the lower judiciary under the Constitution is different from that of the higher judiciary. Unlike the latter, the former is placed fully under the control either of the executive or the High Court. From the construction of the provisions in the Constitution dealing with the subordinate judiciary one finds a balance drawn by the Supreme Court between the power of the executive and that of the High Court. The above cases establish beyond doubt that judiciary itself at times, poses a serious threat to judicial independence and that eternal judicial vigilance is the only remedy against the same. These instances point out that exercise of administrative power even by the judiciary cannot be considered as a reliable alternative for ensuring judicial independence. It is clear that judicial review is the only dependable device for the protection of independence of judiciary. A study of the cases in the area establishes that the Supreme Court was very conscious of the necessity to protect independence of the lower judiciary from both the executive and High Court and the role it has to play for maintaining it.

However, a major criticism that can be leveled against the Supreme Court is its holdings[142] is that it is the Governor and not the High Court who is competent to dismiss, terminate or

141. *Id.* at p. 256.
142. See for instance, *State of West Bengal* v. *Nripendra Bagchi*, 1966 A.I.R. S.C. 447 and *State of Haryana,* v. *Inder Kumar*, A.I.R. 1976 S.C. 1841.

otherwise remove or reduce in rank of judges of the subordinate judiciary. It appears that such a conclusion is reached by the Court by reading Articles 233 and 234 in the light of Article 311[143] which provides that no public servant shall be dismissed from service by an authority subordinate to one who appointed him and that since the Governor is the authority to appoint judges of the subordinate judiciary, he alone should terminate them. Does Article 311 operate as a bar for vesting the power to dismiss judges of the subordinate courts in the High Court? It is submitted that Article 311(1) does not mean that the appointing authority and the authority for terminating a servant should be one and the same. It just means that the terminating authority should not be subordinate to the appointing authority.[144] It does not bar termination of an officer by an authority equal or higher to the one who appointed him. High Court could not be considered as an authority subordinate to the Governor. Hence, removal of a judge by High Court does not violate Article 311. Further, Article 311 is a general provision applicable to all civil servants including judicial officers while Articles 233, 234 and 235 are special ones enacted for judicial officers specifically for protecting independence of the judiciary. In case of a conflict between a general and a special provision governing the same subject matter, the general one should give way for the special one.[145] Therefore, the Court cannot be considered as wrong if the power to terminate and dismiss judges of the subordinate judiciary was construed to have been vested on the High Court. Such a construction enjoys the advantage that it is conducive to independence of judiciary. Though the rigour of these decisions has been considerably reduced by the holding that such

---

143. Article 311(1) reads, "No person who is member of a civil service of the Union or an all India service or a civil service of a State or holds a civil post under the Union or a State shall be dismissed or removed by an authority *subordinate* to that by which he was appointed". (Emphasis supplied)
144. "Article 311 (1) does not mean that the removal must be by the very same authority who made the appointment or by his direct superior. It is enough that the removing authority is of the same rank or grade. Article 311(1) contemplates subordination in respect of rank and not subordination in respect of powers and duties." Seervai, *Constitutional Law of India*, Vol. III (1996), pp. 3017-18.
145. *Generalia specialibus non derogant.*

termination should be effected only on recommendation of the High Court,[146] by a more creative interpretation of the provisions, the Court could have totally avoided intervention of the executive in the matter of termination of judges of the subordinate judiciary with a view to upholding judicial independence.

Can the judicial office be an emblem of immunity for each and every act of the person who holds it? Or can a judicial officer be arrested and dealt with by the police officers as every other citizen? Answers to both these questions are in the negative. In *Delhi Judicial Service Association v. Union of India,*[147] the Supreme Court took note of these aspects. The Court observed that arrest and prosecution of the judges pose a very serious quibble. Judges, as every other person should be available for prosecution and punishment for the offences committed by them. But a free hand of the police officers in dealing with them may pose a serious threat to their independence as judges, as the police personnel may exercise their discretion and authority indiscriminately. In short, arrest and prosecution of judges without thwarting independence of the judiciary is a conundrum. How can the offending judge be brought to book and punished without damaging independence of the judiciary? The Court laid down the following guidelines.

Before arresting a judicial officer the District Judge or High Court should be intimated. If immediate arrest is called for by the facts and circumstances, a technical or formal arrest may be effected. The factum of arrest should immediately be communicated to the District Judge or the Chief Justice of the High Court. The judge so arrested should not be taken to the police station without the order or direction of the District and Sessions Judge. Immediate facilities shall be provided to the judicial officer for communication with his family members,

---

146. *Baldev Raj, supra,* n. 66.

147. A.I.R. 1991 S.C. 2178. That was a writ petition under Article 32. The facts leading to the petition were horrendous. A Chief Judicial Magistrate was arrested and handcuffed. The police tied him with a rope and exhibited him in that condition before the public. He was sent for medical examination on the allegation that he had consumed liquor and violated the prohibition law. The Inspector of Police who arrested him photographed him and published the photograph in newspapers.

legal advisers and judicial officers including the District Judge. No statement of the judge be recorded, punchnama drawn up or medical tests conducted except in the presence of his legal adviser or another judicial officer of equal higher rank. No handcuffing of the judge be made. But if it was necessary the same should immediately be intimated to the District Judge and the Chief Justice of the High Court. The burden to the necessity of handcuffing would be with the police officer. If the same was found to be unjustified, the police officer would be guilty of misconduct and would be personally liable for compensation.[148] The Court made it clear that these guidelines were not exhaustive but contain only the minimum safeguard to be observed in case of arrest of a judicial officer.[149]

Thus decisions dealing with the provisions relating to the subordinate judiciary form a saga of creativity for protecting judicial independence. The prime concern of the Court in these cases was checking of intrusion by the executive into the freedom and independence of judges of the subordinate courts. By a creative interpretation of Article 233, the Court restricted the content of the power of the executive. Through successive decisions the Court provided a meaningful content to 'consultation' in it as a result of which the thrust of the power to appoint district judges was shifted from the executive to the High Court. Likewise, by interpreting Article 234 the Court was able to bring selection of judges other than district judges under the control of the High Court by holding that the opinion of the judge of the High Court who is the expert member of the interview board will be determinative and that the view of the judges should prevail over that of the Public Service Commission. While dealing with the conditions of service of judges of the subordinate courts, the Court by innovative construction of Article 235, managed to introduce more concepts into the parameters of the provision and to make it all comprehensive and self-sufficient. Analyzing the relationship between Article 233 and 235, the Court brought almost all of the incidents of service under the purview of control and supervision of the High Court. In short, by providing flesh and

148. *Id.* at pp. 2212-13.
149. *Id.* at p. 2213.

blood to the provisions dealing with the subordinate courts, the Court was able to effect a divorce between the executive and the judiciary which is a declared constitutional goal[150] and was virtually transferring the entire control of the subordinate judiciary to the High Court.

However, the Court did not permit High Court to wield arbitrary power over the subordinate courts in the guise of its power to control and supervise them. The decisions prove that in cases which the administrative power of the High Court under Article 235 ran mad, the Supreme Court put effective checks upon it through judicial review. To conclude, in every respect decisions dealing with subordinate judiciary exemplify another instance of high judiciary creativity designed to achieve independence of judiciary setting a healthy climate for judges to work without fear or favour.

150. See, the Constitution of India, Article 50. For the text, see *supra*, n. 22.

PART II

6

The Doctrine of Basic Structure

I. INTRODUCTION

Legal system is a system of laws. It means that every law necessarily belongs to the legal system. It is important that legal system shall have unity[1] and coherence. They can be achieved only if the system maintains a hierarchical order or a 'genetic structure' as it is called.[2]

Legal systems are subject to changes with elapse of time and concomitant to the changes in the social, economic and political spheres. Such changes may pose serious threats to the legal system if they go to the extent of destroying the identity of the legal system. It is not desirable that the essential features or elements of the legal system are swept away by such changes. Hence a major problem which legal systems face is one of

1. Joseph Raz, "The Identity of Legal Systems", *California Law Review*, Vol. 59, 795 (1971).
2. "The fundamental relation of the genetic structure is the genetic relation namely the relation between a law and another law authorising its existing." Joseph Raz, *The Concept of a Legal System* (1980), p. 184

balancing itself between demands of continuity and stability on the one hand and change and flexibility on the other.[3] A legal system has to adjust to the required changes without losing its identity. Success of the legal system depends upon maintaining its identity while offering solutions to the problems that arise.

Legal system is often characterized as a hierarchical normative order.[4] Each norm in such a structure derives its authority from a higher norm.[5] In such a legal system Constitution[6] is of highest importance[7] since it contains the norm of high authority.[8] A constitution, written or unwritten, is therefore the highest level of national law in a normative order. It is the basis from which individual norms develop. The constitution draws its nature, character and content from the basic norm of the legal system,[9] as it lives closest to the basic norm. However, being part of the legal system it also is subject to changes. It cannot be expected that constitution would offer permanent solutions to the problems of all times. In the case of an unwritten constitution such changes occur involuntarily while constitutions framed through deliberate action are subject to changes through deliberation. Such wilful changes of the written constitutions are known as amendments. Amendment is the most important method of changing constitutions.[10]

3. Paras Diwan and Piyush Diwan, *Amending Power and the Constitutional Amendments* (1997), p. 10.
4. See, Kelsen, *General Theory of Law and State* (1949), p. 110.
5. "'Norm' is the meaning of an act by which a certain behaviour is commanded, permitted, or authorised." Kelsen, *Pure Theory of Law* (1970), p. 5.
6. Constitution may be defined as the "organic and fundamental law of a nation or state, which may be written or unwritten establishing the character and conception of its government laying down the basic principles to which its internal life is to be conformed." See *Black's Law Dictionary* (1990).
7. "The organization of the modern state is... divisible into two distinct parts....The first, essential and basic portion is known as the constitution of the State... The more important, fundamental and far reaching any principle or practice is, the more likely is to be classed as constitution". See, Fittzgerald (Ed.) *Salmond on Jurisprudence* (1966), p. 83.
8. *Supra*, n. 5 at p. 124.
9. See, *supra*, n. 1. at p. 796.
10. But there are other modes of altering constitutions such as legislative measures, evolving customs and conventions and judicial interpretation. See, William, S. Livingston, *Federalism and Constitutional Change* (1956), pp. 11-15.

Amendability of the constitution is a *sine qua non*, for, absence of possibility to make changes through amendments may lead to its changes through extra constitutional methods including revolution.[11] Moreover, non-amendability of the fundamental law implies monopoly of a generation over the future, which is an unacceptable proposition.[12] An unamendable constitution is therefore characterised as 'the worst tyranny of time or rather the very tyranny of time'.[13] The amendability of the constitution is therefore an accepted norm. In short, to live upto the needs of the changing times as well as to assume self-existence a constitution should be capable of adjusting to changes; at the same time it should protect itself against self-eradication or the very sweeping of the self.[14] In the absence of appropriate provisions for schematic amendment the changes in the constitution may run riot, and leave the very existence of the constitution doubtful. Therefore, provision for amendment to bring about an orderly change is usually incorporated in constitutions.[15] Written constitutions contain provisions for their amendment. They contain the procedure for amending the constitutions as well as the limitations if any, on amendments.[16]

---

11. H.R. Khanna, "Power to Amend the Constitution", (1983) 2 S.C.C.1. At the time of framing our Constitution M.V. Thyagi observed that in the absence of an amendment procedure the constitution would be a brittle one. *C.A.D.*, Vol. IX, p. 1657.
12. See, Paras Diwan, *op. cit.* at pp. 11, 14.
13. *Per* Subba Rao, C.J. in *Golaknath* v. *State of Punjab*, A.I.R. 1967 S.C. 1643 at p. 1662.
14. "It is the function of a constitution to provide resistance to change nearly as such. If that were not so, a constitution would be an incitement to revolutions rather than a means of avoiding them. On the other hand a constitution which left the door open to an every kind of change could not perform its functions, since the function of a Constitution is to ensure stable progress, and certain types of changes are incompatible with progress." *Per* Dickinson as quoted in Paras Diwan, *op. cit.*, at p. 11.
15. Palekar, J. observed in *Kesavananda Bharathi* v. *State of Kerala*, (1973) 4 S.C.C. 225 at p. 679. "The *raison de'tre* for making provisions for the amendment of the constitution is the need for orderly change."
16. See, for instance the Constitution of the United States, Article V, the Constitution of Irelands, 1937, Article 50 and the Constitution of the Federal Republic of Germany, 1949, Article 79(3).

Article 368[17] of the Constitution of India stipulates the conditions and procedure for amending the Constitution.[18]

2. CONSTITUENT POWERS AND THE POWER TO AMEND THE CONSTITUTION

Amendment of the Constitution is different from its enactment. The former is a modification while the latter is the creation of the Constitution. Nevertheless, both emerge from the

17. The original Article was amended subsequently. Article 368 (1) and (2) as they stand now read as follows: "(1) Notwithstanding anything in this Constitution, Parliament may in exercise of its constituent power amend by way of addition, variation or repeal any provision of this Constitution in accordance with the procedure laid down in this article.
(2) An amendment of this Constitution may be initiated only by the introduction of a Bill for the purpose in either House of Parliament, and when the Bill is passed in each House by a majority of the total membership of that House and by a majority of not less than two-thirds of the members of that House present and voting it shall be presented to the President who shall give his assent to the Bill and thereupon the Constitution shall stand amended in accordance with the terms of the Bill:
Provided that if such amendment seeks to make any change in:
(a) Article 54, article 55, article 73, article 162 or article 241, or
(b) Chapter IV of Part V, Chapter V of Part VI, or Chapter 1 of Part XI, or
(c) any of the Lists in the Seventh Schedule, or
(d) the representation of States in Parliament, or
(e) the provisions of this article,
the amendment shall also required to be ratified by the legislatures of not less than one-half of the States by resolutions to that effect passed by those Legislatures before the Bill making provision for such amendment is presented to the President for assent."
18. The Constitution of India contains three procedures for amending it. Some Articles can be amended by a simple majority; for instance, Articles 4, 169 and 239A. These Articles contain specific provisions to the effect that such changes shall not be deemed to be constitutional amendments under Article 368 of the Constitution. Some provisions can be amended only by a special majority of two-thirds of the members present and voting. Article 368(2) specifies such a special procedure. Some other provisions can be amended by a special procedure of such special majority coupled with ratification by a half of the States by a resolution to that effect. Articles 55, 73, 162, 245, 124 to 147, 214 to 232, 245 to 255, Schedule 7, and amendment of Article 368 itself fall under this category.

exercise of the constituent power.[19] A reflection on amendment of the constitution would necessarily involve examination of questions like the meaning of the term amendment, the nature of the power to amend, the source of such a power, the extent of amendability and the scope of judicial review of amendment. These aspects in relation to written constitutions have claimed the attention of courts abroad. In our country, the Supreme Court had to examine these matters in their diverse aspects during the short span of half a century since independence and it resulted in the emergence of the doctrine of basic structure.

What is the source and nature of the power to amend the Constitution? There is a view that a constitution and the process of its amendment are one and the same.[20] The expression 'constituent power' involves some ambiguity. It has been used to denote the amending power and the power to make, remake and unmake the constitution.[21] Such a power seems to have been recognised by the Supreme Court in *Shankari Prasad v Union of India*[22] when the court distinguished the power to amend the Constitution from the concept of "law" under Article 13(2).[23] This view was approved by some of the Judges in *Golaknath v State of Punjab*[24] also. The decision implies that the power to amend the constitution, unlike the power to legislate, is not placed within the constitution but outside it. It means that the power behind the making of the constitution and its amendment is one and the same. In other words, the power to amend the constitution is also constituent in nature. But there is a strong contrary view on this issue. The view emphasizes that the power to amend the constitution is not supreme and independent as one to make a constitution. The latter, like a

---

19. The expression 'constituent power' denotes "the ability to frame or alter a political constitution" Seervai, *Constitutional Law of India* Vol. III (1996), p. 3119.
20. "We might define a constitution as its process of amendment." Herman Finer, *The Theory and Practice of Modern Government* (1961), at p. 127.
21. Upendra Baxi, "Some Reflections on the Nature of Constituent Power" in Rajeev Dhavan and Alice Jacob (Ed.), *Indian Constitution : Trends and Issues* (1978), p. 122 at p. 136.
22. A.I.R 1951 S.C. 1458
23. *Id.* at p. 463.
24. A.I.R 1967 S.C 16430.

plenary legislative power, is unfettered by any external restrictions while the former is subject to some limitations.[25] The power to frame a constitution is primary in nature whereas the other is derivative—derived from the constitution.[26] In short, according to this view, the power to amend a constitution, though a power higher than the legislative power, is within and not outside the constitution.[27] In other words, the power to amend a constitution is not all-comprehensive as the power to enact a constitution. The power to enact the constitution and the validity of the constitution so enacted are beyond the scope of any examination. The power to amend on the other hand, being one derived from the constitution, cannot transgress the limits constitutionally created. Thus like legislation, an amendment of the constitution is likely to be *ultra vires* the Constitution. In such cases the constitution is the touch-stone of the validity of all powers conferred by it.

What is the meaning of the expression 'to amend'? Is it wide enough to include changes to the constitution even to the level of its abrogation? The expression means, to improve, change for the better by removing defects or faults by modification, deletion or addition.[28] In other words, an amendment does not encompass substantial alteration or modification of a constitution. In general, people think of amendments as rather minor changes while overhauling and adoption of a completely new constitution is implied by the term revision.[29] A question emerges here. What are the features of the Constitution, which can be so altered in exercise of the

---

25. Seervai, *op. cit.* at p. 3119. Such limitations may be substantive or procedural in nature.
26. *Ibid.*
27. Baxi, *supra*, n. 21 at p. 123. He observed, "The amending power is a power given by the Constitution to the Parliament. It is a higher power than other power given to Parliament, but nevertheless it is a power *within* and not *outside* of, the Constitution. (Emphasis original).
28. *Black's Law Dictionary.* But it is opined that even the term addition falls outside the purview of the expression 'amendment'. See, W.F. Dodd, "Amending the Federal Constitution," XXX Yale L.J. 321 at p. 331. (1920-21).
29. However, there is strong juristic view that the expression is wide enough to include sweeping changes including repeal and abrogation. See, for instance, William Anderson, *Fundamentals of American Government* (1940), p. 31.

power to amend and what features are beyond its scope? When such a question was posed before the Supreme Court of India, attempts were made to recognize and harmonize such unamendable features with the amendable ones. The doctrine of basic structure of the Constitution was evolved by the Court in such a context.

3. THE DOCTRINE OF BASIC STRUCTURE : PARADIGM OF JUDICIAL CREATIVITY

(a) The Genesis

A constitutional bench of the Supreme Court, consisting of thirteen judges held in *Kesavananda Bharathi* v. *State of Kerala*[30] (*Kesavananda,* for short), popularly called the *Fundamental Rights Case* that the power to amend the Constitution emanates from Article 368 of the Constitution.[31] It means that unlike the power to make the constitution, the power to amend it is derivative in nature. The judges however assigned different but related reasons for the conclusion.[32] The Court further held that the

30. (1973) 4 S.C.C 225: A.I.R 1973 S.C. 1461. The petitioner approached the Supreme Court under Article 32 for enforcement of his fundamental rights under Articles 25, 26, 14, 19(1)(f) and 31 of the Constitution. He challenged the validity of the Kerala Land Reforms Act, 1963 as amended by the Kerala Land Reforms (Amendment) Act, 1969. During the pendency of the petition the Constitution (Twenty-fourth Amendment) Act, 1971, the Constitution (Twenty-fifth Amendment) Act 1972 and the Constitution (Twenty-ninth Amendment) Act 1972 came into force. As a result of the 29th Amendment Act the Kerala Land Reforms Act as amended was inserted in Schedule IX to the Constitution. Incorporation of statutes in Schedule IX immunizes them from being challenged as unconstitutional. The petitioner therefore challenged also the validity of those amendments to the Constitution.
31. *Id. per* Sikri C.J (at pp. 386-87); Shelat J. (for himself and Grover J.) (at p. 412); Hegde J. (for himself and Mukherjee J.) (at p. 468); Jagmohan Reddy J (at p. 609); Palekar J. (at p. 675); Khanna J. (at p. 739); K.K Mathew J. (at p. 833); Dwivedi J. (at p. 924) and Chandrachud J. (at p. 977).
32. *Id. per* Chief Justice Sikri (at pp. 386-87) and Mathew (at p. 833) Shalet and Grover JJ. (at p. 412) held so on the ground that the petitioner conceded that the power was incorporated in Article 368. Hegde and Mukherjee JJ. held that the power to amend the Constitution is impliedly contained in Article 368 (at p. 469). Moreover, the power cannot be located in Articles 245, 246 and 248 as they provide for exercise of legislative power subject to the Constitution while the amendment

expression 'to amend' was one of wide import even to include the power to repeal or abrogate a legal document.[33] However, the Court by majority held that in Article 368 the expression was used in a narrow and constricted sense.[34] The judges agreed that

---

power has to over ride the Constitution (at p. 468). Reddy J. held so on the ground that the decision in *Golaknath* to that effect was correct (at p. 609). Palekar J. observed that all controlled Constitutions confer on the legislature a special function of constituent power to amend the Constitution in accordance with a special procedure. Article 368 is not entirely procedural in nature. There is a mandate in it that the proposed amendment shall become part of the Constitution. That is a substantive provision. Moreover, the makers of the Constitution could have incorporated a provision in the entries of legislative power if they had treated amendment as legislative in nature. He further held that legislation should be subject to the Constitution while amendment should over ride it (at pp. 672-75). Khanna J. said that the words in Article 368 explained that it contains the power also and not procedure alone. The distinction between amendment and legislation is further clarified by the difference in legislative and constitutional procedures (at pp. 737-38). Dwivedi J. justified the conclusion on the ground that amending power and legislative power are contained in two different parts of the Constitution and hence the former could not reasonably be located in the residuary legislative power (at pp. 925-26). Chandrachud J. held that the history of residuary power since 1935 Act and the scheme of distribution of power show that power to amend is located in Article 368 (at p. 977).

33. *Id. per* Hegde J. (for himself and Mukherjee JJ) (at p. 475). "The power to amend a Constitution in certain contexts may include a power to abrogate or repeal that Constitution"; Ray J. (at p. 537); Mathew J. (at p. 863); Dwivedi J. (at p. 944) and Chandrachud J. (at p. 980).

34. *Id.* "... the expression 'Amendment of this Constitution' does not include a revision of the whole Constitution.... In my view that meaning would be appropriate which would enable the country to achieve a social and economic revolution without destroying the democratic structure of the Constitution and the basic inalienable rights guaranteed in Part III and without going outside the contours delineated in the Preamble". *Per* Sikri C.J. (at p. 346); "The meaning of the words 'amendment of this Constitution' as used in Article 368 must be such which accords with the true intention of the Constitution-makers as ascertainable from the historical background,..." *per* Shelat J. (for himself and Grover J.). (at p. 435); "It does not yet include the power to destroy or emasculate the basic elements or the fundamental features of the Constitution." Hegde, J. (for himself and Mukherjee J.) (at p. 512); "None the less it is apparent that the word 'amendment' as used in Article 368 does not connote a plenitude of power". Jagmohan Reddy J. (at p. 632.) and "It also appears that the whole text of a law cannot be repealed or abrogated in one step; some part of it must remain while the other is repealed", Dwivedi J. (at p. 929).

the power under Article 368 would reach each and every provision of the Constitution. But that did not imply that Parliament could alter any and every aspect of the Constitution. In fact there were certain matters which do not come under the scope and ambit of the power of Parliament to amend. Thus the power does not encompass the one to destroy,[35] repeal,[36] or abrogate[37] the Constitution or to frame a new one.[38] In other words, the power cannot be exercised to destroy the identity of the Constitution.[39] It cannot, in short be used as a prelude to enactment of a fresh Constitution. Over and above that, there are certain features of the Constitution, which cannot be altered in exercise of the amending power. The judges named them as *the basic structure,*[40] *basic elements,*[41] *fundamental features*[42] or *the essential features* of the Constitution. In other words, Parliament cannot exercise its plenary power to amend the Constitution so as to weaken the basic structure or principle underlying the Constitution.[43] Such amendments, the Court held, would be unconstitutional. Even though such a restriction is not contained in any of the specific provisions of the Constitution,[44] the doctrine restricts even the plenary legislative body to amend the Constitution in any manner it

35. *Id. per* Hegde J. (for himself and Mukharjee J.) (at p. 481). He said, "In other words, one cannot legally use the Constitution to destroy itself."
36. *Id., per* Sikri C.J. (at p. 320); Palekar J. (at p. 680). See also William L. Marbury, "The Limitations Upon the Amending Power," 33 H.L.R. 223 (1919-20). He observes, "It may be safely presumed that the power to "amend" the Constitution was not intended to include the power to destroy it." (at p. 225).
37. *Supra,* n. 30 *per* Khanna J., (at p. 767); Ray J. (at p. 632) and Mathew J. (at p. 897).
38. *Id. per* Shelat and Grover JJ. (at p. 432).
39. *Id. per* Khanna J. (at p. 767).
40. *Id. per* Sikri C.J. (at p. 366); Shelat and Grover JJ. (at p. 454); Jagmohan Reddy J. (at p. 637).
41. *Id. per* Shelat and Grover JJ. (at p. 454) and Hegde and Mukharjea JJ. (at p. 486).
42. *Id. per* Shelat and Grover JJ. (at p. 472).
43. Rajeev Dhavan, "The Basic Structure Doctrine—A Footnote Comment", in Rajeev Dhavan and Alice Jacob, *op. cit.* at p. 160.
44. *Supra,* n. 30. Sikri J. observed, "The above foundation and the above basic features are easily discernibly not only from the preamble but the whole scheme of the Constitution, ..." (at p. 366).

likes. This doctrine evolved by the judiciary therefore is a clear instance of the judicial creativity.[45]

For evolving the doctrine, the judges relied on different reasonings. Chief Justice Sikri,[46] Justice Shelat,[47] and Justice Hegde[48] introduced the principle of implied limitations on the power of Parliament to amend the Constitution to reach the conclusion that there was an unamendable structure to the Constitution. The principle of implied limitations emphasises that apart from the express procedural limitations contained in the Article 368, there are some substantive limitations on the power to amend the Constitution. Justice Jagmohan Reddy[49] reached the conclusion on the ground that destruction of the essential features of the Constitution would amount to its abrogation. Justice Khanna[50] upheld the basic structure on a similar principle that the power to amend does not imply a power destroy the Constitution and, therefore even after amendments the identity of the Constitution should remain unchanged. The judges expressed the view that an unlimited power to amend the Constitution might lead to undesirable consequences. Parliament would be able to convert the

45. Upendra Baxi, "A Pilgrim's Progress : The Basic Structure Revisited" in *Courage, Craft and Contention—The Indian Supreme Court in the 80's* (1985), p. 65.
46. *Supra*, n. 30 at p. 346. He said, "In a written constitution it is rarely that everything is said expressly. Powers and limitations are implied from necessity or the scheme of the Constitution."
47. *Id.* at p. 453. (For himself and Grover J.) He said, "We are equally unable to hold that in the light of the Preamble, the entire scheme of the Constitution, the relevant provisions thereof and the context in which the material expressions are used in Article 368 no implied limitations arise to the exercise of the power of amendment."
48. *Id.* at p. 483. (For himself and Mukharjea J.) He observed, "From what has been said above, it is clear that the amending power under Article 368 is also subject to implied limitations."
49. *Id.* at p. 633. He held, "If the entire Constitution cannot be abrogated, can all the provisions of the Constitution leaving the Preamble, or one article, or a few articles of the original Constitution be repealed... and the fundamental features substituted therefor? In my view, such an attempt would equally amount to abrogation of the Constitution,..."
50. *Id.* at p. 767. He said, "The word 'amendment' postulates that the old Constitution survives without loss of its identity despite the change and continues even though it has been subjected to alterations....It means the retention of the basic structure or framework of the old Constitution."

democratic system of government to one of dictatorship or hereditary monarchy[51] or make the Constitution extremely rigid.[52] The creative judicial approach in this regard has been succinctly explained by a jurist in the following words,

> "In other words, the need and power to make changes in the Constitution has been conceded to Parliament... but the power thus conceded is the power to make changes in, and not of, the Constitution. Changes in the Constitution, singly and cumulatively, should not amount to a change of the Indian Constitution. The constituent power is no longer the power to make and unmake the Constitution; it is no longer to repeal and replace the Constitution. The constituent power is the power to make changes in the Constitution, a power that can be exercised within the framework of the Constitution. And if the Parliament and the Supreme Executive are unable to understand fully, in the wielding of the constituent power, the basic frame work of the Indian Constitution, the Supreme Court offers itself as a pedagogue, explaining to all concerned the meaning of a State based on freedom and Justice."[53]

(b) Ingredients of Basic Structure: Paradigms of Judicial Innovation

Though the Court held that the power of Parliament to amend the Constitution was impliedly limited by the doctrine of basic structure, what constituted the basic structure was not

---

51. *Id. per* Khanna J. (at p. 767).
52. *Id. per* Sikri C.J. (at p. 365). He said, "Article 368 can itself be amended to make the Constitution completely flexible or extremely rigid and unamendable. If this is so, a political party with a two-third majority in Parliament for a four years could so amend the Constitution as to debar any other party from functioning, establish totalitarianism, enslave the people, and after having effected these purposes make the Constitution unamendable or extremely rigid." Shelat J. observes, "The effect of limitless amending power in relation to amendment of Article 368 cannot be conducive to the survival of the Constitution because, the amending power can itself be taken away and the Constitution can be made literally unamendable or virtually unamendable by providing for an impossible majority."(at p. 431).
53. Upendra Baxi, *supra,* n. 45 at pp. 65-66.

clearly defined and explained by the judges. Chief Justice Sikri suggested that supremacy of the Constitution, republican and democratic form of government, secular characteristic of the Constitution, separation of powers and federal character of the Constitution were its ingredients. He opined that the structure was built upon the dignity and freedom of the individuals.[54] Justice Shelat and Justice Grover were of the view that in addition to the above the mandate to build a welfare state contained in Part IV and the unity and integrity of the nation also formed basic structure.[55] Justice Hegde and Justice Mukherjee illustrated the basic structure with reference to sovereignty of India, democratic nature of our polity, unity of the nation, essential features of the individual freedoms secured to citizens and the mandate to build a welfare state and egalitarian society.[56] Justice Khanna identified the democratic and parliamentary forms of government and secularism as constituting the basic structure of the Indian Constitution.[57] Justice Jagmohan Reddy catalogued Sovereign Democratic Republic; Justice, social, economic and political; Liberty of thought, expression, belief, faith and worship and equality of status and of opportunity as the contents of the basic structure.[58] It is clear that there was hardly any consensus among the Judges as to the contents of basic structure.[59] It is true that no features of the Constitution could be unanimously identified as basic structure by the court. The ratio of *Kesavananda* is that there are certain elements in the Indian Constitution beyond the reach of the power of Parliament to amend, though the Court did not identify unanimously which features of the Constitution constituted its basic structure.

A corollary of the doctrine is that if any amendment is found to be violative of basic structure it would be considered

54. *Kesavananda, supra,* n. 30 at p. 366.
55. *Id.* at p. 454.
56. *Id.* at p. 472.
57. *Id.* at p. 767.
58. *Id.* at p. 638.
59. I.P. Massey, "Theory of Basic Features—A Dogma or Doctrine", 7 J.B.C.I. 38, 43 (1977). See also Ramesh D. Garg, "Phantom of Basic Structure of the Constitution : A Critical Appraisal of the *Kesavananda* Case", 16 J.I.L.I. 243 (1974).

as unconstitutional and struck down. It implies two things. The Constitution being the touch stone to determine the validity of its alterations, like ordinary legislation, constitutional amendments are also likely to be held unconstitutional.[60] It further implies the supremacy and finality of judicial review in determining the validity of constitutional amendments.[61]

Introduction of the doctrine of basic structure can be considered as one of the instances in which the Supreme Court of India was at the zenith of its creativity. Primarily, it is the direct outcome of the view of the Court that the power of Parliament under Article 368 was subject to certain implied limitations. Implied limitations are not legislatively incorporated in a statute, but are incorporated by the judiciary.[62] They could be either substantive or procedural in nature. Article 368 does not contain any substantive limitations on the amending power. However the Court incorporated some implied substantive limitations upon the power of Parliament to amend the Constitution and the doctrine of basic structure is built upon such limitations. In other words, the very foundation upon which the doctrine is built up and the doctrine itself are products of creative dialect of the judiciary. When the scope and extent of the power of Parliament to amend the Constitution is explained in the light of the doctrine of basic structure based on implied limitations, the doctrine would not be eaten away by amendment of the Constitution.

Further, by the doctrine, the Court was able to lay down the criteria for determining the validity of constitutional amendments. The Court evolved the criteria by basing on postulates like the scheme or 'spirit' of or the 'philosophy'[63] that

60. Naturally a question arises here. Can a constitutional amendment be treated as 'law'? The importance of such a question is that if it can be treated so, constitutional amendments can be also subjected to limitations to which ordinary legislation is subject. Such a question was raised before and answered by the Supreme Court in *Shankari Prasad* v. *Union of India,* A.I.R 1950 S.C. 458 and *Golaknath* v. *State of Punjab,* A.I.R. 1967 S.C. 1643.
61. See *infra,* n. 66.
62. See Rajeev Dhavan *op. cit.* at p. 142. There are objections to recognition of the doctrine of implied limitations on the power to amend Constitutions. See, Orfield, *The Amendment of the Federal Constitution* (1942), pp. 115-25.
63. "Every Constitution has a philosophy of its own." D.D. Basu, *Introduction to the Constitution of India* (1985), p. 20.

permeates the Constitution.[64] In the earlier cases[65] while dealing with the power of Parliament to amend the Constitution, the Court had no opportunity to lay down such criteria applicable to all constitutional amendments since the only question posed in those cases was whether fundamental rights could be amended by Parliament. No question regarding the scope and extent of the power to amend was discussed in those cases. The issues raised in *Kesavananda,* on the other hand, extended the Court an opportunity to lay down the standard to evaluate the validity of all constitutional amendments.

Yet another innovative feature of the decision is that by the doctrine the Court brought constitutional amendments within the purview of judicial review. Judicial review of the constitutional amendments is a corollary of the doctrine of basic structure. It also is an example of high judicial creativity and innovation. The Supreme Court of India "is probably the only Court in the history of human kind to have asserted the power of judicial review over amendments to the Constitution."[66] The extent of creativity of the decision will be clear when it is compared with the response of the Supreme Court of the United States in this respect. In the United States, the Supreme Court was reluctant to impose limitations on the constituent body. In *Coleman v. Miller*[67], when the validity of an amendment proposed to the Constitution of the US was challenged, the Supreme Court refused to look into the matter on the ground that it was a political question which the Congress and not the Court was competent to determine.[68] The creativity of the

64. M.K. Bhandari, *Basic Structure of the Indian Constitution* (1993), Preface, at p. xv.
65. *Sankari Prasad* v. *Union of India,* A.I.R. 1951 S.C 458; *Sajjan Singh* v. *State of Punjab,* A.I.R 1965 S.C 745 and *Golaknath* v. *State of Punjab,* A.I.R 1967 S.C 1463.
66. Upendra Baxi, *Courage, Craft and Contention* (1985), p. 64.
67. 307 U.S. 433 (1939). In 1924, the Congress proposed an amendment to the US Constitution for legislating on Child Labour. In 1925 the Kansas Senate voted on it. A *mandamus* was claimed in the State Supreme Court against considering the amendment as passed on the ground that it was not ratified in a reasonable time.
68. In the U.S. the question relating to validity of constitutional amendments was considered as political in nature. See, Richard B. Bernstein with Jerome Agel, *Amending America* (1993), pp. 255-56.

Supreme Court of India becomes clear when it is realised that by introducing the doctrine of basic structure, the Court was trudging through an untrodden area and laying down the law imposing restrictions on powers of Parliament to amend the Constitution.

The doctrine of basic structure as introduced by the Court enjoys the merit that it brought constitutional amendments under judicial review, even when it recognizes the well-accepted distinction between 'law' and 'constitution'. It therefore provided a jurisprudentially acceptable standard for evaluating constitutional amendments. In *Golaknath's Case,* on the other hand, to bring constitutional amendments under judicial review, the Court held that amendments to the Constitution were also 'law' under Article 13(2). Such a holding led to the vanishing of the distinction between 'law' and 'constitution'.[69] Therefore, it was subjected to criticisms. But, by the incorporation of the doctrine of basic structure the Court was able to keep constitutional amendments subject to judicial review without destroying the accepted distinction between constitutional and ordinary laws. It is clear that the doctrine does not suffer from the jurisprudential imbalances to which the decision of *Golaknath* fell a prey.

Yet another remarkable aspect of creativity of the decision lies in the wisdom of the Court in not keeping the doctrine a closed concept. In *Kesavananda,* the judges illustrated the concept with certain examples. The examples only illustrated the contents of the concept and hence were not exhaustive. The doctrine, in other words is a fine example of legal category of indeterminate reference.[70] By the enunciation of the doctrine, the Court opened up ample scope for leeways of choices, so that in future the concept could be given added colour and content according to the requirements of the time.

---

69. *Golaknath v. State of Punjab,* A.I.R 1967 S.C 1463. In this case the Supreme Court invalidated a constitutional amendment on the ground that the concept "law" under Article 13(2) encompassed constitutional amendments also and therefore fundamental rights could not be abridged even by constitutional amendments.
70. For the concept of legal category of indeterminate reference see Julius Stone, *Legal System and Lawyers' Reasonings* (1968), p. 263 *et. seq.*

Moreover, though the doctrine limited the power of Parliament to amend the Constitution, the Court did not close all avenues for substantially altering or repealing the basic document. There is at least one mode of thoroughly revising the Constitution without violating the parameters of the doctrine as evolved in *Kesavananda*. It does not prohibit repeal or revision of the Constitution in any manner including through referendum by the people who are the real sovereign. In other words, the doctrine left the power of the people to amend the Constitution untouched and it limited only the power of the delegate—the Parliament. The doctrine is intended to operate only as a shield against the arbitrariness of Parliament and not against the interests of the people. Thus, viewed from any angle, one finds the decision of *Kesavananda* is replete with creativity of the judiciary. As Baxi has aptly observed,[71] "I heralded *Kesavananda* by saying that the judgement from now is the Constitution of India, no matter what the Government Press puts out a document called 'Constitution of India'."

(c) *Raison d'être* of Basic Structure

Innovative in many respects, the decision of *Kesavananda* has been subjected to strong criticisms. Introduction of the doctrine has been objected as amounting to assertion of superiority of judicial power in the arena of the constitution. It has been condemned as a judicial attempt to limit the constituent power of Parliament. Such criticisms are based on some crucial questions. Is the Supreme Court justified in reading implied limitations into the Constitution? Is the doctrine of basic structure jurisprudentially correct? Is the Court right in subjecting the power of Parliament to amend the Constitution to judicial review?

For a meaningful examination of these questions, a study of the meaning of the expression Constitution and its place and function in a legal order[72] becomes necessary. A legal order may

71. *Supra*, n. 45. at p. 66. See also Upendra Baxi, "The Constitutional Quicksands of Kesavananda Bharathi and the Twenty-fifth Amendment," (1974) 1 S.C.C. 45.

72. "The function of a constitution is the grounding of validity." Kelsen, "The Functions of A Constitution", (1980) tr. of an essay published by I. Stewart as part of an Article, "The Basic Norm as Fiction" (1990) 199, 214-24 as cited in *Lloyd's Introduction to Jurisprudence* (1985), p. 385.

be seen as a hierarchy of norms. Each norm looks up for its validity to the higher general norm.[73] The higher the norm, the more general it would be. The basic norm of the legal system which gives validity to the other norms cannot therefore be a purely legal one. Constitution forms the highest norm in the level of legal order.[74] But the term 'Constitution' has different connotations and covers both material and formal constitutions. A material constitution is different from a formal one. The material constitution is the legal basis of the legal order.[75] It consists of the rules for creation of the general legal norm itself. It is because of the material constitution that the Constitution emerges in its formal shape.[76] A formal constitution is the solemn document, a set of legal norms, created by the material constitution changeable only under special prescriptions.[77] It represents the regularity of matters.[78] The material constitution is the highest level of national law[79] and formal constitution is the result of creation, enactment, amendment and annulment in accordance with the material constitution. Amendment or abolition of the contents of the formal constitution serves to stabilise the material constitution.[80] This implies that amendment, alteration or change in the formal constitution is to give effective expressions to the material constitution that lies closest to the basic norm. It is not difficult to understand that the doctrine of basic structure was an attempt of the Court to make the Constitution of India—the formal constitution—in tune with the material constitution that gave shape to it.

Validity of a constitution depends upon its conformity with a historically earlier constitution, which provided the basic norm of the legal order. The question of validity of a constitutional norm therefore depends upon its conformity with the basic norm, which is the "constitution in the transcendental-logical sense as distinct from the constitution in the positive

73. *Supra*, n. 4 at p. 120.
74. Kelsen, *Pure Theory of Law* (Tr. Max Knight) (1970), pp. 221-22.
75. *Id.* at p. 222.
76. *Supra*, n. 4 at p. 116.
77. *Id.* at p. 124.
78. *Supra*, n. 5 at p. 222.
79. *Supra*, n. 4 at p. 124.
80. *Supra*, n. 5 at p. 222.

legal sense".[81] If the Constitution is amended the amended form also forms part of the Constitution. Hence, just like the enactment of the formal Constitution, amendments also should conform to the earlier constitutions. It should satisfy the general norms of the constitution as well as the basic norm. Does not an amendment of the formal constitution counter to the historically earlier constitution or the material constitution lay down a bad norm? The answer seems to be in the affirmative. For, amendment also is a product of human will. The validity of amendment of the formal constitution has to be tested and the scope of the power to amend determined with reference to the basic norm. It is in this context that introduction of the concept of basic structure becomes highly relevant.

It is clear that there is a surprising semblance between the concept of basic structure of the Constitution as projected by the Supreme Court and the concept of the basic norm of the legal order as envisaged by Kelsen. Basic structure is considered by the Supreme Court as immutable while Kelsen conferred such a status to the basic norm of the legal order which but is a natural reality laying down the norms of the legal order.[82] The basic norm is considered by Kelsen as not a product of free invention. The expressions 'basic structure', 'basic feature', 'the essential features' or 'the principle' of the constitution stand in close similarity with the "Constitution in the transcendental—logical sense". The view of the Supreme Court in *Kesavananda* that the power to amend the Constitution under Article 368 does not envisage alteration of the basic structure naturally emanates from the reasoning that an amendment has to be in conformity with the basic norm. Illustrations of the doctrine of basic structure also establish that the 'basic structure' forms the basic norm, the highest in the hierarchy of norms. Validity of the provisions in the Constitution, which contain individual norms,

81. Kelsen, "The Functions of A Constitution", (1980) tr. of an essay published by I. Stewart as part of an Article, "The Basic Norm as Fiction" (1990) 199, 214-24 as cited in Lloyd, *op. cit.* at p. 379.

82. See, Kelsen, "The Function of the Constitution" quoted in Lloyd, *op. cit* at p. 382. He observes, "The basic norm is thus not a product of free invention. It refers to particular facts existing in natural reality, to an actually laid down and effective constitution and to the norm-creating and norm-applying facts in fact established in conformity with the constitution."

depend on their conformity with the general norms.[83] Amendment of the constitutional provisions being alteration of individual norms contained in the constitution should be in conformity with the general norms. It consequently implies that the power to amend the constitution cannot be exercised in such a manner contrary to the general norms. It is clear from the holding of the majority in *Kesavananda* that though Parliament could amend each and every provision of the Constitution, they could not be altered in such a fashion as to affect the fundamentals from which they emerge. Such reasoning reveals that there is nothing wrong in subjecting the power of Parliament to amend the Constitution to certain implied limitations. A similar restriction on the power of Parliament, which is a sovereign, to alter the norms of English legal order can be found in the celebrated words of Edward Coke,

> ... it appears in our books that in many cases the common law will control Acts of Parliament and sometimes adjust them to be utterly void: for when an Act of Parliament is against common right or reason or repugnant, or impossible to be performed, the common law will control it and adjudge such Act to be void."[84]

The doctrine of basic structure can therefore be justified as an attempt of the Court to identify the permanent elements of the constitution and the legal system and to distinguish them from the impermanent ones. The doctrine was an innovation by the Court to limit the power of Parliament to alter the permanent elements of the legal system. The holding is certainly a creative one in the sense that it avoids total amendment of the Constitution, which is as dangerous as its total non-amendment. The former may lead to uncertainty and incoherence in the legal system, while the latter may prepare the ground for a revolution. In short, the doctrine can be justified as an effective

83. "The validity of the lower, individual norms is grounded by the validity of the higher general norms. And the Judge, in fact, so grounds his judgements that it conforms to a valid general legal norm that authorizes him." See, Kelsen, *supra*, n. 72.
84. *Bonham's Case*, (1610) 8. Co. Rep. 114 at p. 118.

check on the possibility of alteration of the general norms contained in the Constitution by Parliament.

The doctrine gets justification on another ground also. There is a strong view that law is the product of "internal, silently-operating forces"[85] and not exclusively the product of human will. Law, a child of national conviction[86] develops as a response to the impersonal powers to be found in the peoples' national spirit, the *volkgeist*, which is a "unique, ultimate and often a mystical reality".[87] Law, "like language, is a product not often arbitrary and deliberate will but of a slow, gradual and organic growth."[88] Like civilisation, law is the emanation of unconscious, anonymous, gradual and irrational forces in the individual life of a particular nation.[89] Such a view implies that deliberate legislation should obey the forces operating above human forces in a State. Enactment of a Constitution and its amendment are no exceptions to this process.

Enactment of the Constitution of India was the culmination of certain historical incidents and forces that took place prior to independence. It is the outcome of a variety of factors like struggle for freedom, national aspirations, national objectives and the complex structure of the nation due to different religions and languages.[90] In other words, in the Constitution there are some elements formed due to forces other than human will. Such elements are not therefore amenable to legislative will, but legislation will be attuned to them. The concept of basic structure can be considered as a product of such constitution-making forces. Viewing from such an angle it can be seen that

---

85. Savigny, *of the Vocation of Our Age for Legislation and Jurisprudence*, tr. A. Hayward (1831), p. 30 as cited in Bodenheimer, *Jurisprudence* (1974), p. 71.
86. Lloyd, *op. cit.* at p. 869.
87. *Id.* at p. 868
88. Bodenheiner, *op. cit.* at p. 72.
89. Herman Kantorowicz, "Savigny and the Historical School of Law", 53 L.Q.R. 326 at pp. 332-33 (1937).
90. Chief Justice Sikri observes, "... the background of the struggle for freedom, various national aspirations outlined during the struggle, the national objectives as recited in the Objective Resolution dated January 22, 1947 and the Preamble, the complex structure of the Indian Nation consisting as it does of various peoples with different religions and languages and in different stages of economic stages of economic development." *supra*, n. 30 at pp. 1541-42.

alteration of the Constitution will be acceptable only to the extent it does not affect the elements brought out by such forces. The power to amend the Constitution therefore cannot include within it the power to alter such factors.

Further, it is clear from the Constitution that Parliament wields both legislative[91] and constituent powers.[92] There is a view that a body, which wields constituent powers, acts in that capacity as a delegate or trustee of the people.[93] The ultimate and absolute power is vested in the people. This may be a development of the theory that the political sovereign rests with the people and that Parliament is only a representative of the people.[94] Such a proposition gets justification from the fact that constitutions which came into existence after the Second World War declare that they are given by the people unto themselves.[95] This view gets further support from the provisions in some Constitutions that powers not explicitly conferred to any

---

91. The Constitution of India Article 245(1), "Subject to the provisions of this Constitution, Parliament may make laws for the whole or any part of the territory of India, ..."
92. *Id.* Articles 4 and 368.
93. Edward, S. Corwin, *The Constitution and What it Means Today* (1958), p. 177. He observes, "*The amending, like all other powers is in form a delegated and hence a limited power*, although this does not imply necessarily that the Supreme Court is vested with the authority to determine its limits." (Emphasis supplied).
94. See, for example, A.V. Dicey, *Introduction to the Study of the Law of the Constitution* (1962), p. 73. "That body is 'political' sovereign or supreme in a state what will of which is ultimately obeyed by the citizens of the State. In this sense of the word the electors of Great Britain may said to be, together with the Crown and the Lords, in strict accuracy, independently of the King and the Peers, the body in which sovereign power is vested. For, as things now stand, the will of the electorate, and certainly of the electorate in combination with the Lords and the Crown, is sure ultimately to prevail on all subjects to be determined by the British government. The matter indeed may be carried a little further, and we may assert that the arrangements of the constitution are now such as to ensure that the will of the electors shall by regular and constitutional means always in the end assert itself as the predominant influence in the country."
95. K.C. Wheare, *Modern Constitutions* (1966), p. 55. He observes at another place thus, "Most modern Constitutions have followed the American model and the legal and political theory that lies behind it. The people, or a constituent authority *acting on their behalf*, has authority to enact a Constitution." (Emphasis added) (at pp. 54-55).

authority would be reserved to people[96] and from the provisions for referendum[97] or initiation[98] for their amendments in some others. In such a context, a pertinent question arises. Can an authority with delegated power exercise its powers in an absolute and arbitrary manner? Scanning through this aspect some of the judges who constituted majority in the *Kesavananda* held that since Parliament was only a delegate of the people, it should exercise the power to amend the Constitution only in a limited way. They read the implied limitations into the Constitution since it did not contain any such limitations and the basic structure was ultimately justified by them on the theory of delegation.[99] It is an accepted principle in the legislative sphere that the legislature cannot delegate the essential legislative powers.[100] They are to be exercised by the legislature itself. This principle can be accepted in the constitutional matters with much advantage. It can be inferred that people being the ultimate sovereign, they cannot confer an unlimited power on Parliament enabling it to abrogate the Constitution or to amend its basic aspects without their consent. Just as the essential legislative function cannot be delegated, the essential constituent power cannot be parted with. In other words, the power to amend the Constitution is to be understood as a scheme for conveniently altering the constitutional provisions without destroying its identity. Therefore, Article 368 cannot be construed as a provision conferring a representative body with a licence to alter the existing fundamental constitutional norm in any manner and fashion it likes.

However, the delegation theory has been criticized[101] on various grounds. The main objection is based on the holdings of

---

96. See, for instance, the Constitution of the United States, Amendment X. It reads, "The powers not delegated to the United States by the Constitution, nor prohibited by it to the States are reserved to the States respectively, or to the people."
97. See, for example, The Federal Constitution of the Swiss Federation, 1874, Article 120.
98. *Id.* Article 121.
99. *Supra*, n. 30 *per* Sikri C.J. (at p. 377); Shelat and Gover JJ. (at pp. 432-33) and Hegde and Mukharjea JJ. (at p. 481).
100. *Re Article 143 of the Constitution of India,* A.I.R. 1951 S.C. 332.
101. See, for instance, Rajeev Dhavan, *The Supreme Court of India and Parlimentary Sovereinty* (1977), pp. 169-78.

the Supreme Court of the U.S. in *Hawke* v. *Smith,*[102] *Rhode Island* v. *Palmer*[103] and *U.S.* v. *Sprague.*[104] It is submitted that these cases do not support the view that the constituent body is not the delegate of the people. In *Hawk's Case,* what the Court held was that in view of the provision in Article V of the Constitution, Congress was at liberty to decide whether an amendment was to be carried out by ratification or by a convention. But the Court did not negate the premise that the powers derived from the Constitution were derived from the people. The question that arose for consideration in the *Palmer's Case* was whether the eighteenth amendment to the Constitution was effected in excess of the constituent power conferred by Article V of the Constitution. In *Sprague's Case,* the Court held specifically that the Congress was the delegate of the people in exercising the constituent power.[105] Therefore, it may not be proper to reject the theory of delegation in matters of constituent power on the basis of the cases decided by the Supreme Court of the United States. A further objection to the delegation theory is based on

102. 253 U.S. 231 (1919). The plaintiff prayed for injunction to enjoin the Secretary of the State of Ohio from spending money to prepare ballot papers for reference to ratify the questions in relation to the enactment of the XVIII Amendment Act. The question raised in this case is whether the provisions in the Ohio Constitution extending ratification of the XVIII Amendment Act of the U.S. Constitution by reference to people was in conformity with Article V.
103. 253 U.S. 350 (1919). The Constitution of the U.S. was amended by the XVIII Amendment Act whereby manufacture, sale or trade of intoxicating liquor within and import into or export from, the U.S. for the beverage purposes was prohibited. The power of Congress to amend the Constitution was challenged on the ground that it did not have the power to deal with matters relating to liquor. The Court rejected the argument on the ground that it fell within Article V of the Constitution.
104. 282 U.S. 716 (1930). District court quashed an indictment charging the petitioners with unlawful transportation and possession of intoxicating liquor in violation of the National Prohibition Act. The court held that the XVIII amendment act by whose authority the statute was enacted has not been properly ratified to become part of the Constitution. Appeal against the order was filed in the Supreme Court. The Court held that it is for the Congress, the delegate of the people, to determine the mode of referendum.
105. *Id.* at p. 733. The Court held, "Until and unless that Article be changed by amendment, Congress must function as the delegated agent of people in the choice of the method of ratification."

the view prevalent in England that Parliament is a sovereign body and not a delegate of the people[106] and that therefore it was not subject to any limitations whatsoever.[107] Unlike in India, in England, Parliament derives authority not from a Constitution given by the people unto themselves. It, on the other hand, is the creator of every law. Therefore, it may not be wise to explain the constitutional principles of India, a nation with a limited Constitution on the basis of the English law.[108]

It is submitted that the construction that Parliament wields absolute power to amend the Constitution can be grounded only on the positivist imperative theory of law[109] which emphasizes that validity of a law has to be determined with reference to procedural regulations and not on the contents of law. On that basis alone can it be argued that validity and legality of constitutional amendments have to be decided solely on the basis of satisfaction of the procedural requirements expressly provided in the Constitution and not on the impact of such alterations. Such an approach has to be branded as one of legal formalism and hence is not acceptable.

The relevance and necessity of the doctrine of basic structure could be assessed and understood better if we contemplate what may happen in its absence. Constitution of India has accepted the theory of separation of powers though

---

106. *In Re Article 143, Constitution of India,* A.I.R. 1951 S.C. 332 Justice Fazal Ali took such a view on the basis of the English position that legislature was not the agent of the people. (at p. 349).
107. For a discussion of parliamentary sovereignty, See, Ivor Jennings, *The Law and the Constitution* (1959), p. 137 *et. seq.*
108. Even in England there is a contrary view which holds that authority of Parliament in Britain is based on the consent of the people. "The legislative supremacy of the British Parliament, as well as being a legal concept, is also the result of political history and is ultimately based on fact, that is, general recognition by the people and the courts. It is therefore at the same time a legal and political principle." O. Hood Phillips, *Constitutional and Administrative Law* (1973), p. 47. Moreover, entry of U.K. into the European Union has shaken the traditional doctrine of parliamentary sovereignty. See e.g. H.W.R. Wade, "Sovereignty Revolution or Evolution?" (1996) 112 L.Q.R. 568 and T.R.S. Allen, "Parliamentary Sovereignty: Law, Politics and Revolution", (1997) 113 L.Q.R. 443.
109. The Classical Imperative theory propounds that law is the command of the sovereign and it has no correlation with morality. See for a discussion Bodenheimer, *op. cit.* at pp. 91-99.

not in the traditional legal style.[110] One of the concomitants of the theory of separation of powers is that the organs of government can exercise only a limited power and none of the organs of the government can act arbitrarily. Such an arrangement is envisaged by the makers of the Constitution only to check the arbitrary exercise of power by the legislature or the executive. If the power to alter the Constitution is not restricted, Parliament would be able to amend the Constitution in any manner it likes. Parliament would then be able to constitutionalise any law enacted, by altering the provisions of the Constitution. In other words, by exercising the power under Article 368 Parliament would able to tide over the limitations imposed upon it as a legislature by the Constitution and thereby escape the constitutional orbit. Parliament being a body constituted on the basis of political parties, the views of the members of parliament are guided by the policies of those parties to which they subscribe. Hence, decisions in Parliament including amendments of the Constitution depend upon the strength of those parties. A political party, which wields a two-thirds majority in the house, will not find it difficult to amend the Constitution. In other words, in such a context Parliament would play the role of an autocrat. It would be able to politicize the Constitution.[111] It could for instance, "change the democratic government into dictatorship or hereditary monarchy."[112] A political party with a two-thirds majority for a few years could so amend the constitution as to debar any other party from functioning. Through constitutional amendments it would be possible to establish totalitarianism, to enslave the people and "after having effected these purposes make the Constitution unamendable or extremely rigid."[113] In short, if the power under Article 368 is treated as one of unlimited nature and content,

110. *Ram Jawaya Kapoor* v. *State of Punjab,* A.I.R 1955 S.C 549.
111. Politicizing the Constitution is a very bad thing. The very idea of the Constitution turns on the separation of the legal and political realms. The Constitution sets up a few fundamental political ideals such as equality, independence, liberty placing fetters on the temporary majority in the House. See, for a discussion, Alan Brinkley, Nelson W. Polsby and Kathleen M. Sallivan, *New Federalist Papers* (1997), pp. 63-64.
112. *Kesavanda, supra,* n. 30 at p. 767 (*per* Khanna J.)
113. *Id. at* p. 365. (*per* Sikri J.)

limitations imposed on Parliament as a creature of the Constitution would be overcome by it. The very separation of powers and the consequent balance of powers within the constitutional framework could be upset and Parliament could emerge as the sole power holder if a mad Parliament decided to usurp the powers buried in Article 368.[114] These considerations establish beyond doubt that the Supreme Court was not wrong in reading the implied limitations into the concept of power of Parliament to amend it and in incorporating the doctrine of basic structure.

4. THE REASON FOR THE DELAYED ARRIVAL OF THE DOCTRINE

A question arises here. Why did not the doctrine raise its head earlier when the question of amendment was mooted before the Supreme Court? Why did the Court adopt an approach of self-restraint on those occasions? Analysis of the earlier cases would reveal that many factors contributed simultaneously to the non-emergence of the doctrine earlier. Primarily, the earlier cases arose and decided at a time when India had just won independence. Indian democracy was at a very nascent stage. Political set-up in India was very unstable. Legislatures were invoking widest possible powers for the political and economic stability of the nation and for the well-being of the people. It appears that in the early decades of independence, the apex court was not inclined to interfere with the progressive legislative measures unless it was absolutely

114. Later constitutional and political developments in the country indicate that the apprehensions expressed in *Kesavananda* that unlimited power of Parliament to amend the Constitution may lead to arbitrary and autocratic rule of a party. The 39th and 42nd amendments to the Constitution stand testimony to this fact. By the 39th Amendment Act, the then government tried to make elections to the posts of the Prime Minster and the Speaker unquestionable before the courts of law. Similarly, the 42nd amendment act also has been condemned as an expression of sweet will of the ruling party.
The former was struck down in *Indira Gandhi's Case,* 1975 (Supp.) S.C.C. 1 while the latter was declared null and void in *Minerva Mills v. Union of India,* A.I.R 1980 S.C. 1789.

necessary.[115] Considering the fact that the nation had to fight fissiparous tendencies, the Supreme Court attuning itself to the social and political circumstances then prevailing in India rendered very restrictive construction to constitutional provisions so as to enable the State to check those fissiparous tendencies.[116]

The earlier cases relating to amendments to the Constitution are to be analysed in this background. Though questions relating to amendments to the Constitution came up before the Court in those cases the nature and issues involved in them were somewhat different from those in *Kesavananda*. *Sankari Prasad v. Union of India*[117] was the first case where the issue of the amendment of the Constitution was discussed. The only serious question raised in that case was whether 'amendment' under Article 368 could be considered as 'law' for the purpose of Article 13(2).[118] If constitutional amendments come under the concept of law, Parliament would not be competent to amend the Constitution in derogation of fundamental rights. Therefore, answering that question was necessary to determine whether fundamental rights could be abridged by amending the Constitution. Other issues raised in that case were those relating to the formalities and procedure for amending the Constitution.[119] Later in *Sajjan Singh* v. *State of*

115. See for instance, *A.K. Gopalan* v. *State of Madras*, A.I.R 1950 S.C 25 where the Court refused to interfere with the legislative and executive move in imprisoning persons as a preventive measure. But see *State of Madras* v. *Champakam Dorairajan*, A.I.R 1950 S.C 226 where the Court struck down a social welfare legislation as violative of the Constitution.
116. See for instance, *Sankari Prasad* v. *Union of India*, A.I.R 1951 S.C 458. See also *A.K. Gopalan*, *supra*, n. 115.
117. A.I.R 1951 S.C 458. Certain States enacted agrarian reforms legislation. They were challenged as violative of fundamental rights by zamindars. To end such litigations, Parliament enacted Constitution (First Amendment) Act, 1951 incorporating Articles 31A and 31B to the Constitution. The amendment is challenged under Article 32 as unconstitutional.
118. Article 13(2) reads, "The State shall not make any *law* which takes away or abridges the rights conferred by this Part and any *law* made in contravention of this clause shall, to the extent of the contravention, be void." (Emphasis supplied)
119. They *interalia* included the question whether the power to amend the Constitution was conferred on two Houses of Parliament and whether Constitution provides for amending the amendment bill after its introduction in the House. *Supra*, n. 117 at p. 460.

Rajasthan[120] the main questions were whether Parliament under Article 368 could amend fundamental rights and if it could what the procedure for it was. The question of amendability of fundamental rights was again raised before the Court in *I.C Golaknath v. State of Punjab*.[121] In other words, the question in those cases centered mainly on the amendability of fundamental rights in exercise of the power conferred by Article 368. The general question of Parliament's power to amend the Constitution or any part of it other than fundamental rights did not arise for consideration of the Court.

In both *Sankari Prasad and Sajjan Singh* the Court had the same view. In those cases it was held that in exercise of Article 368 Parliament could amend the fundamental rights. The Court reasoned that the makers of the Constitution did not want to keep the fundamental rights beyond the scope of amendment. Moreover, in both those cases the Court held that a constitutional amendment under Article 368 was not law as defined in Article 13(2) and therefore validity of a constitutional amendment under Article 13(2) could not be examined by the judiciary.[122]

However in *Golaknath* a constitutional bench of the Court consisting of 11 judges considered the issue afresh. Examining the issue from the general point of amending the Constitution including the fundamental rights, the majority held that the power to amend the Constitution was contained in Entry 98 of the VII Schedule of the Constitution and therefore amendments to the Constitution were in the nature of legislative procedure.

120. A.I.R 1965 S.C. 845. The Constitution was amended by the first Constitution Amendment) Act, 1951. By it some social welfare legislation were protected. Similarly, some other legislation were protected by the XVII amendment to the Constitution in 1964. These legislation led to the cases of *Sankari Prasad* and *Sajjan Singh* on the ground that they violated the fundamental rights of the petitioner.

121. A.IR. 1967 S.C. 1643. Properties of the petitionrs in different States were acquired under the provisions of different land laws. Such legislation were put in the IX Schedule by the the Constitution (Seventeenth Amendment) Act, 1964 bringing them beyond the pale of judicial review. Three writ petitions were filed challenging the constitutional validity of the Amendment.

122. See, *Shankari Prasad, supra*, n. 117 at p. 463 and *Sajjan Singh, supra*, n. 120 at p. 857.

The Court therefore concluded that constitutional amendments carry with them the characteristics of law and held that in view of Article 13(2) Parliament acting under Article 368, was incompetent to abridge or amend fundamental rights enshrined in the Constitution.[123]

Thus for the first time the Court, in the context of Article 368 read with Article 13(2) introduced some limitations on the power of Parliament to amend the Constitution. To tide over the effect of the decision in *Golaknath,* Parliament amended the Constitution.[124] Provisions were incorporated[125] in the Constitution to the effect that constitutional amendments could not be treated as law for the purpose of Article 13(2) so as to keep constitutional amendments beyond the pale of judicial review.[126] That amendment was in fact a turn in the history of Indian constitutional jurisprudence. Obviously, unlike the past amendments, the twenty-fourth amendment was enacted solely for the purpose of assuring that constitutional amendments would not be nullified on the ground that they violated Part III of the Constitution and to assert supremacy of the constituent power of Parliament. The previous amendments to the Constitution on the other hand were exclusively for the purpose of public welfare. This amendment was a reply to *Golaknath* that constitutional amendments are also amenable to judicial review. It can be considered as a signal of displeasure of Parliament against the judicial restriction of its power to amend the Constitution. It is a declaration that unlike in the legislative sphere, in exercise of constituent power Parliament could wield unlimited power. The peculiarity of the amendment is that unlike the past amendments, it was an assertion of the supremacy of the Parliament in matters of amendments to the

123. *Supra,* n. 121 at p. 1669.
124. The Constitution (Twenty-fourth Amendment) Act, 1971 was enacted for the purpose. By the Act two important changes were brought to effect. By section 2 of the amendment, clause 4 to Article 13 was incorporated. By section 3 of the Act, clauses 1, 2 and 3 were incorporated to Article 368.
125. Articles 13(4) and Article 368(3) introduced by Constitution (Twenty-fourth Amendment) Act, 1971.
126. Article 13(4) reads: "Nothing in this article shall apply to any amendment of this Constitution made under Article 368."
Article 368(3) reads : "Nothing in article 13 shall apply to any amendment made under this article."

Constitution. This amendment opened up an era of tussle for supremacy between Parliament and the judiciary. It was in such a context that the Supreme Court in *Kesavananda* held that though not law, constitutional amendments were amenable to judicial review, which in its turn led to the forty-second amendment of the Constitution.[127]

Thus the amendment of the Constitution by the twenty-fourth amendment altered the nature and content of the issues involved in matters of amendments to the Constitution. It raised the issue from one of amendability of the fundamental rights to one of nature, scope and extent of the constituent power of Parliament. Moreover, the question whether constitutional amendments could be judicially reviewed also was one of serious consideration before the Court. Small wonder that the Court in *Kesavananda* considered all these issues. The main issue in that case was whether the power of Parliament to amend the Constitution was limited in nature and not whether it could amend fundamental rights. It is in such a context that the Court expounded and incorporated the doctrine of basic structure to hold that the power of the Parliament to amend the Constitution was not unlimited. The doctrine was introduced by the Court as an objective criterion for determining the validity of constitutional amendments. In other words, the doctrine was necessary to prevent the arbitrary exercise of power of Parliament to amend the Constitution and thereby to preserve the nature and identity of the Constitution. In the earlier cases like *Sankari Prasad, Sajjan Singh, and Golaknath* the Court was able to decide the limited issue relating to amendment of fundamental rights without the help of any such doctrine.[128] But

127. The constitutionality of the forty-second amendment act was challenged on the basis of the doctrine of basic structure in *Minerva Mills* v. *Union of India*, A.I.R. 1980 S.C. 1789. See, *infra*, Chapter VI, n. 68.

128. Though the wider question of the power amend the Constitution was raised in *Golaknath*, the Court did not make use of the opportunity to examine the scope and extent of the power. The petitioner raised the argument that the amendment "has a positive and negative content and that in exercise of the power of amendment Parliament cannot destroy the structure of the Constitution, but it can only modify the provisions thereof within the framework of the original instrument for its better effectuation. If the fundamentals would be amenable to the ordinary process of amendment with a special majority... the sovereign

the issues in *Kesavananda* being wider, necessitated introduction of the doctrine to base the judicial inclusion of limited nature of the powers to amend the Constitution.

However, *Kesavananda* cannot claim full credit for the doctrine. It cannot be said that the doctrine was originated in *Kesavananda*. It is true that the doctrine got the content and present form in that case. But the idea that the Indian Constitution has some aspects and features beyond the power of Parliament to amend was first projected by Justice Mudholkar in his concurring judgement in the *Sajjan Singh's Case*.[129] However, one finds some fundamental differences between the doctrine as developed in *Kesavananda* and the observations of Justice Mudholkar. To identify such unamendable features Justice Mudholkar used the expression "basic features". Moreover, he observed that such features remain unchangeable only in so far as the Preamble of the Constitution was left unamended. The Preamble according to him was an "epitome of the basic features of the Constitution." Nevertheless, it may not be wrong to state that the doctrine of basic structure was given birth to by Justice Mudholkar. The concept of 'basic features', the mother of the doctrine of basic structure was not, however, elaborately dealt with, discussed or developed by him. The fundamental difference between the doctrine of basic features evolved by Justice Mudholkar and that of the basic structure developed in *Kesavananda* lies in the fact that whereas Justice Mudholkar expounded the view that inalterability of the Constitution would exist only in so far as the Preamble—the epitome of the basic features—was not amended, the *Kesavananda* doctrine of basic structure proclaims that Parliament can under no circumstance amend the basic

---

democratic republic can be converted into a totalitarian system of Government. *There is considerable force in this argument....* But we are relieved of the necessity to express our opinion on this all important question, as, so far as the fundamental rights are concerned, the question can be answered on a narrower basis" *Supra*, n. 121 at p. 1664 (Emphasis applied).

129. He said that the Constitution "formulated a solemn and dignified preamble which appears to be an epitome of the Constitution. Can it not be said that these are indicia of the intention of the Constituent Assembly to give a permanency to the *basic features* of the Constitution. *Supra*, n. 120 at p. 864 (Emphasis added).

structure of the Constitution. It is clear that the doctrine became necessary in *Kesavananda* because Parliament asserted to invoke its power to amend the Constitution in any manner without being struck down by the judiciary. The doctrine is a novel solution to a novel issue.[130]

What is the impact of *Kesavananda* on the earlier cases? Are they overruled? Though *Kesavananda* dealt with novel issues relating to the power of Parliament to amend the Constitution, the Court had to reconsider the questions raised in the previous cases also. The most important question raised in those cases was whether Parliament could amend the fundamental rights. To decide that, it is to be determined whether fundamental rights formed part of the basic structure of the Constitution. The majority held that it did not.[131] In other words the Court held that the fundamental rights were amenable to the amendment jurisdiction of Parliament under Article 368. Such holding in effect is an approval and acceptance of the holding in *Sankari Prasad and Sajjan Singh* that fundamental rights could be amended. It therefore negatives the holding in *Golaknath* that fundamental rights could not be amended. However, the holding of the Court that the power of Parliament to amend the Constitution in accordance with Article is limited amounts to overruling of *Sankari Prasad and Sajjan Singh*. For, in those cases Judges proceeded on a presumption that the power of Parliament to amend the Constitution was unlimited. In this respect *Kesavananda* can be considered as reassertion of *Golaknath*.[132] In short the decision of *Kesavananda* partly overrules all the previous decisions reducing them to academic and historical importance. After *Kesavananda*, constitutionality of an amendment solely depends upon the question whether it alters the basic structure of the Constitution and on nothing else.

---

130. There is a view that no constituent bodies in the world exercised the power to amend the respective Constitutions but for the public weal. See Seervai, *Constitutional Law of India* (1984) at p. 2691.
131. Of the Judges who constituted majority, viz., Sikri C.J., Shelat, Grover, Hegde, Mukharjee, Reddy and Khanna JJ., only Khanna J. opined that fundamental rights did not constitute an ingredient of basic structure. (*Supra*, n. 30 at pp. 764-65). The others held that fundamental rights also formed part of the basic structure. (*Supra*, nn. 54, 55, 56 and 58).
132. Rajeev Dhavan, "The Basic Structure Doctrine—A Footnote Comment," in Rajeev Dhavan and Alice Jacob, *Indian Constitution: Issues and Trends*, (1978) p. 160 at p. 163.

5. AN APPRAISAL OF THE DOCTRINE

The doctrine of basic structure has been acclaimed by a few[133] and scathingly criticised by others.[134] The criticisms are based on several grounds. The doctrine is condemned on the ground that it is an assertion of the supremacy of the judiciary over the constituent powers of Parliament.[135] The doctrine is viewed as objectionable also on the ground that the concept of basic structure was a vague one[136] disabling Parliament at every instance of amendment from knowing whether it affected the basic structure of the Constitution.[137] It is also alleged that the doctrine would place embargoes on the attempt of Parliament to amend the Constitution in the public interest for implementing socio-economic reforms in furtherance of Directive Principles of State Policy.[138] There are views that the doctrine is the outcome of partisan and non-neutral approach of the judiciary in interpreting the Constitution.[139] Another criticism is that the doctrine is based on wrong precedents[140] and that it pushed

133. See, for instance, Upendra Baxi, "Some Reflections on the Nature of Constituent Power", in Rajeev Dhavan and Alice Jacob, *op. cit.* at p. 122 and A. Lakshminath, "Justiciability of Constitutional Amendments," in *id.* at p. 144.
134. See for example T.S. Ramarao, "Constitutional Amendments, Judicial Review and Constitutionalism in India," and M.H. Beg, "The Supremacy of the Constitution", in R. Dhavan and Alice Jacob (Ed.) *Indian Constitution: Trends and Issues* (1978), at p. 108 and p. 113 respectively. See also H.M. Seervai, "The Fundamental Rights Case: At the Cross Roads", 74 Bom. L.R. (Jour) 47 (1973); R.D. Garg, "Phantom of basic structure of the Constitution: A Critical Appraisal of the Kesavananda Case", 16 J.I.L.I. 243 (1975) and D. Conrad, "Constituent Power, Amendment and Basic Structure of the Constitution: A Critical Reconsideration" at pp. 6-7, Delhi L.R. 24 (1977-78).
135. S.P. Sathe, "Limitations on Constitutional Amendment: "Basic Structure" Principle Re-examined" in Rajeev Dhavan and Alice Jacob, *op. cit.* at p. 179.
136. Koteswara Rao, "Does the Indian Constitution Need a Basic Overhauling: A Case for Convening a Constituent Assembly," in Rajeev Dhavan and Alice Jacob, *op. cit.* 99 at p. 101.
137. Seervai, *Constitutional Law of India*, Vol. III (1996), p. 3159.
138. *Id.* at pp. 3159, 3161.
139. Rajeev Dhavan, *The Supreme Court and Parliamentary Sovereignty* (1975), p. 245.
140. P.K. Tripathi, "Kesavananda Bharathi *v.* The State of Kerala, Who Wins?" (1974) 1 S.C.C. 1

judges into politics.[141] In addition to these specific criticisms there were charges that it lacked logical consistency and philosophical background.[142] Small wonder that amidst such varied criticisms, even the Supreme Court doubted the conceptual accuracy and logical precision as well as feasibility of the doctrine of basic structure in the Indian constitutional panorama. Therefore, at the earliest opportunity, the Court made an attempt[143] to review the doctrine. Such a decision was taken at the time of hearing *Indira Gandhi v. Raj Narayan*[144] in which the doctrine was sought to be invoked. The attempt of the Court in reviewing the doctrine was criticised as "a truly extraordinary occurrence replete with puzzles and improprieties."[145] The Court later dropped the steps to review the doctrine.

The juristic condemnation of the doctrine and the lack of self-confidence of the Court are not unexpected. For, the doctrine was unheard of anywhere in the world before, and the results of the doctrine in the constitutional and the legal parlance were yet to be known. Implications of the doctrine were not fully exposed. What was discussed by courts abroad was only the implied limitation on the power of the constituent bodies to amend the Constitution. They did not deal with an objective criterion like the doctrine of basic structure to determine such limitations. Moreover, what the doctrine establishes is that it is the Constitution and not the Court or the Parliament that is supreme.[146] The holding can therefore be treated as "...a remarkable feet of judicial activism unparalleled in the history of world constitutional adjudication."[147] The doctrine represents the features of the Constitution, which give

---

141. Rajeev Dhavan, "The Basic Structure Doctrine—A Footnote Comment" in Rajeev Dhavan and Alice Jacob, *op. cit.* 160 at pp. 166-67 and 178.
142. See generally Rajeev Dhavan, *The Supreme Court and Parliamentary Sovereignty* (1975).
143. See for a narration, Upendra Baxi, *The Supreme Court and Politics* (1980), pp. 70-76.
144. 1975 supp. S.C.C. 1.
145. *Id.* at p. 70.
146. Upendra Baxi, "Some Reflections on the Nature of Constituent Power in Rajeev Dhavan and Alice Jacob *op. cit.* at p. 123.
147. Upendra Baxi, *Courage Craft and Contention* (1985), p. 65.

life to certainty, uniformity and continuity to the legal system which therefore are beyond the scope of amendment without the sanction of the people. Absence of a provision in the Constitution for reference to people for fundamental alteration of Constitution also would justify introduction of a limitation on the power of amendment, for, "if you do not apply brakes, the engine of amending power would soon overrun the Constitution".[148]

Further, the decision cannot be disapproved on the ground that the principle of implied limitations upon which doctrine is based was rejected by the Supreme Court of United States[149] and Courts of Ireland. There is a fundamental difference between the constitutions of those countries and that of India. The Constitutions of those States contain some explicit restrictions on the power of the respective constituent bodies to amend the Constitution. Presence of such limitations excludes any kind of implied limitations on the amendment power.[150] The Constitution of India, on the other hand, does not contain explicit substantive restrictions on the power of the amending body. Such a situation calls for incorporation of some implied limitations. Moreover, in the federal countries like U.S., Australia and Canada, the fundamental features of the respective Constitutions have not been altered in exercise of the power to amend.[151] Amendment of the U.S. Constitution on an important matter like abolition of slavery was only the consequence of the civil war.[152] Therefore, there is no meaning in rejecting the doctrine of basic structure in India on the ground that it was not acceptable to foreign countries.

However, it is to be admitted that some of the criticisms levelled against the decision are not without some merit. Though full of creativity, it cannot be said that the decision in *Kesavananda* is without defects. While introducing the principle

148. *Id.* at p. 68.
149. For example, *Rhode Island* v. *Palmer*, 253 U.S. 350. (1919).
150. *Expressio Unius Exclusio Alterius*.
151. Seervai, *op. cit.* at p. 2691.
152. *Ibid.*, He observed, "However, the problem of slavery was solved not by the exercise of the amending power but by victory in a civil war; the 13th, the 14th and the 15th amendments in so far as they relate to slavery only confirmed what the war had accomplished in fact."

of implied limitations and developing the doctrine of basic structure, the Court referred to some foreign decisions and relied upon others. They include decisions of the Privy Council, Supreme Court of the United States, High Court of Australia and the Supreme Court of Ireland. However, those decisions were either irrelevant or do not support the holding of the Court in *Kesavananda*. Thus, the questions addressed in *Bribery Commissioner* v. *Pedrick Ranasinghe,*[153] and *Liyange* v. *The Queen*[154] referred to by the judges[155] were not similar to those in *Kesavananda*. In *Ranasinghe,*[156] the issue was the power of the legislature to enact laws contrary to the Constitution of Ceylon. The question in *Liyange*[157] on the other hand, related to exercise of judicial power by the Ceylon Parliament. Some of the decisions rendered by the High Court of Australia[158] referred by the judges[159] also deal with constitutional validity of certain statutes.[160] The observation of Chief Justice Kennedy in the

153. [1965] A.C 172.
154. [1967] 1 A.C 259.
155. See for instance, *Kesavananda, supra,* n. 30 at pp. 441-44. (*per* Shelat and Grover JJ.).
156. In this case the respondents were punished in accordance with the Bribery Act, 1954 as amended in 1958. Some of the provisions of the act where in conflict with the Constitution of Ceylon. It as provided in the Act that in case of conflict with the Constitution, those provisions should be considered as amendments to it. But the Constitution provided for a procedure for its own amendment. However the impugned enactment was not in accordance with the procedure. Hence the petition for invalidating the conviction.
157. The Ceylon Parliament passed Criminal Laws (Spl. Provision) Act, 1962 to try accused persons who participated in an abortive coup. Fresh legislation was enacted as the existing legislation was held unconstitutional. The Privy Council struck down that law also on the ground that Parliament usurped the judicial functions, which by virtue of the Constitution Parliament was not competent to hold.
158. *Melbourne Corporation* v. *Commonwealth,* (1947) 74 C.L.R and 31, *Victoria* v. *Commonwealth,* (1971) 45 A.L.J. 251.
159. See, for instance, *Kesavananda, supra,* n. 30 at pp. 349-53. (*per* Sikri C.J.)
160. *Melbourne Corporation* dealt with the question of constitutional validity of section 48 of the Banking Act, 1945 which prohibits a bank from conducting any banking business for a State without the permission of the Commonwealth Treasury. *Victoria,* on the other hand deals with the question of validity of the Pay-Roll Tax Act, 1941 and the Pay-Roll Tax Assessment Act, 1941.

decision, *Jeremiah Ryan* v. *Captain Michael Lenons*[161] of the Irish Supreme Court, heavily relied upon by the judges for identifying the implied limitations was in fact the dissenting view. Moreover, none of the cases deals with the power of the constituent body to amend the respective constitutions. That is so, because, in any of the above countries, no amendments altering the basic structure were effected.

The criticism that the concept of basic structure is vague and that for deciding whether any amendment is violative of the basic structure will be known only when the issue is decided by the Court is true to a certain extent. *Raghupath Rao Ganpath Rao* v. *Union of India*[162] is such an example. The question raised in that case was whether the expression 'integral part of the Constitution' used in *Madhava Rao Scindia* v. *Union of India*,[163] was synonymous with 'basic structure'? In *Raghupath Rao*, the validity of the Constitution (twenty-sixth Amendment) Act, 1971[164] by which the payment of Privy Purse to the erstwhile rulers of the princely states was discontinued, was challenged on the ground that it destroyed the basic philosophy, personality, structure and feature of the Constitution. The Court held that the expression 'integral part' of the Constitution did not mean the concept of 'essential feature' of the Constitution because they are totally distinct and qualitatively different concepts. Each and every provision, concept and institution in

161. 1935 Irish Reports 170.
162. 1994 Supp. (1) S.C.C. 191. That consisted of two writ petitions challenging the validity of the Constitution (Twenty-sixth Amendment) Act, 1971 *inter alia* on the ground that it violated the basic structure and essential features of the Constitution and hence outside the power of the Parliament to amend the Constitution.
163. See, *Madhava Rao Scindia* v. *Union of India*, (1971) 1 S.C.C. 85. It was observed in that case that the institution of Rulerships—*is an integral part of the constitutional scheme.*" And "an order mere 'de-recognising' A Ruler without providing for continuation of the institution of Rulership which *is an integral part of the constitutional scheme* is, therefore, plainly illegal."
164. By the impugned amendment Act Parliament deleted Articles 291 and 362 and inserted Article 363-A and substituted a fresh clause (22) under Article 366. The cumulative effect of the above alterations was to terminate the privy purse privileges of the former Indian Rulers and to terminate expressly the recognition already granted to them under those two deleted Articles.

the Constitution is an integral part of the Constitution; but that does not mean that all of them constitute its essential feature.[165]

Further, it is clear from the discussion of *Kesavananda* that what the Judges meant by the doctrine is the fundamental feature of the legal system. If so, not only a constitutional amendment but also enactment of statute and even action of the Executive can be assailed on the basis of the doctrine. However, in *Kesavananda*, the Court did not make use of the doctrine to test the constitutionality of the impugned statute. It is perhaps this approach that led to the decision in *Indira Gandhi* v. *Raj Narain*, that the doctrine of basic structure was not applicable for testing the validity of statutes.[166]

However, such criticisms do not show that the doctrine of basic structure is defective. The defect lies not in the innovation and introduction of the doctrine, but in the failure of *Kesavananda* in reaching a consensus as to what its contents are and in properly and comprehensively exploring and developing the doctrine. In spite of these defects in the formulation of the doctrine, the Supreme Court deserves appreciation for its contribution in *Kesavananda*.

The doctrine of basic structure implies that Parliament cannot exercise its constituent power under the Constitution so as to destroy the identity of the Constitution. Does it mean that constitutionality of all amendments right from the first one in 1951 is liable to be evaluated on the basis of the doctrine of basic structure enunciated in *Kesavanamda* in 1973? This aspect came up for consideration before the Court in *Waman Rao* v. *Union of*

---

165. The Court observed thus, "It is clear that the learned Judge used the words 'integral part' in their ordinary and connotation—not in any lexicographical sense. Ordinarily speaking, 'integral' means "of a whole or necessary to the completeness of a whole" (Concise Oxford Dictionary). Our Constitution is not a disjointed document. It incorporates a particular socio-economic and political philosophy. It is an integral whole. Every provision of it is an integral part of it—even the provisions contained in Part XXI, "Temporary, Transitional and Special Provisions". One may ask which provision, which concept or which 'institution' or concept is an integral part of the Constitution? He will not find an answer. To say that a particular provision or a particular 'institution' or concept is an integral part of the Constitution is not to say that it is an essential feature of the Constitution. Both are totally distinct and qualitatively different concepts." (*Supra*, n 162 at p. 219).

166. For a discussion, see, *infra*, Chapter, 7 nn. 167-79 and the text thereof.

India.[167] The issue considered by the Court in that case was whether Articles 31A[168] and 31B[169] incorporated by the First Amendment Act and 31C[170] incorporated by the twenty-fifth amendment act were violative of the concept of basic structure and hence unconstitutional. The Court held that Articles 31A and 31C were not violative of the basic structure.[171] It was further held that the first amendment has made the constitutional goal of equal justice a living truth and hence it strengthened the basic structure.[172] However, in determining the constitutionality of Article 31B,[173] the Court did not check up its

167. A.I.R. 1981 S.C. 271. That was a bunch of writ petitions filed challenging the validity of Maharashtra Agricultural Lands (Ceiling on Holdings) Act, 1961 amended by subsequent Acts. Originally the challenge was before the High Court of Maharashtra in writ petitions entitled *Vithalrao Udhaorao* v. *State of Maharashtra,* A.I.R 1977 Bom. 99 on the ground that the Act violated Part III rights. The challenge was repelled by the Court on the ground that the statute and the amendments were protected by being included in the Ninth Schedule of the Constitution and also because of the suspension of the fundamental rights due to the operation of emergency. The Court held that Article 31B as incorporated by the first amendment to the Constitution supported the basic structure rather than destroyed it. Appeals against the decision were filed before the Supreme Court. They were also dismissed while the emergency was on operation. After the revocation of emergency, the Court agreed to review the decision of those cases also.
168. It was inserted into the Constitution by section 4 of the Constitution (First Amendment) Act, 1951.
169. It was inserted into the Constitution by section 5 of the Constitution (First Amendment) Act, 1951.
170. It was inserted into the Constitution by section 3 of the Constitution (Twenty-fifth) Amendment Act, 1971.
171. *Supra,* n. 167 at pp. 285 and 291.
172. The Court held, "The First Amendment has thus made the constitutional ideal of equal justice a living truth. It is like a mirror that reflects the ideals of the Constitution; it is not the destroyer of its basic structure....The Fist Amendment is aimed at removing social and economic disparities in the agricultural sector. It may happen that while existing inequalities are being removed, new inequalities may arise marginally and incidentally. Such marginal and incidental inequalities cannot damage or destroy the basic structure of the Constitution." (*Id*. at p. 285).
173. It was *inter alia* provided by Article 31-B that notwithstanding any judicial decision the laws incorporated in the Ninth Schedule of the Constitution should not be considered as invalid on the ground that they violated the rights conferred by Part III of the Constitution. In other words, the provision has restricted the scope of judicial review.

validity on the basis of the doctrine of basic structure. Instead, the Court proceeded to examine the constitutionality of amendments incorporating of statutes into the Ninth Schedule and held that amendments before 24 April, 1973[174] would not be open to challenge on the ground that they violated the basic structure. Amendments to the Constitution and incorporation of laws in the Ninth Schedule subsequent to that date alone were liable to be judicially reviewed on the anvil of basic structure doctrine. The Court reached the conclusion that the doctrine had only a prospective operation on the ground that if amendments prior to the decision were also evaluated on the doctrine, it would upset the settled claims and titles of the people who acted on the then existing constitutional position.[175] After twenty-five years of *Waman Rao*, in *I.R. Coelho* v. *State of Tamil Nadu*,[176] the court reiterated the holding that judicial review of constitutional amendments was limited to post-*Kesavananda Bharathi*. The court held,[177]

> "[A]ll amendments to the Constitution made on or after 24-4-1973 by which the Ninth Schedule is amended by inclusion of various laws therein shall have to be tested on the touchstone of the basic or essential features of the Constitution as reflected in Article 21 read with Article 14,

174. It was on that day that the Supreme Court decided *Kesavananda* and incorporated the doctrine of basic structure.
175. The Court observed thus, "We propose to draw a line, treating the decision in *Kesavananda Bharathi* (AIR 1973 SC 1461) as the landmark. Several Acts were put in the Ninth Schedule prior to that decision on the supposition that the power of the Parliament to amend the Constitution was wide and untrammeled. The theory that the Parliament cannot exercise its amending power so as to damage or destroy the basic structure of the Constitution, was propounded and accepted for the first time in *Kesavananda Bharathi*. This is one reason for upholding the laws incorporated into the Ninth Schedule before 24 April, 1973, on which date the judgment in *Kesavananda Bharathi* was rendered. A large number of properties might have changed hands and several new titles must have come into existence on the faith and belief that the laws included in the Ninth Schedule were not open to challenge on the ground that they were violative of Articles 14, 19 and 31. We will not be justified in upsetting settled claims and titles and in introducing chaos and confusion into the lawful affairs of a fairly ordered society. (at p. 290).
176. (2007) 2 SCC 1. For a discussion of the case, see, *infra* Chapter 7, nn. 160-164.
177. *Id*. at p. 111.

Article 19, and the principles underlying them. To put it differently even though an Act is put in the Ninth Schedule by a constitutional amendment, its provisions would be open to attack on the ground that they destroy or damage the basic structure if the fundamental right or rights taken away or abrogated pertains or pertain to the basic structure".

The implication of the decisions is very clear. The Court was trying to reduce the operation of the doctrine of basic structure to amendments subsequent to its introduction. Such a limitation is an innovation by the Court, which helped leaving the settled claims and titles arising from such legislation untouched. But it is doubtful whether what the Court has done is correct. The concept of basic structure gives identity not only to the Constitution but it is the very foundation of the legal system. Amendment of the Constitution affecting its basic structure amounts to alteration of its personality. Therefore, limiting the application of the doctrine to the future is likely to lead to certain undesirable results. The dimensions of the doctrine of basic structure are not finally settled. New ingredients are being introduced into the doctrine. In such a situation, if any pre-*Kesavananda* amendment was found to have damaged any feature identified as an ingredient of basic structure, the Court would not be able to strike it down in so far it relates to pre-*Kesavananda* period. It is doubtful whether such implications were taken into account by the Court when it held in *Waman Rao* and *I.R. Coelho* that basic structure had only a prospective application. Considering the significance of the doctrine, the court could have limited the exclusion of the doctrine to the pre-*Kesavananda* issues instead of excluding the pre-*Kesavananda* amendments from its purview.

In spite of such conceptual errors, the Supreme Court has no doubt indulged in a highly creative exercise in introducing of the doctrine of basic structure in *Kesavananda*. It is beyond doubt that by the doctrine the Court tried to protect and maintain the identity of the Indian Constitution acting as the guardian of the Constitution.[178]

178. In *Marbury* v. *Madison,* (1803) 1 Cranch. 137. Chief Justice Marshall observed that the judiciary was to uphold and guard the Constitution (at pp. 178-79).

Basic Structure : Crystallisation of the Doctrine

I. PARLIAMENT-JUDICIARY CONFRONTATION AND THE TAKE-OFF OF THE BASIC STRUCTURE

In *Kesavananda* the Court was at the pinnacle of creativity. By the introduction of the doctrine of basic structure into our Constitution, the Court brought out unforeseen changes in the history of constitutional jurisprudence of the world.[1] Though some aspects were identified as the ingredients of the doctrine, in *Kesavananda Bharathi* the Court was not able to clarify and explain fully the ingredients of the doctrine due to the lack of consensus among the judges. The doctrine unleashed a lot of criticisms from different quarters.[2] Such criticisms had their impacts in the judicial attitude also.[3] As a consequence, the

1. For a discussion of the case, see *supra*, Chapter 6, nn. 30-58.
2. For the criticisms, see *supra*, Chapter 6, nn. 134-42.
3. "Some scholars have clapped and some scholars have scoffed at the decisions in the Fundamental Rights. Case. These criticisms I cannot deny, cause a flutter in the ivory tower". *Per* Chandrachud J. in *Indira Gandhi*, *infra*, n. 6 (at p. 246).

Court decided to review the case and it was feared that the death knell of the doctrine was sounded. But the Court dropped the programme of reviewing the case presumably because, the Bar did not cooperate with the Court.[4] The doctrine had a colourful life thereafter and played a vital role in the constitutional, legal, political, social and economic developments in India.

One of the major criticisms levelled against *Kesavananda* was that there was no consensus among the judges as to the contents of the doctrine.[5] The Court had therefore a twin task before it. First, it had to concretize and provide a more firm conceptual basis for the doctrine. Second, the Court had to explain the essential ingredients of the doctrine of basic structure. The Court had opportunity to deal with and develop the doctrine of basic structure in a lot of cases after *Kesavananda*. Apart from concretizing and fixing firmly what *Kesavananda* said, the train of cases dealing with the doctrine delineated its ingredients.

Democracy and the Rule of Law

In *Indira Gandhi* v. *Raj Narain*,[6] (*Indira Gandhi*, for short) popularly called the *Election Case* the question of applicability of the doctrine came up before the Court for the first time since *Kesavananda*.[7] The Court consisted of five judges who were judges in *Kesavananda* also.[8] It may be an irony that four[9] of

4. *Cf.* Upendra Baxi, *The Supreme Court and Politics* (1985), pp. 70-76.
5. *Supra*, Chapter VI, n. 59.
6. 1975 Supp. S.C.C. 1. The respondent had filed an election petition against the appellant, the then Prime Minister on the ground that she committed corrupt practices during the election in 1971. The High Court of Allahabad rendered verdict in his favour and set aside the election of the appellant. She appealed against it in the Supreme Court.
7. Unlike the earlier cases dealing with the power of Parliament to amend the Constitution under Article 368, in which the main issue was the amendment of the fundamental rights, the *Election Case* dealt with the essential feature of representative government namely free and fair elections and the nature and location of judicial power. See Seervai, *Constitutional Law of India*, Vol. III (1996) pp. 3129-30.
8. Chief Justice A.N. Ray, H.R. Khanna, K.K. Mathew, M.H. Beg and Chandrachud JJ.
9. A.N. Ray, Mathew, Beg and Chandrachud JJ. Only Khanna J. held in *Kesavananda* that the power of Parliament to amend the Constitution as limited by the doctrine of basic structure.

them, who had rejected the doctrine of basic structure and stood for unlimited power of Parliament to amend the Constitution holding that there was no implied limitation on it, had to deal with the doctrine in *Indira Gandhi*. In *Indira Gandhi*, the Court had to examine the doctrine of basic structure as the validity of the 39th amendment to the Constitution by which Article 329A was incorporated[10] into the Constitution was challenged. It was challenged that clauses (4) and (5) of Article 329A were invalid on the ground that they excluded operation of any law in the

10. Article 329A read thus "(1) Subject to the provisions of Chapter II of Part V [Except sub-clause (e) of clause (1) of Article 102], no election—to either House of Parliament of a person who holds the office of Prime Minister at the time of such election or is appointed as Prime Minister after such election; to the House of the People of a person who holds the office of Speaker of that House at the time of such election or who is chosen as the Speaker for that House after such election; shall be called in question, except before such authority [not being any such authority as is referred to in clause (b) of Article 329] or body and in such manner as may be provided for by or under any law made by Parliament and any such law may provide for all other matters relating to doubts and disputes in relation to such election including the grounds on which such election may be questioned.
(2) The validity of any such law as is referred to in clause (1) and the decision of any authority or body under such law shall not be called in question in any court.
(3)...
(4) No law made by Parliament before the commencement of the Constitution (Thirty-ninth Amendment) Act, 1975, in so far as it relates to election petitions and matters connected therewith, shall apply or shall be deemed ever to have applied to or in relation to the election of any such person is referred to in clause (1) to either House of Parliament and such election shall not be deemed to be void or ever to have become void on any ground on which such election could be declared to be void or has, before such commencement, been declared to be void under any such law and notwithstanding any order made by any court, before such commencement, declaring such election to be void, such election shall continue to be valid in all respects and any such order and any finding on which such order is based shall be and shall be deemed always to have been void and of no effect.
(5) Any appeal or cross-appeal against any such order of any court as is referred to in clause (4) pending immediately before the commencement of the Constitution (Thirty-ninth Amendment) Act, 1975, before the Supreme Court shall be disposed of in conformity with the provisions of clause (4).
(6) The provisions of this article shall have effect notwithstanding anything contained in this Constitution.

matter of election of the Prime Minister and the Speaker of the Lok Sabha and divested the judiciary of the power to determine the validity of the elections of those persons. The impugned amendment was therefore alleged to have violated the principles of democracy, rule of law, separation of powers and judicial review, which according to the petitioner were essential ingredients of the basic structure of the Constitution of India.

Examining the scope of the doctrine of basic structure, the Court held that democracy was an ingredient of basic structure of the Constitution.[11] It meant that if an amendment damaged any feature of democracy in any manner, it would be unconstitutional. In other words, Parliament was incompetent to amend the Constitution to the extent of altering the democratic foundation of the Constitution of India.

What is meant by the term 'democracy'? How can it be determined whether an amendment damaged democracy? Does it imply a presidential or parliamentary form of government? The judges addressed themselves to these questions and tried to find answers. The expression cannot have a precise meaning nor can it be comprehensively defined. Justice Chandrachud observed that the concept 'democracy' is very broad and complex[12] and that equality was the faith and creed of democracy.[13] Justice Khanna said that democracy postulates that there should be free and fair periodic elections enabling people to choose and re-elect or change representatives and that it postulates the presence of a mechanism for the settlement of election disputes.[14] Popular sovereignty and equality among the people were also identified by Justice Mathew as part and parcel of democracy.[15] Though the concept of democracy was not an easy one to explain, from the above observations of the judges as also from the juristic expositions,[16] it is clear that it

11. *Supra*, n. 6. *per* Khanna J. (at p. 198); Mathew J. (at p. 119) and Chandarachud J. (at p. 255).
12. *Id.* at p. 255
13. *Id.* at p. 256
14. *Id.* at pp. 87-88
15. *Id.* at p. 135.
16. See, for instance, W. Friedman, *Legal Theory* (1949), p. 435. He observes, "A discussion of the principal legal values of modern democracy can be grouped around four themes of legal theory: (1) The legal rights of the individuals. (2) *Equality before the law.* (3) *The control of government by the people.* (4) *The rule of law.* (Emphasis supplied)

envisages free and fair election on the basis of equality of individuals and an independent dispute settlement mechanism.

Evidently, if the 39th amendment to the Constitution adversely affected any of the above aspects, it is liable to be struck down. Elections to Parliament and State legislatures are conducted in accordance with the provisions of the Representation of the People Act 1950. By the impugned amendment to the Constitution, it was stipulated that elections of the Prime Minister and the Speaker would not be governed by the existing election laws. It further provided that their elections would not be amenable to the jurisdiction of any court.[17] It implied that their elections were made beyond the purview of any law of the realm and beyond the reach of the judiciary. In other words, the amendment struck at the root of the concept of equality which the judges identified as an essential ingredient of democracy by keeping Prime Minister and Speaker above and beyond the reach of law. The Court identified clause (4) of Article 329A as incorporated by the impugned Amendment Act as one which suffered from certain vices. It abolished the existing forum for settling disputes relating to elections of Prime Minister and Speaker of Lok Sabha without creating a new one. This led to a situation were there was no law for regulating elections to the posts of the Prime Minister and the Speaker of the Lok Sabha.[18] The absence of a forum for settling disputes relating to elections denied the aggrieved persons the right to a remedy. It therefore did away with the concept of free and fair elections, which is an essential ingredient of democracy.[19] Justice Mathew alleged that non-application of any law to certain elections was despotic in nature and would damage the democratic structure of the Constitution.[20] He also observed that dispensation of the judicial forum for settling election disputes also resulted in damaging an essential ingredient of democracy.[21] According to

17. Constitution of India, Article 329A(4) as incorporated by the Constitution (Thirty-ninth Amendment) Act, 1975.
18. *Supra*, n. 6 *per* Ray C.J. (at p. 44) Khanna J. (at p. 87-88) Mathew J. (at pp. 129, 133). Chandrachud J. (at p. 257).
19. *Id.*, at p. 88 (*per* Khanna J.)
20. *Id.*, at p. 128.
21. *Id.*, at p. 129.

Justice Chandarachud the provisions happened to violate democracy on the ground that they made the existing law inapplicable to the elections of the Prime Minister and the Speaker and thereby denied equality and were therefore arbitrary in nature.[22] In short, the majority of the judges found the provisions of the impugned constitutional amendment contrary to the concept of democracy on different grounds.[23] The Court therefore struck down clause (4) of Article 329A as incorporated by the 39th amendment Act as violative of democracy an aspect of basic structure of our Constitution.[24]

Earlier, in *Kesavananda,* the Court had accepted that the contents of the Preamble were indicia of the concept of basic structure. Democracy forms part of the Preamble.[25] Therefore, democratic form of government also was held as part of basic structure of the Constitution. Obviously, in *Kesavananda* the judges included democratic form of life within the concept of basic structure not because they thought it to be of great importance, but because, it was included in the Preamble. Thus holding of the Court in *Indira Gandhi* that democracy formed an ingredient of the basic structure of the Constitution is undoubtedly an advancement of the decision of *Kesavananda.*

It is evident from the above discussion that democratic set up is essentially based on equality among the people. From the very concept of right to equal representation in the government each individual in a democratic state is entitled to equality in all respects.[26] There must be equality in holding rights and

---

22. *Id.,* at pp. 257-58.
23. Ray C.J. however did not deal with the question whether democracy formed part of the basic structure of the Constitution. But he held that free and fair elections did not form part of the basic structure of the Constitution. See, *supra,* n. 6 at pp. 43-44. Similarly, Beg J. also surprisingly remained silent on the issue.
24. *Id., per* Khanna J. (at p. 87); *per* Mathew J. (at p. 134) and *per* Chandrachud J. (at pp. 258-59).
25. It reads, "We, the People of India, having solemnly resolved to constitute India into a Sovereign Socialist Secular *Democratic* Republic ..." (Emphasis supplied)
26. See, Friedman, *supra,* n. 16 at p. 435. He said thus, "The main forces in the development of modern democratic thought have been the liberal idea of individual rights protecting the individual and the democratic idea proper, proclaiming equality of rights and popular sovereignty. *The gradual extension of the idea of equality from the political to the social and economic field has added the problems of social security and economic planning.*" (Emphasis supplied.)

shouldering duties irrespective of the status of individuals. Such a concept of equality is based on the doctrine of Rule of Law. In other words, a real democratic set-up would be possible only where there is rule of law. "Rule of Law postulates that the decisions must be made by applications of known principles and rules and in general such decisions should be predictable and the citizen should know where he is."[27] It also means that "the exercise of the power of government shall be conditioned by law and that subject to the exceptions to the doctrine of equality, no one shall be exposed to the arbitrary will of the government."[28] Further, rule of law confers power on the judiciary to look into the allegations of corrupt practices and abuse of constitutional power of the Prime Minister.[29] Rule of law is highly necessary for excluding arbitrary interference by the government.[30] Democratic set-up is therefore possible only if the presence of the rule of law is assured. In other words, democracy postulates rule of law. It implies that since democracy is a feature of basic structure, 'rule of law' also should be. The Court therefore held that rule of law also forms part of the basic structure of the Constitution of India.[31] Some of the judges[32] went to the extent of holding that the concept of equality also constituted an ingredient of the basic structure as it has a thick relation with the rule of law. Though the majority did not hold that the concept of equality was part of the basic structure, the holding of the Court that rule of law is an element of basic structure is an instance of judicial creativity.

---

27. *Supra*, n . 6 at p. 91. (*per* Khanna J.)
28. *Id.* at p. 252 (*per* Chandrachud J.)
29. *Id.* at p. 148 (*per* Beg J.).
30. *Cf.* A.V. Dicey, *Introduction to the Study of the Law of the Constitution* (1962), pp. cxvii-cxviii
31. *Supra*, n. 6 at pp. 90-91. "In any case, the vice of clause (4) [of the 39th Amendment Act] would still lie in the fact that the election of the appellant was declared to be valid on the basis that it *was not to be governed by any law for settlement of election disputes*." (*per* Khanna J.) (Emphasis supplied); at p. 136 (Mathew J.) and at p. 252 (Chandrachud J.)
32. *Id.* Mathew J. (at p. 137). He observes, "Leaving aside these extravagant versions of rule of law, there is a genuine concept of rule of law and that concept implies equality before the law or equal subjection of all classes to the ordinary law" and Chandrachud J. (at p. 252).

The holding of the Court in *Indira Gandhi* that democracy and rule of law are ingredients of the basic structure of the Constitution of India claims our attention for more reasons than one. It is the first instance where the Court has given a fresh life to the doctrine of the basic structure. Till this decision was made, the Court was in a state of flux and there was no unanimity among the judges as to the contents of the basic structure. It is in this case that the Court gave confirmation to the doctrine and tried to explore the contents of basic structure. The decision in *Indira Gandhi* is a creative step of the Supreme Court in interpreting the power of Parliament to amend the Constitution. *Indira Gandhi* identified some of the instances of limitation on the power of the Parliament to amend the Constitution and thus gave firm root to the doctrine of basic structure. Further, the holding of the Court that both democracy and rule of law are to be recognized as ingredients of the basic structure deserves our attention for yet another reason. Democracy and rule of law are the twin devices, which serve the common end of correcting the government. They are complementary to each other and one cannot exist without the other.[33] The decision by bringing both democracy and rule of law as unamendable features of our Constitution upheld the identity of the Constitution of India, can be considered as a worthy successor of *Kesavananda*.

Though *Indira Gandhi* is an instance of judicial creativity, can we say that the decision is an ideal instance of judicial innovation? It seems that the decision of *Indira Gandhi* cannot be considered as an ideal instance of creativity as it suffers from some shortcomings. The Court in this case had an occasion to examine the scope and extent of the expression, 'constituent power' under Article 368.[34] Is it subject to the concept of separation of powers? In other words, is separation of powers an essential ingredient of the basic structure? The Court was not able to form any opinion on the question of the meaning of the expression, 'constituent power' and lay down any law. Four of

33. P.K. Tripathi, *Spotlights on Constitutional Interpretation* (1972), pp. 169-70.
34. For the text of the Article, see *supra*, Chapter 6, n. 17.

the judges equally divided on this issue and the fifth judge expressed no opinion. Two of the judges namely, Chief Justice A.N. Ray and Justice Mathew held that 'constituent power' and the doctrine of separation of powers operate at different levels. Chief Justice A.N. Ray held that the constituent power was independent of the doctrine of separation of powers.[35] Justice Mathew also observed in more or less similar terms[36] and went to the extent of holding that exercise of judicial power by Parliament could not be considered as an act of damaging the basic structure of the Constitution embodied in the separation of powers.[37] Thus Chief Justice A.N. Ray[38] and Justice Mathew[39] held that separation of powers was not an unamendable feature of the Constitution. In other words, according to them it did not form part of the basic structure of our Constitution.

Two other judges namely Justice Beg and Justice Chandrachud on the other hand, held that the doctrine of separation of powers was an important one, it went to the root of the Constitution of India, it was an ingredient of the basic

35. *Supra*, n. 6 at p. 42. He justified the conclusion thus, "When the constituent power exercises powers the constituent power comprises legislative, executive and judicial powers. All powers flow from the constituent power through the Constitution to the various departments or heads. In the hands of the constituent authority there is no demarcation of powers. It is only when the constituent authority defines the authorities or demarcates the areas that separation of power is discussed."
36. *Id.*, at p. 132. He observed, "But this doctrine which is directed against the concentration of these powers in the same hand has no application as such when the question is whether an amending body can exercise judicial power. In other words, the doctrine is directed against the concentration of these sovereign powers in one or other organ of Government. It was not designed to limit the power of a constituent body."
37. "And if the amending body exercised judicial power in adjudging the validity of the election, it cannot be said that by that act, it has damaged a basic structure of the Constitution embodied in the doctrine of separation of powers (*Id.* at pp. 132-33).
38. *Id.* at p. 42. "The rigid separation of powers as under the American Constitution or under the Australian Constitution does not apply to our country."
39. *Id.* at p. 132. He observes, "Whereas in the United States of America and in Australia, the judicial power is vested exclusively in courts, there is no such exclusive resting of judicial power in the Supreme Court of India and the courts subordinate to it."

structure of the Constitution and hence even the constituent body could not escape its impact.[40] They held the view that the Constitution could not be altered in such manner as to damage the separation of powers as envisaged by the Constitution and to upset the ensuing balance of powers. Justice Khanna refused to make any opinion on the scope of the constituent power and held that settlement of that issue was not necessary for deciding the main issue posed before the Court, viz., constitutionality of clause (4) of Article 329A.[41] In view of the reservation of opinion by Justice Khanna, the matter was left undecided. The result of the decision was that the question whether the doctrine of separation of powers is part of the basic structure and restricts 'constituent power' of Parliament remained unsettled even after the decision in *Indira Gandhi*.[42]

It appears that the view taken by Justices Beg and Chandrachud represents the correct exposition of law. Acceptance of the contrary view leads to appalling and undesirable consequences. The view that the doctrine of

40. *Id.* at p. 198. Justice Beg held, "The majority view in that case, [*Kesavananda*] which is binding upon us, seemed to be that both the supremacy of the Constitution and separation of powers are parts of the basic structure of the Constitution."
Justice Chandrachud observed thus, "The truth of the matter is that the existence, and the limitations on the powers of the three departments of government are due to the normal process of specialisation in governmental business which becomes more and more complex as civilization advances....The reason of this restraint is not that the Indian Constitution recognizes any rigid separation of powers. Plainly it does not. The reasons is that the concentration of powers in any one organ may, by upsetting that fine balance between the three organs, destroy the fundamental premises of a democratic government to which we are pledged....The Parliament, by clause (4) of Article 329A, has decided a matter of which the country's courts were lawfully seized....I find it contrary to the basic tenets of our Constitution to hold that the amending body is an amalgam of all power, legislative, executive and judicial." (at pp. 259 to 261).
41. *Id.* at p. 86.
42. Such an unsettled position arose only because Justice Khanna took such a stand. It is worthwhile to remember that in *Kesavananda* the question whether fundamental rights formed part of the basic structure of the Constitution ultimately depended upon the stand of Justice Khanna as other judges were equally divided upon the issue. Fundamental rights were held as not forming part of the basic structure as he held so. See, *supra*, Chapter 6, n. 131.

separation of powers operates only at the sub-constitutional level, that too only if the Constitution so stipulated and that the doctrine cannot have any application when one deals with the constituent power—an amalgam of legislative, executive and judicial powers—is a dangerous one. It would lead to a situation where the doctrine becomes inapplicable in the matter of amending the Constitution. The application of the doctrine would then be limited to exercising the powers of the government in accordance with the Constitution. In such a context, in amending the Constitution, and by enacting the enabling legislation, any and all powers could be wielded by Parliament. Such a proposition makes an absurd distinction between the concept of power and its exercise.[43] In other words, though exercise of the legislative power by Parliament may be subject to the doctrine of separation of powers and the ensuing balance of powers, the constituent power is held to be beyond the doctrine. Such a distinction does not appear to be a real one.[44] It suffers from another defect also. It equates enactment of a Constitution with amendment of the Constitution. There is a distinction between them. Enactment of a new Constitution is totally different from its amendment. The former can even be an extra-constitutional one while the latter is always subject to the Constitution. Unlike the enactment of a new Constitution, its amendment is derivative in nature. It is derived from the

43. Such a view is clear from the opinion of Justice Mathew. He holds, "The possession of power is distinct from its exercise. The possession of legislative power by the amending body would not entitle it to pass an ordinary law, unless the Constitution is first amended by passing a constitutional law authorising it to do so. In the same way the possession of judicial power by the amending body would not warrant the exercise of the power, unless a constitutional law is passed by the amending body enabling it to do so....The doctrine of separation of powers which is directed against the concentration of the whole or substantial part of the judicial power in the Legislature or the Executive would not be a bar to the vesting of such a power in itself." (*Supra*, n. 6 at p. 133).
44. This is so because when Parliament finds that it was not able to exercise the legislative power conferred by Article 245 due to the operation of the doctrine of separation of powers, it would be able to invoke Article 368 so as to upset separation of powers and thereafter exercise the legislative powers accordingly.

Constitution itself.[45] Therefore, the power to amend the Constitution is certainly subject to the limitations envisaged by the Constitution. The doctrine of basic structure is devised to operate on the power to amend the Constitution. Obliteration of the distinction between the enactment of the Constitution and its amendment would defeat the very purpose of the doctrine.

It is true that the Constitution of India has not adopted the doctrine of separation of powers in the traditional sense. For, unlike the Constitution of the United States, it does not contain any specific provision laying down that legislative, executive and judicial powers should be wielded by the legislature, executive and judiciary respectively. However, from the various provisions of the Constitution, it is clear that it worked out the aspects of administration on the basis of separation of powers and the consequential balance of powers. An alteration of the provisions of the Constitution to erase the separation of powers and to vest those powers in one and the same body may damage the very foundation of the basic document and would lead to the possibility for the exercise of arbitrary powers. In other words, the doctrine of separation of powers certainly forms an essential ingredient of the basic structure of our Constitution. Moreover, the Constitution of India as originally enacted postulates separation of powers, though not in the traditional style and manner as developed in the U.S. Therefore, recognition and conferment of power on the constituent body to amend the Constitution to upset the separation of powers as envisaged by the Constitution of India and confinement of the application of the doctrine of separation of powers over the exercise of power by the government organs alone defeats the very purpose for which the doctrine of basic structure was introduced. Earlier in *Kesavananda,* some of the judges recognized the doctrine as an essential element of the basic structure.[46] In short, the view of Chief Justice A.N. Ray and Justice Mathew coupled with the non-expression of any opinion

45. *Cf.* Seervai, *op. cit.* at p. 3119 where he observes, "...the power to frame a Constitution is a primary power, whereas a power to amend a rigid Constitution is a derivative power—derived from the Constitution and subject at least to the limitations imposed by the proscribed procedure."
46. Sikri C.J., Shelat and Grover JJ.

on the issue by Justice Khanna in *Indira Gandhi's Case* pulls the Constitution to the pre-*Kesavananda* stage.

A related issue that sprung up before the Court in *Indira Gandhi* was whether judicial review formed part of the basic structure. It is an issue related to the concept of democracy, rule of law and especially separation of powers. As referred to by one of the judges,[47] democracy is founded on free and fair elections.[48] An important feature of democracy is redressal of election disputes through an independent and impartial forum.[49] Democracy can be preserved only on survival of equality of individuals before such judicial fora. Similarly, rule of law also can be assured only if arbitrariness of governmental action is proscribed for which there must be courts of law.[50] Separation of powers envisages mutual checks and balances between the organs of the government. It includes independence of the judiciary from the executive and the legislature.[51] All these indicate the necessity of judicial review for maintaining democracy and rule of law. Is not then judicial review a necessary ingredient of the Constitution of India? Can it not be treated as a feature of its basic structure in the light of the holding of the Court that democracy and rule of law are ingredients of the basic structure of the Constitution of India? The majority in *Indira Gandhi's Case* held that judicial review was not part of the basic structure of the Constitution.[52] The judges justified such a conclusion on different grounds. They held that

47. Khanna, J.
48. *Supra*, n. 6. at p. 87. He observed, "Democracy further contemplates that the elections should be free and fair, so that the voters my be in a position to vote for candidates of their choice."
49. *Id.* at p. 88. *Per* Khanna J. "Not much argument is needed to show that unless there be a machinery for resolving an election dispute and for going into the allegations that elections were not free and fair being vitiated by malpractices, ..."
50. See, A.V. Dicey, *Introduction to the Study of the Law of the Constitution* (1950), p. cxviii,
51. "The key stone of separation of powers in contemporary democracy and one that is crucial to the maintenance of some balance of powers in the mixed economy—is the independence of the judiciary." See, Friedman, *The State and the Rule of Law in a Mixed Economy* (1971), p. 74.
52. Chief Justice Ray observed, "Judicial review in many matters under statute may be excluded." (*supra*, n. 6 at p. 38.) "Judicial review is one of the distinctive features of the American Constitution al Law...These

for maintenance of democracy, what was required was only a process of settling disputes relating to elections. That, according to the judges, did not necessitate a judicial process for settling them.[53] In many democratic countries, election disputes are settled without recourse to judiciary but by the legislature itself.[54] Moreover, the Constitution of India as originally enacted did contain some provisions, which indicate that judicial review was not treated as its essential part.[55] On these grounds, the Court held that judicial review was not an essential feature of the basic structure of the Constitution.

The fragrance of the holding that democracy and rule of law are the ingredients of the basic structure is considerably watered down by the decision of the Court that separation of powers and judicial review were not the unamendable aspects of the Constitution of India. Undoubtedly, identification of democracy and rule of law as features of basic structure is a creative holding of the Court. As a result of the decision, Parliament is denuded of its power to amend the Constitution destroying those aspects and converting our Constitution as a totalitarian and undemocratic one. Evidently, separation of powers and judicial review are conditions precedent for the existence of a healthy democracy and rule of law. Therefore, it is very much necessary that in exercise of the constituent power, Parliament is not permitted to obliterate judicial review from the Constitution. In other words, much of the favourable consequences of the identification of democracy and rule of law as features of basic structure of the Constitution are lost by the denial of the same status to separation of powers and judicial

---

features are not in our Constitution." (at p. 41) Chandrachud J. held thus, "Since the Constitution, as originally enacted, did not consider that judicial power must intervene in the interests of purity of elections, judicial review cannot be considered to be a part of the basic structure in so far as legislative elections are concerned". (at p. 254) and Khanna J. at pp. 90-91).

53. *Id. per* Ray C.J. (at p. 43); Khanna. J. (at p. 91) and Chandrachud J. (at p. 254).

54. See instances of U.K., U.S., Australia, Japan, Norway, France, Germany, Turkey etc. Ray, C.J. Khanna, J. (at p. 88) and Chandrachud J. (at p. 254) have noted this fact.

55. See for instance, the Constitution of India, Articles 31(4), (6), 103, 136(2), 2 27(4), 262(2) and 329 (a), (b).

review. As mentioned by the Court, democratic life and rule of law would successfully operate only if the presence of an independent arbitrator is assured by the Constitution itself. Absence of such a body is likely to lead to the gradual decadence of the rule of law. If the dispute-settling scheme were wielded by the government or the legislature, possibility of arbitrariness and political influence would be very high. In such a context, generality, and its counterpart equality may also get eroded.

Even in the midst of the creative and progressive aspects of the decision, the holding in *Indira Gandhi* is defective in the above respects. Further, the holdings of the judges cannot be considered as fine examples of judicial craftsmanship. Though the Judges incorporated some aspects as ingredients of the doctrine of basic structure, it is pointed out that they were not much confident and they based their decisions on the doctrine of basic structure only for judicial self-discipline and not because they subscribed to the doctrine.[56] That may perhaps be the reason that they were not much emphatic and vociferous in invoking the doctrine of basic structure in determining the validity of the 39th amendment to the Constitution. The judges fell back upon the doctrine as if they had no other option. It was observed that the law stood as decided in *Kesavananda,*[57] that the decision was to be accepted dutifully and without reserve as good law,[58] that it need not be challenged,[59] and that *Kesavananda* was binding upon the Court[60] though the judges did not share the view of the majority in it.[61] These observations implicitly make it clear that the judges did not agree with the majority decision in the *Kesavananda Bharathi*. They held democracy and rule of law as part of the basic structure of the Constitution only because of their inability to ignore the *Kesavananda* decision. The desire of judges not to lay too much

56. See, Upendra Baxi, *Courage, Craft and Contention* (1985), p. 79. He observes, "These Justices had applied the doctrine of basic structure in *Indira Nehru Gandhi*, partly as a response to the need for institutional survival and partly as a matter of judicial self-discipline.
57. *Supra*, n. 6 at p. 78 (Khanna J.).
58. *Id.* at p. 246 (Chandrachud. J).
59. *Id.* at p. 35 (A.N. Ray C.J.).
60. *Id.* at p. 198. (Beg. J).
61. *Id.* at p. 119. (Mathew J.).

stress on the basic structure and rely upon it is clear from another aspect also. After the conclusion of the 35 daylong arguments but before the decision was delivered, the Court decided to review the decision of *Kesavananda*.[62] The attempt of the Court undoubtedly was to trim if not to overrule the scope and extent of *Kesavananda*.[63]

Similarly, the rationale adopted by the judges to invalidate and strike down Article 329(4) also reveals that they were not in agreement with the earlier decision. Though the Court struck down the amendment as invalid, some of the judges either did not seek the help of the doctrine of basic structure for invalidating the impugned provision[64] or sought its help in a roundabout manner. Thus Chief Justice Ray declared the amendment invalid on the ground that it left elections of Prime Minister and Speaker beyond the reach of any law and without any forum for settling disputes in relation to their election.[65] Similarly, Justice Mathew also struck it down on the ground that it left those elections beyond the reach of any law.[66] A reading of the judgements indicate that Chief Justice A.N. Ray and Justice M.H. Beg were totally indifferent to the doctrine of basic structure and they wanted to avoid the doctrine at any cost. While the holdings of Justice Mathew and Justice Chandrachud indicate that they were forced to the conclusion out of sheer helplessness. Only Justice Khanna followed the doctrine as expounded in an unconditional style. In short, though the judges recognized the doctrine of basic structure, there was a visible diffidence on their part to seek support from the doctrine

62. "Under the leadership of Chief Justice Ray, the Supreme Court endeavored with to match the expedition with which Parliament had amended the election law and the Constitution. This was done by the announcement that a Full Court would be convened to re-examine *Kesavananda* sometime after the hearings in *Indira Nehru Gandhi* were completed (after October 9, 1975) but before the decision to that case was announced (November 7, 1975) Upendra Baxi, *op. cit.* at pp. 78 79.
63. *Id.* at p. 79.
64. Ray C.J. and Mathew J. However, Justice Khanna held that Article 329A (4) was invalid as it violated the basic structure of democracy. While Justice Chandrachud struck down it on the ground that it violated the basic structure of rule of law
65. *Supra*, n. 6 at p. 44.
66. *Id.* at p. 135.

for striking down the impugned amendment.[67] But one need not be surprised over such an approach of the Court. For, the majority of the judges who decided *Indira Gandhi* was in the minority in *Kesavananda* and they had rejected the doctrine of basic structure in that case. Among those who subscribed to the formation of the doctrine in *Kesavananda* only Justice H.R. Khanna was there in the bench, which decided *Indira Gandhi's Case*.

The judicial dialect in *Indira Gandhi,* in short, exhibits an unusual rendezvous of creativity and restraintivism. It was creative in identifying some features of the Constitution of India as its basic structure and giving a firm basis to the doctrine. The diffidence of the Judges to make the doctrine the ratio of their decision to nullify the amendment and the refusal of the Court to recognize important pillars such as separation of powers and judicial review as the basic structure of the Constitution illustrate the restraintivism of the Court. However, with the decision in *Indira Gandhi,* the position of the doctrine of basic structure was more or less secured. For, even the Judges who did not agree with the *Kesavananda* doctrine, applied it in the *Indira Gandhi*.

What is to be analyzed next is whether the Supreme Court invoked the doctrine in all necessary cases and also whether it made use of the doctrine in the correct and proper way. The decision in *Indira Gandhi* was not the end of the doctrine. It, on the other hand, was only the beginning.

2. FORTY-SECOND AMENDMENT AND THE JUDICIAL GALLOP

Limited Amendability, Judicial Review and Balancing of Fundamental Rights and Directive Principles

A few years later the question of application of the doctrine of basic structure again came up before the Court in *Minerva Mills* v. *Union of India*.[68] In this case the scope and ambit of the

67. "*Indire Nehru Gandhi* did not decide what the ratio of *Kesavananda* was. Rather it assumed it *ex-concessionis* and proceeded to apply it, not without much strain and difficulty." Upendra Baxi, *op. cit.* at p. 71.
68. A. I.R. 1980 S.C. 1789.

power of Parliament to amend the Constitution and the role of the judiciary in reviewing the exercise of such a power again came up for consideration when the validity of the amendments to Articles 31 C and 368 made by 42nd amendment to the Constitution was challenged.[69] By section 4 of the Amendment Act, Article 31 C was amended to save laws inconsistent with Articles 14 or 19 enacted for giving effect to the directive principles. It further provided that no such law should be called in question on that ground.[70] By the same amendment Act, Article 368 was amended to include in it new clauses (4) and (5). Those clauses conferred on Parliament unlimited power to amend the Constitution and prohibited judicial review of constitutional amendments.[71] These amendments were challenged on the ground that they violated the basic structure of the Constitution. The Court held that the power of Parliament to amend the Constitution was not unlimited. The Constitution conferred on Parliament only a limited power to alter it. Limited amenability of the Constitution was a feature of the basic structure. Unlimited power to amend the Constitution, wielded by Parliament by the impugned amendment was counter to the basic structure of the Constitution namely, the limited

---

69. It was a writ petition filed under Article 32 of the Constitution against the acquisition of the petitioner company by the Government of India under the Sick Textiles Undertaking (Nationalisation) Act, 1974. The legislation was incorporated in the IX Schedule of the Constitution by the Constitution 39th Amendment Act. It means that it was beyond the scope of challenge of Courts. However the petitioner could not challenge the validity of the amendment by virtue of Article 368 clauses (4) and (5) which incorporated into the Constitution by the Constitution 42nd Amendment Act, 1976 as they conferred unbridled power on Parliament to amend Constitution and excluded judicial review. Therefore the petitioner inter *alia* challenged the validity of the 42nd amendment Act on the ground that it violated the basic structure of the Constitution.
70. For the provision, see, *infra*, n. 89.
71. Article 368(4), "No amendment of this Constitution (including the provisions of Part III) made or purporting to have been made under this Article [whether before or after the commencement of section 55 of the Constitution (42nd Amendment) Act, 1976] shall be called in question in any court on any ground.
(5) For the removal of doubts it is hereby declared that there shall be no limitation whatever on the constituent power of Parliament to amend by way of addition, variation or repeal the provisions of this Constitution under this Article."

amendability.[72] Therefore, Parliament could not amend the Constitution to confer unlimited amending power on it. The Court therefore struck down clauses (4) and (5) of Article 368 as incorporated by the 42nd amendment Act.[73]

It is true that in *Kesavananda* the Court limited the power of Parliament to amend the Constitution. But the Court did not conclusively hold in that case that limited amendability of the Constitution was a feature of its basic structure. In such a context, Parliament could undo the results of *Kesavananda* by a declaration that its power to amend the Constitution is unlimited. In other words, Parliament by amending the Constitution could dispel the limitations on its amending power since limited amendability had not been held as a feature of the basic structure of the Constitution. That exactly is what was done by Parliament by incorporating clause (5) to Article 368 by the 42nd Amendment, Act.[74] Obviously, such an understanding of the constituent power of Parliament would take back the amendment jurisprudence to the pre-*Kesavananda* stage, leaving Parliament the sole, unlimited and ultimate custodian of amendment powers.[75] The holding of the Court in *Minerva Mills* that limited amendability itself is a feature of the basic structure is to be appreciated against this background. Such a holding foreclosed any future possibility of nullifying the consequences of *Kesavananda* on the power of Parliament to amend the Constitution. By the decision, the Court has done away with the possibility of converting the power of Parliament to amend the

---

72. The Court held, "Since the Constitution had conferred a limited amending power on the Parliament, the Parliament cannot under the exercise of that limited power enlarge that very power into an absolute power. Indeed, a limited amending power is one of the basic features of our Constitution and therefore, the limitations on that power cannot be destroyed. In other words, Parliament cannot, under Article 368 expand its amending power so as to acquire itself the right to repeal or abrogate the Constitution or to destroy its basic and essential features. The donee of a limited power cannot by the exercise of that power convert the limited power into an unlimited one." *Supra*, n. 68 at p. 1798 (*per* Chandrachud, CJ.)
73. *Supra*, n. 68 at pp. 1799 and 1826-27.
74. *Supra*, n. 71. See also Baxi, *op. cit.* at p. 84. He observes, " The removal of the basic structure limitation was the sole objective of the Forty-second Amendment Act legislated during the emergency".
75. *Supra*, n. 68 at p. 1798.

Constitution as an unlimited one. The decision in *Minerva Mills* therefore has a very innovative operation. It deserves specific mention that the decision was reached after taking into account the consequence of a contrary interpretation. The Court reached the conclusion that Parliament has got only a limited power to amend the Constitution after examining what might happen if the limited amendability theory was rejected. Chief Justice Chandrachud, speaking for the Court observed that clause (5) of Article 368 could abrogate democracy and substitute it with a totally antithetical form of government denying people social, economic and political justice by emasculating liberty of thought, expression, belief, faith and worship and by abjuring commitment to the ideal of a society of equals.[76] In other words, no "constitutional power can conceivably go higher than the sky-high power conferred by clause (5)..."[77] It is on these grounds that the Court held that limited amendability itself was an ingredient of the basic structure. Justice Bhagwati in his separate and concurring judgement agreed with this view holding that what was conferred by the Constitution was only a limited amending power which therefore cannot be converted into an absolute and unlimited one[78] and therefore clause (5) of Article 368 was unconstitutional.

It is clear that incorporation of limited amendablity itself was very much essential for the continued life of *Kesavananda*.

76. *Ibid.*
77. *Ibid.*
78. Justice Bhagwati held, "Therefore, after the decisions in *Kesavananda Bharati's case*, and *Smt. Indira Gandhi's Case*, there was no doubt at all that the amendatory power of Parliament was limited and it was not competent to Parliament to alter the basic structure of the Constitution and Cl. (5) could not remove the doubt which did not exist. What Cl.(5) really sought to do was to remove the limitation on the amending power of Parliament and convert it from a limited power into an unlimited one. This was clearly and indubitably a futile exercise on the part of Parliament. I fail to see how Parliament which has only a limited power of amendment and which cannot alter the basic structure of the Constitution can expand its power of amendment so as to confer upon itself the power of repeal or abrogate the Constitution or to damage or destroy its basic structure.... This clause seeks to convert a controlled Constitution into an uncontrolled one by removing the limitation on the amending power of Parliament which, as pointed out above, is itself an essential feature of the Constitution and it is therefore violative of the basic structure." (*Id.* at pp. 1826-27)

Therefore, in the absence of *Minerva Mills* decision, *Kesavananda* might have been left to oblivion by arbitrary invocation of Article 368. In short, the decision of *Minerva Mills* that limited amendability of the Constitution is an essential ingredient of the basic structure provides a creative addition to the concept of constituent power of Parliament and the meaning of amendment under Article 368. The decision therefore guarantees the continued existence of the doctrine of basic structure in the Indian constitutional jurisprudence.

However the holding is liable to be frowned at by traditional constitutional lawyers. It can be criticized on the ground that the constituent power contains in it legislative, executive and judicial powers and is *sui generis* in nature. The holder of the constituent power is recognized as absolutely supreme. Like legislature in the legislative sphere, it is supreme within its sphere and is not liable to be interfered with by any other authority including the judiciary. The judiciary cannot dictate terms to such an authority as to how the power is to be exercised. But such a criticism has another side also. Who is the holder of constituent power? Can we say that the constituent power is wielded by Parliament alone? Does not judiciary have a share in its exercise? Is it true that Article 368 confers Parliament with the power to amend the Constitution in any manner it likes? The power to enact a Constitution is different from the one to make alterations in it. The former may be extra-constitutional in nature while the latter is one derived from the Constitution. Consequently, the former is not subject to any limitations. But the latter would be subject at least to the limitations expressly envisaged by the Constitution. The Court also seems to have accepted such a difference between the enactment of the Constitution and its amendment.[79] Further, it is well accepted that interpretation of the Constitution is a function conferred on the judiciary. The power to amend the Constitution being one derived from the Constitution, the final authority to determine its scope and ambit is the judiciary. In such a sense, the judiciary also can be said to have a share in the

79. *Id* at p. 1798. It was held, "Since the Constitution had conferred a limited amending power on the Parliament, the Parliament cannot under the exercise of that limited power enlarge that very power into an absolute power."

constituent power. Viewed from such an angle, the holding of the Court cannot be considered as one, which lays down wrong law.

Another question that was looked into by the Court was whether judicial review could be abolished by amending the Constitution. The Court had to address itself to such a question in view of incorporation of clause (4) in Article 368 which sought to deprive the courts of their power to examine the validity of amendments to the Constitution. The answer to that question depends upon whether judicial review formed part of the basic structure of the Constitution. Deprivation of judicial review may lead to upset of the nice balance of power established by the Constitution. This in its turn may lead to deprivation of fundamental rights including that provided by Article 32. It may then lead to a circumstance when even the ordinary laws may escape judicial scrutiny.[80] The Court therefore held that judicial review was also a part of the basic structure of the Constitution. It was held that judicial review could not be amended out of the Constitution and the Court struck down clause (4) of Article 368.[81] The response of Justice Bhagwati on this issue was more vociferous. Agreeing with the view of the Court, he observed that judicial review was part of the basic structure of the Constitution on the ground that

80. *Id.* at p. 1799. The Court held, "The newly introduced Clause (4) of Art. 368 must suffer the same fate as Clause (5) because the two clauses are inter-linked. Clause (5) purports to remove all limitations on the amending power while Clause (4) deprives the courts of, their power to call in question any amendment of the Constitution.... It is the function of the Judges, nay their duty, to pronounce upon the validity of laws. If courts are totally deprived of that power the fundamental rights conferred upon the people will become a mere adornment because rights without remedies are as writ in water. A controlled Constitution will then become uncontrolled. Clause (4) of Article 368 totally deprives the citizens of one of the most valuable modes of redress which is guaranteed by Article 32. The conferment of the right to destroy the identity of the Constitution coupled with the provision that no court of law shall pronounce upon the validity of such destruction seems to us a transparent case of transgression of the limitation on the amending power.... If Clause (5) is beyond the amending power of the Parliament, Clause (4) must be equally beyond that power and must be struck down as such."

81. *Ibid.*

without it, government of laws and rule of law would cease to exist and hence its absence may lead to the death knell of democracy and rule of law.[82] Thus he considered judicial review as part of the basic structure of the Constitution on the ground that its absence may adversely affect the existence of two other aspects which are already recognized as basic structure of the Constitution of India, viz., democracy and Rule of Law. If judicial review was held as not an essential ingredient of the basic structure and hence amenable to the amending powers, it would be convenient for Parliament to exclude judicial review in areas it poses a serious threat to the arbitrariness of Parliament and the executive.

A careful examination of this aspect reveals a slight deviation in judicial craftsmanship and the approach of the Court in developing the concept of basic structure from the earlier cases. In the earlier instances, the Court identified certain aspects as ingredients of basic structure on the ground that they themselves were the pillars upon which the Constitution of India rests. In this case, on the other hand, the Court held that judicial review was an ingredient of the basic structure not merely because it formed one of the foundation pillars of the Constitution, but it was so, because the Court thought that its absence might silently and gradually eat away the features

82. *Id.* at pp. 1825-26. He observed, "The power of judicial review is an integral part of our constitutional system and without it, there will be no Government of laws and the rule of law would become a teasing illusion and a promise of unreality. I am of the view that if there is one feature of our Constitution which, more than any other, is basic and fundamental to the maintenance of democracy and rule of law , it is the power of judicial review and it is unquestionably, to my mind, part of the basic structure of the Constitution.... So also if a constitutional amendment is made which has the effect of taking away the power of judicial review and providing that no amendment made in the Constitution shall be liable to be questioned on any ground, even if such amendment is violative of the basic structure and, therefore, outside the amendatory power of Parliament, it would be making Parliament sole Judge of the constitutional validity of what it has done and that would, in effect and substance, nullify the limitation on the amending power of Parliament and affect the basic structure of the Constitution. The conclusion must therefore inevitably follow that clause (4) of Article 368 is unconstitutional and void as damaging the basic structure of the Constitution."

which the Court had already identified as very basic to the Constitution.

Nevertheless, the holding of the Court in *Minerva Mills* that judicial review formed part of the basic structure is another facet of its creativity. The holding on this count is the disapproval and overruling of the decision in *Indira Gandhi's Case* in which the Court held that judicial review did not form part of the basic structure.[83] For the maintenance of judicial review separation of powers becomes unavoidable. Hence if judicial review forms part of the basic structure of the Constitution, separation of powers also should be an element of the basic structure. Though the Court did not explicitly hold so, there are some indications in *Minerva Mills* to such an effect.[84] In short, by the decision in *Minerva Mills* Case, the holdings to the contrary in the *Indira Gandhi* were overruled and the discussions of the concept of basic structure were more crystallized.

Another question that sprung up in *Minerva Mills* was the relative importance of fundamental rights and directive principles. This question was dealt with by the Court in the context of the amendment of Article 31C. From the very inception of the Constitution, the question whether fundamental rights were to be given pride of place or whether the directive principles were entitled to be so placed was a matter of heated dispute.[85] The question is not easy to answer. If either of them is considered as more important, the other is to be sacrificed for it. If fundamental rights were treated as of higher importance, the State cannot legislate in such a manner as to abridge the fundamental rights even in furtherance of the directive principles. If on the other hand, directive principles were considered to be of much importance, legislative power could be exercised even to the level of abridging or abrogating fundamental rights. Can either of them claim pride of place over the other? There are two schools of thought in this issue. One school holds that the fundamental rights should be given

83. *Supra*, nn. 53-55.
84. *Supra*, n. 68 at p. 1799. It was held, "Our Constitution is founded on a nice balance of power among the three wings of the State, namely, the Executive, the Legislature and the Judiciary. (*supra*, n. 68 at p. 1799)
85. For a treatment of the subject, see, *infra*, Part III, Chapter 8.

predominance over the directive principles. The other school gives pride of place to directive principles on the view that the directives are more important than the rights. In the earlier stages the Court conferred priority to fundamental rights.[86] Later, the Court changed its view and held that in case of conflict, it is the directive principles, which should prevail over the fundamental rights.[87] Still later the Court took a view that neither of the above views would solve the problems of Indian society and held that that there was no conflict between fundamental rights and directive principles and that there was a balance between them.[88] However, the issue came afresh before the Court in *Minerva Mills,* since by the 42nd Amendment Act, Parliament amended Article 31C to give superiority to directive principles over the fundamental rights.[89] It empowered the State to legislate in furtherance of directives even to the level of extirpation of the basic rights. The holding of the Court that the contents of Parts III and IV had equal importance[90] was upset by the 42nd Amendment Act. It is likely that conferment of such a power on Parliament may lead to legislative autocracy. The Court is the guardian of the fundamental rights of the people.[91] The Constitution provides that legislation contrary to fundamental rights is void *ab initio*.[92] The Court therefore held in the *Minerva Mills Case* that Part III and IV together constituted the core of commitment to social revolution. They were like two wheels of a chariot. Hence, the

86. See for example, *State of Madras v. Champakam Dorairajan,* A.I.R. 1951 S.C and *Hanif Quareshi* v. *State of Bihar,* A.I.R. 1961 S.C. 448.
87. See for example, *Bijay Cotton Mills* v. *State of Ajmir,* A.I.R. 1955 S.C. 33 and *Mumbai Kamgar Sabha* v. *Abdulbahi,* A.I.R. 1976 S.C. 1455.
88. *C & B Lodging* v. *State of Mysore,* A.I.R. 1970 S.C. 2042.
89. The relevant portion of Article 31-C as amended by the 42nd Amendment Act reads, "Notwithstanding anything contained in Article 13, no law giving effect to the policy of the State towards securing *all or any of* the principles *laid down in Part IV* shall be deemed to be void on the ground that it is inconsistent with, or takes away or abridges any of the rights conferred by Article 14 or Article 19... and no law containing a declaration that it is for giving effect to such policy shall be called in question in any court on the ground that it does not give effect to such policy. (Emphasized clauses were incorporated by the 42nd Amendment Act).
90. *Supra,* n. 88.
91. See the Constitution of India, Article 32.
92. *Id.,* Article 13(2).

Constitution of India is built to run smoothly on a fine balancing of the two wheels namely, Parts III and IV. Therefore, one cannot be given primacy over the other. The harmony and balance between them, according to the Court was an essential feature of the basic structure of the Constitution of India.[93] The Court therefore concluded[94] that section 4 of the 42nd Amendment Act, by which Article 31C was amended, was beyond the scope of the power of Parliament under Article 368 as it breached the benign balance between fundamental rights and directive principles, which is an ingredient of the basic structure of the Constitution.[95] Thus the holding in *Minerva Mills* projects

93. *Supra*, n. 68 at p. 1806. Justice Chandrachud for the Court observed thus, "The significance of the perception that Parts III and IV together constitute the of core commitment to social revolution and they together are the conscience of the Constitution is to be traced to a deep understanding of the scheme of the Indian Constitution.... In other words, the Indian Constitution is founded on the bedrock of the balance between Parts III and IV. To give absolute primacy to one over the other is to disturb the harmony of the Constitution. This harmony and balance between fundamental rights and directive principles is an essential feature of the basic structure of the Constitution." Agreeing with this view, Justice Bhagwati held, "There can be no doubt that the intention of the Constitution makers was that the Fundamental Rights should operate within the socio-economic structure or a wiser continuum envisaged by the Directive Principles, for then only would the Fundamental Rights become exercisable by all and a proper balance and harmony between Fundamental Rights and directive Principles secured." (at p. 1851)
94. *Id.* at p. 1811. But on the very same ground, Justice Bhagwati held that the amendment did not violate the basic structure of the Constitution and hence valid. He observed that 31C was amended with a view to provide that in case of conflict, directive principles should prevail over the fundamental rights. He opined that such a conflict was not envisaged by the makers of the Constitution and so no solution was proposed by them. That was the reason for the proposal for the amendment. He further observed that amendment far from damaging the basic structure, strengthens and re-enforces it by giving importance to the fundamental rights of the community as against the rights of a few. The amendment, therefore just codifies the existing position by providing that legislation in furtherance of directives would not be invalid on the ground that they breach Articles 14 and 19. (See the discussion of the issue by Bhagwati J. at pp. 1842-57)
95. But for a contrary view, see, the observations of Justice O. Chinnappa Reddy in *Sanjeev Coke Mfg. Co.* v. *M/s Bharat Coking Coal Ltd.*, A.I.R 1983 S.C. 239. In that case, he generally agreed with the view of Justice Bhagwati in the *Minerva Mills Case*. He further held that the view of the majority in that case was invalid. (at p. 248.)

another aspect of innovation of the Supreme Court in relation to the doctrine of basic structure.

On the whole, *Minerva Mills* is a comprehensive decision bringing three things to the limelight. Parliament cannot treat on its sweet will and pleasure the Constitution as the play thing since its power to amend itself is limited in nature; its power to amend can be exercised only without disturbing the balance between the rights conferred on the people and the legislative power of the State and Parliament cannot do away with the judicial review contained in the provisions of the Constitution. By bringing these aspects under the rubric of basic structure, the Court was able to concretize the concept of basic structure and put it as a stumbling block on the arbitrary exercise of constituent power by Parliament.

The value of these creative aspects gets increased for the reason that such drastic changes have been brought about by a Judge who at the nascent stages of the evolution of the doctrine of the basic structure stood against the doctrine. Chief Justice Chandrachud who rendered the decision of the Court in *Minerva Mills* was the only Judge who had participated in the earlier two cases, namely *Kesavananda* and *Indira Gandhi*. In *Kesavananda*, he had stood for unlimited amending power of Parliament and rejected the theory of implied limitations and the doctrine of basic structure.[96] In *Indira Gandhi*, on the other hand, even though he recognized the doctrine of basic structure and decided that case accordingly, he held that judicial review did not form part of the basic structure.[97] In *Minerva Mills* in which Chief Justice Chandrachud rendered the judgement of the Court is proof of the unconditional acceptance and widening of the doctrine of basic structure by a Judge who once had stood against it. Such a creative development of the judicial process has been appreciated by a renowned jurist as "a pilgrim's progress."[98]

3. ARE THERE ALTERNATIVES TO BASIC STRUCTURE?

It is clear from the above discussion that the Court was

96. *Supra*, Chapter 6, n. 30 at pp. 988-89.
97. *Supra*, n. 52.
98. Upendra Baxi, *op. cit.* at p. 86.

able to identify some important aspects of the Constitution as the ingredients of the basic structure. Inclusion of any aspect into the doctrine naturally implies that it becomes a basic feature of the Constitution. A question springs up here. Can there be a substitute for a feature that has been recognized as an ingredient of basic structure? The expression basic structure *ex facie* means that it is basic and cannot be altered or substituted since the basic structure constituted the unalterable features of the Constitution. But the Supreme Court was not emphatic of that view when the issue came up before the Court in *S.P. Sampath Kumar* v. *Union of India*.[99] While challenging the vires of the Administrative Tribunals Act, the question mooted was whether judicial review could have an alternative. The Court did not disagree with the decision on *Minerva Mills* that judicial review formed part of the basic structure of the Constitution. But the Court held in *Sampath Kumar* that a legislation could be considered violative of the Constitution only if it took away judicial review in toto. This means that partial prohibition of judicial review would not be bad on the ground that it violated the basic structure. Agreeing with and drawing conclusions from the holding of Justice Bhagwati in the *Minerva Mills*,[100] the Court further held that the presence of effective alternative mechanisms or arrangements for settling disputes would be a constitutionally viable alternative for judicial review.[101] Justice Bhagwati who rendered a separate

---

99. A.I.R 1987 S.C. 386. A petition was filed under Article 32 challenging the vires of the Administrative Tribunals Act, 1985. The Act framed under Article 323-A (incorporated by the 42nd Constitutional Amendment Act) was challenged on the ground that Section 28 of the Act, which exclued jurisdiction of the High Court under Articles 226 and 227 struck at the root of one of the features of the basic structure viz., judicial review.

100. *Supra*, n. 82.

101. *Supra*, n. 99 at p. 395. The Court held, "We have already seen that judicial review by this Court is left wholly unaffected and thus there is a forum where matters of importance and grave injustice can be brought for determination or rectification. Thus exclusion of the jurisdiction of the High Court does not totally bar judicial review. This Court in Minerva Mills Case did point out that 'effective alternative institutional mechanisms or arrangements for judicial review can be made by Parliament. Thus it is possible to set-up an alternative institution in place of the High Court for providing judicial review."

opinion concurred with it.[102] Hence the Court refused to strike down the statute as violative of judicial review. However the Court incorporated a word of caution of substituting judicial review thus, [103]

> "What, however, has to be kept in view is that the Tribunal should be a real substitute of the High Court-not only in form and dejure but also in content and defacto."

The Court held that the impugned Act did not annul judicial review since the jurisdiction of the Supreme Court under Articles 32 and 136 remained in tact even after the amendment of the Constitution and incorporation of Article 323A. The Court did not agree with the view that the Tribunals should be supplemental to and not substitution of High Courts.[104] Clearly, as a result of the holding, importance of judicial review as a basic structure is watered down since it was held substitutable by alternatives.

By holding that the Administrative Tribunals Act was constitutionally valid, the Court digressed from the real issue involved in the case. The question that really emerged before the Court was the validity of the 42nd Amendment Act, which added Article 323A to the Constitution, which permitted reduction of the scope of judicial review. However instead of dealing with this issue, the Court preferred to deal with the vires of the statute. The Court avoided dealing with the validity of the amendment act by examining the vires of the impugned statute, striking down some of the provisions and proposing some changes to others. Justice Bhagawati observed that in view of *Minerva Mills*, judicial review could not be abolished and so the amended provision in the Constitution is to be viewed as one which provided for effective alternative schemes for judicial review.[105] Such an interpretation of the amendment amounts to

102. *Id.* at pp. 389-90.
103. *Id.* at p. 396.
104. *Id.* at p. 395.
105. *Id.* at p. 390. He observed, "If this constitutional amendment were to permit a law made under Cl. (1) of Art. 323A to excludes the jurisdiction of the High Court under Arts. 226 and 227 without setting up an effective alternative institutional mechanism or arrangement for judicial review, it

an attempt on the part of the Court to save the 42nd Amendment Act.[106] It is submitted that the decision does not fully take the purpose of the introduction of the concept of basic structure into account and hence reduces its status in the constitutional jurisprudence. Is the holding an indication that each and every feature of basic structure could be substituted? Such a state of affairs is certainly dangerous and would defeat the very purpose for which the doctrine has been introduced.

In *P. Sambamurthi* v. *State of A.P.*,[107] the Court exhibited a consistent view in this respect. In that case, the constitutional validity of clauses (3) and (5) to Article 371D as inserted by the 32nd Amendment Act, 1973[108] were challenged on the ground

---

would be violative of the basic structure doctrine and hence outside the constituent power of Parliament. It must, therefore, be read as implicit in this constitutional amendment that the law excluding the jurisdiction of the High Court under Arts. 226 and 227 permissible under it must not leave a void but it must set-up another effective institutional mechanism or authority and vest the power of judicial review in it."

106. It is worthwhile to mention that the vires of the amendment act was not challenged by the petitioner either.

107. A.I.R. 1987 S.C. 663. They were writ petitions challenging the constitutional validity of clauses (3) and (5) of Article 371-D of the Constitution

108. Article 371-D is a special provision with respect to the State of Andhra Pradesh. Clause (3) of the Article reads thus, "The President may, by order, provide for the constitution of an Administrative Tribunal for the State of Andhra Pradesh to exercise such jurisdiction, power and authority [including any jurisdiction, power and authority which immediately before the commencement of the Constitution (Thirty-Second Amendment Act), 1973, was exercisable by any court (other than the Supreme Court) or by any tribunal or other authority] as may be specified in the order with respect to the following matters namely:-
appointment, allotment or promotion to such class or classes of posts in any civil service of the State, or to such class or classes of civil posts under the State, as may be specified in the order;
seniority of persons appointed, allotted or promoted to such class or classes of posts in any civil service of the State, or to such class or classes of civil posts under the State, or to such class or classes of posts under the control of any local authority within the State, as may be specified in the order;
such other conditions of service of persons appointed, allotted or promoted to such class or classes of posts in any civil service of the State or to such class or classes of civil posts in any civil service of the State or to such classes of posts under the control of any local authority within the State, as may be specified in the order;

that they ran counter to judicial review which was a feature of the basic structure. The Court struck down Proviso to clause (5) of Article 371D, which declared that the order of Administrative Tribunals could be modified or annulled by the government. The impact of the amendment is clear. Even if the Tribunal rendered a decision, without the consent of the government, its order could not be implemented. The Court observed that such a provision ran counter to the basic principle of rule of law. The Court held,[109]

> "It is through the power of judicial review conferred on an independent institutional authority such as the High Court that the rule of law is maintained and every organ of the State is kept within the limits of the law. Now if the exercise of the power of judicial review can be set at naught by the State Government by overriding the decision given against it, it would sound the death knell of the rule of law. The rule of law would cease to have any meaning, because then it would be open to the State Government to defy the law and yet to get away with it. The Proviso to clause (5) of Article 371-D is therefore clearly violative of the basic structure doctrine."

In other words, the Court struck down[110] the impugned clause of Article 371-D on the ground that it did not constitute an effective alternative for judicial review, which is an ingredient of basic structure of the Constitution and not because it excluded judicial review.[111]

Clause (5) reads thus, "The order of the Administrative Tribunal finally disposing of any case shall become effective upon its confirmation by the State Government or on the expiry of three months from the date on which the order is made, whichever is earlier";

Provided that the State Government may, by special order made in writing and for reasons to be specified therein, modify or annul any order of the Administrative Tribunal before it becomes effective and in such a case, the order of the Administrative Tribunal shall effect only in such modified form or be of no effect as the case may be.

109. *Supra*, n. 107 at p. 667.

110. *Id.* at p. 668.

111. For, the Court held, "No constitutional objection to the validity of Cl. (3) of Art. 371-D could be possibly be taken since we have already held in *S.P. Sampath Kumar* v. *Union of India*, decided on 9th December 1986 that

4. JUDICIARY AND THE BASIC STRUCTURE

(a) Judicial Review as Basic Structure Further Explained

The decisions in *Minerva Mills,*[112] *Sampath Kumar*[113] and *Samba Murthi*[114] share some common features. In all of them judicial review was recognised as part and parcel of basic structure not in an independent capacity but as one necessary for guaranteeing the continuance of the aspects of the Constitution which the Court recognized as ingredients of the basic structure. Incorporation of judicial review in the category of basic structure was out of the fear of the Court that its absence might lead to termination of democracy and decadence of rule of law. That perhaps is the reason for the Court to hold in all of these cases that though judicial review cannot be abrogated, it could be partially excluded and substituted by an equally efficacious and alternative remedy.[115] The idea that even if a feature is an ingredient of basic structure, it could have a substitute was raised for the first time by Justice Bhagwati in the *Minerva Mills Case.*[116] It is doubtful whether feasibility of such a proposition was examined by the Court in a proper perspective in *Sampath Kumar* and *Sambamurthy*. If a feature is identified as an ingredient of the basic structure, it implies that it is so important for the maintenance of the identity of the Constitution. In such a context it is doubtful whether it can be substituted by any other scheme at all. For, substitution of such a feature by any other concept may help destroy some ot the characteristics of the basic structure and amounts to watering down its contents. Further, it would also imply that the feature is not so essential one. Moreover, judicial review is imbued with certain features that cannot exist in its absence. The training of

---

judicial review is a basic and essential feature of the Constitution and it cannot be abrogated without affecting the basic structure of the Constitution, but Parliament can certainly without in any way violating the basic structure doctrine amend the Constitution so as to set-up an effective alternative institutional mechanism or arrangement for judicial rcview."

112. A.I.R. 1980 S.C. 1789.
113. A.I.R. 1987 S.C. 386.
114. A.I.R. 1987 S.C. 663.
115. *Supra*, nn. 82, 101 and 111.
116. *Supra*, n. 68 at pp. 1825-26.

a judicial mind and the independence extended to the judicial officers are some of the prerequisites for effective judicial review, which are absent in any mechanism other than judicial review howsoever efficient it be. Therefore, the holding of the Court that though judicial review constitutes a part of basic structure, it can be substituted by equally efficient methods is certainly open to objection.

It is in such a context that the decision of *L. Chandra Kumar* v. *Union of India*[117] becomes highly relevant. This case was decided by a constitutional bench consisting of nine Judges.[118] The Court reiterated its stand in *Minerva Mills* that judicial review was a feature of the basic structure of the Constitution. The Court further held that the jurisdiction of the Supreme Court under Article 32 and that of the High Courts under Articles 226 and 227 also formed part of the basic structure of the Constitution and therefore they cannot be ousted or excluded at all.[119] It was justified on the ground that the jurisdiction of High Court under Articles 226 and 227 was as important as that of the Supreme Court under Article 32.[120] The Court highlighted the importance of judicial review on the basis of the independence enjoyed by the judiciary.[121] In reaching the

---

117. A.I.R. 1997 S.C. 1125. It was a group of special leave petitions, civil appeals and writ petitions with certain common questions. Questions raised in these cases were whether the power under Article 323A(2)(d) or Article 323B(3)(d) of the Constitution conferred on Parliament totally exclude jurisdiction of all courts except that of the Supreme Court under Article 136;whether the disputes and complaints raised in respect of the exercise of power under Articles 323A clause (1) or Article 323B(2) were beyond the scope of the power of judicial review of High Courts under Articles 226 and 227 and that of the Supreme Court under Article 32 and whether the Tribunals constituted under Articles 323A and B be considered as effective substitutes for High Court.
118. Justice A.M. Ahmadi, C.J. M.M. Punchhi, K. Ramaswamy, S.P. Barucha, S. Saghir Ahmed, K. Venkitaswamy and K.T. Thomas JJ.
119. *Supra*, n. 117 at p. 1150.
120. *Ibid*. The Court observed, "If the power under Article 32 of the Constitution, which has been described as the "heart" and "soul" of the Constitution, can be additionally conferred upon "any other Court," there is no reason why the same situation cannot subsist in respect of the jurisdiction conferred upon the High Courts under Article 226 of the Constitution."
121. *Id*. at p. 1149.

conclusion that Article 32 formed part of the basic structure, the Court might have been influenced by the observation made by Dr. Ambedkar at the time of enacting the provision in the Constituent Assembly that it was the most important one in our Constitution.[122] On a variety of grounds, the Court considered the powers vested in High Courts under Articles 226 and 227 as very important which therefore could not be excluded.[123] The Court observed that administration of justice by Tribunals leaves much to be desired[124] and the remedy under Article 136 was too costly and would lead to crowding of cases in the Supreme Court.[125] Therefore, the Court held that decisions of Tribunals were reviewable by Division Bench of High Courts.[126] The Court further extended the scope of judicial review to include specifically jurisdiction of judicial superintendence by High Courts over the decisions of all courts and tribunals within their respective jurisdictions as envisaged by the Constitution of India.[127] In short, the Court deviated from its earlier stand in *Minerva Mills, Sampath Kumar* and *Samba Murthi* that judicial review could be substituted by equally effective methods and clarified that judicial review as envisaged by Articles 32, 226 and 227 cannot in any way be substituted. The Court further held that the jurisdiction of Tribunals was only supplemental to

---

122. *C.A.D.*, Vol. VII, p. 953. He said, "If I was asked to name any particular Article in this Constitution as the most important—an Article without which the Constitution would be a nullity—I could not refer to any other Article except this one. It is the very soul of the Constitution and the very heart of it and I am glad that the House has realised its importance."
123. *Supra*, n. 117 at p. 1150.
124. *Id.* at p. 1153.
125. *Id.* at p. 1154.
126. *Ibid.* It is worth-mentioning that the Court specifically held that review of decisions of Tribunals and questions regarding the validity of the constitution of Tribunals were to be dealt with only by Division Benches of High Courts.
127. *Id.* at p. 1150. The Court held, "We also hold that the power vested in the High Courts to exercise judicial superintendence over the decisions of all Courts and Tribunals within their respective jurisdictions is also part of the basic structure of the Constitution. This is because a situation where the High Courts are divested of all other judicial functions apart from that of constitutional interpretation, is equally to be avoided".

and not in substitution of the review power of High Courts.[128] Clearly, it is only after the decision of *Chandra Kumar* that the concept of judicial review got the full-fledged status as a feature of basic structure. The change in the view of the Court in *Chandra Kumar* reflects the correct perception of the Court that judicial review is so important in our legal system that it is a basic feature which cannot be substituted. While in the earlier decisions the Court had given importance to judicial review only as an accessory to some other goals to be achieved by the Constitution, in *Chandra Kumar*, the Court has raised judicial review from its status of an accessory element to the level of a salient feature of the basic structure of the Constitution.

It is evident from the decision in *Chandra Kumar* that the Court considered the status of the higher judiciary as different from that of any other authority. On what reasons can the higher judiciary enjoy superiority over other institutions so as to claim immunity to its review? The Court in *L. Chandrakumar*, addressed itself to these questions and explained the reasons thus,[129]

> "While the Constitution confers the power to strike down laws upon the High Courts and the Supreme Court, it also contains elaborate provisions dealing with the tenure, salaries, allowances, and retirement age of Judges as well as mechanism for selecting Judges to the superior Courts. The inclusion of such elaborate provisions appears to have been occasioned by the belief that, armed by such provisions, the superior Courts would be insulated from any executive or legislative attempts to interfere with the making of their decisions.... The constitutional safeguards

128. *Id.* at p. 1156. However, the Court pointed out that in the prevailing circumstances, the workload pending in High Courts was very high and therefore, the jurisdiction conferred on Tribunals need not be trimmed to vest full power on High Courts. The Court therefore held that Tribunals could hear and decide matters where vires of statutory provisions are questioned. They have the power to test the vires of subordinate legislation and rules. In other words, litigants would not have the right to approach High Courts in the first instance unless the question involved includes one regarding the vires of the parent statute which created the Tribunal. (*Id.* at pp. 1154-55.)
129. *Id.* at pp. 1149-50.

which ensure the independence of the Judges of the superior judiciary are not available to the Judges of the subordinate judiciary or to those who man Tribunals created by ordinary legislations. Consequently, Judges of the latter category can never be considered full and effective substitute for the superior judiciary in discharging the function of constitutional interpretation."

In other words, conferment of a higher status to judicial review by the higher judiciary is justified in view of the independence enjoyed by it. Moreover the role of the judiciary is becoming more and more important in the modern world. It means that independence of the judiciary is very vital for the maintenance and upkeep of the confidence reposed upon it in respect of judicial review. Judicial independence[130] would then have to be recognized as an ingredient of the basic structure.

(b) Independence of Judiciary—Another Dimension of Basic Structure

The question of importance of independence of the judiciary was raised before the Supreme Court on many occasions. In *Shri Kumar Padma Prasad* v. *Union of India*[131] the question raised was whether the person who held only non-judicial posts could be appointed District Judge or Judge of High Court. The Court observed that though Judges were used to be appointed from among the members of executive offices, after independence Judges were not being appointed from such offices. One of the Directive Principles also mandates the State to separate judiciary from the executive,[132] which means that judiciary shall be free from executive control. Such a separation of the judiciary from the executive was necessary for the

130. For a detailed discussion of the concept of judicial independence, see, *supra*, Part I, Chapter 1.
131. (1992) 2 S.C.C. 428. That was an appeal from a petition filed before the High Court of Gauhati against appointment of a person as Judge of the High Court on the grounds inter alia that he did not satisfy the constitutionally required qualifications and that the appointment was sought to be effected without the process of consultation envisaged by Article 217(1) of the Constitution.
132. The Constitution of India, Article 50.

maintenance of judicial independence. Hence, Justice Kuldip Singh speaking for the Court held that independence of the judiciary was one of the features of the basic structure of the Constitution of India.[133] Addition of judicial independence as a feature of the basic structure is certainly a creative stride of the Court. It was very much necessary also. The necessary implication and clear consequence of the decision is that Parliament cannot amend the Constitution in a manner damaging the independence of judiciary.

Independence of the judiciary received further consideration by a constitutional bench of the Court consisting of nine Judges in *S.C. Advocates-on-Record* v. *Union of India*.[134] In that case the Court had to deal with important questions relating to appointment of judges to the Supreme Court, appointment and transfer of judges to High Courts and the importance and weight the opinion of the Chief Justice of India would carry in these matters. While construing the related provisions in the Constitution, the Court observed that those questions were to be dealt with in the light of the concept of independence of the judiciary. The Court unanimously held that the concept of independence of judiciary was very important from the point of view of the Constitution.[135] The Judges quoted the views of legal luminaries, judicial decisions and other authorities with approval to hold that independence of the judiciary was a cardinal virtue. It was observed that independence of judiciary was very much necessary for the maintenance of rule of law[136] and democracy.[137] Considering its importance in the modern society, the Court unanimously held that the concept of independence of the judiciary formed an

---

133. *Supra*, n. 131 at p. 456. Earlier, in *S.P. Gupta* v. *Union of India*, 1981 Supp. S.C.C. 87. Bhagawati J. (at p. 221) and Fazl Ali J. (at p. 408) held that independence of the judiciary was also a feature of the basic structure of the Constitution of India.
134. (1993) 4 S.C.C. 441.
135. *Id. per* Verma J. (for Dayal, Ray, Anand, Barucha and for himself) at p. 680; Pandian J. at p. 522; Ahmadi J. at p. 601 and Kuldip Singh J. at p. 649.
136. *Id. per* Pandian J. at p. 523 and Kuldip Singh J. at p. 647.
137. *Id. per* Pandian J. at pp. 523-25.

essential and basic feature of the Constitution of India.[138] The Court construed the constitutional provisions and rendered the decision in tune with the requirements of the concept of independence of the judiciary.[139]

5. NEW HORIZONS OF BASIC STRUCTURE

(a) Basic Structure—A Norm for Interpretation of the Constitution

By the decisions of *Shri Kumar* and *S.C. Advoctes* the Court added one more feature to the basic structure. The magnitude and the direction of creativity of those decisions are noteworthy. In none of them was there any question regarding amendment of the Constitution with adverse impact on independence of the judiciary. The main question involved in *Shri Kumar* was the conditions to be satisfied by an appointee of a High Court while *S.C. Advocates* dealt with the construction of the expression "after consultation with the Chief Justice of India" appearing in Articles 124(2), 217(1) and 222(1).[140] The Court held that these provisions should be construed in consonance with the concept of independence of the judiciary, which according to the Supreme Court is an essential ingredient of the basic structure. In other words, the Court evolved a new rule of constitutional construction by holding that the provisions in the Constitution

138. *Id.* Verma J. (for the Court) held "These questions have to be considered in the context of the independence of the judiciary, as part of the basic structure of the Constitution, to secure the 'rule of law', essential for the preservation of the democratic system."(At p. 680).
Pandian J. observed, "To say differently, it is the cardinal principle of the Constitution that an independent judiciary is the most essential characteristic of a free society like ours." (at p. 522).
Ahmadi J. held, "The concept of judicial independence is deeply ingrained in our constitutional scheme and Article 50 illumines it." (at p. 640).
Kuldip Singh J. held, "Independence of the judiciary is the basic feature of the Constitution." (at p. 665).

139. For a detailed discussion of the case and the decision of the Court on those points, see *supra*, Part I, Chapters 3 & 4.

140. Article 124(2) deals with the procedure for appointing Judges to the Supreme Court, Article 217(1) with the procedure for appointing Judges to High Courts and Article 222(1) regulates the procedure for transferring Judges of High Courts.

should be construed in accordance with a feature of its basic structure, namely, independence of judiciary. The creativity of the decision lies in the holding of the Court that the doctrine of basic structure can be a norm for constitutional construction. Till then the Court was invoking the doctrine of basic structure only to limit the power of the Parliament to amend the Constitution under Article 368. Thus the decisions in *Shri Kumar* and *S.C. Advocates* are creative on two counts. Without any room for doubt the Court held that judicial independence constituted a feature of the basic structure of the Constitution. The Court further by using the doctrine as a touchstone for constitutional construction created a new technique of constitutional interpretation. *S.C. Advocates* is remarkable for the advancement in the technique of judicial dialect also. In the earlier cases, while construing the provisions dealing with judiciary, the Court was considering independence of the judiciary as a desideratum to be achieved through such interpretation.[141] But in *S.C. Advocates,* the Court on the other hand construed those provisions with a presupposition that judicial independence was ingrained in the Constitution of India and that constitutional construction has to be made keeping that in mind.

(b) Basic Structure—A Norm for Actions of Constitutional Authorities

Another decision relevant in this context is *S.R. Bommai* v. *Union of India.*[142] The Supreme Court had to deal in that case

141. See, for instance the decision of *S.P. Gupta* v. *Union of India,* 1981 Supp. S.C.C. 87. In this case the Court had to deal with the question of appointment and transfers of Judges to the higher judiciary. The Judges held that the concept of independence of the judiciary was very important as far as the Constitution of India is concerned. However, the Court did not deal with those issues in the light of the concept. For a discussion of these issues, see *supra,* Part I, Chapters 3 and 4.

142. (1994) 3 S.C.C. 1. That is a collection of cases either by special leave appeal or by transfer from High Courts. They however involve a common question as to the interpretation of Article 356, which stipulates for declaration of presidential rule in certain States and judicial review of such proclamation. Those cases arose out of the dismissal of the Governments of Nagaland in 1987, Karnataka in 1989, and dismissal of the governments and dissolution of the Legislative Assemblies of Rajasthan, M.P. and H.P., in 1992 following the crisis that took place on demolition of the Babri Masjid in Ayodhya.

with the scope and ambit of Article 356[143] which lays down the conditions and procedure for imposing President's rule in the States. Two important questions were raised *inter alia* before the Court. One was how it could be determined that the State government failed to carry out the administration of the State in accordance with the provisions of the Constitution enabling the President to invoke Article 356 and dismiss the State government. The provision just says that the power could be invoked by the President if he is satisfied from the report of the Governor or otherwise that the government could not carry out the administration in accordance with the provisions of the Constitution. But it does not explain the circumstances under which it could be inferred whether the State government failed to carry out the administration in accordance with the provisions of the Constitution. The second question was whether such a decision of the President could be judicially reviewed. While dealing with the first question, the Court held that secularism formed an essential ingredient of the basic structure.[144] The Court held that determination of the issue whether the State Government failed to carry out the administration of the State in accordance with the provisions of the Constitution depended also upon the question whether it failed to uphold and maintain secularism

---

143. Article 356 reads, "If the President, on receipt of a report from the Governor... of a State or otherwise, is satisfied that a situation has arisen in which the government of the State cannot be carried on in accordance with the provisions of this Constitution, the President may by proclamation—assume to himself all or any of the functions of the Government of the State and all or any of the functions of the Government of the State and all or any of the powers vested in or exercisable by the Governor... or any body or authority in the State other than the Legislature of the State;
declare that the powers of the Legislature of the State shall be exercisable by or under the authority of Parliament; make such incidental and consequential provisions as appear to the President to be necessary or desirable for giving effect to the objects of the Proclamation, including provisions for suspending in whole or in part the operation of any provisions of this Constitution relating to any body or authority in the State;
...."

144. *Supra*, n. 142 *per* Ahmedi J. (at p. 78); Sawant and Kuldip Singh JJ. (at p. 149); Ramaswamy J. (at p. 170) and Jeevan Reddy and Agarwal JJ. (at p. 298). Justice Pandian was in agreement with the views of Justice Jeevan Reddy (at p. 66).

which is an essential ingredient of the basic structure.[145] Such a conclusion was drawn by the Court from the various provisions of the Constitution like Articles 25, 26, 27, 28,[146] 29,

145. *Id. per* Sawant J. speaking for himself and Kuldip Sing said, "One thing which prominently emerges from the above discussion on secularism under our Constitution is that whatever the attitude of the State towards the religions, religious sects and denominations, religion cannot be mixed with any secular activity of the State.... religious tolerance and equal treatment of all religious groups and protection of their life and property and of the places of their worship are an essential part of secularism enshrined in our Constitution.... If therefore, the President had acted on the aforesaid 'credentials' of the Ministries in these States...it can hardly be argued that there was no material before him to come to the conclusion that the Governments in the ...States could not be carried on in accordance with the provisions of the Constitution." (at pp. 146, 147 and 148). Justice Ramaswamy observed, "They/he should not mix religion with politics. ... Programmes or principles evolved by political parties based on religion amounts to recognising religion as a part of the political governance which the Constitution expressly prohibited. It violates the basic features of the Constitution....Any act done by a political party or the Government of the State run by that party in furtherance of its programme or policy would also be in violation of the Constitution and the law. When the President receives a report from a Governor or otherwise had such information that the Government of the State is not being carried on in accordance with the provisions of the Constitution, the President is entitled to consider such report and reach his satisfaction in accordance with law." (at pp. 206-07). B.P. Jeevan Reddy J. speaking for himself and Aggarwal J. observed, "If the President was satisfied that the faith of these BJP Governments in the concept of secularism was suspect in view of the acts and conduct of the parties controlling these Governments and that in the volatile situation that developed pursuant to the demolition, the Government of these States cannot be carried on in accordance with the provisions of the Constitution, we are not able to say that there was no relevant material upon which he could be so satisfied.... If the President was satisfied that the Governments, which have already acted contrary to one of the basic features of the Constitution, viz., secularism, cannot be trusted to do so in future, it is not possible to say that in the situation then obtaining, he was not justified in believing so." (at pp. 295-96). Justice Pandian agreed (at p. 66) with what Justice Jeevan Reddy said. Justice Ahmadi (at p. 78) agreed with the observations of Justice Ramaswamy and Justice Jeevan Reddy on this count.

146. Articles 25 to 28 deal with the right to freedom of religion. Article 25 provides for freedom of conscience and free profession, practice and practice of religion, 26 with the freedom to manage religious affairs, 27 with freedom as to payment of taxes for promotion of any particular religion and 28 with freedom as to attendance at religious instruction or religious worship in certain educational institutions.

30,[147] 31 and 51A.[148] Thus, for the first time the concept of basic structure has been invoked by the Court as a criterion to determine the constitutionality of administration carried out by a State Government.

The decision is innovative in that the concept of secularism was recognized as a feature of basic structure. Though the concept of secularism has been considered as an ingredient of basic structure by some of the Judges in various cases right from the decision of *Kesavananda,* in none of them the Court had held that it formed part of basic structure. Unlike the western concept, in our Constitution, it envisages not an anti-religious idea, but equal treatment of persons irrespective of religion. In other words, secularism indubitably forms an essential feature of the concept of rule of law[149] which, according to the Supreme Court, is a part and parcel of the concept of basic structure.[150] Therefore, the thrust of the directive force of the decision need not be doubted. The consequence of the holding is that Parliament cannot amend the Constitution to impair any aspect of the concept of secularism in the Constitution. The decision is creative in another way also, in so far as it implies that the act of constitutional authorities can be tested on the basis of the doctrine of basic structure. The Court rendered a wide interpretation to the expression, 'provisions of the Constitution' in Article 356 by including within it secularism—a feature of basic structure. Thus for the first time, the doctrine has been utilized by the Court as a touchstone of the functions of constitutional authorities when it was held that constitutionality of actions of the State Government and justifiability of invocation of Article 356 by the President could be evaluated on the basis of a feature of basic structure namely, secularism.

Dealing with the question whether the 'satisfaction' and action of the President under Article 356 were amenable to

147. Articles 29 and 30 deal with the cultural and educational rights. Article 29 deals with the protection of interests of minorities and Article 30 with right of minorities to establish and administer educational institutions.
148. Article 51A of the Constitution deals with fundamental duties of citizens.
149. The concept of secularism is related to tolerance, qualified religious freedom, qualified religious equality or non-discrimination. See, V.M. Bachal, *Freedom of Religion and the Indian Judiciary* (1975), p. 6.
150. See, *Indira Gandhi, supra,* n. 31.

judicial review, the Judges observed that the power of the President under the provision could not be exercised in an arbitrary or *malafide* manner,[151] and that it was conditional in nature.[152] All of the Judges were of the opinion that the presidential power under the provision was not unlimited and hence it was unanimously held[153] that the power of the President to dismiss the State government was subject to judicial review.[154] Such a conclusion was reached by the Court on the ground *inter alia* that arbitrary exercise of the power under Article 356 runs counter to the federal structure of the Constitution which according to the Court[155] was an element of basic structure of the Constitution[156] and that the President had to exercise the power under Article 356 in such a manner as not to whittle down the federal structure.[157]

151. *Supra,* n. 142. at p. 374. (*per* Sawant J., for Kuldip Singh and himself).
152. *Id.* at p. 280. (*per* Ramaswamy J.)
153. *Id. per* Ahmadi J. (at p. 80); Verma J. (for Yogeshwar Dayal and himself) (at p. 83); Ramaswamy J. (at pp. 177-78) and Jeewan Reddy (for Aggarwal J. and himself) (at pp. 246-47).
154. However, there was difference of opinion among the judges as to the scope and extent of judicial review in this respect.
155. Though all of the Judges have not used the expression basic structure, it is evident from their holding that they conferred the federal structure of the Constitution the status of basic structure. See, *infra,* n. 157.
156. *Supra,* n. 142 *per* Sawant and Kuldip Singh JJ. They held, "Democracy and federalism the essential feature of the Constitution and are part of its basic structure. (at p. 112);
Ramaswamy J. observed thus, "Federalism envisaged in the Constitution of India is a basic feature in which the Union of India is permanent within the territorial limits set in Article 1 of the Constitution and is indestructible." (at p. 205);
Jeewan Reddy and Dayal JJ. held "Let it be said that the federalism in the Indian Constitution is not a matter of administrative convenience, but one of *principle*—the outcome of our own historical process and a recognition of the ground realities." (at p. 217). (Emphasis supplied)
157. *Id. per* Sawant and Kuldip Singh JJ. It was held, "Democracy and federalism are the essential features of our Constitution and are part of its basic structure. Any interpretation that we may place on Article 356 must therefore help to preserve and not subvert their fabric. The power vested *de jure* in the President but *de facto* in the Council of Ministers under Article 356 has all the latent capacity to emasculate the two basic features of the Constitution and hence it is necessary to scrutinise the material on the basis of which the advice is given and the President forms his satisfaction more closely and circumspectly". (at p. 112);
Ramaswamy J. held, "The exercise of power under Article 356 by the

Thus, in the *Bommai's Case*, the doctrine of basic structure has been invoked by the Court for two different purposes. The assistance of one of the features of basic structure-secularism—was sought for assessing the validity of the action of the State Government so as to determine whether it was liable to be dismissed under Article 356. Assistance of another feature-federalism—was sought for checking the possibility of arbitrariness of the presidential action. Thus, the Court has projected the doctrine of basic structure as a criterion for assessing the validity of the action of the authorities created by the Constitution.

The decisions in *S.C. Advocates*, and *S.R. Bommai*, project the creative attempts on the part of the Apex Court to use for the doctrine of basic structure in innovative ways. In the former case, the Court has for the first time used it as a tool for constitutional construction while, in the latter it has been used by the Court as a criterion for testing the constitutionality of actions of certain authorities under the Constitution namely the State Government and the President. These decisions clearly indicate the forewarning that in future any exercise of constitutional power by an authority in a way prejudicial to any of the features of basic structure of the Constitution is likely to be struck down as unconstitutional.

6. FUNDAMENTAL RIGHTS—WHETHER PART OF BASIC STRUCTURE

The question whether fundamental rights were part of the basic structure has been a moot point before the Supreme Court from *Kesavananda* and the Court has not given a conclusive

---

President through Council of Ministers places a great responsibility on it and.... It is to reiterate that the federal character of the Government reimposes the belief that the people's faith in democratically elected majority or coalition Government would run its full term, would not be belied unless the situation is otherwise unavoidable..." (at p. 191).
Jeevan Reddy J. observed, "Article 365 merely says that in case of failure to comply with the directions [of the centre] given, "it is lawful" for the President to hold that the requisite type of situation [contemplated by Article 356(1)] has arisen. It is not as if each and every failure *ipso facto* gives rise to the requisite situation." (at p. 273).

answer to it for long. In *I.R. Coelho* v. *State of Tamil Nadu*[158] in which the validity of the 34th and 66th amendments to the Constitution by which certain laws limiting the right to hold land,[159] enacted by the State of Tamil Nadu and State of West Bengal were included in the ninth schedule. Since the questions raised in the case was the vires of the constitutional amendments by which laws were included in the ninth schedule, it called for reconsideration of *Waman Rao*, the matter was referred to a larger bench consisting of 9 judges and was decided as *I.R. Coelho* v. *State of Tamil Nadu*.[160] While dealing with the scope of the constituent power of Parliament to include the law into the ninth schedule, the court widened the scope of basic structure in so far it held that basic structure "includes reference to Article 21 read with Article 14, Article 15, etc."[161] and "the triangle of Article 21 read with Article 14 and Article 19."[162] The court criticized the practice of invoking Article 31B to put laws into the ninth schedule as "insertion in the Ninth Schedule is not controlled by any defined criteria or standards by which the exercise of power may be evaluated" and that insertion of laws in the ninth schedule "nullifies entire Part III of the Constitution."[163] It was held that the same would make "the entire Part III inapplicable at the will of Parliament" and the doctrine of basic structure redundant which "is likely to make the controlled Constitution uncontrolled."[164] Thus, *I.R. Coelho* has categorically held that fundamental rights also constituted a part of the basic structure. The holding is certainly innovative in so far as the most essential rights viz., rights to life, equality and the rights to freedoms are brought outside the purview of the constituent power of Parliament.

158. (1999) 7 SCC 580.
159. The Gudalur Janman Estates (Abolition and Conversion into Ryotwari) Act, 1969 enacted by the State of Tamil Nadu and the Land Holding Revenue Act, 1979 enacted by the State of West Bengal.
160. (2007) 2 SCC 1 : AIR 2007 SC 861.
161. *Id.* at p. 106.
162. *Id.* at p. 108.
163. *Id.* at p. 98.
164. *Id.* at p. 108.

7. BASIC STRUCTURE—A NORM FOR LEGISLATION?

A pertinent question springs up here. Can the doctrine be invoked for evaluating and striking down legislation?[165] Such a question was raised for the first time before the Court in *Indira Gandhi* v *Raj Narain*.[166] The Court per majority[167] held[168] that the doctrine of basic structure was to be the touchstone of constitutional amendments only and that it could not be a yardstick to determine the constitutionality of exercise of legislation.[169] Such a legal proposition leads to a situation in

---

165. This question becomes relevant mainly because, some of the ingredients of basic structure developed by the Court are not referable to any specific provision of the Constitution. Democracy, federalism and independence of judiciary are some of them. In such a context, if basic structure does not form a criterion for testing the validity of legislation, a law not violating the provisions of the Constitution, but violative of basic structure would remain valid, which is an absurd proposition.
166. 1975 Supp. S.C.C. 1. The respondent challenged the validity of two amendments made to the Representation of Peoples Act, 1950,viz., amendment 58 of 1974 and 40 of 1975. By those amendments, Parliament had validated certain election practices which otherwise would have been invalid. These amendments were challenged by the respondent on a host of grounds including that they violated democracy, which was a feature of basic structure of the Constitution. For a detailed discussion of the case on other issues, see *supra*, nn. 6-67.
167. The majority consisted of Ray C.J., Mathew and Chandrachud JJ. (M.H. Beg J. *contra*) However, Justice H.R. Khanna refused to express any opinion on this issue as he thought that the case could be decided on other grounds.
168. Justice Ray C.J. held, "The contention of the respondent that the Amendment Acts of 1974 and 1975 are subject to basic features or basic structure of basic framework fails on two grounds. First, legislative measures are not subject to the theory of basic features or basic structure or basic framework." (at p. 66)
Justice Mathew observed, "Besides, those cases being cases of legislative validation, need not pas the test of the theory of basic structure which, I think, will apply only to constitutional amendments." (at p. 131.)
Justice Chandrchud held, "The constitutional amendments may, on the ratio of the Fundamental Rights Case, be tested on the anvil of basic structure. But apart from the principle that a case is only an authority for what it decides, it does not logically follow from the majority judgment in the Fundamental Rights case that ordinary legislation must also answer the same test as a constitutional amendment."(at p. 261.)
169. Only Justice M.H. Beg held that even legislative powers could be subjected to the doctrine of basic structure. *Id.* at p. 236.

which the legislative authority would be able to do certain things, which the constituent authority, the mother of legislative, executive and judicial power cannot do. Undoubtedly such a proposition of law would be absurd. It defeats the very purpose for which the doctrine of basic structure has been introduced into the Indian legal system. Moreover, a theoretical discussion reveals that the doctrine of basic structure carries the characteristics of the basic norm of the legal system. The *grundnorm* being the basic norm of the legal system, is the criterion for testing the validity of all other norms of the legal system. In other words, to be valid, even the lowest legal norm has to satisfy the requirement of the *grundnorm*.[170] Further, it is clear from the decisions in which the doctrine has been developed and applied that the Court has recognized the doctrine of basic structure as part and parcel of our Constitution. Obviously legislation has to satisfy the requirements of the Constitution including the basic structure. Since the basic structure constitutes the essential aspect of our Constitution, it forms the very foundation of the Indian legal system. The decision in *Indira Gandhi* that the doctrine of basic structure is not applicable to test the validity of ordinary legislative action is therefore incorrect.

However, in *Sampath Kumar*,[171] the Court tested the validity of the Administrative Tribunals Act, 1985 on the basis of basic structure.[172] This issue got reconsideration later in *G.C. Kanungo* v. *State of Orissa*.[173] The question before the Court was the constitutionality of an amendment effected to the Arbitration Act, 1940 by the State of Orissa to nullify an arbitration award. Holding that the enactment amounted to an encroachment on the judicial power of the State "resulting in infringement of a

170. For a discussion of the concept of basic norm evolved by Kelsen, see, *supra*, Chapter 6, nn. 72-83.
171. *Supra*, n. 99.
172. *Supra*, nn. 101 and 104.
173. (1995) 5 S.C.C. 96. The amount to be paid by the State to the petitioners (contractors) was fixed by arbitration proceedings. To nullify the liability, the government enacted the Arbitration (Orissa Amendment) Act, 1991 amending Arbitration Act, 1940. It was a petition under Article 32 challenging the constitutionality of the amendment on the ground that it was violative of Article 14.

basic feature of the Constitution—the Rule of Law"[174] the Court struck down the amendment. These decisions which accept the doctrine of basic structure as a norm for evaluating the exercise of legislative power recognize it as a grundnorm of our legal system.

Later, reconsidering *Waman Rao*, the court examined this issue in detail in *I.R. Coelho*[175] the court made it crystal clear that the doctrine of basic structure applied to both to the constitutional amendments by which laws were included in the ninth schedule as well as the statutes so added into it. The court held,

> "Every amendment to the Constitution whether it be in the form of amendment of any article or amendment by insertion of an Act in the Ninth Schedule, has to be tested by reference to the doctrine of basic structure which includes reference to Article 21 read with Article 14, Article 15, etc. As stated, law included in the Ninth Schedule do not become part of the Constitution, they derive their validity on account of the exercise undertaken by Parliament to include them in the Ninth Schedule. That exercise has to be tested every time it is undertaken."[176]

and that

> "This court being bound by all the provisions of the Constitution and also by the basic structure doctrine has necessarily to scrutinise the Ninth Schedule laws. It has to examine the terms of the statute, the nature of the rights involved, etc. to determine whether in effect and substance the statute violates the essential features of the

174. *Id.* at p. 114.
175. *Supra,* n. 160.
176. *Id.* at pp. 106-07. Accepting the reasoning of *Waman Rao,* the court explained method of finding out whether the basic structure was violated. It held, 'the measure of the permissibility of an amendment . . . is how far it is consistent with the original; you cannot by an amendment transform the original into opposite of what it is. For that purpose, a comparison is undertaken to match the amendment with the original.' (*Id.* at p. 99)

Constitution. For so doing, it has to first find whether the Ninth Schedule law is violative of Part III. If on such examination, the answer is in the affirmative, the further examination to be undertaken is whether the violation found is destructive of the basic structure doctrine. If on such further examination, the answer is in the affirmative, the result would be invalidation of the Ninth Schedule law. Therefore, first the violation of rights of Part III is required to be determined, then its impact examined and if it shows that in effect and substance, it destroys the basic structure of the Constitution, the consequence of invalidation has to follow."[177]

Though the decision of *I.R. Coelho* is only a reiteration of *Waman Rao*, unlike the latter, it deserves commendation for the novelty of approach it exhibited. The court has vivified and explained that the doctrine of basic structure applied for evaluating both the constitutional amendments and the laws included in the ninth schedule which, was not examined in *Waman Rao*.

8. VALIDITY OF CONSTITUTIONAL AMENDMENT—HOW DETERMINED?

Though various aspects regarding the doctrine of basic structure has been discussed by the Supreme Court since 1973, except for some stray indirect references made by some of the judges in the course of rendering their opinions,[178] there were no discussion as to the mode of determining how an amendment

177. *Id.* at p. 110. The court also observed that validation under Article 31B is only fictional immunity and the validity of the amendment is to be guided by the impact test.

178. "For determining whether a particular feature in the scheme of our Constitution is a part of its basic structure, one has perforce to examine in each individual case the place of the particular feature in the scheme of our Constitution, its object and purpose; and the consequences of its denial on the integrity of the Constitution as a fundamental instrument of country's governance. But, it is needless for the purpose of these appeals to ransack every nook and cranny of the Constitution to discover the bricks of the basic structure". *Per* Chandrachud J. in *Indira Gandhi* v. *Raj Narain*, 1975 Supp. SCC 1 at 252.

was violative of basic structure. The Supreme Court however, expressed its opinion in this regard in *M. Nagaraj* v. *Union of India*,[179] in which the petitioners under Article 32 challenged the constitutionality of the Constitution (Seventy-seventh Amendment) Act, 1995, Constitution (Eighty-first Amendment) Act, 2000, Constitution (Eighty-second Amendment) Act, 2000 and the Constitution (Eighty-fifth Amendment) Act, 2001 as violative of equality which is an aspect of the basic structure of the Constitution. Accepting that basic structure is 'based on the concept of constitutional identity',[180] and that 'recognition of a basic structure in the context of amendment provides an insight that there are, beyond the words of particular provisions, systemic principles underlying and connecting the provisions of the Constitution,' it was held that 'these principles give coherence to the Constitution and make it an organic whole, that they are 'part of constitutional law even if they are not expressly stated in the form of rules and that they are 'the overarching principles that one would be able to distinguish essential from less essential features of the Constitution.' The court thereafter observed that to qualify as an essential feature,[181]

> "it must be established that the principle is a part of the constitutional law binding on the legislature. Only thereafter, is the second step to be taken, namely, whether the principle is so fundamental as to bind even the amending power of Parliament i.e. to form a part of the basic structure. ...This is the standard of judicial review of constitutional amendments in the context of the doctrine of basic structure."

Being based on constitutional identity and constitutional limits,[182] the court held that application of the principle of basic structure to constitutional amendments depends on the twin tests namely, the "width test" and the test of "identity."[183] By

179. (2006) 8 SCC 212.
180. *Id*. at p. 244.
181. *Id*. at p. 243.
182. *Ibid*.
183. *Id*. at p. 268.

width test the court would examine whether by the impugned amendment obliterates any of the constitutional limitations while the identity test examines whether the amendment altered the structure of the Constitution.[184] Finding that the impugned amendment did not breach any of these aspects, the court held them as constitutionally valid.

Later, in *I.R.Coelho* v. *State of T.N.*,[185] though referred to these tests for determining the validity of the constitutional amendments impugned in it, the court held that validity of an amendment depended upon the impact it causes on the Constitution and not on its form.[186] But, the dimension of the issue had a substantial change in *Ashoka Kumar Thakur* v. *Union of India*.[187] It was a cluster of petitions under Article 32 challenging the validity of the Constitution (Ninety-third Amendment) Act, 2005[188] on the ground that it violated the principle of equality which is part of the basic structure of the Constitution. The Chief Justice[189] held that basic structure was 'a larger principle on which the Constitution is framed' and the question whether a feature formed part of the basic structure had to be examined in each case, keeping in mind the scheme of the Constitution, its objects and purpose as well as the integrity of the Constitution as a fundamental instrument for

184. *Id*. at p. 269. These tests have been alluded to by the Supreme Court in *I.R. Coelho* (2007) 2 SCC 1, 111 and still later by one of the judges (Justice Bhandari) in *Ashok Kumar Thakur* v. *Union of India*, (2008) 6 SCC 1, 676
185. (2007) 2 S.C.C. 1.
186. *Id*. at p. 111. The court also observed that the measure of permissibility of amending a pleading that it should not 'transform the original into opposite of what it is' could be used for evaluating the constitutional amendments also. (*Id*. at p. 99)
187. (2008) 6 S.C.C. 1.
188. By the Constitution (Ninety- third Amendment) Act, 2005 clause (5) was inserted into Article 15. It reads: "Nothing in this article or in sub-clause (g) of Clause (1) of Article 19 shall prevent the State from making any special provision, by law, for the advancement of any socially and educationally backward classes of citizens or for the Scheduled Castes or the Scheduled Tribes insofar as such special provisions relate to their admissions to the educational institutions including private educational institutions whether aided or unaided by the State, other than the minority educational institutions referred to in Clause (1) of Article 30."
189. It was decided by a five-judge bench, consisting of the Chief Justice K.G. Balakrishnan,. Arijit Pasayat, C.K.Thakker Dalveer Bhandari and R.V. Raveendran JJ.

governance.[190] He observed that though equality as contained in Articles 14, 15 and 16 of the Constitution was a feature of basic structure, as its contents were variable according to the changing conditions, the question whether an amendment of those provisions violated the basic structure depended upon its implication on the constitutional identity.[191] Justice Bhandari, in his separate opinion held that an amendment could be considered to have altered basic structure "if its actual or potential effect would be to damage a facet of the basic structure to such an extent that the facet's original identity is compromised"[192] and not if the amendment merely abridges the basic structure, as in that case, "the structure's identity remains" intact.[193]

An examination of the cases from *Nagaraj* through *Ashoka Kumar Thakur* leaves room for tendencies unsettling the precession set by *Kesavanandabharathi* and *Minerva Mills*. While in *Nagaraj* the court held that to be valid, an amendment should pass the twin tests of the width test and the identity test, in *I.R. Coelho*, the court adopted the 'impact test' according to which the validity of an amendment would be determined on the basis of the impact it would create on the basic structure. According to the Court, considering "the actual effect and impart of the law,"[194] "the rights test" was more appropriate than "the essence of the rights test".[195] Application of the essence of the rights test would bar only substantial changes of the basic structure while the rights test prohibits even minor alterations to it. In *Ashoka Kumar* on the other hand, in the guise of relying upon *Nagaraj* and *I.R. Coelho*, the court held that the validity of an amendment was evaluated on the identity test instead of the impact test, thereby permitting abridgment of the basic structure. Unlike the precedents, in *Ashoka Kumar* the issue of validity of the constitutional amendment has been reduced to examination of identity of the Constitution. Now, after *Ashoka Kumar*, an amendment would not be held invalid unless it

190. *Supra*, n. 187. at p. 482.
191. *Id*. at p. 483. Justice R.V. Raveendran in his separate judgement agreed with the Chief Justice on this count. (*Id*. at p. 710).
192. *Id*. at p. 665.
193. *Ibid*.
194. *Supra*, n. 185. at p. 111.
195. *Id*. at p. 108.

totally destroys the basic structure.[196] Thus with *Ashoka Kumar*, one finds gradual decrease in the severity of norms for examining the validity of constitutional amendments. It is submitted that this trend would enable Parliament to transgress the constitutionally set limits on its powers reducing the sacrosanct principle of basic structure to insignificance.

9. ALTERATION OF BASIC STRUCTURE

Can the basic structure be altered in any manner? Can we in some way change the identity of our Constitution? If possible, what is the method for doing it? These are some of the doubts that naturally arise at this juncture. The Supreme Court has not so far ventured to make any observation on these issues. But we can deduce some clues from the various decisions of the Supreme Court in this regard. If we say that the basic structure is inalterable, it means that the future generations are always bound by the declarations of the past ones. Incorporation of provisions for amending Constitutions has been justified on the ground that unalterable Constitutions are always prone to be swept away through revolutions.[197] The same is true of basic structure also. Even though basic structure constitutes the fundamental principle upon which the Constitution is erected, there may be occasions on which a nation requires alteration of such fundamentals of the legal system. Therefore the proposition that the basic structure is unalterable on any account cannot be treated as a wise one. Nor have the Judges in any of the cases observed that the basic structure of the Constitution is totally unalterable. The doctrine was introduced

196. *Id. per* Balakrishnan C.J. "The variability of changing conditions may necessitate the modifications in the structure and design of these rights, but the transient characters of formal arrangements must reflect the larger purpose and principles that are the continuous and unalterable thread of constitutional identity. It is not the introduction of significant and far-reaching change that is objectionable, rather it is the content of this change insofar as it implicates the question of constitutional identity. (*Supra*, n. 187. at p. 483).
Bhandari J., "If legislation merely abridges the basic structure, the structure's identity remains. The legislation is upheld. In this sense, Parliament may take away or destroy fundamental rights by amending the Constitution, provided that the basic structure is not altered." (at p. 665).

197. See, *supra*, Chapter, 6, n. 11.

by the Apex Court as a limitation on the *constituent power* of Parliament i.e. the Executive and not on the *alterability* of the Constitution as such. The doctrine was only a precautionary measure against arbitrary exercise of the constituent power by Parliament. In the absence of such a doctrine, if a government wielded a thumping majority in Parliament, it would be able to amend the Constitution in any fashion it likes.[198] Such a check on the constituent power was considered necessary to prevent the possibility of the Constitution becoming a plaything in the hands of the Parliament, which is only a delegate of the real sovereign, namely the people. Undoubtedly the identity of the Constitution can be altered with the concurrence of the people. In a truly democratic state, nothing should stand in the way of altering the Constitution by the people themselves. In other words, to repeal the Constitution or to alter its identity and to bring forth a new Constitution, referendum can be resorted to even though alteration of the fundamentals of the Constitution cannot be left to the sweet will of the representative body. It may be difficult for a representative legislative body like Parliament to keep themselves away from politics as they are constituted on the basis of political alignments. Constitutions of other nations contain provisions for referring important matters relating to their alteration to the people.[199] The decisions delineating the doctrine of basic structure do not stand in the way of changing them through referendum. Though there is no specific provision in the Constitution of India sanction of the people is the only possible way to get the basic structure amended. But there is a view that basic structure could be amended by Parliament if it has been converted as the Constituent Assembly. This view does not appear to be correct since, every time when it seeks to amend the Constitution, Parliament sits as, and exercises the powers of, the Constituent Assembly and does not act merely in the legislative capacity. In short, there is only one safe and possible method for amending the basic structure and that is a

---

198. The 24th, 39th and 42nd amendments are the best example for exercise of such a power. In fact such indiscriminate exercise of the power to amend the Constitution has invited the doctrine of basic structure into the legal system. For a detailed discussion on the origin of the doctrine, see *supra*, Chapter 6.
199. See for instance, Federal Constitution of the Swiss Federation, Article 120.

referendum.[200] Perhaps, the future development of case law may indicate such a course as the permissible method.

8. CONCLUSION

A discussion of the cases dealing with basic structure reveals the development in the judicial thinking in explaining it. There are two significant aspects to the judicial creativity in this respect. One lies in developing and crystallizing the doctrine. The other rests in the development of the doctrine as a norm for testing the validity of legislative and executive acts and as a tool for interpreting the Constitution.

There has thus been a high degree of judicial creativity in the process of crystallization and ramification of the concept of basic structure in India. A study of the above cases proves that the doctrine has gained an undeniable place in the Indian legal system. The cases testify a saga of assertion of constitutionalism and constitutional principles over the policies of government. They further evidence judicial assertion over actions of other constitutional authorities. These cases testify that the doctrine is ingrained into the Indian constitutional ethos in an unrootable manner. That is evident from the rethinking of Parliament to incorporate the doctrine of basic structure into the Constitution.[201] It is clear that the doctrine is available now not only for limiting the power of the Parliament to amend the Constitution but also for interpreting the basic document as well as for restraining arbitrary actions of different authorities envisaged by the Constitution. Above them all, the doctrine has now been accepted as a norm for evaluating statutes also.

In short, the doctrine of basic structure has gained an incontrovertible status in the Indian constitutional system. It is unlikely that in the future the doctrine would be abrogated rolling back the constitutional position to the pre-*Kesavananda* days. Nor is it desirable also. It is yet to be seen whether the doctrine will satisfy the requirements of the next millennium. Nevertheless, it is beyond dispute that the Supreme Court of India will be remembered for the unique contribution in the constitutional jurisprudence namely, the basic structure.

---

200. For a discussion of these three methods, see, D.D. Basu, *Shorter Constitution of India* (1996) pp. 1147-48.

201. That is clear from the 45th Constitution amendment bill, which was an attempt on the part of Parliament to incorporate some restrictions on its constituent power under Article 368 by stipulating that in exercise of that power it could not amend the basic structure of the Constitution.

PART III

8

Individual Rights and Social Justice

I. INTRODUCTION

The Constitution of India reflects the sense of justice that rallied in the minds of its makers. This is evident from the Preamble,[1] and the importance given by the makers of the Constitution to the Fundamental Rights and Directive Principles of State Policy. It is rightly opined that the fundamental rights and directive principles explain the concept of justice contained in the Preamble[2] and could be characterized as elements constituting the conscience of the Constitution of India.[3]

However, there are some basic differences between the rights and the directives. The fundamental rights contained in

1. See, The Constitution of India, Preamble. The relevant portion reads, "We the people of India, having solemnly resolved ... to secure to all its citizens; JUSTICE, social, economic and political;..."
2. D.D. Basu, *Commentaries on the Constitution of India*, Vol. E (1981), p. 94. See also, Sudesh Kumar Sharma, *Directive Principles and Fundamental Rights, Relationship and Policy Perspectives* (1990), p. 11.
3. Granville Austin, *The Constitution of India—The Cornerstone of a Nation* (1966), p. 50.

Part III deal with justice in its dimensions as individual,[4] political and civil rights,[5] while directive principles contained in Part IV, spell out justice at the social level[6] and deal with social and economic progress.[7] Fundamental rights operate as a source of restriction on the powers of the 'State'.[8] The powers of the state, whether legislative, executive or administrative, are subject to those rights. Directive principles, on the other hand, are incorporated in the Constitution to guide the State in matters of legislation and administration. They can be treated as provisions that streamline the legislative and administrative activities of the State. That may be the reason why Dr. Ambedkar compared[9] the Directive Principles with the Instruments of Instructions.[10] Like Instruments of Instructions they are directions to the future legislatures and executives to show in what manner they should exercise their powers. Ambedkar therefore observed that directive principles were the

4. Seervai, *Constitutional Law of India* (1993), p. 1937. He observes, "The thing to note is that fundamental rights are conferred on each and every person or on each and every citizen or on each and every specified community or denomination."
5. V.S. Deshpande, "Rights and Duties under the Constitution," 15 J.I.L.I. 94 at p. 99 (1973).
6. R.B. Sreevasthava, *Economic Justice under the Indian Constitution* (1989), pp. 49, 181.
7. K.C. Markandan, *Directive Principles in the Indian Constitution,* (1966), p. 25. Gajendragadkar observers in *The Indian Parliament and the Fundamental Rights* (1972), p. 62. "...Article 37, in fact, enunciates the basic socio-economic policy which the Constitution demands must form the subject-matter of legislative action on the part of the State in order to achieve the goal set before the country by the Preamble and the relevant provisions of the Constitution." See also Sirajud-Islam Laskar, *Directive Principles of State Policy in Indian Constitution* (1988), p. 13.
8. See, Constitution of India, Article 12. It reads, "In this Part, unless the context otherwise requires, "the State" includes the Government and Parliament of India and the Government and the Legislatures of each of the States and all local or other authorities within the territory of India or under the control of the Government of India."
9. *C.A.D.*, Vol. VII, p. 474.
10. The Instrument of Instruction "is the executive instruction by the Crown. It cannot be enforced by judicial process." See, C.L. Anand, *Constitutional Law and History of Government of India* (1990), p. 405.

ready index for the legislatures of the future.[11] It is opined that they can be treated as guidelines for the courts also.[12] Incorporation of a provision in the Constitution that directive principles are "fundamental in the governance of the country"[13] implies that they are normative in character setting before the State the goals to be achieved.[14] Fundamental rights and directive principles represent the negative and positive aspects of State obligations.[15] As a sequel to such a difference, the Constitution also provides that the fundamental rights are enforceable through courts of law[16] while the directive principles are outside the pale of judicial enforcement.[17] Moreover, it can be said that fundamental rights are static in nature while directive principles are dynamic in character.[18] To

11. See, C.A.D., Vol. VII, p. 476. He said, "*In enacting this part of the Constitution, the Assembly is giving certain directions to the future legislature and the future executive to show in what manner they are to exercise the legislative and the executive power they will have*. Surely it is not the intention to introduce in this part these principles as mere pious declarations. *It is the intention of the Assembly that in future both the legislature and the executive should not merely pay lip service to these principles but that they should be made the basis of all legislative and executive action that they may be taking hereafter in the matter of the governance of the country.*" (Emphasis supplied). See also R.B. Sreevasthava, *op. cit.* at p. 181. See also Ram Jeth Malani, "Fundamental Rights v. Directive Principles". 8 J.B.C.I. 392 at p. 397. (1981).
12. Austin, *op. cit.*, at p. 114. "...the Directive Principles have been a guide for the Union Parliament and state legislatures; they have been cited by the courts to support decisions; governmental bodies have been guided by their provisions. The Government of India Fiscal Commission of 1949, for example, recognized that its recommendations should be guided by the Principles."
13. The Constitution of India, Article 37. It reads, "The provisions contained in this Part shall not be enforceable by any court, *but the principles therein laid down are nevertheless fundamental in the governance of the country* and it shall be the duty of the State to apply these principles in making laws." (Emphasis supplied).
14. Seervai, *Constitutional Law of India*, Vol. II (1984), p. 1602.
15. Austin, *op. cit.*, at p. 50.
16. The Constitution of India, Article 32.
17. *Supra*, n. 13.
18. P.B. Gajendragadkar, The *Indian Parliament and the Fundamental Rights* (1972). He observes (at p. 43) that the directive principles set out the goal of bringing about an egalitarian society in India. The adoption of the concept of welfare State, fighting of poverty, ignorance, squalor, disease and unemployment raise hopes and aspirations in the minds of the people. Though legitimate, at all times they remain unsatisfied. Their

use the Dworkian terminology, it may not be wrong to state that fundamental rights are 'principle-based' and directive principles are 'policy-based'.[19] In other words though both aim at justice and fairness, fundamental rights and directive principles differ in colour, content and character.

In spite of all these differences between them there is a common thread running through fundamental rights and directive principles. They have a common origin and share common objectives, viz., 'to ensure the welfare of the society envisaged by the Preamble'.[20] It cannot be disputed that both strive for justice. Directive Principles deal with the concept of justice at macro-level while fundamental rights lay down the concept at micro-level. Further, directive principles form the distributive aspect of justice while fundamental rights constitute its corrective aspect.[21]

A question remains unanswered in the structural arrangement of the fundamental rights and directive principles in the Constitution. What is the relationship between the fundamental rights and directive principles? Even the members of the Constituent Assembly could not reach a consensus on this

horizon expands along with that the contents of economic concepts. In this theoretical sense, directive principles are dynamic. Since these features are lacking in the case of fundamental rights, though important and significant, they are static.

19. Ronald Dworkin, *Taking Rights Seriously*, (1995) p. 22 He observes, "I call a 'policy' that kind of standard that sets out a goal to social feature of the community....I call a 'principle' a standard that is to be observed, not because it will advance or secure an economic, political, or social situation deemed desirable, not because it is a requirement of justice or fairness or some other dimension of morality."
20. D.D. Basu, *op. cit.* at pp. 92, 94.
21. For a discussion on the distributive and corrective aspects of justice, see, Fitzgerald (Ed.) *Salmond on Jurisprudence* (1966), p. 63. See also W. Friedmann, *Legal Theory* (1949), p. 9, where he observes, "...distinction between 'distributive' and 'corrective' justice still forms the basis of all theoretical discussions on the subject. The former directs the distribution of goods and honours to each according to his place in the community; it orders the equal treatment of equals before the law.... The second form of justice is essentially the measure of the technical principles which govern the administration of law. In regulating legal relations a general standard of redressing the consequences of actions must be found..."

issue.[22] The relation between the fundamental rights and directive principles was a matter of heated debate over the years before the judiciary. The judiciary had to struggle, formulating different versions to figure out a sensible content to their relationship. In the interpretation of the relationship between the fundamental rights and directive principles and in explaining the contents of the former in the light of the latter, the judiciary has been highly creative. For a proper understanding of the creative process, a glance into the genesis and evolution of fundamental rights and directive principles is essential.

2. EVOLUTION OF FUNDAMENTAL RIGHTS AND DIRECTIVE PRINCIPLES

A study of different Constitutions reveals that almost all of the written constitutions have incorporated certain rights which are considered as either essential, inviolable or sacred and therefore beyond the reach of the powers of the 'State'. Such rights are accorded a status higher than the ordinary legal rights and are therefore called the Bill of Rights, Fundamental Rights or Basic Rights. The origin of such basic rights inviolable even by the State can be traced to the contents of Magna Carta 1215, Petition of Rights 1628 and Bill of Rights 1688 in England. The Constitution of the United States introduced certain rights by constitutional amendments.[23] Following suit, different nations[24] incorporated certain important rights into their Constitutions. India is also no exception to this.[25]

In India, the concept of rights beyond the reach of legislature was there in the minds of the freedom fighters right

22. There was a view in the Constituent Assembly itself that there were some elements of conflict between the fundamental rights and directive principles. See, *infra*, n. 69.
23. Amendments I to X to the Constitution of the U.S. contain what is called fundamental rights. Hence, those amendments together are called the Bill of Rights
24. See, for instance, Constitutions of German Democratic Republic, Articles 6-18; Constitution of France 1946 which reaffirmed the Declaration of the Rights of Man and Citizens adopted in 1789.
25. Cf. Seervai, *Constitutional Law of India*, Vol. I (1991), p. 349. He observes, "Our Constitution followed the United States precedent and enacted fundamental rights in the Constitution itself."

from the early stages of the freedom movement. The demand for minimal rights is as old as the formation of the Indian National Congress in 1885.[26] However the idea of fundamental rights as such was embodied for the first time in the Constitution of India Bill, 1895.[27] The demand was repeated in various Congress resolutions between 1917 and 1919. The Common Wealth of India Bill, 1925 presented to the House of Commons contained some provisions[28] dealing with fundamental rights.[29] Recommendations for incorporating social and economic rights were made for the first time in the All Parties Conference, 1928.[30] This view continued in the I.T.R. First Session, where grant of economic rights and conferment of political rights were claimed by the Indian Labour Organization.[31] Later in 1931, Indian National Congress in its 47th session adopted a resolution with four topics in which Fundamental Rights and Economic Programme had a prominent place.[32] However, the peculiarity of the concept of such fundamental rights during that period was that they envisaged no distinctions between individual, political and civil rights on the one hand and social and economic rights on the other. In other words, there was no distinction between what is presently contained in Parts III and IV of the Constitution of India. The Commonwealth of India Bill, 1925, for instance, incorporated liberty of persons, free expression of opinion, free elementary education and use of roads as fundamental rights.[33] Similarly, the Nehru Report 1928 also made no such distinction and we find in it a conglomeration of topics under the rubric

26. D.D. Basu, *op. cit.* at p. 92.
27. Austin, *op. cit.* at p. 53. Article 16 of this Bill laid down a variety of rights including those of free speech, imprisonment only by competent authority, and of free state education. For an authentic summary of the Bill, see, Shiva Rao, *Select Documents I* at p. 43 *et. seq.*
28. Article 8.
29. For the Text of the Bill, see K.C. Markandan, *op. cit.*, at pp. 28-29.
30. *Id.* at p. 30. They included rights for primary education and for improvement of labour conditions.
31. *Id.* at p. 32.
32. *Id.* at p. 43.
33. The Commonwealth of India Bill, 1925, Sec. 4. For the text, see. B. Siva Rao, *Framing of India's Constitution*, Vol. I (1966) p. 44.

Rights, which we presently find as fundamental rights and directive principles.[34]

It was the Sapru Committee 1945,[35] which for the first time drew such a distinction between civil rights on the one hand and social and economic rights on the other. The criterion for such a distinction was the enforceability through courts of law. The Committee opined that the civil rights were judicially enforceable while the others were not.[36] Later, at the time of the framing of the Constitution of India, the Sub-Committee on Fundamental Rights divided the concept of Fundamental Rights into two. They were those "which require positive action by the State and which can be guaranteed only if such an action is practicable, while the other merely requires that the State shall abstain from prejudicial action.... It is obvious that rights of the first type are not either capable of, or suitable for, enforcement by legal action, while those of the second type may be so enforced."[37] Hence, the Sub-Committee proposed that the judicially unenforceable part of rights might be called as Fundamental Principle and the enforceable ones as Fundamental Rights.[38] Such a difference between the two was maintained by the makers of the Constitution on the ground of the fundamental difference between them. According to them the fundamental rights had negative contents while the directive principles were positive in nature. Such a distinction implies that enforcement of fundamental rights calls only for a restraint on the part of the State while implementation of the directive principles requires a positive action on its part which may cause huge expenditure of state funds. That is why they held fundamental rights alone as justiciable in nature permitting

34. The Nehru Committee Report, 1928. Clause 4. For the text, see, Shiva Rao, *op. cit.* at p. 58.
35. Sapru Committee was constituted for the purpose of eliciting information regarding future constitutional set-up. See, Markandan, *op. cit.* at p. 46.
36. *Ibid.*
37. B. Shiva Rao, *Framing of India's Constitution* Vol. III (1967), p. 33.
38. *Ibid.* The unenforceable rights would include the duty of the State to secure the citizens right to work, maintenance in old age and sickness, free education, protection of economic interests of the weaker sections and State protection of the culture, language and script of various communities and linguistic areas in India. (*Id.* at p. 34).

individuals to enforce them through courts of law and to approach the courts for preventing and prohibiting their violation[39] and considered Directive Principles of State Policy as not enforceable through courts of law.[40] Such a bifurcation is seen to have been effected in some other Constitutions also.[41] It is on the basis of such logic that the concept of directive principles came to have a place in the Constitution of India. The idea of incorporation of directive principles in our Constitution is said to be based on the declarations in the Constitution of Ireland 1937,[42] which can be accepted as the precursor of the Constitution of India in this respect.[43] Provisions in Part IV in our Constitution have much in common[44] with the contents of Article 45[45] of the Irish Constitution. However, some

---

39. See, The Constitution of India, Articles 13 (2) and 32.
40. *Id.* Article 37.
41. See for instance, the Constitution of Ireland, 1937 Article 45.
42. For the text, see, Amos J. Peasle, (Ed.) *Constitutions of Nations* Vol. II.
43. Incorporation of the directive principles has been ascribed also due to the Irish-Congress relationship dating back to the nineteenth century and the consequent long standing affinity of the Congress to the Irish nationalist movement. See, Granville Austin, *op. cit.,* at p. 76.
44. Joseph Minattur, "Directive Principles and Unconstitutional Law," in V. Grover, (Ed.) *Political Process and Role of Courts* (1997), 436 at p. 437.
45. It reads, "The principles of social policy set forth in this Article are intended for the general guidance of the Oireachtas. The application of those principles in the making of laws shall be the care of the Oireachtas exclusively, and shall not be cognisable by any Court under any of the provisions of this Constitution.

    The State shall strive to promote the welfare of the whole people by securing and protecting as effectively as it may a social order in which justice and charity shall inform all the institutions of the national life.

    The State shall, in particular, direct its policy towards securing

    That the citizens (all of whom, men and women equally, have the right to an adequate means of livelihood) may through their occupations find the means of making reasonable provision for their domestic needs.

    That the ownership and control of the material resources of the community may be so distributed amongst private individuals and the various classes as best to subserve the common good.

    That, especially, the operation of free competition shall not be allowed so to develop as to result in the concentration of the ownership or control of essential commodities in a few individuals to the common detriment.

    That in what pertains to the control of credit the constant and predominant aim shall be the welfare of the people as a whole.

    That there may be established on the land in economic security as many families as in the circumstances shall be practicable.

Constitutions do not provide for anything like our directive principles[46] while some other Constitutions which contain concepts similar to those in Part III and Part IV of our Constitution make no such distinction between and among the concepts.[47]

It is clear that in India, both Fundamental Rights and Directive Principles share a common origin though the conceptual background of these two is different. It is also evident that they have a common target to achieve. They in general can be identified as the attempt of the Constitution-makers to assure justice and secure progress at the individual and collective (social) levels simultaneously. The fundamental rights represent the political freedom of individuals while the directives identify their social and economic freedoms. They together constitute a comprehensive whole. Therefore, in the absence of one, the other may become meaningless and ineffective.. The directives contain the social and economic aspects of individual rights without which the political and civil

---

3(1) The State shall favour and, where necessary, supplement private initiative industry and commerce.

(2) The State shall endeavour to secure that private enterprise shall be so conducted as to ensure reasonable efficiency in the production and distribution of goods and as to protect the public against unjust exploitation.

4(1) The State pledges itself to safeguard with especial care the economic interests of the weaker sections of the community, and, where necessary, to contribute to the support of the infirm, the widow, the orphan, and the aged.

(2) The State shall endeavour to ensure that the strength and health of workers, men and women, and the tender age of children shall not be abused and that citizens shall not be forced by economic necessity to enter avocations unsuited to their sex, age or strength."

46. For instance, the Constitution of the United States of America.
47. See for example, the Constitution of the erstwhile Union of Soviet Socialist Republic. Chapter 7 deals with "the Basic Rights, Freedom and Duties of Citizens of the U.S.S.R." which includes the rights of citizens to rest and leisure (Article 41); health protection (Article 42); education (Article 45); cultural benefits (Article 46); to profess or not to profess religion (Article 52d); not to be arrested without court order or warrant of a prosecutor (Article 54); and to privacy (Article 56). See also the Constitution of the Weimer Republic.

liberties as contained in Part III cannot be realized.[48] That may be the reason why it was observed that in the absence of the directives, revolution might take place.[49] Similarly, without proper enjoyment of fundamental rights, it cannot be said that the objects for which directives exist are satisfied.[50] In other words, enforcement of fundamental rights against directive principles is meaningless and implementation of directive principles contrary to fundamental rights is constitutionally not envisaged. It is a truism that the individual rights guaranteed by the Constitution might either lose their content or become unenforceable when directive principles are absent.[51] In this sense, fundamental rights can be considered as that built upon the background of directive principles.[52] In such a context,

48. *Cf.* Upendra Baxi, (Ed.) *K.K. Mathew on Democracy, Equality and Freedom* (1978), p. 55. See also *People's Union for Democratic Rights* v. *Union of India*, A.I.R. 1982 S.C. 1473. The Court observed, (at p. 1486) "Political freedom had no meaning unless it was accompanied by social and economic freedom and it was therefore necessary to carry forward the social and economic revolution with a view to creating socio-economic conditions in which every one would be able to enjoy basic human rights and participate in the fruits of freedom and liberty in an egalitarian social and economic framework. It was with this end in view that the Constitution-makers enacted the Directive Principles of State Policy in Part IV of the Constitution setting out the constitutional goal of a new socio-economic order."
49. See, Austin, *op. cit.* at p. 51. For a contrary view, see, Seervai, *op. cit.* at p. 1644.
50. See, *Minerva Mills* v. *Union of India*, A.I.R. 1980 S.C. 1789. Chandrachud J. speaking for the majority observes (at p. 1807) "But just as the rights conferred by Part III would be without a radar and a compass if they were not geared to an ideal, in the same manner, the attainment of the ideals set out in Part IV would become a pretence or tyranny if the price to be paid for achieving that ideal human freedoms."
51. This idea is reflected in the following observations, "The formulation of social and economic objectives in national constitution owes its origin essentially to the realization that the content of political freedom is impaired by the abuse of social justice and that without adequate protection for social and economic rights, constitutional guarantees of what are known as "classical individual liberties" such as the right to equality, liberty of persons and freedom of speech and association may lose much of their significance." B. Siva Rao, *Framing of India's Constitution—A Study* (1968), p. 319.
52. This idea is reflected in the following words of Roosevelt, "We have come to the clear realization of the fact that true individual freedom cannot exist without economic security and independence. Necessitous men are not free men... In our day these economic truths have become accepted as self-evident." B. Siva Rao, *supra*, n. 37 at p. 46.

fundamental rights and directive principles can be considered as complementary and supplementary to each other[53] and they derive their life breath from each other.

It is clear that the makers of the Constitution had certain specific objectives in their mind in introducing the directives into the Constitution. They attempted to lay down (a) the limits within which the State should work, (b) the ideals, particularly economic and social, which the state should strive to achieve, (c) the directions to the future legislature and executive about the manner in which they should work,[54] and (d) the ground for proper enjoyment of the individual rights popularly called Fundamental Rights.[55] Hence it may not be wrong to say that in every respect the directive principles of state policy simulate the *Rajadharma*[56] of ancient India.[57] It is therefore improper for the Government to ignore the directive principles while administering the nation.

3. NATURE OF DIRECTIVE PRINCIPLES

What is the nature and status of the directive principles contained in the Constitution? There is a view that the directives contain mere pious wishes or declarations,[58] ideals, goals or principles of constitutional morality rather than reality of government.[59] In view of Article 37 of the Constitution,[60] judiciary cannot interfere with questions relating to implementation of the directives. It rests fully with the pure will

53. K.S. Hegde, "Directive Principles of State Policy in the Constitution of India," (1971) 1 S.C.J. 50 at p. 61.
54. C.A.D., Vol. VII, p. 476. See also D.D. Basu, *Commentary on the Constitutional Law of India*, Vol. E (1981), p. 82.
55. *Cf.* Shailaja Chander, *Justice V.R. Krishna Iyer on Fundamental Rights and Directive Principles*, (1992) p. 52.
56. Rajadharma is the fundamental social and political principle exposing complete fulfilment of human ends as well as universal security. T. Sundara Rami Reddy, "Fundamental Rights and the Directive Principles," 22 J.I.L.I. 399 (1988).
57. *Supra*, n. 55 at p. 56.
58. *C.A.D.*, Vol. VII, p. 476.
59. Such a view is said to have been pioneered by Ivor Jennings. See, Rajeev Dhavan, *Supreme Court of India: Its Socio-Juristic Techniques* (1977), p. 88. See also, Seervai, *op. cit.* at p. 1613.
60. See, *supra*, n. 13.

and pleasure of the 'State' to decide whether the mandates contained in the directives should be looked into for framing legislative policies and discharging executive functions. There is no assurance that the various governments would implement them through legislative and executive actions. On such a view, they are characterised as constitutional ideals. However, there is a contrary view that they are not mere ideals and that any law against them is ultravires.[61] The directives are sufficient to give protection against arbitrary legislation. Non-implementation of the directives would be questioned by the people and the government would be answerable to the electorate.[62] The holders of this view therefore assert that directive principles serve a definite constitutional purpose.

Notwithstanding such a difference of opinion over their effectiveness, and the existence of completely contrary views that they are bereft of any force of law,[63] and that non-compliance with the directives brings forth unconstitutionality,[64] it is undisputed that the directive principles adorn a very important place in the administration of the nation. Directive Principles are important for more reasons than one. Proper implementation of the directives is very much necessary for the social and economic progress of the nation. In them lie the secrets of upliftment of the masses. They are the talismans for the social and economic progress of the downtrodden. Moreover, only a proper implementation of the directive principles would enable realization of the fundamental rights conferred by the Constitution.[65] It is therefore constitutionally inappropriate on the part of the administrators to ignore the directive principles.

61. *C.A.D.*, Vol. VIII, p. 482.
62. *C.A.D.*, Vol. VII, p. 41 (*per* Ambedkar).
63. For a nice treatment of the question whether directive principles have got the characteristics of law, see, Upendra Baxi, "The Little Done the Vast Undone, Some Reflections on Reading Granville Austin's The Indian Constitution." 9 J.I.L.I. 323 especially pp. 344-67 (1967); Jagat Narain, "Equal Protection Guarantee and the Right of Property under the Constitution of India", 15 I.C.L.Q. 199 and Upendra Baxi, "Directive Principles and Sociology of Indian Law—A Reply to Dr. Jagat Narain", 11 J.I.L.I. 248 (1969).
64. Jagat Narain, "Judicial Law-making and the Place of Directive Principles in Indian Constitution", 27 J.I.L.I. 198 at p. 219 (1985).
65. *Supra*, n. 48.

4. RELATION BETWEEN FUNDAMENTAL RIGHTS AND DIRECTIVE PRINCIPLES

Examination of some crucial questions is necessary for a proper understanding of the constitutional status of the directive principles. What is the relationship between the fundamental rights and directive principles? Is there any conflict between them? In case of such a conflict, can directive principles prevail over the fundamental rights? Or, in such a case, will fundamental rights prevail over directives? Is there any remedy against non-implementation or wrong implementation of directive principles by the State while carrying out administration?[66] Neither constitutional history nor provisions in our Constitution does provide a satisfactory answer to these questions. However, these are some of the questions to which the Indian judiciary particularly the Apex Court, has addressed itself. What is the contribution of the judiciary in making a proper alignment between the rights and the directives? Has the judiciary played any significant role for the proper implementation of the directives? A study of the judicial response on these issues is very important for many reasons. Indiscriminate exercise of power by the State for implementing directives may override the fundamental rights. This may lead in some of the cases to virtual deprivation of the constitutionally guaranteed rights. Such cases open up much scope for judicial review of state action against abridgment of

66. One may find many instances in which the governments carry out administration of the country either in a manner contrary to or in ignorance of the mandate of the directive principles. There are innumerable occasions in which law was enacted and administration carried out by the government without taking the directives into account. For example, enacted law has not been sufficient for giving effect to of Article 45, which provides for free and compulsory education. Similarly, it is doubtful whether enacted law has been sufficient to protect the interests of the workers by stipulating a living wage as required by Article 43 and their participation in management as contemplated by Article 43-A. Similar is the case with protection of environment and wild life warranted by Article 48-A. Likewise, there are instances in which the mandates of the directives have remained dead letters even after 50 years of independence. Thus even in the wake of Article 44, no law has been enacted for uniform civil code.

fundamental rights. Since fundamental rights are established on the bedrock of directive principles,[67] failure on the part of the legislature or the executive to implement the directives may make realization of fundamental rights difficult. The role the judiciary has played in cases of non-implementation of the directives by the State also assumes significance in such a context.

The approach of the judiciary in classifying the relationship between fundamental rights and directive principles fall into two stages. In the first stage, the Court was considering the two Parts as in conflict.[68] In the second, on the other hand the rights and directives were considered as supplementary and complementary to each other and on that basis the Court began to explain fundamental rights in the light of directive principles. It is in this second stage that the Court exhibited remarkable innovation. For a proper evaluation of the role played by the Court in this stage, an analysis of the cases touching upon the relationship between Part III and Part IV is necessary.

(a) The Initial Approach

In the early stages, the Court had the approach that in some cases steps to implement the directive principles may amount to violation of fundamental rights. At the time of bifurcation of the rights into fundamental rights and directive principles, the Constituent Assembly was warned by the constitutional Advisor B.N. Rau about the possibility of such an understanding of those two parts.[69] The Supreme Court had to deal with cases in which legislation in furtherance of directive principles was impugned on the ground that it infringed the

67. *Supra*, n. 48.
68. This stage can further be divided into three based on the difference of the view of the Court. See, Seervai, *Constitutional Law of India*, Vol. II (1984), p. 1578. For a different type of classification of stages, see, Paramjith S. Jaiswal, *Directive Principles and Socio-Economic Justice in India* (1990), pp. 150-215.
69. He said, "There is a danger which ought to be pointed out. It may be necessary for the State for the proper discharge of one of its fundamental duties...to invade private rights. In other words, there may be a conflict between the Directive Principles of State Policies and of the rights or freedom of the individual guaranteed in the fundamental rights." See K.C. Markandan, *op. cit.* at p. 81.

fundamental rights conferred by the Constitution and therefore unconstitutional. In the earlier stages, the Court held that in case of such a conflict, the fundamental rights would prevail over the directives. In *State of Madras* v. *Champakam Dorairajan*[70] the Court held that the unenforceable directive principles could not override the judicially enforceable fundamental rights.[71] Reiterating the stand, later in *Mohemmed Hanif Quareshi v. State of Bihar*[72] the Court held that the directives could not override the fundamental rights in so far as there is a categorical statement in Article 13(2) that nothing contrary to Part III rights could exist. Hence the Court advocated a harmonious construction whereby the State could implement directive principles without abridging fundamental rights.[73] In *Re Kerala Education Bill, 1957*[74] the Court observed that though the law referred for its consideration was in furtherance of Article 46, such legislative power should not be exercised in a manner overriding and subverting Part III of the Constitution.[75]

(b) The Changing Note

A significant change is visible in the attitude of the Court

70. A.I.R. 1951 S.C. 226. In this case, a government order reserving seats in professional colleges in the State on communal lines was challenged as violative of Article 29(2). The order was sought to be justified on the ground that it was for implementing the directive contained in Article 46.
71. *Id.* at p. 228. The Court observed, "The directive principles ... which by Article 37 are expressly made unenforceable by a Court, cannot overrule the provisions found in Part III which notwithstanding other provisions, are expressly made enforceable by appropriate writs... The directive principles of State policy have to conform to and run as subsidiary to the Chapter on Fundamental Rights."
72. A.I.R. 1958 S.C. 731. That was a bunch of writ petitions under Article 32 challenging the validity of certain enactment banning slaughter of certain animals by some States as violative of Article 19(1)(g). The States sought to justify the legislation on the ground that they were in furtherance of Article 48.
73. *Id.* at p. 739.
74. A.I.R 1959 S.C. 956. After passing the Kerala Education Bill, 1958 the State sent for the assent of the President. The President sent it to the Supreme Court under Article 143(1) seeking its advice whether the provisions of the Act violated the Constitution. The Court held that some of the provisions of the Act violated the minority rights under Article 30.
75. *Id.* at p. 966.

in the subsequent decade. During that term, the Court began to construe the directive principles as on par with fundamental rights. This trend was inaugurated by the decision in *C & B Boarding and Lodging* v. *State of Mysore*.[76] Discarding the attitude of finding an intrinsic imbalance between fundamental rights and directive principles, the Court in this case, tried to confer equal status to fundamental rights and directive principles. The Court was on its way to find co-existence of rights and directives on the ground that they were supplementary and complementary to each other. Justice Hegde speaking for a five Judge bench held,[77]

> "While rights conferred under Part III are fundamental, the directives given under Part IV are fundamental in the governance of the country. We see no conflict on the whole between the provisions contained in Part III and Part IV. They are complementary and supplementary to each other."

A changing note is thus visible in the judicial approach towards the relationship between fundamental rights and directive principles. The Court identified the rights and directives as the media for attaining social and national welfare, and observed that the provisions of the Constitution could not be treated as barriers to progress but were on the other hand instruments which proposed orderly progress.[78] The Court therefore held that there was no fundamental right to carry on

---

76. A.I.R 1970 S.C. 2042. A bunch of cases were filed as Writ Petitions and appeals by certificate challenging the validity of a notification under the Minimum Wages Act, 1948, fixing minimum wages for different classes of employees in different residential hotels and eating houses on the ground that the provision in the Act empowering the government to issue the notification confers unguided and arbitrary powers on the government. The notification was challenged as violatve of the fundamental rights of the petitioners under Article 14 and Article 19(1)(g).
77. *Id.* at p. 2050.
78. *Ibid.* Speaking for the Court, Justice Hegde observed, "The provisions of the Constitution are not enacted as the barriers to progress. They provide a plan for orderly progress towards the social order contemplated by the preamble to the Constitution. They do not permit any kind of slavery, social-economic or political."

a profession to the extent of exploitation which directive principles sought to prevent. In short, the Court was reaching a conclusion that the rights and directives were pointers to the same direction.

This approach was given further colour and content a decade later in *Minerva Mills* v. *Union of India*.[79] This case further explained the supplementary and complementary nature of fundamental rights and directive principles. Holding that Parts III and IV of our Constitution constitute the core of the commitment for a social revolution, the Court observed:[80]

> "(T)hey together, are the conscience of the Constitution to be traced to the deep understanding of the scheme of the Indian Constitution.... Parts III and IV are like two wheels of a chariot, one no less important than the other. You snap one and the other will lose its efficacy. They are like a twin formula for achieving the social revolution, which is the ideal which the visionary founders of the Constitution set before themselves. In other words, the Indian Constitution is the bedrock of the balance between Parts III and IV."

The Court placed emphasis on the point that Parts III and IV of the Constitution were only a means for achieving certain ideals and not ends in themselves. Those ideals would be realized only if the rights set out in Part III are fulfilled and the duties laid down in Part IV are discharged. Such a point of view calls for conferment of equal status and importance to the provisions in Parts III and IV. Both share the same responsibility in building up a society in which 'Justice, Equality, Fraternity and Liberty' exist. In other words, there is a duty on the State to ensure that the fundamental rights of the people are not breached and that the directive principles are implemented. The Court gave up the view that there was a conflict between Directive Principles and fundamental rights. The Court stopped the approach of putting one category as superior to the other. From experience, the Court understood that for the welfare of the society and progress of the State both are equally required.

79. A.I.R. 1980 S.C. 1789.
80. *Id.* at p. 1806. (*per* Chandrachud J.)

This undoubtedly is a new trend in the attitude of the Apex Court which accepts the modern view that distinguishing individual rights based on principles and social goals based on policies, at times, is difficult.[81] Can the State in such a situation avoid implementation of the socially relevant directive principles? Will not non-implementation of the directive principles adversely affect the progress of the nation and the enjoyment of fundamental rights? Is not implementation of the directive principles as necessary as the enforcement of fundamental rights? Answers to all these questions are in the affirmative.

It is clear from the decisions in cases like *Re Kerala Education Bill*, *Chandrabhawan* and *Minerva Mills* that the Court realized the necessity of checking wrong implementation of directives as well as the necessity of proper and timely implementation of the directives by the State. What would happen if the legislature and the executive refuse to implement the directives? Will the Court in such cases remain helpless, as directives are not justiciable? Apart from this aspect, will not such non-implementation restrict the scope of judicial review under Article 32 if the Court could not do anything to implement the directives so as to give effect to fundamental rights? What role could the judiciary play in protecting the enjoyment of fundamental rights in such a context? Can the Court prepare the background by implementing the directive principles without violating the constitutional provision prohibiting justiciability of the directive principles?

5. THE CREATIVE JUDICIAL APPROACH

It is in a context of such complex questions that the second stage in judicial approach reflecting a new trend in interpreting the relationship between Parts III and IV is developed by the Supreme Court. The changed approach is developed by a new

81. Dworkin, *op. cit.* at p. 90. He observes, "Arguments of principles are arguments intended to establish an individual right; arguments of policy are arguments intended to establish a collective goal. Principles are propositions that describe rights; policies are propositions that describe goals. But what are rights and goals and what is the difference. It is hard to supply any definition that does not beg the question."

judicial technique of construing the provisions contained in Part III of the Constitution. The technique was of giving fundamental rights wider content with the help of the concepts contained in directive principles. The Court started construing fundamental rights by reading them in the light of the constitutional guidelines for legislation contained in the directives. The Court so engaged itself in an act of creativity by a more progressive interpretation of the law through adoption of a new judicial technique. In this process, the Court infused the concept of social justice into fundamental rights and gave a go by to the earlier view that they contained only individual rights.

This change in the judicial approach will be clear from the decisions dealing with the construction of the constitutional provisions relating to the concepts of equality and the right of life. The right to equality is contained in Articles 14[82] and further explained by Articles 15 to 18 and the concept of right to life is contained in Article 21.[83] Undoubtedly, some facets of these two concepts are discernible in different provisions contained in Part IV also. Facets of the concept of equality are perceivable in Articles 38[84], 39(a), (b), (c) and (d)[85],

---

82. Article 14 reads, "The State shall not deny to any person equality before the law or the equal protection of the laws within the territory of India."
83. Article 21 provides, "No person shall be deprived of life or personal liberty except according to the procedure established by law.
84. Article 38(1) reads, "The State shall strive to promote the welfare of the people by securing and protecting as effectively as it may a social order in which justice, social, economic and political, shall inform all the institutions of the national life."

    (2) The State shall, in particular, strive to minimise the inequalities in income, and endeavour to eliminate inequalities in status; facilities and opportunities, not only amongst individuals but also amongst group of people residing in different areas or engaged indifferent vocations."
85. Article 39(a) to (d) reads as follows:

    "The State shall, in particular, direct its policy towards securing—
    that the citizens, men and women equally, have the right to an adequate means to livelihood;
    that the ownership and control of the material resources of the community are so distributed as best to subserve the common good;
    that the operation of the economic system does not result in the concentration of wealth and means of production to the common detriment;
    that there is equal pay for equal work for both men and women;
    ...."

43[86], 44[87] and 46.[88] Similarly, some of the basic requirements of a decent human right to life can be seen in Articles 39A,[89] 41,[90] 42[91], 43[92], 45[93] and 47.[94] An examination of the cases dealing with these two concepts reveals how the Supreme Court explained fundamental rights in the light of social justice by reading directive principles into them.

(a) The Concept of Equality

The concept of equality enshrined in Part III of the Constitution has ever been a matter of judicial discourse. The

86. Article 43 reads, "The State shall endeavour to secure, by suitable legislation or economic organization or in any other way, to all workers, agricultural, industrial or otherwise, work, a living wage, conditions of work ensuring a decent standard of life and full enjoyment of leisure and social and cultural opportunity and, in particular, the State shall endeavour to promote cottage industries on an individual or co-operative basis in rural areas."
87. Article 44 runs, "The State shall endeavour to secure for the citizens a uniform civil code throughout the territory of India."
88. Article 46 reads, "The State shall promote with special care the education and economic interests of the weaker sections of the people, and, in particular, of the Scheduled Castes and Scheduled Tribes, and shall protect them from social injustice and all forms of exploitation."
89. Article 39-A reads as follows, "The State shall secure that the operation of the legal system promotes justice, on a basis of equal opportunity, and shall, in particular, provide free legal aid, by suitable legislation or schemes or in any other way, to ensure that opportunities for securing justice are not denied to any citizen by reason of economic or other disabilities."
90. Article 41 reads, "The State shall, within the limits of its economic capacity and development, make effective provision for securing the right to work, to education and to public assistance in case of unemployment, old age, sickness and disablement, and in other cases of undeserved want."
91. Article 42 reads, "The State shall make provision for securing just and humane conditions of work and for maternity relief."
92. *Supra*, n. 86.
93. Article 45 runs: "The State shall endevour to provide, within a period of ten years from the commencement of this Constitution, for free and compulsory education for all children until they complete the age of fourteen years."
94. Article 47 runs: "The State shall regard the raising of the level of nutrition and the standard of living of its people and the improvement of the public health as among its primary duties and, in particular, the State shall endeavour to bring about prohibition of the consumption except for medicinal purposes of intoxicating drinks and of drugs which are injurious to health.

Court had occasion to have a thorough excursus into the concept of equality contained in Article 14 in various instances when the right to equality was alleged to have been violated by State action. The concept of equality means equal treatment of equals and unequal treatment of unequals.[95] Hence, right to equality is violated when there is discrimination among persons who are equally placed. The fundamental right to equality is violated when the State discriminates individuals who are equally posited. This leads us to a question of classification of persons through legislation. If the State classifies or categorizes individuals on certain wrong and unacceptable principles, the right to equality under Part III would be deemed to be violated. It means that there are certain principles on which classification or discrimination of individuals could be effected by State without violating the right to equality. But, what are those principles on which such classification could be made? To be valid, such classification effected by the state action should be reasonable. There are two tests judicially laid down to evaluate whether the classification is reasonable. A valid classification, the Apex Court held, must be founded on an intelligible differentia which distinguishes persons or things that are grouped together from others left out of the group and that differentia must have a rational nexus with the object sought to be achieved by the state action.[96] The right to equality is violated, if the impugned state action failed to satisfy the requirements of the judicially evolved twin tests. It means that all cases of unequal treatment by classification of persons or things would not be struck down as violative of equality. The biped test of valid classification determines the scope and extent of the right to equality under Article 14. However, determination of the concept of equality on such tests reflects a

---

95. For a discussion, see Mahendra P. Singh (Ed.) *V.N. Sukla's Constitution of India* (1990), p. 32.
96. *Budhan Choudhary* v. *State of Bihar,* A.I.R. 1955 S.C. 191, 193. The Court held, "In order, however, to pass the test of permissible classification two conditions must be fulfilled, namely, (I) that the classification must be founded on an intelligible differentia which distinguishes persons or things that are grouped together from others left out of the group and (ii) that the differentia must have a rational relation to the object sought to be achieved by the statute in question."

purely legalistic and positivist approach of the Court. The concept of right to equality and the validity of state action revolve in such a circumstance only around the technical, logical and semantic aspects of law.

Later, the Supreme Court recognized the need to concentrate on the content of the concept of equality. In *E.P. Royappa* v. *State of Tamilnadu,*[97] the Court observed the concept should not be subjected to a narrow, pedantic or lexicographic approach. The Court observed that the concept of equality envisaged by Article 14 is a dynamic one with many aspects and dimensions. The concept of equality cannot therefore be "cribbed, cabined and confined" within traditional and doctrinaire limits.[98] It was observed that the concept of equality was antithetic to arbitrariness and hence every instance of arbitrariness should be considered violative of equality. Hence, Article 14 was emphasized to strike at the root of arbitrariness of state action. The Court widened the scope of the concept of equality in accordance with the changed demands of time and gave a new dimension to the concept with a view to controlling arbitrariness. The decision is certainly the evidence of rejection of a mere positivist approach in the interpretation of the concept.

In spite of the progressive interpretation rendered by the Court in *Royappa,* certain questions regarding the concept were left unanswered. Though the Court held that the concept of equality was dynamic in nature and antithetical to arbitrariness, it did not clarify what were the contents of equality and what were the instances of violation of equality? How can arbitrariness be determined? These questions are related to social facts and hence the scope and content of the right and the

---

97. (1974) 4 S.C.C. 3. This was a petition under Article 32 of the Constitution. The petitioner was a member of the Indian Administrative Service. He was posted to act as Chief Secretary. The Government of the State had made the posts of Additional Chief Secretary, Chief Secretary and the Revenue Member on par. However, later the petitioner was appointed as Deputy Chairman of the State Planning Commission and later still as Officer on Special Duty. The government posted his junior as the Chief Secretary. This petition was filed on the ground *inter alia* that the act of the State was violative of Articles 14 and 16.

98. *Id.* at p. 38. (*per* Bhagwati J.)

instances of violation have to be determined in relation to the social ideals. It is in such a context that the Court introduced the concept of social justice into the concept of equality and read the concept of equality contained in Part III in the light of and in accordance with the directive principles in Part IV of the Constitution, which contain some aspects of equality.

(i) Equal Pay for Equal Work

One of the most creative attempts of the Court in this respect is found in the matter of protection of the interests of employees. It is well established that payment of wages to workers is correlated to the volume and nature of work undertaken by them. If the power, duty, responsibility and functions of different persons are similar, they all should be paid on par. There cannot be differential treatment between and among them. Or, in other words, discrimination among employees who have same responsibility and duty under an employer for purposes of payment of wages would be violative of the concept of equality. However, this aspect of equality has not been explicitly covered by Article 14, or Article 16(1).[99] The Supreme Court had occasion to deal with that issue in *Randhir Singh* v. *Union of India.*[100] The Court observed that though not a fundamental right, without the right to equal pay for equal work, the concept of equality as a fundamental right would be meaningless. Dealing with the plea of equal pay for equal work, the Court observed:[101]

> "But, it certainly is a constitutional goal... Directive Principles, as have been pointed out in some of the judgements of this Court have to be read into fundamental right as a matter of interpretation.... *To the vast majority of*

99. Article 16(1) reads, "There shall be equality of opportunity for all citizens in mattes relating to employment or appointment to any office under the State."

100. A.I.R. 1982 S.C. 879. A petition under Article 32 of the Constitution was filed by a driver-constable in the Delhi Police Force alleging that there was disparity between his scale of pay and that of other drivers in the services of the Delhi Administration. The petition is filed against such disparity.

101. *Id.* at p. 881. (Emphasis supplied).

the people ... the equality clause will have some substance if equal work means equal pay."

The Court therefore held:[102]

> *"Construing Articles 14 and 16 in the light of the Preamble and Article 39(d),* we are of the view that the principle of equal pay for equal work is deducible from those Articles and may be applied properly applied to cases of unequal scales of pay based on no classification or wrong classification..."

The Court clarified that the fundamental right to equality was wide enough to include the right to equal pay for equal work. The creativity of the decision lies not simply in widening the concept of equality but also in the technique adopted in widening it namely, the projection of the relevant provision in Part IV to the relevant provision in Part III of the Constitution making equal pay for equal work a facet of right to equality in Part III. The creativity of the decision becomes clear when it is compared with the earlier view the Court has taken in *Kishsori Mohanlal Bakshi* v. *Union of India,*[103] where the concept of the concept of equal pay for equal work was held to have no nexus with the concept of equality as enshrined in Article 14.[104]

(ii) Equality and the Socialistic Goals

The Court had an occasion to deal with another aspect of equality in *Atam Prakash* v. *State of Haryana.*[105] The issue raised in that case was the validity of the Punjab Preemption Act, 1913, which was in operation in the State. It was challenged as

102. *Id.* at p. 882 (Emphasis added). This view was followed in *P.K.R. Iyer* v. *Union of India,* (1984) 2 S.C.C. 141, *P. Savitha* v. *Union of India,* 1985 Supp. S.C.C. 94, *Surinder Singh* v. *Eng. in Chief, C.P.W.D.,* (1986) 1 S.C.C. 639. *Federation of All India Customs and Central Excise Stenographers* v. *Union of India,* (1988) 3 S.C.C. 91. *Mewa Ram Kanojia* v. *All India Institute of Medical Sciences,* (1989) 2 S.C.C. 235. *Harbanslal* v. *State of H.P.,* (1989) 4 S.C.C. 459. *State of M.P.* v. *Pramod Bhattia,* A.I.R. 1993 S.C. 286 and *State of U.P.* v. *Karamchari Sangh,* A.I.R. 1998 S.C. 203.
103. A.I.R. 1962 S.C. 1139.
104. *Id.* at p. 1141. The Court observed: "The abstract doctrine of equal pay for equal work has nothing to do with Article 14."
105. (1986) 2 S.C.C. 249.

violative of the fundamental right to equality.[106] The Court observed that while expounding the Constitution, or while checking up the constitutional validity of a statute, the cardinal rule was to look up to the Preamble as the guiding light and the directive principles as a Book of Instruction. The directive principles embody the hopes and aspirations of the people. Hence, when constitutionality of a statute is evaluated under Article 14, it should be checked whether the classification effected by it is consistent with "the socialistic goals set out in the Preamble and the directive principles."[107] It was further held that a classification not in tune with the Constitution *per se* was unreasonable and invalid.[108] The consequence of such a holding is that if any classification was made contrary to the mandate contained in Part IV of the Constitution, it is a sufficient ground for striking it down as violative of equality. The Court construed the concept of equality in Part III in the light of the directive principles in Part IV. It was made clear that validity of a classification is to be determined not only with reference to Part III but also to Part IV. Though no reference was made to any specific provision in Part IV for explaining the concept of equality, the Court widened the horizons of the concept of equality by holding that the concept of reasonable classification should be consistent with the socialistic goals set out in the Directive Principles.[109] The decision transforming the legalistic tests of classification into socialistic ones can be considered as a clarification by the Court that Directive Principles will also form the criteria for determining constitutionality of state action and hence the concepts in Part IV could be treated on par with fundamental rights.

Sri Srinivasa Theatre v. *Government of Tamil Nadu,*[110] *is* another example where the Court construed and developed the

106. The petitioner challenged the constitutional validity of the archaic right to preemption based on consanguinity contained in the Punjab Preemption Act, 1913 as violative of Articles 14 and 15.
107. *Supra,* n. 105 at p. 257
108. *Ibid.*
109. The Court held that the doctrine of preemption was a relic of the feudal past and that it was inconsistent with the constitutional scheme. It was further held that the concept effected no reasonable classification. (*Id.* at p. 263).
110. A.I.R. 1992 S.C. 999. The Tamilnadu Entertainment Tax Act, 1939

concept of equality in the light of directive principle. The validity of classification of theatres for the purpose of taxation was challenged as violative of equality in Part III. The Court clarified that the concept 'equality before law' was a dynamic one and it had many facets[111] and that a more equal society envisaged in Article 38[112] was one such facet. The Court held:[113]

> "A facet which is of immediate relevance herein is the obligation upon the State to bring about, through the machinery of law, a more equal society envisaged by the preamble and *Part IV of our Constitution. For, equality before law can be predicted meaningfully only in an equal society, i.e. in a society contemplated by Article 38 of the Constitution...*"

The Court held that taxation was not only a means to raise revenue but also a method to reduce inequality and hence, it could be employed for the goals adumbrated by Article 38.[114] It means that when taxation is challenged as violative of fundamental right to equality, decision as to its validity is to be taken with reference to what is contained in Part IV. In this case the Court refused to construe the concept of equality in an independent and isolated manner and proposed to explain it in the light of and in relation to the corresponding ideas in Part IV. It was in fact an attempt of the Court to explain the concept in the light of the provision in Article 38(2) that the State should

---

provided for levy of entertainment tax on admission to cinema theatres. The percentage of tax varied from locality to locality. In 1978, the Act was amended changing the method of collection of tax. But the change was applied to the areas not within certain municipal corporations and special grade municipalities. In 1989, the Act was again amended and the old method of collection of tax was reintroduced to some of the theatres situated in the municipal areas and those withing a radius of five kilometers. This amendment was challenged before the High Court on the ground that it violated rights under Articles 14 and 19(1)(g). The High Court dismissed the petition. Appeal was filed before the Supreme Court. The Supreme Court dismissed the appeal on the ground that there was no violation of Article 14 nor was there any unreasonable restriction on the right to trade.

111. *Id.* at p. 1004. Cf. *E.P. Royappa* v. *State of Tamilnadu*, (1974) 4 S.C.C. 3
112. For the text of Article 38, see, *supra*, n. 84.
113. *Supra*, n. 110 at p. 1004. (Emphasis added).
114. *Ibid.*

strive to minimize the inequalities in income, status, facilities and opportunities among individuals and groups of people residing in different areas or engaged in different vocations. The holding that classification of individuals for the purpose of attaining the goals contained in Article 38 would in no way violate Article 14 means that the directive principle in Article 38 nurtures the concept of equality contained in Part III.

The makers of the Constitution had never believed in numerical equality.[115] They instead advocated the right to proportional equality.[116] That may be the reason why from its very inception the Constitution of India permitted classification on certain reasonable criteria. It thus contained provisions for discrimination in favour of socially and educationally backward classes of people including Scheduled Castes and Scheduled Tribes[117] and provided that such a favour to backward classes would not be violative of the concept of equality.[118] In other words, the concept of equality contained in Part III of the Constitution is inextricably inter-linked with the concept of protective discrimination in favour of certain sections of the people. The Court had occasion to highlight the importance of the scheme of reservation extended in favour of such classes and to hold that such a discrimination would also be in accordance with the concept of equality. The Court in very many cases held that the right of members of the backward classes for reservation in various government posts is a facet of the fundamental right to equality.[119] The scope and extent of the

---

115. Numerical equality means identical amounts be distributed or identical burden be imposed.
116. Proportionate equality indicates distribution according to merit. For a discussion of numerical and proportional equality, see, Upendra Baxi (Ed.) *K.K. Mathew on Democrary, Equality and Freedom* (1978), p. 53.
117. Articles 15(4) and 16(4).
118. Article 15(4) reads, "Nothing in this Article or in clause (2) of Article 29 shall prevent the State from making any special provision for the advancement of any socially and educationally backward classes of citizens or for the Scheduled Castes and the Scheduled Tribes."
    Article 16(4) provides, "Nothing in this article shall prevent the State from making any provision for the reservation of appointments or posts in favour of any backward class of citizens which, in the opinion of the State, is not adequately represented in the services under the State."
119. See for instance, *State of Kerala* v. *N.M. Thomas*, A.I.R. 1976 S.C. 490; *A.B.S.K. Sangh* v. *Union of India*, A.I.R 1981 S.C. 298.

right to reservation is a multi-dimensional question. It, for instance, includes issues like the extent of reservation, the persons and classes eligible for such a consideration, the criteria to be adopted for extending reservation and also the instances and stages in which reservation is to be effected. The Supreme Court had to grapple with these questions from the very early stages of the Constitution. One of the serious issues that arose in this respect was whether reservation is to be adopted and extended at the stage of promotion also. The Supreme Court had to decide this issue on more occasions than one. In *General Manager, Southern Railways* v. *Rangachari,*[120] the Court held that the right included the right to be reserved in matters of promotion. The Court held that the right to reservation even at the stage of promotion was part and parcel of right to equality envisaged by Part III of the Constitution. Later, in *Indraw Sahney* v. *Union of India,*[121] the Court held that the right to reservation was limited to initial posting and it did not extend to promotions. In the earlier cases the Court reached the conclusion simply by hanging on the idea of protective discrimination contained in Article 16(4). The issue was re-agitated before the Court in the later 1990's. In *Viswas Anna Sawant v. Municipal Corporation of Greater Bombay,*[122] the Court confirmed that the right to reservation in matters of promotion for the backward classes was an aspect of their fundamental right to equality. However, in this case the Court had a different reason for the conclusion. The Court held that the right to be considered for promotion was also a fundamental right

120. A.I.R. 1962 S.C. 36
121. A.I.R. 1992 S.C.477.
122. (1994) 4 S.C.C. 434. That was an appeal by Special Leave. The respondents decided to provide reservation for backward classes in matters of promotion also. Later it took the decision to promote such persons on the basis of interview. The High Court of Bombay held that the backward classes should be given promotion as per the earlier decision without an interview. Implementation of the order has led to the special leave petition before the Supreme Court.
123. *Id.* at p. 436. The Court held, "The right to consideration for promotion is a fundamental right guaranteed to Scheduled Castes and Scheduled Tribes in fulfilment of the mandate under Article 16(1) read with Article 46 to render socio-economic justice."
124. (1997) 9 S.C.C. 662.

guaranteed to the Scheduled Castes and Scheduled Tribes by virtue of the provisions contained in Article 16(1) *read with Article 46* of the Constitution for rendering socio-economic justice to them:[123]

In *State of Uttar Pradesh* v. *Dr. Dina Nath Sukla*,[124] Court pointed out that the right to reservation in matters of promotion was a feature of equality. But to reach the conclusion, the Court reasoned that the concept of legal equality has to be understood and read in the light of the concept of social equality and held that the idea of social equality is to be deduced from what is contained in Part IV of the Constitution. The Court observed thus:[125]

> "When there is a clash of interests and competing claims there is a craving for equality of opportunity amongst the people and for emancipation from the pangs of absolute prohibition, *Articles 15(2) to (4), 16(4) and 4-A read with Directive Principles, poured forth practical content, softened the rigour of legal equality and gave practical content of equality in opportunity resulting through distributive justice in favour of unequals to hold an office or post under the state in the democratic governance*".

A common feature of these decisions[126] dealing with the concept of equality is that in construing the concept they lay down a path different from the earlier cases[127] where the Court expounded the concept of equality on the basis of what is called 'legal equality' which did not recognize the social aspect of the idea of equality. The creative element of the decisions is that the Court shifted the thrust of the concept of right to equality from a purely legal and logical one to a social terrain. For giving the concept of equality such a social content and thus to provide flesh and blood, the Court sought the help of the directive principles in Part IV which in some way or the other championed the cause of equality at a larger social level. The attempt of the Court to explain the concept of equality in the

125. *Id.* at pp. 666-67. (Emphasis added)
126. *Supra*, nn.110, 120, 121, 122 and 124.
127. *Supra*, nn. 96 and 103.

light of provisions contained in Part IV as one including reservation is very sensible. For, the mandate[128] in Part IV to extend reservation to socially and educationally backward classes envisages a social aspect while the right under Articles 15 and 16 deal with reservation at an individual level. Undoubtedly, in these cases the view of the Court was formed after taking into account the aspect of social welfare envisaged by the makers of the Constitution. In other words, these decisions reveal the creative judicial technique adopted with a view to giving up a formal approach in matters of interpreting the concept of equality contained in Part III of the Constitution and adopting an alternative approach of defining in terms of the ideals contained in Part IV. As a result of these decisions, the Court was able to give a more sensible content to the concept of equality.

(b) The Concept of Life Under Article 21

Another aspect of construction of the fundamental rights in which the Court exhibited creative response was the interpretation of the concept of right to life contained in Article 21. *Maneka Gandhi* v. *Union of India,*[129] inaugurated a new era in understanding the concepts in Part III, especially Article 21. As a result of the decision in *Maneka Gandhi,* the Court was able to figure out new concepts in fundamental rights. In *Maneka Gandhi,* the Court held that fundamental rights were not distinct and mutually exclusive and that legislative and executive acts should satisfy the test of validity under different Articles.[130]

(i) Article 21 and Social Justice

The post *Maneka* decisions reveal new trends in the construction of the concepts of rights to 'life' and to 'personal liberty' in Article 21. Finding that the contents of the provision were ill-equipped to meet the requirements of the contemporary society, the Court started pouring into them the contents of social justice. Two trends of constitutional construction are perceivable in this respect. In some cases the Court interpreted

128. Article 46. For the text of the Article, see, *supra*, n. 88.
129. (1978) 1 S.C.C. 248.
130. *Id. per* Ray C.J. (at pp. 394-95); Chandrachud J. (at p. 323); Bhagwati J. (at pp. 282-83) and Krishna Iyer J. (at pp. 374-75).

the provision in Article 21 without reference to any other provision in the Constitution. In these cases we find the Supreme Court adding more aspects to Article 21. In some others, questions relating to the scope and violation of right to life were dealt with by the Court in the light of similar concepts in directive principles contained in Part IV of the Constitution. The earliest instance in which the latter kind of interpretation was given was *Bandhua Mukti Morcha* v. *Union of India*.[131] An important question that came up before the Court in that case was whether violation of the provisions of the Bonded Labour System (Abolition) Act 1976 could be dealt with under Article 32. The Court held that it could be. Dealing with the concept of right to life under Article 21, Justice Bhagawti speaking for the Court observed:[132]

> "*This right to live with human dignity enshrined in Article 21 derives its life breath from the Directive Principles of State Policy and particularly Clauses (e) and (f) of Article 39 and Articles 41 and 42* and at the least, therefore, it must include protection of the health and strength of workers, men and women, and of the tender age of children against abuse, opportunities and facilities for children to develop in a healthy manner and in conditions of freedom and dignity, educational facilities, just and humane conditions of work and maternity relief. These are the minimum requirements which must exist in order to enable a person to live with human dignity and no State . . . has the right to take any action which will deprive a person of the enjoyment of these basic essentials."

The peculiarity of the holding is that the Court tried to give content to the fundamental right to life enshrined in Article 21 in Part III of the Constitution in the light of some of the directive principles contained in Part IV. It is a clear instance of reading fundamental right to life in accordance with social justice. This

---

131. A.I.R. 1984 S.C. 802. The petitioner was an organisation dedicated to the cause of release of bonded labourers in the country. It conducted a survey in the various States and sent a letter to the Supreme Court regarding the inhuman condition of those working in the mines. The Court considered the letter as a writ petition and issued notice.

132. *Id.* at pp. 811-12. (Emphasis added).

can be treated as an attempt of the Court to link the concepts contained in Article 21 with the social ideals envisaged in Part IV.[133] The holding is certainly innovative. It laid down a principle, which became the guideline for the future.

In *State of Himachal Pradesh* v. *Umed Ram,*[134] the Court held, construing the right to life under Article 21 in conjunction with Article 19(1)(d) and in the background of Article 38(2), that it included the right to travel throughout the territory of India. The right, according to the Court, does not mean a mere right for simple physical existence. It, on the other hand, includes the right to a quality of life for the residents of the hilly areas. A road confers right to communication and hence the Court held that denial of that right to road means denial of the right to life in its richness and fullness. The Court therefore held that "(A)ccess to road is access to life itself."[135]

The repercussions of the decision in *Maneka Gandhi* in the interpretation of Article 21 were multi-dimensional. While dealing with the rights of accused persons and prisoners, the Court held that the right to life envisaged by Article 21 was available to persons who face the legal procedure. One finds a significant contribution of the judiciary in the incorporation of the right to speedy trial and free legal aid[136] as part and parcel of the right to life under Article 21. However, in those cases, the Court was incorporating the concepts without seeking any assistance from the directives contained in Part IV. The rights of free legal aid and speedy trial as part of the right to life under Article 21 got a new dimension in *State of Maharashtra* v. *Manubhai Pragaju Vashi.*[137] The question that came up for

133. The creative feature of the holding will be more clear when it is compared with the holding of Justice A.N. Sen who simply held that wrongful and illegal employment of a person in violation of the Bonded Labour System (Abolition) Act, 1976 was deprivation of his liberty under Article 21.
134. A.I.R. 1986 S.C. 847. Construction of a road was delayed or abandoned due to the resistance of some persons. A letter sent to the High Court was treated as writ petition. The High Court directed the State to allot sufficient fund for the construction of the road. An appeal was filed in the Supreme Court by the State against the decision of the High Court.
135. *Id.* at p. 851.
136. *Hussainara Khatoon* v. *Union of India,* A.I.R. 1979 S.C. 1377 and *Suk Das* v. *Union Territory of Arunachal Pradesh,* (1986) 2 S.C.C. 401. But for a contrary view, see, *Ranjan Dwivedi* v. *Union of India,* A.I.R. 1983 S.C. 624.
137. (1995) 5 S.C.C. 730.

consideration before the Court was whether the government could be directed to pay grants-in-aid to law colleges in the private sector. The Court observed that for free legal aid and speedy trial which in the wake of Article 39-A guaranteed under Article 21,[138] vast number of legally trained persons are required for protecting them. Only if students are able to study in private law colleges, without paying high fees, the fundamental right to free legal aid and speedy trial of masses would be ensured.[139] Thus, the Court concluded that effective protection of the right to free legal aid and speedy justice, which form part of "life" under Article 21, calls for payment of grants-in-aid to private law colleges by the government irrespective of its financial capacity.[140] Though the reasoning of the Court appears to be very round about, the holding echoes the pain the Court takes to infuse fundamental rights with social justice in the light of directive principles.

(ii) Right to Equality and Article 21

Equality itself is a fundamental right. But, can it be said that any aspect of that concept is an ingredient of the right to life under Article 21? The concept of equality is correlated to the idea of economic empowerment of the people. Hence, conferment of equality with social content would mean equality in economic matters. Disparity in economic matters may defeat the very object of enacting the right to life in the Constitution. The concept of right to life would be meaningless unless there is equality in the economic sphere. Therefore, it is quite natural that the right to life would be considered as violated in the absence of economic equality. In such a context, can a law, which furthers the cause of equal economic empowerment of people, be treated as violative of the fundamental rights to equality and life? Such a question was posed before the

138. *Id.* at p. 743. The Court observed, "In the light of the above, we have to consider the combined effect of Article 21 and Article 39-A of the Constitution of India. The right to free legal aid and speedy trial are guaranteed under Article 21 of the Constitution."
139. *Id.* at pp. 743-44.
140. *Id.* at p. 745. The Court held, "In this perspective, we hold that Article 21 read with Article 39-A of the Constitution mandates or castes a duty on the State to afford grants-in-aid to recognized private law colleges, similar to other faculties..."

Supreme Court in *Muralidhar Kesekar* v. *Viswanath Borde*.[141] In that case, constitutional validity of a law, which prohibited transfer of immovable property by members of Scheduled Tribes, was challenged on the ground that it violated the concept of equality. The Court observed that economic empowerment to the poor was an integral constitutional scheme of socio-economic democracy which therefore is a basic human fundamental right as part of rights to equality, life, status and dignity to the poor, weaker sections, dalits, etc. The Court therefore held that legal restriction on the right to purchase the property owned by the members of the Tribes was one to protect their rights to life and equality in the light of the Directive Principles contained in Articles 38, 39 and 46.[142]

This view was re-emphasized by the Court later in *Ahmedabad Municipal Corporation v. Nawabkhan Gulab Khan*.[143] In that case, while explaining the right of certain pavement dwellers not to be evicted, the Court held that the right to life in Article 21 included the right to live with human dignity. The Court sought the help of the provisions contained in Part IV of the Constitution and held:[144]

> "Articles 38, 39 and 46 mandate the State, as its economic policy, to provide socio-economic justice to minimise inequality in income and in opportunity and status. *It positively charges the State to distribute its largessses to the weaker sections of the society envisaged in Article 46 to make social and economic justice a reality, meaningful and fruitful so as to make life worth living with dignity of person and equality of status....*"

141. 1995 (Supp.) 2 S.C.C. 549. The appellant purchased a land belonging to the respondent who was a member of the tribal community. The property was transferred to the respondent by the government. The purchase of immovable property from the tribal community had been legally prohibited for the protection of the tribal community. The purchase by the appellant was therefore held invalid. In this case, the constitutionality of that law was challenged by the purchaser.
142. *Id.* at p. 559.
143. (1997) 11 S.C.C. 121. The respondents, who were unauthorised pavement dwellers on a main road in huts, were decided to be removed. The High Court prohibited their removal till alternative accommodation was provided. Appeal was filed against in the Supreme Court the order of the High Court.
144. *Id.* at pp. 139-40. (Emphasis added).

Clearly, the decisions in *Muralidhar* and *Nawabkhan* are attempts of the Court to raise the ideals of socio-economic justice, equality of opportunity and dignity to the weaker sections of the population to the level of fundamental rights by reading the right to life in the light of Articles 38, 39 and 46. It certainly is a creative step of the Court. The creative content of the decision can be properly appreciated only when it is viewed against the decision of *Francis Corellie v. Union of India*[145] where the Court had held that the right to life under Article 21 encompassed the right to decent existence.[146] In *Francis Corellie* the Court did not seek the help of the provisions contained in Part IV of the Constitution to construe and widen the scope of right to life under Article 21. *Muralidhar Kesikar* and *Nawab Khan Gulab Khan* set a different line in the sense that they tried to widen the concept of right to life in the light of the directive principles.

Recognition of rights of workers to humane conditions of work find a place in Part IV of the Constitution.[147] Being directive principles they were left judicially unenforceable. It is unfortunate that even after five decades of independence, the State could not take effective steps to protect these rights of the workers. Naturally, it became a matter of judicial concern. It was in such a context that the Supreme Court in *Bandhua Mukti Morcha*[148] declared that in the light of Articles 39, 41 and 42, Article 21 included rights of workers to health and strength, just and humane conditions for work and maternity relief.[149] In

145. A.I.R. 1981 S.C. 746. A writ petition was filed under Article 32 by a detinu of British national challenging the validity of some of the provisions in the Conditions of Detention Order which restricted her right to have interviews with lawyer and members of her family as violative of right to life under Article 21.
146. The Court held, "Now obviously, the right to life enshrined in Article 21 cannot be restricted to mere animal existence. It means something much more than just physical survival . . . . We think that the right to life includes the right to live with human dignity and all that goes along with it, namely, the bare necessaries of life ..." (*Id.* at pp. 752-53).
147. Article 39(e), *supra*, n. 85, and Article 42, *supra*, n. 91.
148. A.I.R. 1984 S.C. 802.
149. *Supra*, nn. 131-132.

Consumer Education and Research Centre v. *Union of India,*[150] the Court developed the concept of right to life as including workers' right to health, in a more innovative style. The Court held that the right of workers to health was "an integral facet of meaningful right to life."[151] The reason for reaching such a conclusion by the Court was that lack of health would denude workers of their livelihood.[152] In the context of *Olga Tellis* v. *Bombay Corporation,*[153] in which the Supreme Court recognized right to livelihood as a right to life under Article 21, it is clear that denying workers their right to health amounts to denial of their right to life. The Court concluded that the facilities mentioned under Article 38 should be provided to workers to enable them to protect their health. Therefore, the Court held that the right to health and medical aid would form fundamental right under Article 21 read with Articles 39(c), 41, 43 and 48A.[154] The decision can be considered as another instance of high creativity. The Court was construing the concept of right to life under Article 21 as one, which encompasses the right of the working class to health and medical care on the ground that their absence may destroy their right to livelihood which is part and parcel of right to life. This case therefore can be considered as the extension of the holding in *Olga Tellis*. The impact of the decision is very clear. The right of workers to have humane conditions for work provided in Article 42 and protection of their health envisaged in Article 39 (e), which were mere guidelines for legislation got as a result of the decision transformed as fundamental right. It may be the

---

150. A.I.R. 1995 S.C. 922. A writ petition was filed under Article 32 seeking directions from the Court to maintain records of health and certain standards for protection of the health of workers in the asbestos industries, who are open to fatal occupational diseases like cancer of the respiratory organs.
151. *Id.* at p. 940.
152. *Ibid.*
153. A.I.R. 1986 S.C.180.
154. *Supra,* n 150 at p. 940. The Court held, "Therefore, we hold that right to health, medical aid to protect the health and vigour of a worker while in service or post-retirement is a fundamental right under Article 21 read with Articles 39(c), 41, 43 and 48A and all related Articles and fundamental human rights to make the life of the workman meaningful and purposeful with dignity of person."

lethargy on the part of the State in initiating appropriate legislation that prompted the Court to raise the directives to the status of fundamental rights enabling workers to approach the Court under Article 32 for enforcement. But for the decision, there would not have been a constitutional duty for the State to protect these rights of workers. The decision in effect infuses the concept of social justice into Article 21 enabling the weaker sections of the population to enjoy right to life in a more meaningful manner. In *State of Punjab* v. *Ram Lubhaya Bugga*,[155] in a different fact situation the Court held that the concept of right to life under Article 21 cast an obligation on the state to secure health to its citizens in view of Article 47.[156]

(iii) ***Right to Education and Right to Life***

The view that fundamental rights cannot be enjoyed without proper implementation of the directive principles is perfectly true in relation to primary education. Without primary education, it may not be possible for an individual even to realize that there are certain rights guaranteed to them in the Constitution. The stipulation that the State shall endeavour to provide free and primary education within ten years of enactment of the Constitution[157] therefore gains much importance. Despite such constitutional provisions we find that there is a continued lethargy and inaction on the part of the State in assuring free and primary education.[158] It is against

155. (1998) 4 S.C.C. 117. As a result of the change in the policy of the government of Punjab in 1995, government employees were denied sanction to be treated in non-government hospitals with a right to reimbursement for treatment expenses unless the facility was not available in government hospitals. This was challenged before the Supreme Court as violative of the right to life under Article 21.
156. The Court observed, "When we speak about a right, it correlates to a duty upon another, individual, employer, government or authority. In other words, the right of one is an obligation on another. Hence, the right of a citizen to live under Article 21 casts obligation on the State. This obligation is further reinforced under Article 47, it is for the State to secure health for its citizen as its primary duty." (*Id.* at p. 129).
157. Article 45. *Supra*, n. 93.
158. "Universal primary education and opportunity for employment are inscribed as principles fundamental in the governance of the country. But this directive, in the decades after Freedom, has proved a Dead Sea Fruit, Educational justice and employment justice, facets of human dignity and

such a background that the decision of *Mohini Jain* v. *State of Karnataka*[159] is to be analyzed. In this case, the Court had to deal with the status of the right to education under the Constitution. The question was whether it formed part of the fundamental right to life or not. The Court held that directive principles, which were fundamental in the governance of the country, were to be read into the fundamental rights. The right to education flows directly from the right to life under Article 21 as the latter could not be enjoyed without the former. The Court therefore concluded that the State was under an obligation to provide education to citizens.[160] Without making the right to education guaranteed by Article 41[161] a reality, fundamental rights would remain beyond the reach of the majority of the people.[162] Such

---

personality, are in crisis, whatever the periodical national Plans and hyperbolic budget speeches may paint in fine phrases." V.R. Krishna Iyer, *Justice at Crossroads,* (1992) at p. 9. See also, Sirajul Islam Laskar, *op. cit.* at p. 80.

159. A.I.R. 1992 S.C. 1858. The State of Karnataka passed the Educational Institutions (Prohibition of Capitation Fee) Act 1984 for regulating the tuition fee to be charged by private medical colleges in the State. The State issued a notification in 1989 under section 5(1) of the Act thereby fixing the tuition fee and other deposits to be made by students. The notification created three categories of students namely those admitted against "Government seats", "the Karnataka Students" and the "Indian students from outside Karnataka." The fee structure of these categories also varied. The petitioner being a person from Meerut, outside Karnataka had to pay high fees for getting admission. She was not able to pay such a high fee. Hence, she was denied admission. She challenged by a writ petition under Article 32 the notification permitting the private Medical Colleges to charge exorbitant fees from students from outside the State.

160. *Id.* at p. 1864. The Court held, "The directive principles which are fundamental in the governance of the country cannot be isolated from the fundamental rights guaranteed under Part III. These principles have to be read into the fundamental rights.... "Right to life" is the compendious expression for all those rights which the Courts must enforce because they are basic to the dignified enjoyment of life. The right to education flows directly from right to life. The right to life under Article 21 cannot be assured unless it is accompanied by the right to education."

161. *Supra,* n. 90.

162. *Supra,* n. 159 at p. 1864. The Court held, "The State is under a constitutional mandate to create conditions in which fundamental rights guaranteed to the individuals under Part III could be enjoyed by all. Without making right to education under Article 41 of the Constitution a reality the fundamental rights under Chapter III remain beyond the reach of large majority."

a constitutional position means that an individual had a right to call upon the State to provide educational facilities within its economic capacity and development as the State is under a constitutional obligation to create conditions in which fundamental rights would be enjoyed by all. The Court therefore held that the right to education was concomitant to the fundamental rights and so every citizen has a fundamental right to education.[163]

The holding in *Mohini Jain* was reconsidered by the Court in *J.P. Unnikrishnan* v. *State of Andhra Pradesh*.[164] Observing that fundamental rights get their life breath from directive principles[165] the majority of a constitutional bench consisting of five Judges held[166] that the concept of right to life in Article 21 should be explained and understood in the light of what is contained in directive principles. The Court concluded that right to education was implicit in the right to life under Article 21.[167] The right, according to the holding of the Court implied the right of citizen to call upon the State to provide educational facilities to him. In other words, if the State failed to provide

163. *Id.* at p. 1866. The Court went to the extent of holding that the State was under obligation to establish educational institutions to enable citizens to enjoy the said right to education and that charging of capitation fee was denial of that right.
164. A.I.R. 1993 S.C. 2178. In a bunch of writ petitions filed under Article 32 by private educational institutions engaged in or proposing to engage in medical or engineering education the correctness of *Mohini Jain v. State of Karnataka*, A.I.R. 1992 S.C. 1853 was challenged. It was alleged that if the decision was implemented, the petitioners would have to close down their institutions.
165. *Id.* at p. 2191 (*per* Mohan J.); and at p. 2230 (*per* Jeevan Reddy J.)
166. *Id.* at p. 2234.
167. Justice Mohan held, "If really Art. 21, which is the heart of fundamental rights has received expanded meaning from time to time there is no justification as to why it cannot be interpreted in the light of Art. 45 wherein the State is obligated to provide education up to 14 years of age, within the prescribed time limit.... This right to live with human dignity enshrined in Art. 21 derives its life breath from the Directive Principles of State Policy and particularly clauses (e) and (f) of Art. 39 and Arts. 41 and 42 ..." (*id.* at p. 2191).
Jeevan Reddy and Pandian JJ held, "The right to education which is implicit in the right to life and personal liberty guaranteed by Article 21 must be construed in the light of the directive principles in Part IV of the Constitution." (at p. 2231).

education, people would be able to approach the Court for enforcing it *a la* fundamental right. It is a fine instance of reading fundamental rights in the light of the directives.[168] However, the decision in *J.P. Unnikrishnan* has not approved the decision of *Mohini Jain* in toto. It is a modified version of the holding in *Mohini Jain*. In *Unnikrishnan*, the Court held that only primary education up to the age of 14 envisaged in Article 45, which formed part of the fundamental right to life under Article 21. Right to higher education would therefore be there only subject to the economic capacity of the State as envisaged in Article 41. Such a construction of right to life would be possible only when the directives contained in Articles 41 and 45 are read into Article 21.[169] The decision in *Unnikrishnan* is an instance where the Court explained the right to life in accordance with what is contained in the directive principles for championing the cause of social justice. *Unnikrishnan* therefore is an improvement of *Mohini Jain* in the sense that it develops the concept of right to life in the context of social justice in a more realistic way and strictly in tune with the contents of the directives of Article 41. Article 45, making education beyond primary level subject to economic capacity of the government. It is clear that *Unnikrishnan* is another illustration for the interpretation of the fundamental right in view of social justice for which the Court sought the help of directive principles.[170]

The holding that right to life under Article 21 encompasses within it the right to education was subject to judicial analysis

168. While rendering the decision, Justice Jeevan Reddy clarified that by such transformation of the right to education as a fundamental right, all the provisions in Part IV do not get transformed to Part III. It just implied that the Court was "merely relying upon Article 41 to illustrate the content of the right to education flowing from Article 21. It was observed that such incorporation was out of the inherent fundamental importance of the right. The Court further clarified that the decision did not mean that each and every obligation referred to in Part IV got automatically within the purview of Article 21.
169. *Supra*, n. 164 at p. 2232 (Justices B.P. Jeevan Reddy and Pandian).
170. Evidently, it is in acceptance of the view of the Supreme Court in *Unnikrishnan* that the Constitution was amended by the 86th Amendment Act, 2002 to incorporate Article 21A provides that "The State shall provide free and compulsory education to all children of the age of six to fourteen years in such manner as the State may, by law, determine."

again in *State of H.P.* v. *H.P. State Recognized and Aided Managing Committee.*[171] The questions were whether teachers working in different schools were entitled to parity of pay and whether the State was bound to extend grants-in-aid for payment of salary of teachers of schools recognized and aided by the State. The Court held that after *Unnikrishnan,* right to education up to the age of 14 has been declared as an essential ingredient of fundamental right to life. If the State were not meeting the expenses for paying salary of teachers of schools recognized and aided by the State, the students in such schools would have to pay more fees. Such a situation may amount to circumvention of the decision in *Unnikrishnan* and denial of the fundamental right to free primary education. The Court therefore held that the State was duty-bound to meet the expenditure for payment of salary to the teachers of the various recognized and aided schools. The teachers in such schools were entitled to receive parity of pay scales with that of school teachers of the State as well as grants-in-aid from the State.[172] This decision confirms that in view of social justice, the Court has conferred a full-fledged status of fundamental right to the right to education at the primary level.

These decisions exemplify the opinion of the Court that directive principles give fillip to the fundamental rights. The significance of such a construction need not be over-

---

171. (1995) 4 S.C.C. 507. The respondents were teachers in various recognized aided private schools in the State of Himachal Pradesh. Those schools received aid from the State for payment of salary to the teachers in such schools. Though the government had agreed to extent help up to 95% of the total expenditure on salary, limits were fixed by the government for such payment. The teachers filed a writ petition before the High Court for having parity of payment, with the teachers of the State schools from state funds. The High Court allowed the same. The State filed appeal before the Supreme Court.

172. *Id.* at pp. 512, 514 and 515. The issue had another aspect also. The teachers in the government and aided schools were having the same amount of work. Both have the same conditions of service. Moreover, all the schools in the State have the same syllabus. Therefore, disparity in the payment of salary by the government leads to violation of right to equal pay for equal work, which is recognized by the Court in many cases as an aspect of fundamental right to equality under Article 14. (*id.* at p. 511). However, the Court did not deal with this aspect in detail in this case.

emphasized. Incorporation of fundamental rights in the Constitution becomes fruitful only when people are literate and educated. The postulate that fundamental rights depend upon the implementation of directives is absolutely true in the matter of Article 45.

(iv) Right to Life and International Covenants

Another aspect of judicial creativity is the attempt of the Court to expound the contents of Article 21 in the light of international covenants. It is well accepted that principles, agreements and covenants at the international level would not be enforced *qua* law unless enacted in the form of law.[173] There is need for a specific legislation for enforcing what is contained in such agreements.[174] In *Peoples Union for Civil Liberties* v. *Union of India*,[175] the specific question the Court had to decide was whether right to life under Article 21 included within its fold the right to privacy. The question whether international covenants can be used as an aid for construction of constitutional provision in Article 21 was posed before the Court in this case. Article 51 of the Constitution provides

173. A.H. Robertson, *Human Rights—National and International Law*, quoted with approval by Krishna Iyer in *Jolly Geroge Varghese* v. *Bank of Cochin*, A.I.R. 1980 S.C. 470 at p. 473. See also Oppenhiem, *International Law—A Treatise* (1955), pp. 37, 40.
174. That may be the reason why Article 253 has been enacted in our Constitution. It reads thus, "Notwithstanding anything in the foregoing provisions of this Chapter, Parliament has power to make any law for the whole or any part of the territory of India for implementing any treaty, agreement or covenant with any other country or countries or any decision made at any international conference, association or other body."
175. (1997) 1 S.C.C. 301. A public interest litigation was filed under Article 32 by the petitioners challenging the tapping of telephones of politicians by the Central Bureau of Investigation. The petitioner challenged the constitutional validity of section 5(2) of the Indian Telegraphs Act, 1855, which permitted tapping of telephones. The petitioner contended that such tapping violated Article 21.
176. Article 51 reads "The State shall endeavour to—
promote international peace and security;
maintain just and honourable relations between nations;
foster respect for international law and treaty obligations in the dealings of organized peoples with one another; and
encourage settlement of international disputes by arbitration."

inter alia that the State shall endeavour to foster respect for international law and treaty obligations in the dealings of organised peoples with one another.[176] Casting a positive glance at that provision and approving the observation of Chief Justice Sikri in *Kesavananda* that Article 51 of the Constitution recognizes incorporation of international law to India, the Court held that assistance from international law could be sought, in so far as it does not go counter to the municipal law. The Court therefore, held that the concepts of right to life and personal liberty could be explained in the light of International Covenants to which India is a party. Accordingly, it was held that Article 17 of the International Covenant on Civil and Political Rights[177] does not run counter to our municipal law[178] and hence Article 21 could be interpreted in conformity with the international law.[179] The Court therefore concluded that the language of the Constitution should be interpreted in the light of the U.N. Charter and the solemn declarations subscribed by India. It is significant to note that this is an attempt of the Court to raise the fundamental right in Article 21 to the international standards. For making Article 21 of contemporary relevance, the Court relied on the directive contained in Article 51(c) and used it as a device to read the right to privacy contained in the international covenants into the fundamental right in Article 21 of the Constitution. The innovative creativity of the decision lies not in reading privacy as an ingredient of right to life, for, it already had found a place in the concept of right to personal liberty under Article 21 by virtue of judicial decisions.[180] It, on the other hand, lies in using the directive principles contained in Article 51 to give Article 21 the contents of international covenant.

177. For the text of the Covenant, see, Ian Brownlie, *Basic Documents on Human Rights* (1992), p. 125 *et. seq.*
178. Article 17(1) and (2) of the International Covenant on Civil and Political Rights, 1966 reads, (1) "None shall be subject to arbitrary or unlawful interference with his privacy, family or human or correspondence, nor to lawful attacks on his honour and reputation.
(2) Every one has the right to the protection of the law against such interference or attacks."
179. *Supra*, n. 175 at pp. 312-13.
180. See, *Govind* v. *State of M.P.*, (1975) 2 S.C.C. 148 and *R. Rajagopal* v. *State of Tamilnadu*, (1994) 6 S.C.C. 632.

Construction of Article 21 reached sky high limits in *Vishaka* v. *State of Rajasthan*,[181] where the Court held that sexual harassment of women in the places of work amounted to violation of rights to gender equality and life under Articles 14, 15, 19(1) (a) and 21.[182] Since there is no right mentioned in those Articles against sexual assault, the Supreme Court fell back upon Article 51(c) to interpret fundamental rights contained in them and held that in the absence of domestic law, contents of international conventions and norms were significant to interpret provisions in the Constitution guaranteeing gender justice and human dignity to women.[183] Judicial innovation in these cases lies in the method of incorporating the concepts found in the international treaties and conventions into Articles 14 and 21 by relying on the directive contained in Article 51(c). The prime motive of the Court to read the contents of international law into fundamental rights was nothing but its wish to make it vivacious with the presence of social justice in them.

Bandhua Mukti Morcha v. *Union of India*,[184] is another instance in which the Court used the directive principle for interpreting Article 21. Observing that child cannot develop without a benign environment, the Court held that deprivation of the rights of children has a deleterious effect on democracy and rule of law.[185] In the wake of Articles 21 and 24 read with Articles 39(e), (f) and 45 every child is entitled to health, well-

---

181. (1997) 6 S.C.C. 241. This writ petition under Article 32 was spurred by a gang rape of a woman social worker in the State of Rajasthan on the ground that it amounted to violation of her fundamental rights under Articles 14, 19 and 21.
182. *Id.* at p. 248.
183. *Ibid.* For reading those rights into Articles 14 and 21, the Court relied upon Article 11 of the Convention on the Elimination All Forms of Discrimination against Women, 1979. It provides that the States should take appropriate steps to eliminate discrimination against women in the field of employment to ensure right to work as an inalienable right of all human beings and right to protection of health and safety in the working conditions. For the text, see, Ian Brownlie, *op. cit.* at pp. 169 *et. seq.*
184. (1997) 10 S.C.C. 549. A writ petition was filed under Article 32 praying for a *mandamus* directing the government to take steps to prevent employment of children in carpet factories. Employment of children in carpet industry was challenged mainly as violative of Article 24.
185. *Id.* at p. 553.

being, education and social protection.[186] Convention on the Rights of the Child, ratified by the Government of India recognizes the rights of children for full and harmonious development. The directive principles under Articles 39(e) and (f), 45 and 46 read with Articles 21, 23 and 24 cast a duty on the State to render socio-econoic justice to children, their empowerment and full growth of their personality.[187] Observing that various statutes extend only unreal protection, the Court directed the State governments to take steps to provide compulsory education and periodic health check-up to all children.[188] By this decision, the Court proved that a glance to Article 21 in the light of the directives would enable it to render assistance to poor children.

The argument that the concept of right to life in all sense would include the right of a person to have job is not new. Though there is some factual reality in this point, the judiciary has ever been reluctant to uphold the same as part of an ingredient of the right to life enforceable under Article 21 of the Constitution for specific reasons. Of late, in *Secretary, State of Karnataka* v. *Umadevi (3)*,[189] the temporary employees in certain State Departments and instrumentalities claimed that they were entitled to be regularized and made permanent as the right to life under Article 21 encompassed within it the right employment. The court rejected the claim of the petitioners on the ground that acceptance of the claim of the petitioners would deny other aspirants the same right. However, the court upheld

186. *Id.* at pp. 553-54.
187. *Id.* at p. 556.
188. *Id.* at pp. 557-58.
189. (2006) 4 SCC 1. This was a group of appeals against the decision of the High Court of Karnataka which accepted the claims of the petitioners some of whom were working for nearly 10 years as temporary employees in some government departments or in the instrumentalities of the state for regularization. But, *cf. Indian Drugs & Pharmaceuticals Ltd.* v. *Workmen* (2007) 1 SCC 408 where certain temporary workers in the appellant company claimed the right to be permanent, the Supreme Court held that even in the wake of Article 41 which provides for the right to work, "Article 21 of the Constitution cannot be stretched so far as to mean that everyone must be given a job. The number of available jobs are limited, and hence court must take a realistic view of the matter and must exercise self-restraint." (at p. 432).

the proposition that the concept of right to life under Article 21 got nourished by Article 39(a), which cast an obligation on the State to ensure livelihood to all its citizens. The court held:[190]

> "The obligation cast on the State under Article 39(a) of the Constitution is to ensure that all citizens equally have the right to adequate means of livelihood. It will be more consistent with the policy if the courts recognize that an appointment to a post in government service or in the service of its instrumentalities can only be by way of a proper selection in a manner recognized by the relevant legislation in the context of the relevant provisions of the Constitution. In the name of individualizing justice, it is also not possible to shut our eyes to the constitutional scheme and the right of the numerous as against the few who are before the court. The directive principles have also to be reconciled with the rights available to the citizen under Part III of the Constitution and the obligation of the State to one and all and not to a particular group of citizens."

Though the court rejected the plea of the petitioners' right to regularization and permanency in the posts on the ground of their right to life under Article 21, it does not mean that the court rejected the view that right to life encompasses the right to livelihood also. The court was merely rejecting the claim of the petitioners that the right did not clothe them with the right to be regularized and that the right was to be available to all the persons.

(v) Right to Life and Environment

There is an undeniable link between the concepts of environment and life implying the bond between right to environment and right to life under Article 21. The Indian judiciary responded very positively to the clarion call of the international community for protecting environment. The Supreme Court incorporated by judicial interpretation the right

190. *Id.* at p. 41.

to clean environment as part and parcel of right to life.[191] By the early nineties the Court clearly construed Article 21 to include within it the right to pollution free environment.[192] However, in these cases, the Court held the concept of right to life under Article 21 inclusive of right to pollution free environment without the help of any other constitutional provision. As a corollary of such decisions, the Court held in the subsequent cases that the person who pollutes the environment and violates the fundamental rights of another had a responsibility to make good the loss by paying damages.[193] The Court began to evolve certain rules through adjudicatory process for effective protection of the environment not found specifically in any statute. 'Polluter pay principle'[194] and 'precautionary principle'[195] are some of such judicially evolved rules. In *M.C. Mehta* v. *Union of India*,[196] the Court held that the 'Precautionary Principle' has been accepted as part of the law by Articles 21, 47, 48-A and 51-A(g) which *mandates* the State to protect and improve the environment and to safeguard it.[197] The holding thus makes it mandatory for the State government to anticipate,

191. See, for instance, *Rural Litigation and Entitlement Kendra, Dehradun* v. *State of U.P.*, A.I.R. 1988 S.C. 2187 and *M.C. Mehta* v. *Union of India*, A.I.R. 1988 S.C. 1037 *(Ganga Pollution (Tannaries) Case*
192. See, *Subhash Kumar* v. *State of Bihar*, A.I.R. 1991 S.C. 420.
193. See for instance, *M.C. Mehta* v. *Union of India*, A.I.R. 1987 S.C. 1086 and *Union Carbide India Ltd.* v. *Union of India*, A.I.R. 1994 S.C. 101.
194. It means that the polluter of environment is absolutely liable to compensate for the harm caused by him to villagers, soil, water and the like and is also liable to remove all pollution. This principle was accepted as a sound one in *Indian Council for Enviro-Legal Action* v. *Union of India*, (1996) 3 S.C.C. 212.
195. The principle says that where there are serious and irreversible damage, lack of scientific certainty should not be used as a reason for postponing measure to prevent environmental degradation. This principle was accorded international recognition when it was incorporated in the Rio Declaration 1992. See, P. Leelakrishnan, *Environmental Law in India* (1999), p. 59. See also *Vellore Citizen's Welfare Forum* v. *Union of India*, (1996) 5 S.C.C. 647.
196. (1997) 3 S.C.C. 715. This was a continuation of the decision in *M.C. Mehta* v. *Union of India*, (1996) 8 S.C.C. 462. In that case the Court was concerned with control of pollution and preservation of environment from mining operations within 5 km. of the tourist resorts of Badkhal Lake and Surajkund in Haryana.
197. *Id.* at p. 720.

prevent and attack the causes of environmental degradation. Where there are threats of serious and irreversible damage, lack of scientific certainty should not be extended by the State as a reason for postponing the prevention of environmental degradation. The Court imposed a duty on the State to protect the environment as a correlative of fundamental right to life under Article 21 by reading it in the light of the directives in Part IV which enabled State action for the protection of the environment. The right to be protected against environmental degradation was read into Article 21 by the Court, in the light of directives dealing with the duty of the State to raise the level of nutrition, and standard of living and to improve public health;[198] to protect and improve environment, to safeguard forests and wild life[199] and the fundamental duty to promote international peace and security.[200]

In *Intellectuals Forum* v. *State of A.P.*,[201] the court was faced with a unique issue. It was an appeal against the decision of the High Court of Andhra Pradesh which dismissed the petition challenging the decision of the state government to destroy two tanks in the Titupati town which was a drought stricken area, to find adequate space for construction of buildings for the pilgrims to the place. The petitioners contended that Article 48A which mandates the State to maintain the environment demanded non-destruction of the tanks to enable supply of drinking water. The court accepted the proposition that right to life under Article 21 read in the light of Articles 48A and 51A encompassed the right to environment also.[202] Nevertheless, the court observed that shelter also is a requirement next to food and clothing. Balancing these rights, (right to environment and

198. Article 47.
199. Article 48-A.
200. Article 51-A (g).
201. (2006) 3 S.C.C. 549.
202. *Id.* at p. 576. The court held, "These two articles [48A and 51A] are not only fundamental in the governance of the country but also it shall be the duty of the State to apply these principles in making laws and further these two articles are to be kept in mind in understanding the scope and purport of the fundamental rights guaranteed by the Constitution including Articles 14, 19 and 21 of the Constitution and also the various laws enacted by Parliament and the State Legislatures."

right to shelter), the court held that no further constructions were to be made in the locality.

A discussion of the above cases gives rise to certain questions. What prompted the Court to render such an interpretation of fundamental rights? Was the Court justified in embarking upon such a construction of those rights? It is clear from some of the holdings of the Court that the failure of the State organs in implementing directive principles has irked the conscience of the Court.[203] The Court at many times highlighted the importance of the directive principles in the administration of the State and extended support to their implementation.[204] Still the State did not take much care in carrying out the administration in accordance with the principles, which are fundamental in nature. In many instances, such inaction on the part of the State led to denial of social and economic justice to the people. Moreover, the Court realized that without timely implementation of the directives, fundamental rights would become empty promises. Even though in the traditional view social justice was contrary to the concept of right, of late, it is accepted that a "just social system defines the scope within which individuals must develop their aims, and it provides a framework of rights and opportunities and the means of satisfaction within and by the use of which these ends may be equitably pursued"[205] and hence, "in justice as fairness the concept of right is prior to that of the good."[206] It may be in such a context that the Court began to read the contents of Part IV into the provisions of Part III. In other words, it is the inaction of the legislature and the executive that led to the judicial process of implementing directive principles in the form of fundamental rights. Even if the State had taken timely action to implement directive principles, through legislative and executive measures, they would have remained mere statutory

---

203. See, for instance, the decisions in *Mohd. Ahamad Khan* v. *Shah Bano Begum*, (1985) 2 S.C.C. 556, 572 and *Sarala Mudgal* v. *Union of India*, (1995) 3 S.C.C. 635.
204. See, for instance, *State of Bombay* v. *F.N. Balsara*, A.I.R. 1951 S.C. 318; *Bijay Cotton Mills* v. *State of Ajmer*, A.I.R. 1955 S.C. 33.
205. John Rawls, *A Theory of Justice*, Universal Law Publishing Co., New Delhi, (2005), p. 31.
206. *Ibid*.

rights, which require a lengthy process for enforcement. But their incorporation into the fundamental rights by the judiciary paved the way to a situation in which they became enforceable as fundamental rights under Article 32. Though directive principles are not enforceable through courts of law,[207] unlike Ireland, in India directive principles are not outside the pale of judicial cognition.[208] Moreover, though the distinction between fundamental rights and directive principles is an accepted and important classification of social goods, in certain contexts the classification may not be useful.[209] Therefore, the modern approach of taking directives into account in interpreting fundamental rights does not run counter to what is contained in the Constitution. It is only a creative juristic technique to give effect to the directives without violating constitutional provisions. Further, it would be unwise to categorize all the directives under one rubric and hold that all are equally unenforceable. They contain mandates of different nature. Some deal with the general principles of social policy,[210] some with principles of administrative policy,[211] while the third category nurtures the concept of socio-economic rights[212] implementation of which is absolutely necessary for the protection of individual rights and liberties and some others contain a statement of the international policy of the Republic.[213] The directives that

207. Article 37.
208. Joseph Minattur, "The Unenforceable Directives in the Indian Constitution," (1975) 1 S.C.C. 17.
209. "Furthermore, the distinction between fundamental rights and liberties and economic and social benefits marks a difference among primary social goods that one should try to exploit. It suggests an important division in the social system. *Of course, the distinctions drawn and the ordering proposed are bound to be at best only approximations. There are surely circumstances in which they fail.*" Rawls, *op. cit.* at p. 63. (Emphasis supplied)
210. For example, Article 38.
211. For instance, Articles 40 and 50.
212. See, Articles 38 to 39-A, 41 to 43 and 45 to 49.
213. P.B. Gajendragadkar, The *Constitution of India : Its Philosophy and Basic Postulates,* Gandhi Memorial Lectures University College, Nairobi (1969), p. 18. For a classification of directive principles on the basis of values contained in them, see, G.S. Sharma, "The Concept of Leadership Implicit in the Directive Principles of Social Policy in the Indian Constitution," 7 J.I.L.I. 173 at p. 175 (1965).

promulgate the constitutionally desired social order are considered as fundamental while others are treated as directive.[214] It would therefore be incorrect to appraise them all as of equal importance and to make a sweeping statement that judiciary should not take any directives into account for rendering decisions. Those dealing with social policy and socio-economic justice deserve much attention by the administrators. When there is total inaction on the part of the government in taking them into account, the judiciary has a duty to make use of them whenever found necessary for enforcing fundamental rights. Whereas in the past the Court had seen the directives as subservient to fundamental rights,[215] or as reasonable restrictions on the Part III rights,[216] the modern trend in judicial creativity is one of reading directive principles into the fundamental rights with a view to securing social justice. Such a judicial approach gives sensible contents to the fundamental rights.

During the pre-emergency era, the cases in which the Court had to deal with the relationship of fundamental rights and directive principles were cases in which the issue was proprietary rights. Therefore, while interpreting such rights, the Court utilized directive principles as restrictions of those rights. But the post-emergency period witnessed attack on the very person of the people and it called the Court to interpret the personal rights *vis-à-vis* directive principles. It was in such an occasion that the Court developed the technique of reading directive principles into the fundamental rights with a view to achieving social justice. In other words, such a revolutionary and creative approach of the Supreme Court corresponds to the shift in emphasis from proprietary fundamental rights to personal ones.

The interpretation of the provisions in Part III adopted by the Court in the above cases has many consequences. As a result of such a construction, fundamental rights, which mainly have

---

214. Upendra Baxi, "The Little Done, the Vast Undone—Some Reflections on the Reading Granville Austine's The Constitution," (1967) 9 J.I.L.I. 323 at p. 361.

215. For different uses of directive principles, see, Rajeev Dhavan, *Supreme Court of India, Socio-juristic Techniques* (1977), p. 90.

negative contents, were provided with positive contents on an objective basis in the light of the directive principles. Consequently, the State was imposed with positive obligations to implement the directives. Directive Principles, which once were mere guidelines for the State, got transformed themselves as limitations on the power of the state. Thus, the State became duty bound to protect many concepts mentioned in Part IV such as the rights to equal pay for equal work and health of workers, rights of backward classes and right to primary education only because the Court read them into the rights contained in Part III. Non-implementation of a directive by the State considered by the Court as part of the fundamental right would justify invocation of Article 32. Consequently, the power of the Supreme Court under Article 32 to enforce fundamental rights got widened to include enforcement of the directive principles.[217] Such an innovative interpretation changed the nature of directive principles from mere guidelines to constitutional obligations. Enforcement of such directives thus became the duty of the State and hence the right of the people. Though by such a construction, the Court flouted Article 37 of the Constitution, which prohibits judicial enforcement of the directives, such a creative reading is justified from another perspective. Envy of the least advantaged in the society towards the better off[218] can be avoided only when the social institutions are just. Moreover, people in a society would act justly only when they derive benefit from the system.[219] Giving content to fundamental rights in the light of the directives would help eradicate the existing social inequality thereby furthering the progress of the society.

When the Court pointed out that the State could not cast a blind eye to the implementation of directive principles without violating the fundamental rights, the State has to be vigilant in implementing the directives contained in Part IV. Thus, reading

216. See, for instance, *State of Bombay* v. *F.N. Balsara*, A.I.R 1951 S.C. 318.
217. There is a view that the Constitution should be amended to enable judicial enforcement of directive principles contained in Articles 39 (d), 39-A, 41, 42 and 43. See, Mahavir Singh, "Directive Principles and Fundamental Rights—A Correlation : Some Suggestions to Remove the Controversy," (1981) 3 S.C.C. 28.
218. Rawls, *op. cit.* at p. 531.
219. *Id.* at p. 456.

of the directives into Part III fulfills the aim of rendering social justice. The Court by its innovative creativity on the one hand and advancing the cause of social justice on the other, provided more colour and content to the life of individuals. In short, this judicial approach seems to support the cause of social justice for which the makers of the Constitution stood.

Analysis of the above decisions indicates that in the late eighties and in the nineties, the Supreme Court exhibited a highly creative outlook in interpreting some of the vital fundamental rights. The Court in those cases while explaining the contents of those fundamental rights transfused similar ideas contained in Part IV into them. The creativity of the Court lies in the identification of uniformity of ideas in Parts III and IV and explaining fundamental rights in accordance with the directive principles.[220] Such an innovative trend can be said to be out of the development and extension of the view of the Court that neither fundamental right nor the directive principle be given precedence over the other and that they are supplementary and complementary to each other. This creative interpretation of the provisions of the Part III represents the modern, ideal version of the relationship between fundamental rights and directive principles. By such a construction, the Court was able use the directive principles for protecting the rights of the people and thus to circumvent the limitations on the justiciability of the directive principles. These decisions are creative in many ways. Discarding the earlier trend of understanding them as negative mandates, they emphasize the latest version that the rights impose positive duties on the State. Further, these decisions exemplify how fundamental rights could be given effect to in accordance with the contents of directives by raising them from the level of individual rights to

220. Perhaps, the following words of a distinguished constitutional expert were prophylactic, "...whenever our judges perform their creative function through the interpretation of the fundamental rights it is very natural that the presence, in the same Constitution, of the directive principles should exert an inexorable influence and control on their judgement as to the scope of the fundamental rights." P.K. Tripathi, "Directive Principles of State Policy: The Lawyers' Approach to Them Hitherto Parochial, Injurious and Unconstitutional," in *Spotlights on Constitutional Interpretation* (1972), 291 at p. 316.

the plateau of social justice. In short, they also show how fundamental rights could be given content and sense without sacrificing the moral mandates contained in Part IV. They reflect a novel approach to define the inter-relationship between fundamental rights and directive principles. Undoubtedly, these decisions will stand in good stead in the era of liberalization which India is slowly accepting into its legal and constitutional fold as a result of which the rights of the down-trodden and the weak are likely to be neglected.

9

Conclusion

Judicial activism after the inauguration of the era of legislation and written constitutions has been condemned[1] than hailed. Whatever be the theoretical and ideological displeasure to it, experience of the common law and civil law systems stand testimony to the fact that legal systems cannot maintain their stability and accommodate themselves to changes without a sensitive and creative judiciary. In an era of judicial law-making precedent was only a device for self-regulation and an anchor for subsequent decisions of the judiciary.[2] With the arrival of legislation and written constitutions, the role of the rules of precedent has been shifted to and taken over by enacted laws and judicial decisions had necessarily to be tagged to them. Even thereafter, situations arise where the enacted law does not

1. See, for instance, Richard Ekins, "Judicial Supremacy and the Rule of Law", 119 L.Q.R. 127 *et. seq*. (2003)
2. In the earlier stages, in England, judges did not consider themselves bound by the decisions given by their predecessors. They followed the previous decisions for the sake of certainty and convenience. It was considered as procedural and customary in nature *(mos judiciorum)* and precedent was considered as evidence *of* law and not *as* law. See, C.K. Allen, *Law in the Making*, (1964) Chapter III Part I, particularly, pp. 176-235.

meet the societal requirements whereupon the responsibility befalls upon the judiciary to pour in meaning and content into the words used in them. And at times to keep the enacted laws abreast of their modern requirements, certain new concepts had to be launched into the words used in the enacted law without which the law might become desuetude. The focus of this study has been on certain areas in the Indian Constitution where one notices slow and gradual but steady judicial creativity while interpreting the constitutional provisions. The study reveals that judicial innovation was essential to adapt the constitutional provisions to the changed modern context. The primary aspect judicial innovation has been mainly in the creation and introduction of certain new concepts not found in any specific provision of the Constitution which, but, were essential for its meaningful interpretation. Independence of the judiciary, basic structure and certain elements of social justice cherished by the makers of the Constitution are some such concepts infused into the Constitution by the judiciary. The second aspect of creativity lies in the attempt of the Court to construe provisions in the Constitution with a view to maintaining as well as modernizing the concepts so infused into the Constitution. Introduction of those concepts into the Constitution was necessary and is justified. Examination of the above areas proves that the Court was by and large successful in its attempt in construing the constitutional provisions in tune with the judicially introduced concepts.

I

The decisions dealing with the judiciary reveal the consciousness of the apex court as to the necessity of independence of judiciary in a federal, democratic and parliamentary set-up. The significance of the concept, which was absent in the Constitution was recognized initially by the court as an effective check against the arbitrariness of the executive. Decisions dealing with appointment of judges to the higher judiciary and those dealing with transfer of judges of High Courts stand testimony to this. Analysis of cases dealing with appointment of judges to the Supreme Court reveals that the Court construed the provisions with a view to upholding judicial independence. The holding in the *Judges Case*[3] that 'consultation' envisaged by the Constitution was not a formality and that it operated as a check on the executive arbitrariness is indicative of this. By such a holding the Court was able to rule out the possibility of unilateral decision-making by the President. However, the holding did not completely do away with the possibility of executive arbitrariness in selecting judges. But, the holding in the *S.C. Advocates*[4] was to the effect that the process of consultation required the President to act according to the recommendation of the Chief Justice of India in normal cases, and that the only freedom enjoyed by him was not to appoint the recommendee of the Chief Justice of India in appropriate cases. Such a holding has fully ruled out the chances of executive arbitrariness. The holding gave pride of place to the opinion of the Chief Justice of India and thus strengthened the institutional independence of judiciary. The concept of judicial independence as developed by the Court sought to exclude the possibility of arbitrariness of the Chief Justice of India also. In this respect, *Subhash Sharma,*[5] and *S.C. Advocates* developed 'consultation' as one of 'participative consultative process', which implied that before forming an opinion, the Chief Justice of India has to consult a collegium consisting of his senior colleagues. This view got reaffirmation when it was held[6] that in the absence of such a consultative process the President was not bound to appoint the recommendee of the Chief Justice of India and that such appointments were open to judicial review. Thus, in a way, it can be said that the court meaningfully used the requirement of consultation with the Chief Justice of India as a device to protect independence of judiciary. The requirement that in selecting persons as judges of the Supreme Court from among the judges of the High Courts, their seniority on the national basis should also be taken into account reduced chances of arbitrariness of the Chief Justice of India in selecting Judges to the Supreme Court. The holding that the President was not bound to act

3. *S.P. Gupta* v. *Union of India,* 1981 Supp. S.C.C. 87.
4. (1993) 4 S.C.C. 441.
5. A.I.R. 1991 S.C. 631.
6. *Special Reference No. 1 of 1998.* (1998) 7 S.C.C. 739.

unless the Chief Justice of India formed his view after consulting his colleagues and that the President could require the collegium to reconsider the proposal can be appreciated as fine pieces of judicial innovation for promoting judicial independence and for avoiding arbitrariness by the judiciary. While interpreting the provision for appointing judges to High Courts, the Court accepted and recommended the same procedure. To rule out arbitrariness of the Chief Justice of India, and to make 'consultation' meaningful, the Court held that the view of the Chief Justice of the High Court concerned deserved the greatest weight. Thus, the apex court has taken all precautions against the possibility of the Chief Justice of India acting contrary to judicial independence. The requirement that all opinions should be documented and communicated individually excludes chances of exertion of pressure or influence on the consultants.

Speaking of judicial independence without the independence of its head is meaningless. Hence, interpretation of the provision dealing with selection and appointment of the Chief Justice of India deserves significance, especially when the provision in the Constitution does not give any indication in this regard except that the President need not consult the outgoing Chief Justice of India.[7] In such a context, the holding that the Chief Justice of India be appointed on the basis of seniority and on the recommendation of the out going Chief Justice of India[8] is an example of creativity and vision of the Court. It fills up a gap in the constitutional provision and excludes executive arbitrariness in selecting persons to the post of the head of the judicial family. The favourable impact of the holding on independence of judiciary is evident when viewed in the background of the two instances in which, taking advantage of the constitutional provision, the President appointed the Chief Justice of India in supersession of the senior-most judges and their adverse impact on the independence of the institution. In short, the cases dealing with the appointment of judges to the Supreme Court reveal that the Court fathomed the relation between independence of judiciary and the process of

7. See, Article 124(2) Proviso.

appointment of judges and exhibited high creativity in interpreting and giving content to the term 'consultation' in Articles 124(2) and 217(1) with a view to upholding judicial independence.

Cases dealing with appointment of Additional Judges, transfer of judges of High Courts and removal of judges constitute a telltale of the realization of the Supreme Court as to how security of tenure and judicial independence are intertwined. They reveal the innovative response of the Supreme Court in this respect. Ever since the incorporation of Article 224A, it was the door through which judges entered the High Courts irrespective of whether posts of permanent judges in the High Court were vacant. It is in such a circumstance that the court held in the *Judges Case* that the consultative process followed in appointing permanent judges was applicable in appointing temporary judges and that the executive did not enjoy any discretion to determine the term of such appointment. Holding that Additional Judges should not be appointed for short-terms like three or six months and incorporation of the concept of legitimate expectation of Additional Judges to be considered for reappointment and their right to approach the court for non-extension are instances of fine judicial craftsmanship in harmonizing the provision for appointment of temporary judges with the need to preserve independence of judiciary. When a new content was given to consultation, appointment of Additional Judges became fully free from the executive discretion and the cause of judicial independence was advanced.[9] The holding[10] that the writ of *mandamus* could be issued for reviewing the strength of the permanent judges in a High Court reduced the chance of appointment of Additional Judges in cases where appointment of permanent judges was warranted. Nevertheless, had the Court conferred on Additional Judges the right to be re-appointed, the cause of judicial independence would have been protected further.

Transfer of High Court judges is an area in which a high degree of creativity is exhibited by the Supreme Court. The

8. *S.C. Advocates, supra,* n. 4.
9. *S.P. Gupta, supra,* n. 3.
10. *S.C. Advocates, supra,* n. 4.

holding in the *Seth's Case*[11] that for transferring the judge of a High Court, public interest was a *sine qua non* and the discussion as to the relevance of consent of the judge indicate the realization of the apex court as to the nexus between the threat of transfer and independence of the judiciary. A dispassionate reading of the judgement would enlighten one that the judiciary was aware of the threat the power of the executive could inflict in transferring judges of the High Court. The holding that public interest is a condition precedent and the emphasis on consultation with the Chief Justice of India for transfer added flavour to the concept of independence of judiciary. The view was reiterated in the *Judges Case*. Though the court examined the issue from the perspective of the independence of the judiciary, the court left unlimited discretion to the executive in this respect. However, with the holding in the *S.C. Advocates*, concurrence of the Chief Justice of India became the chief element in transferring judges. The subsequent decision[12] that the Chief Justice of India before forming a view has to consult the Chief Justices of the High Courts concerned rules out the possibility of his arbitrariness and hence provided further impetus to judicial independence. The holdings that transfers could be judicially reviewed and that improper transfers could be struck down add strength to these norms. These norms found their way into the Constitution due to creative judicial innovation. However, being elusive, the concept of public interest will have to be elaborated further clearly and meaningfully if judicial independence is to be protected to its fullest extent. But the verdict on the transfer issue is not an unmixed blessing. The holdings in *S.C. Advocates* and *Special Reference* that the opinion of the Chief Justice of India contains elements of public interest and therefore transfers according to his opinion were not open to judicial review will have adverse impact on independence of judiciary. For threat to judicial independence came not only from the executive but also from the judiciary itself. Moreover, though these holdings help protect judiciary from executive arbitrariness, it is yet to be seen how far the judiciary may be protected from the possibility of

11. *Union of India* v. *Sankalchand Seth*, A.I.R 1977 S.C. 2328.
12. *Special Reference, supra*, n. 6.

combined arbitrariness of the President and the Chief Justice of India. It has been accepted that judges of the High Courts are not equivalent to the civil servants who are employees of the State. They, on the other hand are on par with the executive wherefore, there is nothing wrong in the Court's being more creative by incorporating consent of the judge as a condition precedent for transfer and it might have been more effective to protect judicial independence.

Removal of judges of the higher judiciary is another conspicuous area in which the Court exhibited remarkable innovation. The procedure for removal of judges under Article 124(4) is similar to the impeachment procedure prevailing in England, which has political overtones than legal content. The removal drama of Justice Ramaswamy of the Supreme Court brought to light how weak the provisions in our constitution are. Hence, with a view to checking removal of judges of the higher judiciary on political grounds and to ensure that removal is made only on the ground of proved 'misbehaviour' or 'incapacity' the Court held that misbehaviour should be proved under Article 124(5) and the Judges Inquiry Act, 1961 through the judicial process and that the motion for removal of judges could be taken up in Parliament only if misbehaviour is so judicially established.[13] Thus by the holding, unlike in England and America, the court could bring the judicial process under Article 124(5) and not the political process under Article 124(4) as the fulcrum of the removal procedure. Further, the court held in *Sarojini Ramaswamy*[14] that the procedure for removal as subject to judicial review. By bringing the removal procedure subject to judicial review, the Court undoubtedly made a significant contribution to the cause of protection of independence of the judiciary. Shift from the emphasis on the Parliamentary process to the judicial ones and the incorporation of judicial review have brought the process of removal of judges of the higher judiciary out of the uncertainty and the consequential threat of political process. The holding in *Ravichandra Iyyer*[15] that though the procedure for removal under

13. *Sub-Committee on Judicial Accountability* v. *Union of India*, (1991) 4 S.C.C 599.
14. (1992) 4 S.C.C. 506
15. *Ravichandra Iyyer* v. *Justice A.M. Bhattacharjee*, (1995) 5 S.C.C 457.

Article 124 is the only constitutionally envisaged one, every instance of misconduct may not constitute misbehaviour and that minor misconduct could be rectified by self-regulation insulate judges against the threat of arbitrary removal. It was also held that cases of minor misconduct should be dealt with by in-house proceeding by the judiciary disabling Parliament from passing a resolution for removal. As a result of these decisions the procedure for removal is thus brought out of the realm of politics so as to assist the cause of judicial independence. The holdings of the Supreme Court in *Sub-Committee* and *Sarojini Ramaswamy* help insulate the independent and impartial judges from being threatened by the removal procedure. These decisions represent instances in which the Supreme Court indulged in creative interpretation of the provisions of the Constitution whereby judiciary has been saved from onslaughts of the legislature.

Nevertheless, the subsequent constitutional developments proved that the holdings of the court cannot be said to encompass the entire issues relating to removal of judges. They, for instance, do not give any indication as to the course to be adopted if Parliament does not remove a judge who has been found guilty of misbehaviour by the judicial tribunal constituted under Article 124(5). Though Constitution does not deal with such a situation, the court could have made some observations balancing independence of the judiciary on the one hand and the interest of the nation to avoid a judge whose misbehaviour has been proved. Similarly, though the court in *Ravichandra Iyyar* highlighted the significance of self-regulation of the institution through in-house procedure as a means for upholding judicial independence, there are some issues which the court has not addressed. What happens if through an in house proceeding it is revealed that the accused judge has misbehaved? As per the Constitution, the Chief Justice of India or any other authority cannot take any disciplinary measure against the erring judge. The maximum the Chief Justice of India can do is to avoid allotting of cases to him and in the case of a judge of the High Court, to transfer him to another High Court and recommend to the Speaker to take action in accordance with the procedure contained in Article 124(4) and

(5). Then again the ultimate decision is left with Parliament and if it delays or refuses to remove the judge, the judiciary has to bear with him.[16]

Cases dealing with the subordinate judiciary also reveal how the concept of judicial independence was kept in mind by the Supreme Court in interpreting the respective provisions in the Constitution. By giving emphasis on the aspect of consultation with the High Court the Court was able to reduce the influence of the executive in appointments of District Judges. The Court developed the concept and importance of consultation stage by stage. Initially, it was held that for appointing district judges, consultation was to be made with the High Court alone.[17] Later it was held that the recommendations of the High Court had to be implemented,[18] that government could not brush it aside without valid reasons.[19] The thrust of these holdings was carried further by the decision that if the recommendations of the High Court were not implemented without stating the reasons, a writ of *mandamus* could be issued to the government to communicate the reasons for the same.[20] As by the above decisions, the power to appoint District Judges virtually came to be vested with the High Court, the executive could remove District Judges only after consulting the High Court. Similarly, by creatively interpreting Article 235, and by giving wide content to the expression 'control and superintendence' in it the Court was able to bring all incidents of service of judges of the subordinate judiciary except their appointment and removal under the control and supervision of High Courts. The Court construed Article 235 in such a manner that the power of control and superintendence vested in the High Court would not damage independence of judges of the subordinate judiciary.

Insulation of the lower judiciary from the executive and the legislature however, does not mean that it is free from any

---

16. The incident of Mr. Justice Sowmithra Sen of the High Court of Calcutta stands testimony to this. For a discussion of the incident, see, *supra* Chapter 4, n. 275.
17. *Chandra Mohan* v. *State of U.P.*, A.I.R. 1966 S.C. 1987.
18. *Hari Dutt* v. *State of A.P.*, A.I.R. 1980 S.C. 1426.
19. *M.M. Gupta* v. *State of J.K.*, A.I.R. 1982 S.C. 1579.
20. *State of Kerala* v. *Lakshmikkutty*, A.I.R. 1987 S.C. 331.

threat. Many cases that came up for consideration of the Supreme Court reveal that the threat to the independence of the lower judiciary from within the institution is at times more grave than the threat from without. The High Court, in the guise of control of and superintendence over the subordinate courts under Article 235 has invoked the power in a manner subversive of its independence. Highlighting the necessity of independence of the judge, how-low-so-ever he be, and making High Courts aware of their role as the guardian and protector of the lower judiciary, the Supreme Court on many such instances circumscribed the exercise of power by the High Court under Article 235 thereby protecting the members of the lower judiciary from the institutional onslaught. Evidently, the cases dealing with the subordinate judiciary reveal that independence of judiciary was developed as a shield not only against the legislature and executive but also against the judiciary itself. An examination of the cases dealing with the higher and lower strata of the Indian judiciary would reveal how the judicially introduced concept of independence of the judiciary was made use of by the Supreme Court for interpreting the provisions in the Constitution. The court not only introduced the concept into the Constitution but also modernized it, infusing into it the ideas of the institutional, individual and personal aspects.

II

Judicial review of the power of Parliament to amend the Constitution is another sphere of scintillating judicial activism. In this area the Supreme Court of India excelled all other judicial fora at global level. The Court for the first time in the history of constitutional jurisprudence held that the power to amend the Constitution was amenable to judicial review[21] and propounded a norm—the doctrine of basic structure—for evaluating the validity of amendment to the Constitution. By the doctrine the court identified certain features of the Constitution that needed permanency. Though there was no consensus among the judges as to what the ingredients of basic structure were, they by and large agreed as to what the features

21. *Kesavananda Bharathi* v. *State of Kerala*, (1973) 4 S.C.C. 225.

of the doctrine should be and that they were not to be amended in exercise of the constituent power of Parliament. By the doctrine, the first of its kind ever made, the Court was able to overcome the myth that questions of constitutional amendments were political in nature and hence were beyond the purview of judicial review. The creative element of the doctrine lies in bringing constitutional amendments amenable to judicial review without destroying the well-accepted distinction between constitution and ordinary law. To work out a coherent doctrine of basic structure, the Court introduced the theory of implied limitations into the Constitution. The doctrine was invoked to check gradual erosion of the identity of the Constitution—the basic document of the legal system—in exercise of the power for modifying it. History bears testimony to the increased significance of the doctrine. By the doctrine, the Court was able to prevent the Constitution being made a plaything in the hands of the political parties in Parliament. The success of the doctrine is evident from the fact that Parliament did not venture to substantially change the Constitution after the doctrine has made a firm grip in the Indian legal system.

Though the concept of basic structure was beautifully delineated by the court, the lack of consensus as to its ingredients among the judges provided food for many of the criticisms that immediately followed the historic decision. But, this initial hotchpotch among the judges gave way by the 80's to the firm concept when the court began to describe and develop the doctrine in different cases. Likewise the reluctance of the court in *Indira Gandhi* to apply the doctrine for evaluation of the statutes runs counter to the spirit in which it was introduced in the *Kesavananda Bharathi*, which, however was corrected later. The holding in *Waman Rao*[22] limiting the application of basic structure to the amendments after the arrival of *Kesavananda Bharathi* is another shady aspect of the doctrine. Such a holding unfortunately reduced the status of the doctrine as the foundation stone of the legal system as among the other legal concepts.

Notwithstanding the scathing criticisms leveled against the doctrine of basic structure, the Court developed it further and

22. A.I.R. 1980 S.C. 271.

gave it a concrete form. Almost all important features of the Constitution like democratic form of government, federal structure, secularism, judicial review, independence of judiciary and rule of law were thus included in the doctrine to prevent their alteration by amendments. By such a development of the doctrine the Court could undoubtedly prevent abuse of the amendment power to serve political ends. As a further development to the process, the court began to use the doctrine as a criterion for interpreting the provisions of the Constitution,[23] and as a norm for evaluating the acts of constitutional authorities.[24] Further, the doctrine was invoked by the Court as a criterion also for assessing the validity of legislation.[25] In other words, through such a process, the doctrine of basic structure has been developed by the Supreme Court as a criterion for evaluating legislative and executive powers and as a tool to guide exercise of judicial powers. These later decisions are indicative of the realization of the court as to the significance the doctrine of basic structure acquired in the Indian legal system. In short, formulation of the doctrine, which does not have its parallel in other countries is a crowning glory to the creative interpretation of the Constitution by the Supreme Court.

III

Meaning and content of fundamental rights and their relationship with directive principles have ever been a topic of judicial deliberation. Fundamental rights were identified as containing the individual rights while directive principles contained elements of social justice and policy. The conflict between rights and principles on the one hand and policies on the other grasped the relationship between the fundamental rights and directive principles. At one stage, they were therefore considered as conflicting and the court dealt with the former, leaving the latter exclusively to the domain of the government.

23. *S.C. Advocates, supra,* n. 4.
24. *S.R. Bommai* v. *Union of India,* (1994) 3 S.C.C. 1.
25. *G.C. Kanungo* v. *State of Orissa,* (1995) 5 S.C.C. 96.
26. See, e.g. *Mineva Mills* v. *Union of India,* A.I.R. 1980 S.C. 1789.

But, in the later stages, the Supreme Court began to reflect that individual rights cannot be realized without social justice and *vice versa* consequent to which fundamental rights and directive principles were began to be considered as complementary to each other.[26] As a successor to such a version of the fundamental rights and directive principles came the era of exploring the scope of fundamental rights in the light of directive principles.

Interpretation of fundamental rights in the light of the directive principles represents the most modern and creative trend in constitutional interpretation. This trend reveals the judicial perception of the directive principles as a guide for construing the fundamental rights and the attempt of the Supreme Court to construe the scope of fundamental rights in tune with the concept of social justice reflected in the directive principles. Such a judicial response stems from the understanding of the Court that fundamental rights would be meaningless without a tinge of social justice. The creative trend was inaugurated with the interpretation of the fundamental rights to equality and life under Article 14 and Article 21 respectively. By seeking assistance from the related concepts contained in the directive principles, the Court gave more sense and vitality to those rights. Equal pay for equal work[27] and protection of the down-trodden and backward classes were read as facets of the right to equality.[28] Right to easy access to justice,[29] right to primary education,[30] right to pollution-free environment[31] and right to health and medical care for employees[32] were read as part of right to life. Thus the individual rights in Part III were fused with the concept of social justice envisaged in Part IV of the Constitution. Reading of the directive principles into the fundamental rights enabled the

27. *Randhir Singh* v. *Union of India*, A.I.R.1982 S.C. 879.
28. *Atam Prakash* v. *State of Haryana* (1986) 2 S.C.C. 249.
29. See, e.g. *State of Maharashtra* v. *Manubhai Pragaju Vashi*,(1995) 5 S.C.C. 730.
30. *J.P.Unnikrishnan* v. *State of Andhra Pradesh.*, A.I.R. 1993 S.C. 2178.
31. See, e.g. *M.C. Mehta* v. *Union of India*, (1997) 3 S.C.C. 715; *Intellectuals Forum* v. *State of A.P.*, (2006) 3 S.C.C. 549
32. *Consumer Education and Research Centre* v. *Union of India*, A.I.R. 1995 S.C. 922.

Supreme Court to overcome the lethargy of the legislature and the executive in implementing the directives and also to bring in harmony between them. Elucidation of the fundamental rights in the light of social justice reflected in the directive principles can therefore be considered as an instance of high judicial creativity. As a result of such a construction, the nature of those directive principles itself has changed. They ceased to be mere directives for state action but became mandate for it. If left to legislative or executive will for their implementation, the right elements in the directives would not have been enforced as rights. But as a consequence of the innovative interpretation, the Court was able to extend the scope of Article 32 for their enforcement as fundamental rights. This creative judicial response has to be carried further in interpreting other fundamental rights also.

But, unlike the other areas of judicial creativity already discussed, innovation in interpreting fundamental rights in the light of directive principles is at a very nascent stage. Such a vibrant perception of the fundamental rights has yet to be extended as far as the other fundamental rights are concerned. Such a version of the fundamental rights appears to have been the consequence of the judicial response to balance the vehement exercise of state power to implement the directive principles, which, at times extended to the level of denying fundamental rights. The Supreme Court was trying to project the view that fundamental rights contained some elements of social justice, which is contained in the directive principles and that fundamental rights, in the absence of the directive principles would be meaningless. However, the impact of globalization and liberalization bringing with them the emphasis on fundamental rights as against the directive principles in the governance of the country on this innovative judicial attitude is yet to be evaluated.

The examination of the judicial response in the above three areas reveals that overcoming the conventionally accepted and constitutionally envisaged limitations on the judicial power, the Supreme Court directed its authority against the legislative and executive excesses in certain crucial areas in the Indian Constitution. Judicial independence was the idea introduced to prevent onslaughts on the judiciary, basic structure was a judicial essay on Parliament's attempt to cow down other authorities in the country while identifying social justice in fundamental rights was to overcome the inertia of the rulers in promoting the welfare of the common man. To conclude, notwithstanding the lapses of the Supreme Court in construing the provisions in the above three areas, they stand testimony to the innovative attitude and creative response of the Court in interpreting the Constitution. They indicate the relevance and potential of the creative judicial dialetics, nay decisive role it can play in the modern democratic life. It is yet to be seen how far the Indian Supreme Court would maintain its energetic and vibrant attitudes and to what extent the Indian legal system would benefit out of the judicial craftsmanship.

Bibliography

Books

A.M. Bhattacharjee, *Hindu Law and the Constitution,* Eastern Book House, Calcutta (1994).

A.S. Altekar, *State and Government in Ancient India,* Motilal Banarsidas, New Delhi (1949).

A.V. Dicey, *Introduction to the Study of the Law of the Constitution,* McMillan & Co. London (1962).

Alexander Hamilton, James Madison and John Jay, *The Federalist Papers,* Bantam Classic Edition, New York (1982).

Alf Ross on Law and Justice, Stevens and Sons, London (1958).

Alfred Denning, *Road to Freedom,* Sweet and Maxwell (1955).

Allen Brinkley, Nelson W. Polsby and Kathleen M. Sallivan, *New Federalist Papers,* W.W. Norton and Co., New York (1997).

Amos, J. Peasle, (Ed.), *Constitutions of Nations.*

Anson, *The Law and the Custom of the Constitution,* Vol. I, Oxford, Clarendon Press, London (1907).

B. Shiva Rao, *The Framing of India's Constitution, Select Documents,* Vol. I, Indian Institute of Public Administration, New Delhi (1967).

B. Shiva Rao, *The Framing of India's Constitution, Select Documents,* Vol. III, Indian Institute of Public Administration, New Delhi (1967).

———, *The Framing of India's Constitution, Select Documents,* Vol. IV, Indian Institute of Public Administration, New Delhi (1968).

B. Shiva Rao, *The Framing of India's Constitution—A Study*, Indian Institute of Public Administration (1966).

B.N. Hansaria, *Does India Need a New Constitution?* Eastern Book House, Calcutta (1998).

B.P. Singh Seghal, *Judiciary and Justice in India*, Deep and Deep Publications, New Delhi (1993).

B.R. Sharma, *Judiciary on Trial—Appointment, Transfer, Accountability*, Deep and Deep Publications, New Delhi (1989).

Benjamin N. Cardozo, *The Nature of Judicial Process*, Yale University Press, Universal Law Publishing Co. Ltd., Delhi (1995).

Black's Law Dictionary, St. Paul Minn. West Publishing Co. (1990).

Bordenheimer, *Jurisprudence*, Universal Book Traders (1974).

Broom's Legal Maxims, Universal Law Publishing Co., New Delhi. (2000).

C.K. Allen, *Law in the Making*, Universal Law Publishing Co. (P) Ltd. (1964).

C.L. Anand, *Constitutional Law and History of Government of India*, The University Book Agency, Allahabad (1990).

Carlo Guarnieri & Patrizia Pederzoli, *The Power of Judges : A Comparative Study of Courts and Democracy*, OUP (2002).

Chitty's Statutes of Practical Utility, Vol. 3, Sweet and Maxwell, London (1912).

D.D. Basu, *Commentaries on the Constitution of India*, Vol. E., S.C. Sarkar, Calcutta (1981).

D.D. Basu, *Shorter Constitution of India*, Prentice-Hall of India, New Delhi (1996).

D.D. Basu, *Introduction to the Constitution of India*, Prentice-Hall of India, New Delhi (1985).

Dennis Lloyd, *The Idea of Law*, Penguin Books Ltd., England (1977).

E.W. Thomas, *The Judicial Process, Pragmatism, Practical Reasoning and Principles*, Cambridge (2005).

Earnest Barker (Ed.), *The Politics of Aristotle*, Oxford University Press, London (1958).

Edward S. Corwin, *The Constitution and What it Means Today*, Princeton University Press, New Jersey (1958).

Emmettee S. Redford *et. al.*, Politics and Government in the United States, Harcourt, Brace and World Inc. (1965).

Fitzgerald (Ed.), *Salmond on Jurisprudence,* N.M. Tripathi, Bombay (1966).

Francis Bacon, *Advancement of Learning,* Book I, J.M. Dent & Sons Ltd.

Friedmann, *Legal Theory,* Stevens and Sons, Bombay (1949).

Friedmann, *The State and the Rule of Law in a Mixed Economy,* Stevens and Sons, London (1971).

G.W. Paton, *A Text Book of Jurisprudence,* English Language Book Society (1972).

Granville Austin, *The Constitution of India, Cornerstone of a Nation,* Clarendon Press, Oxford (1966).

H.M. Seervai, *Constitutional Law of India,* Vol. II, N.M. Tripathi, Bombay (1984).

H.M. Seervai, *Constitutional Law of India,* Vol. I, N.M. Tripathi, Bombay(1991).

H.M. Seervai, *Constitutional Law of India,* Vol. II, N.M. Tripathi, Bombay (1993).

H.M. Seervai, *Constitutional Law of India,* Vol. III, N.M. Tripathi, Bombay, (1996).

H.R. Khanna, *Judiciary in India and Judicial Process,* Ajoy Law House, S.C. Sarkar & Sons (P.) Ltd. Calcutta (1985).

H.R. Khanna, *Neither Roses Nor Thorns,* Eastern Book Company, Lucknow.

Harold, J. Laski, A *Grammar of Politics,* S. Chand & Co., New Delhi (1979).

Henry, J. Abraham, *The Judicial Process,* Oxford University Press (1962).

Herman Finer, *The Theory and Practice of Modern Government,* Surjeet Publications, New Delhi (1961).

Heuston, *Essays in Constitutional Law,* Stevens and Sons Ltd., London (1961).

Hilaire Barnet, *Constitutional and Administrative Law,* Lawman (India) Pvt. Ltd., New Delhi (1996).

I.M. Copie, *Introduction to Logic,* Prentice-Hall of India, New Delhi (1996).

Ian Brownlie, *Basic Documents on Hunan Rights,* Clarendon Press, Oxford (1992).

Ivor Jennings, *The Law and the Constitution,* University of London Press, London (1959).

J.A.G. Griffith, *The Politics of the Judiciary*, Fontana, Collins, U.K. (1978).

John Rawls, *A Theory of Justice*, Universal, New Delhi (2005).

Joseph Raz, *The Concept of a Legal System*, Clarendon Press, Oxford (1980).

Julius Stone, *Legal System and Lawyers Reasonings*, Maitland Publications Pty. Ltd. (1968).

K.C. Wheare, *Modern Constitutions*, Oxford (1966).

K.C. Markandan, *Directive Principles in the Indian Constitution*, Allied Publishers (P) Ltd., Bombay (1976).

K. Shanmukham, *N.S. Bindra's Interpretation of Statutes*, Law Book Co. Allahabad (1997).

Kelsen, *General Theory of Law and the State*, Cambridge, Harvard University Press (1949).

———, *Pure Theory of Law*, University of California, Berkeley (1970).

L.M. Singvi, *Freedom on Trial*, Vikas Publishing House (P) Ltd., New Delhi (1991).

Lee Epstein (Ed.), *Courts and Judges*, Ashgate (2005).

Lloyd's Introduction to Jurisprudence, Stevens and Sons (1985).

Lord Denning, *What Next in Law*, Butterworths, London (1982).

Louis L. Jaffe, *English and American Judges as Law Makers*, Oxford (1969).

M.K. Bhandari, *Basic Structure of the Indian Constitution*, Deep and Deep Publications, New Delhi (1993).

M.P. Jain and S.N. Jain, *Principles of Administrative Law*, Wadhwa & Co., Nagpur (1986).

M.P. Jain, *Outlines of Indian Legal History*, N.M.Tripathi, Bombay (1981).

M.P. Singh, *V.N. Sukla's Constitution of India*, Easterm Book Company, Lucknow (1990).

Martin Shapiro and Rocco J. Tresolini, *American Constitutional Law*, Macmillan Publishing Co. Inc., New York, (1970).

Martin Shapiro, *Courts: A Comparative and Political Analysis*, University of Chicago Press (1981).

Mohan Kumaramangalam, *Judicial Appointments*, Oxford and IBH Publishing Co., New Delhi (1973).

Montesquieu, *The Spirit of Laws, The Great Books of the World*, Vol. 30, William Banton Pub. Encyclopaedia Britannica Inc., University of Chicago (1978).

Nayar, Kuldip, *The Supersession of Judges,* Indian Book Co., New Delhi (1977).

O. Hood Phillips, *Constitutional and Administrative Law,* Sweet and Maxwell, London (1975).

Oppenhiem, *International Law—A Treatise,* Longman, London (1955).

Orfield, *The Amending of the Federal Constitution,* The University of Michigan Press, Chicago (1942).

P.B. Gajendragadkar, *The Constitution of India: Its Philosophy and Basic Postulates,* Oxford University Press, Nairobi (1969).

P.B. Gajendragadkar, *The Indian Parliament and the Fundamental Rights,* Eastern Law House, Calcutta (1972).

P.H. Levy, *Introduction to Legal Reasoning,* University of Chicago (1948).

P.K. Tripathi, *Spotlights on Constitutional Interpretation,* N.M. Tripathi, Bombay (1972).

P. Leelakrishnan, *Environmental Law in India,* Butterworhs, New Delhi (1999).

P. St. J. Lananglann (Ed.), *Maxwell on Interpretation of Statutes,* N.M. Tripathi, Bombay (1976).

Palkhiwala, Nani A., *Our Constitution Defaced and Defiled,* MacMillan, New Delhi (1974).

Paras Diwan and Piyush Diwan, *Amending Power and Constitutional Amendments,* Deep and Deep Publications, New Delhi (1997).

Patric Devlin, *Samples of Law-making,* Oxford University Press (1962).

R.B. Srivastava, *Economic Justice under the Indian Constitution,* Deep and Deep Publications, New Delhi (1989).

Rajeev Dhavan and Alice Jacob, *Indian Constitution: Trends and Issues,* N.M. Tripathi, Bombay (1978).

Rajeev Dhavan, *Supreme Court of India: Its Socio-Juristic Techniques,* N.M. Tripathi, Bombay (1977).

Rajeev Dhavan, *The Supreme Court of India and Parliamentary Sovereignty,* Sterling Publishers, New Delhi (1977).

Rama Jois, *Legal and Constitutional History of India,* Vol. I, N.M. Tripathi, Bombay (1990).

Raol Berger, *Impeachment the Constitutional Problems,* Harward University Press, Cambridge (1973).

Richard, B. Berstein, *Amending America*, Times Books, Random House, (1993).

Rocco, J. Tresolini and Martin Shapiro, *American Constitutional Law,* Macmillan Publishing Co. Inc., London (1970).

Roger Cotterrell, *The Sociology of Law—An Introduction,* Butterworths, London (1992).

Ronald Dworkin, *Taking Rights Seriously,* Universal, New Delhi (1995).

Rupert, M. Jackson, *The Machinery of Justice,* Cambridge University Press (1972).

S.A. de Smith, *Constitutional and Administrative Law,* Penguin Education, England (1973).

Shylaja Chander, *V.R. Krishna Iyer on Fundamental Rights and Directive Principles,* Deep and Deep Publications, New Delhi (1992).

Simon Shetreet and Jules Descheness, *Judicial Independence: A Contemporary Debate,* Martinus Nijhoff Publishers, Derdrecht (1985).

Sirajud-Islam Laskar, *Direcitive Principles of State Policy under Indian Constitution,* Deep and Deep Publications, New Delhi (1988).

Sudesh Kumar Sharma, *Directive Principles and Fundamental Rights: Relationships and Policy Perspectives,* Deep and Deep Publications, New Delhi (1990).

The Concise Oxford Dictionary.

Upendra Baxi, *Courage, Craft and Contention, The Supreme Court in the 80's,* N.M. Tripathi, Bombay (1985).

Upendra Baxi, *K.K. Mathew on Democracy, Equality and Freedom,* Eastern Book Company, Lucknow (1978).

Upendra Baxi, *Supreme Court and Politics,* Eastern Book Company, Lucknow (1980).

Upendra Baxi, *The Indian Supreme Court and Politics,* Eastern Book House, Lucknow, (1980).

Verinder Grover, (Ed.), *Courts and Political Process in India,* Deep and Deep Publications, New Delhi (1989).

Verinder Grover, (Ed.), *Political Process and Role of Courts,* Deep and Deep Publications, New Delhi (1997).

William Anderson, *Fundamentals of American Government,* Henry Holt and Co., New York (1940).

William Holdsworth, *A History of English Law*, Vol. X, Sweet and Maxwell, London (1966).

William, S. Livingston, *Federalism and Constitutional Change*, Oxford Clarendon Press, U.K. (1956).

Willoughby, *The Constitution of the United States*, Vol. 3 (1929) Baker, Voorhis and Co., New York.

Yardley, *Introduction to British Constitutional Law*, Butterworths, London (1964).

Articles

Ajit Kumar, "Appointments of the Judges of the Supreme Court and the High Courts", 7 Ac L.R., p. 137 (1983).

Alfred, F. Havinghurst, "The Judiciary and Politics in the Reign of Charles II, 66 L.Q.R. 64 (2) (1950).

Alice Jacob and Rajeev Dhavan, "Appointment of Supreme Court Judges and Contemporary Politics in Indian", [1975] C.U.L.R., p. 15.

Amitya, K. Chondhury, "Appointment of a Chief Justice: The Study of a Controversy in a New Perspective" in Verinder Grover (Ed.), *Courts and Political Process in India*, Deep and Deep Publications, New Delhi (1989).

Anand Prakash, "Appointment of High Court Judiciary under the Constitution of India—Issues and Perspectives", 9 J.B.C.I (1982) p. 397.

Chadrapal, "Independence of Judiciary—Some Aspects of Indian Experience", J.I.L.I (1982) p. 282.

Conrad, "Constituent Power Amendment and Basic Structure of the Constitution: A Critical Reconstruction", 67 Delhi L.R. 24 (1977-78).

Ervin, R. Kaufman "The Essence of Judicial Independence", 80 Col. L.R. (1980) p. 671.

Erving, R. Kaufman, "Chilling Judicial Independence", 88Y.L.J 681 (78-79).

G.S. Sharma, "The Concept of Leadership in Directive Principles of SP in Indian Constitution", 7 J.I.L.I. 173 (1965).

H.M. Seervai, "The Fundamental Rights Case at the Cross Roads", 74 Bom L.R. Journal 47 (1973).

H.R. Khanna, "Need to Preserve Image of Judges", 9 J.B.C.I (1982), p. 241 (1973).

H.R. Khanna, "Power to Amend the Constitution", (1983) 2 S.C.C I (Jo).

Harry, T. Edwards, "Regulating Judicial Misconduct and Dividing 'Good Behaviour of Federal Judges", 87 Mich L.R. p. 765.

Herman, Kantorowencz, "Savigny and the Historical School of Law", 53 L.Q.R 326 (1937).

I.P. Massey, "Theory of Basic Features—A Dogma or Doctrine", 7 J.B.C.I (1977) p. 38.

J.C. Dougherty, "Inherent Limitation Upon Impeachment", 23 Y.L.J 16 (1913).

J.N. Mallik, "Removal of Judges", AIR 1964 Jour. 42.

Jagath Narain "Equal Protection Guarantee and Right of Protection under Constitution of India", 15 I.C.L.Q p. 199.

Jagath Narain "Judicial Law Making and the Place" of Directive Principles in I.C 27 J.I.L.I (1985) 198 (1985).

Joseph Minattur, "Directive Principles and Unconstitutional Law", in Verinder Grover (Ed.), *Political Process and Role of Courts*, Deep and Deep Publications, New Delhi (1997).

Joseph Raz, "The Identity of Legal Systems", 59 California L.R 795 (1971).

K.N. Chandrasekharan Pillai, "A Comment on *Shanti Bhrushan* v. *Union of India*", (2009) 2 S.C.C. 46 (J).

K.S. Hegde, "Directive Principles of State Policy in the Constitution of India", I.S.C.J 50 (1971).

Kashmir, Singh, "Appointment of Judiciary of the Supreme Court" in B.P. Singh *Law, Judiciary and Justice in India*, Deep and Deep Publications, New Delhi, at p. 112 (1993).

Khanna, H.R., "Need to Preserve Image of Judiciary", I. J.B.C.I 241.

Koteseara, Rao, "Does the Indian Constitution Need a Basic Overhandling: A Case for Conveying Constitution Assembly in Rajiv Dhawan & Alice Jacob, (Ed.), *Indian Constitution—Trends and Issues* N.M. Tripathi, Bombay, p. 99 (1978).

Kuldip, Nayar, "The Thirteenth Chief Justice" in Kuldip Nayar (Ed.), *Supersession of Judges*, Indian Book House, New Delhi, p. 9 (1973).

Larry, C. Berkson, "Judicial Selections in US", 8 J.B.C.I. 424 (1982).

Laurence, H. Tribe, "A Constitution We are Amending: In Defense of a Restrained Judicial Role", 97 Har. L.R. 433 (1983).

Lord Halesham, "The Independence of the Judicial Process", 7 J.B.C.I., p. 21 (1978).

M.H. Beg, "The Supremacy of the Constitution", in Rajiv Dhawan & Alice Jacob, (Ed.) *Indian Constitution—Trends and Issues*, N.M. Tripathi, Bombay p. 113. (1978).

Mahavir Singh, "Directive Principles and Fundamental Rights—A Co-relation Some Suggestions to Remove the ontroversy", (1981) 3 S.C.C. 28 (Jour.).

Morris, R. Kohen, "The Process of Judicial Legislation in Law and Social Order", in *Essays in Legal Philosophy* (1967).

P.K. Thripathi, "Keshavananda Bharathi *v.* State of Kerala, Who Wins?", (1974) S.C.C I (Jour.).

P.K. Tripathi, "Directive Principles of State Policy: The Lawyers' Approach to Them Hitherto Parochial, Injurious and Unconstitutional", in *Spotlights on Constitutional Interpretation*, N.M. Tripathi, Bombay (1972).

Rajeev Dhawan, "The Basic Structure Doctrine—A Footnote Comment", in "Some Reflections on the Nature of Constitution" in Rajiv Dhavan and Alice Jacob (Ed.), *Indian Constitution- Trends and Issues*, N.M.Tripathi, Bombay p. 160.

Ram Jeth Malani, Fundamental Rights *v.* Directive Principles 8 J.B.C.I., p. 392 (1981).

Ramesh, D. Garg, "Phantom of Basic Structure of the Constitution—A Critical Appraisal of the Keshavananda Case", 16 J.I.L.I (1974) p. 243.

Richard Ekins, "Judicial Supremacy and the Rule of Law", (2003) 119 LQR 127.

S. Sahai, "Role and Status of the Judiciary in Indian Government", J.B.C.I. 442 p. 8 (1981).

S.A. de. Smith, "Tenure of Office by Colony Judges", 16 MLR (1953) p. 502.

S.M. Mehta, "Appointment of Additional India in the High Courts: A Threat to the Independence of Judiciary" in B.P. Singh Seghal (Ed.), *Law, Judiciary and Justice in India*, Deep and Deep Publications (P) Ltd., New Delhi p. 59. (1993).

S.P. Sathe, Limitations on Constitutional Amendments: Basic Structure Principle Re-Gainned" in Rajiv Dhawan & Alice Jacob (Ed.), *Indian Constitution—Trends and Issues,* N.M. Tripathi, Bombay p. 179.

Shariffful Hassan, "Supreme Court and Appointments to Judicial Service: A Need for Judicial Rethinking", 34 J.I.L.I 125 (1992).

Simon Shetreet, "Judicial Independence: New Conceptual Dimension and Contemporary Chellenges in Simon Shetreet and Jules Dischenes (Ed.), *Judicial Independence: A Contemporary Debate,* Martinus Nijhoff Publishers, Dordrecht, p. 590 (1985).

T.S. Rama Rao, "Constitutional Amendments, Judicial Review and Constitutionalism in India", in Rajeev Dhawan & Alice Jacob (Ed.), *Indian Constitution—Trends and Issues,* N.M. Tripathi, Bombay, p. 160 (1978).

T.T. Sundera Ram Reddy, "Fundamental Rights and Directive Principles", 22 J.I.L.I 22 (1988).

Tom. C. Clark, "Judicial Self Regulation—The Potential", 35 Law Contemporary Problems, p. 37 (1970).

Upendra Baxi, "A Pilgrim's Progress: The Basic Structure Revisited" in Upendra Baxi, *Courage, Craft and Contention—The Indian Supreme Court in the 80's,* N.M. Tripathi, Bombay p. 65 (1985).

Upendra Baxi, "Directive Principles and Sociology of India—Reply to Dr. Jagath Narain", 11 J.I.L.I p. 248 (1968).

Upendra Baxi, "Some Reflections on the Nature of Constitution" in Rajeev Dhawan & Alice Jacob, (Ed.), *Indian Constitution—Trends and Issues,* N.M. Tripathi, Bombay (1978), p. 122.

Upendra Baxi, "The Constitutional Quick Sands of Keshavananda Bharati and the 25th Amendment", (1974) I S.C.C 45 (Jour.).

Upendra Baxi, "The Little Done and the Vast Undone, Some Reflections on Reading Granville Austin's The Indian Constitution", J.I.L.I 323, 1967 p. 9.

V.S. Desh Pandey, "Rights and Duties under Constitution", 15 J.I.L.I 94 (1973).

William L. Marbury, "The Limitations upon the Amending Power", 33 H.L.R., p. 223 (1919-20).

Wrisley Brown, "The Impeachment of the Federal Judiciary", 26 H.L.R 68 (1912-13).

Reports and Document

C.A.D., Vol. VII.
C.A.D., Vol.VIII.
C.A.D., Vol. IX.
The Constitution of India, 1950.
The Constitution of France.
The Constitution of Ireland, 1937.
The Constitution of the Swiss Federation, 1874.
The Constitution of the United States of America, 1787.
Convention on Political and Civil Rights, 1966.
Convention on the Elimination of All Forms of Discrimination against Women, 1979.
Law Commission of India, 14th Report, 1958.
Law Commission of India, 80th Report, 1979.
Law Commission of India, 118th Report, 1987.
Universal Declaration of Human Rights, 1948.
The Times of India, Mumbai, Tuesday, July 20the 1998.
Frontline, Vol. 25. Issue 20 Sept. 27-Oct 10, 2008.
The Hindu, 31 May 2009, Kochi.

Statutes

Judicature Act, 1975, 38 & 39 Vict. C. 77.
Act of Settlement, (1700) 12 & 13 Will. C. 2.
Regulating Act, 1773, Stal. 13 Geo. 3 c. 3.
The Indian High Courts Act, 1861, 23 & 25 Vict. C. 104.
The Indian High Courts Act, 1911, 1 & 2 Geo. V. c. 18.
The Government of India Act, 1915, 5 & 6 Geo. V. c. 61.
The Government of India Act, 1935,
The Judges Enquiry Act, 1968.
The Judicial Councils Reform and Judicial Conduct and Disability Act, 1980 (U.S.).
The Supreme Court Rules, 1966.

Index